FOR DURKHEIM

Rethinking Classical Sociology

Series Editor: David Chalcraft, University of Derby, UK

This series is designed to capture, reflect and promote the major changes that are occurring in the burgeoning field of classical sociology. The series publishes monographs, texts and reference volumes that critically engage with the established figures in classical sociology as well as encouraging examination of thinkers and texts from within the ever-widening canon of classical sociology. Engagement derives from theoretical and substantive advances within sociology and involves critical dialogue between contemporary and classical positions. The series reflects new interests and concerns including feminist perspectives, linguistic and cultural turns, the history of the discipline, the biographical and cultural milieux of texts, authors and interpreters, and the interfaces between the sociological imagination and other discourses including science, anthropology, history, theology and literature.

The series offers fresh readings and insights that will ensure the continued relevance of the classical sociological imagination in contemporary work and maintain the highest standards of scholarship and enquiry in this developing area of research.

Also in the series:

Max Weber Matters
Interweaving Past and Present
Edited by David Chalcraft, Fanon Howell, Marisol Lopez Menendez,
Hector Vera
ISBN 978-0-7546-7340-8

Karl Mannheim and the Legacy of Max Weber
Retrieving a Research Programme
David Kettler, Colin Loader and Volker Meja
ISBN 978-0-7546-7224 1

Vilfredo Pareto's Sociology
A Framework for Political Psychology
Alasdair J. Marshall
ISBN 978-0-7546-4978-6

For Durkheim
Essays in Historical and Cultural Sociology

EDWARD A. TIRYAKIAN
Duke University, USA

Routledge
Taylor & Francis Group

LONDON AND NEW YORK

First published 2009 by Ashgate Publishing

2 Park Square, Milton Park, Abingdon, Oxon OX14 4RN
711 Third Avenue, New York, NY 10017, USA

Routledge is an imprint of the Taylor & Francis Group, an informa business

First issued in paperback 2016

British Library Cataloguing in Publication Data
Tiryakian, Edward A.
  For Durkheim : essays in historical and cultural sociology.
  - (Rethinking classical sociology)
  1. Durkheim, Emile, 1858-1917 2. Weber, Max, 1864-1920
  3. Durkheimian school of sociology 4. Sociology
  I. Title
  301'.092

Library of Congress Cataloging-in-Publication Data
Tiryakian, Edward A.
  For Durkheim : essays in historical and cultural sociology / by Edward A. Tiryakian.
    p. cm. -- (Rethinking classical sociology)
  Includes index.
  ISBN 978-0-7546-7155-8
  1. Durkheim, Imile, 1858-1917. 2. Sociology--History. 3. Culture. I. Title.

HM465.T57 2009
301.092--dc22

2008049693

ISBN 13: 978-0-7546-7155-8 (hbk)
ISBN 13: 978-1-138-26236-2 (pbk)

Contents

List of Tables

Series Editor's Preface

With *For Durkheim*, we publish the second volume in our series that engages directly with the work of Durkheim (and in fact Professor Tiryakian the author of the former has reviewed in Contemporary Sociology that first volume in our series by Jonathan Fish), and there are further volumes in the pipeline. These publications verify that even in the context of the contested and expanded canon of classical sociological thinkers and texts, Durkheim, alongside his slightly younger contemporary, Max Weber, and alongside the older Marx, is still a force to be reckoned with and a source that beckons to contemporary theorists. The title *For Durkheim* of course resonates with previous rethinking of classical thinkers-namely, Althusser's *For Marx* (1965) and Bryan Turner's *For Weber* (1981). As Tiryakian says, this was a conscious decision. At the same time, the volume recalls aspects of Gouldner's *For Sociology* (1973) since what is provided is not merely advocacy for a Durkheimian position, but for using Durkheim as both a subject in his own right and as a source for unravelling contemporary social and cultural processes; as such, an advocacy for sociological analysis undertaken in continuity with the sociological tradition – an intent shared with Gouldner's earlier volume.

Professor Tiryakian is a Durkheimian scholar. But he is also so much more than this. As he has written in his essay, *Have Sociological Passport, Will Travel*: "I consider Emile Durkheim and Max Weber as major totems; Talcott Parsons and Pitirim Sorokin as my major personal mentors" (in *Sociologists in a Global Age*, edited by Mathieu Deflem, Ashgate, 2007). Hence, the reader will find a whole section of the volume, *For Durkheim*, engaging with the legacy of Weber in this connection. Moreover, Professor Tiryakian's work, produced now for more than six decades, includes analysis of religion, ethnicity and ethnic conflicts, national identity, development and modernity. The work of Professor Tiryakian demonstrates the relevance to a range of substantive areas, of thinking with classical theory in mind.

For Durkheim is also a volume important to rethinking classical sociology as whole, since it demonstrates, in general and in key chapters, the manner in which sociology is often a part of the very culture it seeks to comprehend. This involves seeing classical sociology as including a classical cultural sociology, as well as approaching classical sociology with cultural sociological questions in mind. Sociological writing, that is to say, is often part of a more general intellectual interaction with social change, such that it shares concerns and tropes with other discourses in theology, literature or art. These interrelations, the interaction of classical sociological and literary and artistic imaginations, can characterise the texts that the classical sociologists composed, affecting their forms and means of expressions. These interrelations also can be detected in the content of classical sociology, in terms of the social problems considered significant, or in a response to modernity or to contemporary malaise that is also appreciated, analysed and reacted to in other cultural movements and productions.

For example, Simmel's *The Metropolis and Mental Life* (1903) provides a well-known cultural sociological response to a gigantic social form that had major consequences, Simmel argued, for individual psychology, the development of specific forms of the division of labour, for particular attitudes (most famously the Blasé outlook) and social types, and of course for social relations. It would be foolish to think that it was only sociology that was conscious of these changes and that it was only sociological writing that wrestled with the phenomena; that it was only sociological narratives and mimetic modes that were altered. On the contrary, the cultural movements in Berlin, in Munich, in London, in Paris, in New York and Chicago equally responded to these cataclysmic changes (for sure, in diverse ways representing, for example, a drive to document, or an embrace and fascination, or a desire to escape for example). The atonality of Schoenberg and the mechanical strident rhythms of Stravinsky, the cityscapes of Kirchner, Knut Hamsun's exploration of modernist shame in Nordic "Christiania" in *Hunger* and Franz Kafka's nightmare story, *The Metamorphosis* to name but a few examples, are traceable to these social changes just as are the social work activity of a Beatrice Webb or a Jane Addams. Simmel himself invokes the names of Nietzsche and Ruskin to connect with the cultural critics of his time who share a concern with the meaning of the metropolis for character and social life. He could have added many a German novelist from Fontane to Raabe and later could have added the example of film, including Charlie Chaplin's *Modern Times* and Fritz Lang's *Metropolis*.

No-one would of course deny these facts: but what is less common is the support of the corollary that such connections need to be explored (and not only by historians of sociology but by social theorists too) and sociological discourse examined in this light, even if it leads to claims that sociology might not always have a monopoly of insight or of "truthful" representation or, indeed, the means to communicate the meaning and explanation of these phenomena to a public keen to understand themselves and others.

These types of connections, however, are brought out very well in the chapters which follow in *For Durkheim*, especially those considering Durkheim's milieu and the relation between Avant-Garde Art and Avant-Garde Sociology in the period 1905-1913. Professor Tiryakian shows, for example, that primitivism is not a phenomenon limited to art, or, one might add, to the literary imagination of Edgar Rice Burroughs in his *Tarzan* novels, but that sociology partakes also in the atmosphere, and not always critically.

Throughout our series, and indeed embedded in its original formulation, has been a concern with how one can and should go about reading the works of classical sociologists in a fashion that does justice to their historicity and to the fact of their transcending of time and place; how to communicate to readers and practising sociologists that whilst each classical work requires painstaking exegesis, the exegesis that is carried out is but one layer of enquiry which is to be added to similar labours on other texts; to then, in turn, arrive at an informed themed imagination where, often, those texts and original formulations are now heard as a melody whose constitution is of a variety of motifs and cadences (including some in discordant keys). It is with the melody in mind, and by 'humming variations during field work', that contemporary and historical processes and events are to be approached and filtered. By melody I mean sets of questions and perspectives, and a range of analogous and contrasting examples of typical patterns, that constitute this active, classically informed, sociological imagination. In short, we cannot be sociologically 'unmusical' if we seek to understand the diverse and significant contours of our concrete realities. Those realities include of course a range of episodes and events, but they certainly include the tragedies of the current global economic slump, as well as the increasing recurrence of campus/school shootings in North America and more recently, Finland.

I mention these cases, and the Finnish connection as an example of contemporary experience, since I have recently returned from spending time at the University of Helsinki as a guest of the Collegium for Advanced Studies. On the morning after the shooting at the vocational college of Kauhajoki, which occurred on September 23rd 2008, during the period of my visit, many of the public buildings and private tenement houses in Helsinki (and across the nation) flew flags at half mast. Flags had not been flying at all in the residential streets during the days before the tragedy. Some of these flags draped low (the wind from the harbour and the Gulf of Finland was hushed that day) and might brush the head of the pedestrian on the payment: they seemed like so many handkerchiefs suspended to wipe the tears of those stirred by the events and sensing, if only momentarily, a Durkheimian feeling of solidarity. Equally striking to me was the fact that it was not sociologists who appeared in the media that week, but psychologists. Did sociology not have anything to say or to offer by way of comfort or explanation? Ironically, I had been touring Amish Country in Pennsylvania only a fortnight before and, as a tourist, had a meal in an Amish household with people closely affined with the families who had lost daughters in the Nickel Mines shooting in an Amish school in 2006. 'Ironic' is the wrong term: rather, here was a coincidence that was no coincidence that was brought home to me because of my connection with place. That there was coincidence was because of the increasing regularity of these murders. That somehow my attention was grabbed more than usual was because the experience was less mediated than normally, although, thankfully, I was very distant from the events themselves and the people and communities bereaved. The shooting in Kauhajoki was the second tragedy in Finland; on November 7th, 2007 the Jokela High School in Tuusula witnessed the murder of 5 school children and 3 adults. The 'massacre' had been eerily 'announced' on *YouTube* only the day before.

Sociology will appear as impotent, and the classical tradition especially so, if effort is not expended on providing a sociological contribution to the debates. It was reassuring therefore to note on leaving Helsinki that at least the tragedy of the shootings at "Virginia Tech" (April 16th, 2007) had given rise to sustained sociological analysis in the volume, *There is a Gunman on Campus* (edited by Ben Agger and Timothy Luke, Rowman and Littlefield, 2008). Further, the remarkable theological response of the Amish community to the evil that stole into their enclave has been well documented and celebrated by Donald Kraybill and co-authors (*Amish Grace: How Forgiveness Transcended Tragedy*. John Wiley and Sons, 2007): Kraybill himself of course being an expert on the anthropology and sociology of Amish culture and hence a media port of call in the wake of the event. The task then, perhaps, is not only to appreciate that the concerns of many discourses are also to be reflected in sociological writing and analysis, but that, since this is the case, the writing of sociology needs to be as effective in communicating its insights as some of these other discourses sometimes seem to be: perhaps often to the chagrin of sociology. Only then can the expertise within sociology show its public face.

In the engagement with classical sociology, and in its rethinking, we are constantly seeking to find the discontinuities and continuities (the interweaving of past and present- the subtitle of a work currently in press in our series) in social thought and sociological analysis and in the social worlds that these developments of theory are meant to parallel as commentary and explication. Authors in our series have therefore been engaged in the hermeneutical tasks of bridging the sometimes quite distant horizons of text and reader. They have been involved in overcoming selective reception histories, and of rethinking contemporary theoretical positions and engaging with contemporary social developments informed by the classical tradition as a whole, or by the particular thinker or sets of thinkers under scrutiny. I am quite sure that Durkheimian perspectives, for example, on 'school shootings' and their aftermaths are possible and are forthcoming. These will not only look to the impact on solidarity of these events but also be aware of the 'suicidal current' that these events can bring in their wake to those who survived the tragedy.

Professor Tiryakian contributes to these concerns of making classical sociology relevant to everyday life and global processes with the voice of an experienced and spirited campaigner: a scholar who, as he puts in it his introduction, is fully conscious of the 'double helix' of the theoretical text; of the need for close historical and contextual exegesis of a classical thinker, coupled with an engagement with contemporary social events and trends, whether these be of more macro scale or of indicative micro proportions. But it is perhaps only here with this volume in our series that there is a consistent and conscious orientation toward what I have called classical cultural sociology. And an interest in classical cultural sociology partakes of the "double helix" too: there are rich sources in the classical tradition – and Tiryakian shows this especially for Durkheim – for the analysis of cultural forms, products and processes; there is also the need to understand classical sociology itself from the perspective of the questions raised by an interest in culture.

Professor Tiryakian demonstrates that he is not sociologically unmusical; that he does not place Durkheim in his intellectual context merely because of an historical interest; that he is not only concerned with accurate and informed analysis of Durkheim's texts and ideas; that he is not unaware of the importance of using classical sociology, and Durkheim in particular, to respond to and unravel the complexities of contemporary social life in which cultural forces play such a significant part. Professor Tiryakian is of course very aware of what constitutes effective reading of the classics and the production of valuable sociological knowledge, and this is due in no small part to his characteristic intelligence and good humour and his global sensitivity and experience. One can associate Professor Tiryakian with the analysis of classical texts and with the past history of the discipline (see for example, the inventory of the "Professor Tiryakian papers, 1963-2008" held at Duke University at Durham in North Carolina); alternatively, but perhaps equally characteristic, one can see Professor Tiryakian on *YouTube* giving the Mayhew Lecture of 2008 on the topic of Danish Mohammed Cartoons. It seems to me, therefore, that Professor Tiryakian, in his work, in his sociology, and in this book, successfully and continually rethinks classical sociology and constantly and creatively interweaves past and present.

David Chalcraft
March 2009
Cumbria

Acknowledgments

John Donne's powerful meditation "No man is an island, entire of itself" has had multiple applications over the centuries. It is certainly appropriate to invoke it in bringing out a volume parts of which as separate essays have benefited from multiple presentations to diverse academic audiences and from the encouragement of colleagues and students along the way. Among those no longer here but who in the past encouraged and stimulated my engagement with Durkheim, I remain indebted to Talcott Parsons, Robert Nisbet, Robert Merton, Georges Gurvitch, and Fernand Dumont. Among my contemporaries who have continued to provide stimulus and feedback with their own deep appreciation and knowledge of Durkheimiana, a special note of appreciation to Robert Bellah, W.S.F. Pickering, Jeffrey Alexander, John Rex, Steven Lukes, and Hans Joas. My thanks also go to Françoise Dauphragne at the Bibliothéque of the École Normale Supérieure for providing invaluable archival assistance. I dedicate this volume to two very special friends each of whom has been my *socius* in all my intellectual travels, including my Durkheimian explorations.

The production of this volume owes to many. For general support and attentive care, I have much benefited from the initial editorial interest of Mary Savigar and her successor at Ashgate, Neil Jordan. For a variety of important technical assistance in the preparation of texts, I am grateful to Duke University personnel: Cheryl Thomas, Rob Marks, and Steven Foy, in particular. Edmund Tiryakian has provided exemplary filial solidarity with a translation from the original French of the essay "Contextualizing the Emergence of Sociology". Dr Josefina Tiryakian has been my unpaid editor *extraordinaire* for this and other writings that have managed to see their way to print.

For Georges Balandier and Shmuel Eisenstadt
Exemplary Scholars, Long-Time Friends

Permissions

Grateful acknowledgments are made to the following publishers and journals for permission to include in this volume various writings of Edward A. Tiryakian originally published through them:

To *Basic Books/Perseus Book Group* for permission to include "Emile Durkheim's Matrix," in Tom Bottomore and Robert Nisbet, editors, *A History of Sociological Analysis,* New York: Basic Books, 1978.

To *Contemporary Sociology/American Sociological Association* for permission to include "On Discovering Durkheim," in my review essay with that title, *Contemporary Sociology*, volume 6, January 1977.

To *Blackwell–Wiley* for permission to include "Emile Durkheim and Social Change," in George Ritzer, editor, *Blackwell Encyclopedia of Sociology*, Malden, MA: Blackwell Publishing, 2007.

To *Brill* for permission to include "Durkheim and Husserl: A Comparison of the Spirit of Positivism and the Spirit of Phenomenology," in Joseph Bien, editor, *Phenomenology and the Social Sciences: A Dialogue,* The Hague: Martinus Nijhoff, 1978.

To *Archives Européennes de Sociologie/European Journal of Sociology* for permission to include "Durkheim, Mathiez and the French Revolution The Political Context of a Sociological Classic," *European Journal of Sociology,* 29 (1988): 373-96.

To *Les Presses de l'Université Laval* for permission to translate and include "Le travail chez Emile Durkheim," pp. 229-50 in Daniel Mercure and Jan Spurk, editors, *Le Travail dans l'Histoire de la pensée occidentale.* Saint-Nicholas, Québec: Les Presses de l'Université Laval, 2003.

To *Cambridge University Press* for permission to include "Durkheim, Solidarity and September 11," in Jeffrey Alexander and Philip Smith, editors, in *Cambridge Companion of Work.* Cambridge and New York: Cambridge University Press, 2005.

To *Cambridge University Press* for permission to include "From Durkheim to Managua: Revolutions as Religious Revivals," in Jeffrey Alexander, editor, *Durkheimian Sociology.* Cambridge and New York: Cambridge University Press, 1988.

To *Social Forces/UNC Press* for permission to include "Sexual Anomie, Social Structure and Social Change," in *Social Forces*, 59 (1981): 1025-1053.

To *Archives Européennes de Sociologie/European Journal of Sociology* for permission to include "A Problem for the Sociology of Knowledge: The Mutual Unawareness of Emile Durkheim and Max Weber," *European Journal of Sociology,* 7 (1966): 330-36.

To *University of Chicago Press* for permission to include "Neither Marx nor Durkheim... Perhaps Weber," in *American Journal of Sociology* 81 (July 1975): 1-33.

To *Sage Publications* for permission to include "Collective Effervescence, Social Change and Charisma," in *International Sociology,* 10 (September 1995): 269-81.

To Kyong-Dong Kim and the Korean Sociological Association for permission to include "On the Shoulders of Weber and Durkheim: East Asia and Emergent Modernity," in Kim Kyong-Dong and Su-Hoon Lee, editors, *Asia in the 21ˢᵗ Century: Challenges and Prospects.* Seoul: Panmun Book Co. 1990.

Introduction:
Why *For Durkheim?*

The present state of sociology may be characterized as a flourishing decentered discipline in different parts of the world, including those in Eastern Europe and Eastern Asia which a quarter of a century ago were for the most part suppressed by political regimes. The internet has opened up new areas of research and new data bases, there has been a significant proliferation of specialty areas in various sections of the American Sociological Association, and new sophisticated statistical techniques have sprung up to demonstrate, hopefully with rigor, new concepts.

Unlike the 1960s and 1970s, it has been a "cool period" for new theorizing. Perhaps the main problem for sociological theory today is how to energize mainstream graduate training to give theory its due in the curriculum and steer the young graduate student Argonauts between the lures of "post-colonial theory," "queer theory", "post-modernism", and "deconstructionism" to make sense analytically and theoretically of "the Global Age" with its development processes of globalization and anti-globalization, of new state formation and state deformation, of new multiple identities both "traditional" and transnational, and of transregional civilizational crossings with new diasporas bringing the East to the West, the South to the North, and all these being part of the modernity of the 21st Century. Still early in this century, we await to renew and go beyond the systemic theorizing of the late 20th Century in major figures like Parsons, Habermas, Wallerstein, Castells, Eisenstadt, and Albrow. To do justice to the emergent global reality of our situation and its interrelationships at various levels, economic, political, cultural and technological, calls for sociology to reinvent itself or at least to put the dynamics of the global societal system as the hub, and regions and nation-states as the spokes. Yet, far from throwing aside the legacies of the past, there is need to know these legacies well enough to recombine them, following the example of genomics and the mapping of the human genome.

In a "new" world of "global complexities",[1] with its many "butterfly effects" that can have manifold political, economic, and social repercussions from one corner on earth to another, sociologists might well give emphasis to a cooperative mapping of the social genome. It is with such a tacit project that sociologists can recognize with freshness the ongoing importance of major classical figures: Tocqueville, Marx, Weber, Simmel and Durkheim, who formulated basic inquiries of modernity that continue to prod the sociological imagination. They were not

---

1   John Urry, *Global Complexity*, Cambridge and Malden, MA: Polity/Blackwell, 2003.

the only ones "at the beginning", as the history of sociology continues to unravel, particularly with documentation of the contributions of minorities and marginalized figures coming to light, to say nothing of bringing into the fold of sociological theory figures from non-Western regions who constitute part of the story of modernity. That said as necessary for the "reinvention" of sociology in the twenty first century, it is also important to retain the figures just mentioned as essential cornerstones, as both reminders of where sociological thought is anchored and as stimulants for seeking major patterns and tendencies in the new century.

My chapters in this volume bring together a lifelong interest in one sociological cornerstone. The title *For Durkheim* is indirectly a response posed by two earlier remarkable volumes waiving the banners of two other giants of sociological analysis: *For Marx* by Louis Althusser and *For Weber* by Bryan Turner.[2] Althusser in the 1960s, amidst competing perspectives on Marxism, sought to reclaim the hard core of Marx's structural approach; Turner, some years later, was responding to Marxist critiques of Weber's idealism and subjectivism carried in his "methodological individualism".

At least symbolically, the "trilogy" (some might view it as a tryptich) of the major figures of sociological theory merits completion with a volume marking the sustained *engagement* by its author for the figure in focus. My engagement – and enthusiasm – for Emile Durkheim is extensive and intensive, going back to my graduate training in theory with Talcott Parsons at Harvard University, who in an initial discussion, after finding that I could read French with ease, suggested that I read Durkheim in the original. Parsons himself, as I was much later to understand,[3] was thoroughly familiar with Durkheim (whom he reread with great interest in his later years), albeit identified as a Weberian scholar. Reading Durkheim – his entire corpus – has been for me immensely satisfying, intellectually and even aesthetically exciting as one can follow the reasoning of a great mind to establish sociological truths and uncover patterns under the façade of quotidian reality.

My engagement with Durkheim has other layers. It took me to become aware that Durkheim did not do sociology as an isolated individual, but rather as team leader, a team that he began forming while he was a young faculty at Bordeaux, providing them with a division of labor that was an empirical manifestation of the justification for his own doctoral dissertation, *The Division of Labor in Society*. It was only near my mid-career that I thought of making contact with the team, a remarkable set of first-rate scholars who, like Robert Hertz and Marcel Granet, established their academic credentials with major studies in the sociology of religion, yet could write with idealistic but rigorous fervor about causes of social

---

2   Louis Althusser, *For Marx* (1965), Ben Brewster, trans. New York: Pantheon Books, 1969; Bryan S. Turner, *For Weber. Essays on the Sociology of Fate* (1981). London & Thousand Oaks, CA: Sage, 1996.

3   "Parsons's Emergent Durkheim*s*," *Sociological Theory*, 18 (March 2000): 60-83.

democracy; the same can be said for François Simiand and Maurice Halbwachs as major contributors to economic sociology.[4]

During a sabbatical leave in 1971, besides doing archival research in Épinal (Durkheim's birth place, where I discovered one of his earliest unpublished pieces), and in Bordeaux (where he spent half of his career), I went around Paris looking to meet, if not Durkheimians, then their relatives. Georges Davy, well in his nineties, was the only one still alive, but I did meet widows and children of several, along with students of Marcel Mauss, like Georges Dumézil. The composite picture reinforced my appreciation and respect for Durkheim and his team of collaborators: there really was an *organic solidarity* that drew them together in their dedication to establish sociology. In one sense, if they did not present Durkheim with a *Festschrift*, their work during and after his unfortunately short lifetime, could well have been entitled *Pour Durkheim (For Durkheim)*.

There is still another layer to my engagement. I spent my childhood years in France, attending primary school, until the war clouds in the summer of 1939 led to my impromptu return to America (I left France literally on the eve of WWII). I lived in France, accordingly, during the last decade of the Third Republic. What led to its downfall like putty at the hands of the German army, repeating what had happened seventy years previously, became something more than a comparative historical question. It became an existential question regarding the broader temporal frame of childhood.

As a mature social scientist, this prompt led me to progressively become fascinated with the entire period of the Third Republic, and thereby to seek an understanding of the total *milieu* in which Durkheim flourished, which was over three decades the cultural, educational and political flourish of the Third Republic, as it surmounted internal crises. Why republican democracy was viable and thrived in a new century, with unequaled bursts of creativity in the arts, sciences, and technology, but why this faltered in the 1930s (as did Weimar Germany) with bitter internal divisions that I have vague childhood memories of have provided me with continuing terrain to explore. And perhaps the engagement with the Third Republic is also tacitly an engagement with the American republic, which in recent years seems as bitterly divided as France was in my youth and with the same need for sociological intervention as the Durkheimians sought to provide in their teaching and research. So perhaps *For Durkheim* is also an invoking of a sociological presence for new cadres of sociologists, in the classroom or in their career, to take to heart Durkheim's mission of making sociology central in reframing the twin problem of integration and solidarity in advanced modernity.

What then will the reader find in this volume? It is not a systemic, chronological work in the nature of an intellectual biography. For that, one is better served with

---

4 Robert Hertz, *Socialisme et Dépopulation*, Les Cahiers du Socialiste, no. 10. Paris, 1910; Marcel Granet, *Contre l'Alcoolisme. Un Programme Socialiste*, Les Cahiers du Socialiste, no. 11, Paris 1911; Maurice Halbwachs, *La Politique Foncière des Municipalités*, Les Cahiers du Socialiste, no. 3, Paris 1908.

two large-scale studies, the first which has served well for many years, Steven Lukes's excellent intellectual biography *Émile Durkheim*, and the recent immense labor of Marcel Fournier, *Émile Durkheim*.[5]

What *For Durkheim* brings together is a set of chapters that span thirty years, including two original ones recently prepared for this volume. There are three foci which I have used to frame the 17 chapters selected among my writings on Durkheim.

In Part 1, I seek to engage the reader to (re)discovering Durkheim, his major projects and his major concerns. While most sociologists, students and practitioners, have some general knowledge of Durkheim, mainly on an ad hoc basis of reading scattered texts, there are trails leading to and from him which have tended to be less well surveyed. Conversely, some already surveyed ones deserve a second look in terms of their actuality, including whether they need upgrading in light of our modernity, a century after his.

As a general methodological note, I take it as a directive that to *understand* more fully the import of a text (taken singly or as the total oeuvre of a major figure like Durkheim), one should look at both the manifold contexts of his or her productions and also how they apply to a deeper understanding of the situation of the contemporary, here and now reader. A classic theoretical text can gain appreciation (i.e., vitality) lifting it out of the bins of the catacombs of dusty shelves by seeing how it relates to broad currents and influences, some commonly known, some to be discovered by new historical data or new interpretations. To make it theoretically relevant for today's practitioners, the text further needs to be related to today's epistemological and ontological concerns, to the problematic of contemporary sociology. The first dimension is the domain of the history of sociology; the second, of contemporary sociology. The two intertwine in what might be thought of as the "double helix" of a theoretical text.

Accordingly, I begin Part 1 with three chapters to help in the discovery and recovery of Durkheim, beginning with a lengthy study of the basic projects of Durkheim in laying out, tacitly a broad scientific research program for sociology. The historical and philosophical contexts in which he and his dedicated team carried this out are, in my judgment, essential parts of the Durkheimian matrix. Two other brief chapters follow, one a review chapter of a three-volume publication (in French) of his works and their major themes, a publication which also made available a correspondence of Durkheim that showed him not as a detached intellectual but as a caring human being. The other brief chapter is intended to dispel an earlier (and fallacious) view that Durkheim's theorizing about social structure and social organization did not address the question of social change.

Two other figures that are germane in contextualizing Durkheim are treated in subsequent chapers. The first is Edmund Husserl founder of modern

---

5   Steven Lukes, *Émile Durkheim; his life and work, a critical study*. New York: Harper & Row, 1972;   Marcel Fournier, *Émile Durkheim (1858-1917)*. Paris: Arthème Fayard, 2007.

phenomenology, born shortly after Durkheim, and like him, attended the same world-famous research laboratory of Wilhelm Wundt in Leipzig. Given Durkheim's training and keen appreciation of philosophy, it seemed appropriate to compare Durkheim and Husserl whose respective methodologies appear as polar opposites. The second figure was an historian at the Sorbonne, where at the turn of the century sociology and history seemed to be at loggerheads methodologically. What I have found as an exciting bridge is how the early writing on religion by Durkheim stimulated the young historian of the French Revolution Albert Mathiez to look for a new dimension of the French Revolution in religious cults, and that in turn provided Durkheim with an important comparative dimension for his own seminal study of religion.

The last two chapers in this first part deal with well-known substantive themes of Durkheim, but I seek in these not only to discuss the social and intellectual context in which they were written, but also their actuality a century later.

Part 2 draws together various chapters which have as a central focus the question of the dynamics of cultural change, not only the place of culture in the sociological analysis of change but also the cultural context of sociological analysis, the latter often overlooked. The first two chapters are complementary though written nearly thirty years apart. In the first, I had been intrigued in looking at the composition and works of the Durkheimian school at the importance of *symbolism* in the later Durkheim and in the works of major associates who worked with him in the sociology of religion. A stimulus from Robert Nisbet's *Sociology as Art Form* led me to consider the context of avant-garde art in the Bordeaux period of the Durkheimian school, and it struck me that the symbolists in art and the sociological search for symbols in the Durkheimians had a not insignificant affinity. The second chapter was undertaken in the present decade, initially on the occasion of an invited presentation at the British Centre for Durkheim Studies in Oxford. Although there is some overlap in the focus on avant-garde art, new aspects of the cultural context unfolded, and not only because what was avant-garde art in Durkheim's Bordeaux period changed rapidly, just about when he left his university position there to become a professor at the Sorbonne. Almost the same year as he received his professorship at the Sorbonne, Picasso and Braque shook the cultural scene, going beyond the Fauves to cubism. In the second chapter, then, I relate the radical innovations in representational and performance arts to the radical innovation of Durkheim, both, I propose, part of a broad cultural context of *primitivism*.

Durkheim is well noted for his critique of utilitarianism, and its offshoot today in rational choice theory, for his critique of Spencer's individualism, a critique which in so many words points to the cultural embededness of markets (in laws, regulations, mores, etc.). Cultural sociology has taken a new lease on life by going beyond the critique of Spencer found in *The Division of Labor in Society* to finding new stimuli for theorizing and application as derivative of the later *Elementary Forms of the Religious Life*. The cultural scene has greatly become illuminated in sociology with one window (that is particularly associated with Foucault and

Bourdieu, but also Gramsci) opening to the place of culture in the (re)production of domination and hegemony in a social order. As Jeffrey Alexander has keenly seen in framing cultural sociology,[6] Durkheim's window on culture is wider, in the full panorama of his seminal *The Elementary Forms of the Religious Life*, which has well deservedly become seen as his *magnum opus* and a foundational work for the sociology of culture. At one level, the analysis on rituals and symbols as key elements of the structuration of the social order is in keeping with this opening.

But in keeping with the complementary aspects of culture as "order-maintaining" and "order- transforming", to follow Eisentadt,[7] there is an unstated dialectic in *The Forms*: the lifeblood of society are endogenous forces of social mobilization, of creative moments of regeneration and enthusiasm, with a rebirth of the sphere of the sacred, even if that may itself become subject in time for the *extraordinary* to become *ordinary*, quotidian. The destructuring and restructuring of the social order in societal movements and collective effervescence is thus given in a complementary view of the cultural scene. For comparative purpose, how this may be applied to revolutionary change that appeared pretty much at the same time in several countries ("From Durkheim to Managua") provides us with material for the actuality of Durkheim in the contemporary world.

I also include a chapter that examines a cultural potential for destructuring the social order as much as any political revolution, namely what may be termed "sexual anomie". On the surface, it might appear that Durkheim's views on marriage and monogamy are a straight reflection of Victorian patriarchal biases. This is partly true, but putting together various parts of his dealing with sexuality, one can see the potential for far-reaching changes in social organization that Durkheim intuitively sensed, and which have increasingly become actualized in our modern period.

The cultural sphere has other dimensions that bring the sacred into play. Durkheim grasped at the potential explosive force if the separation of the sacred and the profane, a cardinal aspect of social organization, were violated or broken. The eruption of Muslim outrage over a set of cartoons appearing in a Danish newspaper, as well as the reaction of the Western world to the outrage, caught my attention as providing materials for the relevance and actuality of Durkheim's sacred/profane dichotomy. The Danish Cartoons affair has marked this decade as a *cause célèbre*, a cultural maelstrom involving new and old identities, new and old values, as complex a totality as the *cause célèbre* that shook Durkheim's France, the Dreyfus affair.

---

6   "Introduction: Durkheimian sociology and cultural studies today," pp. 7-21 in J.C. Alexander, ed., *Durkheimian Sociology: cultural studies.* Cambridge and New York: Cambridge University Press, 1988.

7   S.N.Eisenstadt, "The Order-maintaining and Order-Transforming Dimensions of Culture," pp. 64-87 in Richard Münch and Neil J. Smelser, eds, *Theory of Culture.* Berkeley: University of California Press, 1992.

Part 3 contains a set of chapters which explore the complex relationship, intellectually and otherwise, of Durkheim and his great contemporary, Max Weber, the two being central nodes of French and German sociology before World War I. Going to Germany as a young promising student was decisive for Durkheim's career, and Weber made several visits to Strasburg and Paris, so their criss-crossing the Rhine has provided me with another set of comparative and historical materials. In the first two chapters, I have put the stress on differences between them, in the initial chapter on their seeming unawareness if not benign neglect of the other, and in the second chapter, the advantage over Durkheim (and Marx) of utilizing Weber as ingress to making sense of American society. In this vein, it is not too far-fetched to view Durkheim and Weber as collective representations of France and German social science competing to open up fields of sociology the way Pasteur and Koch competed to bring glory to France and Germany in the field of microbiology.

However, the last three chapters in this part tacitly opt for inviting readers to viewing Durkheim and Weber as complementary rather than antipodal theorists, engaged in a heuristic dialogue in the analysis and understanding of our modern situation, in particular the directions of large-scale societal change, the definitive challenge for the sociological enterprise. Ultimately, that is the rationale *For Durkheim.*

Figure 1   **Emile Durkheim (top row, second left) and his first-year cohort at the École Normale Supérieure (ENS), Paris, 1879-80**

Courtesy of the Blibliothèque of the École Normale Supérieure of Paris.

PART 1

(Re) Discovering Durkheim

Chapter 1

Emile Durkheim's Matrix[1]

Introduction

Emile Durkheim is the crucial figure in the development of sociology as an academic discipline. Before Durkheim sociology was a provocative idea; by his professional endeavors it became an established social fact. Durkheim inherited a nineteenth-century sociological tradition, one with a distinctive French flavor of social realism and social reconstruction; much of contemporary sociology's framework reflects basic features which were imparted by Durkheim's refashioning of sociology into a systematic discipline. Two such features, "positivism" and "structural-functional analysis," became in the 1960s and 1970s targets of much criticism (ideological as well as conceptual); nonetheless, one can also say that Durkheim's visibility and esteem are presently at higher levels in both francophone and anglophone sociological circles than perhaps any previous period, including that of his own lifetime. Perhaps the quest for "roots of identity" is also operative in sociology as it has become in popular culture, and Durkheim is surely, alongside Max Weber and Karl Marx, one of the deepest roots of the sociological imagination. Whatever the reason, every self-respecting sociologist has read at least *The Division of Labor* and *Suicide* as an undergraduate or graduate student, and quite likely most sociologists will also have read during their career *The Rules of the Sociological Method* and *The Elementary Forms of the Religious Life*. Each is a seminal study: the first in industrial sociology, the second in deviance, the third in methodology, and the fourth in the sociology of religion and of knowledge. Each is a venture in sociological analysis which does not fade with time, in a discipline where most works disappear from reading lists within ten years after publication. How many other sociologists have three or four of their works read firsthand by succeeding sociological generations? Moreover, Durkheim is not only still widely read but he is also more and more commented and reflected upon by new generations of sociologists, who are also producing new collections of his writings, some seeing print for the first time. Truly, it may be said that the past ten years have seen the production of the most extensive and high-caliber Durkheimiana of any comparable period since his death in 1917.

The understanding of such a major figure as Durkheim is, like any historical benchmark or event, not a once-and-for-all matter but rather more of an emergent process. Consequently, this essay will be selective in its emphasis, while trying

---

1   First published as "Emile Durkheim," in Tom Bottomore and Robert Nisbet, eds., *A History of Sociological Analysis*. New York: Basic Books, Inc., 1978, pp. 187-236.

to give the reader a general orientation to Durkheimian sociology. I have been fascinated by Durkheim for twenty years, but I do not feel there is anything definitive in my present understanding of his writings; still, some things, some connections seem clearer to me now than previously, and these I propose to share with readers of this volume. In particular, I wish to advance as a thesis that Durkheim's sociological analysis, though it makes sense in itself, would better be understood as one component of a threefold life project.

Although the entelechy for this vast project cannot be documented in the form of a letter or journal entry kept by Durkheim, nonetheless there are sufficient indications to propose that his life project was constituted by three interwoven goals:

1. to establish sociology as a rigorous scientific discipline
2. to provide the basis for the unity and unification of the social sciences
3. to provide the empirical, rational, and systematic basis for modern society's civil religion.

Durkheim was successful in achieving the first. By the age of forty Durkheim had produced sociology's "manifesto" in the guise of the trilogy consisting of *The Division of Labor*, *The Rules of Sociological Method*, and *Suicide*. Equally significant, he celebrated his fortieth birthday with the publication of the first volume of the *Année Sociologique*, a collective enterprise of the first real sociological school, whose formation was entirely due to Durkheim's intellectual charisma. When Durkheim began his teaching career in the 1880s, sociology was highly suspect in academic circles, in the Old as well as in the New World, for it ran counter to the dominant individualism of the nineteenth century. But Durkheim, in the pre-First World War French university setting which prided itself in intellectual elitism, became one of the most respected and influential members of the faculty of the prestigious Sorbonne. Symbolic of his conquest of the academic setting on behalf of the discipline which reflected so much his imprint, he was eventually given the first chair of sociology in France in 1913.

The second component of the project entailed establishing the unity of the social (or cultural) sciences on a positivistic basis. Here Durkheim was heir to the Comtean idea of the essential unity of scientific knowledge, with sociology as the last emergent science, furnishing the pinnacle of man's cognitive mastery of the world. The social world was understood by Durkheim as a moral ensemble, with its structure and organization subject to rational understanding. Durkheim saw that such an understanding was necessarily a collaborative undertaking, for science progresses only through a division of labor; the latter became for Durkheim both a moral principle and a scientific principle of essential importance for the modern world. *The Division of Labor* and the *Année Sociologique* are complementary in providing the theory and practice of what Durkheim thought of this fundamental principle of organization.

Social science deals with conventions, mores, ideals; in brief, Durkheim viewed it as investigating scientifically the normative infrastructure of human society. Economics, history, law, and religion are some of the familiar chambers of the human house, and sociology provides the thread which interrelates all the chambers. From Claude Bernard, the founder of modern physiology, Durkheim was well aware that the hallmark of science is experimentation and comparative analysis; however, direct experimentation (such as Bernard had done for experimental medicine with vivisection) is not possible in the social world.

Nevertheless, the comparative analysis of social phenomena in a systematic, organized way was a project which Durkheim partially realized with the *Année Sociologique*. As Terry Clark has aptly commented,[2] this was in its operation a sociological laboratory as much as a journal, one in which recruits served an apprenticeship learning the craft of the new science; the paramount endeavor of this journal was to codify the forms and contents of sociology. Durkheim's academic collaborators in this project were not for the most part professional sociologists, yet they formed a highly integrated interdisciplinary team, sharing various academic and social bonds, and they translated to their own specialty areas the core sociological view obtained from Durkheim.[3] The *Année Sociologique* (still published today) reflected under Durkheim's editorship his acceptance of the essential unity of all social phenomena and his belief that their structural characteristics may be studied scientifically, objectively. But the journal was only a partial success in terms of unifying the social sciences, for the First World War terminated the life of its organizing spirit and decimated the ranks of the second generation of the project. Durkheim's successor and nephew, Marcel Mauss (1872-1950), was acknowledged as a great erudite – "he knew everything," has been said of Mauss – but there was one thing which this genial man of genius did not possess, and that was the discipline and rigor of organization. Mauss himself did not complete his dissertation, and was unable to carry on successfully the editorship of the *Année*, which suspended publication after two issues.[4] Lacking a forum for its development and lacking effective instrumental leadership, Durkheim's project of the unity of the social sciences became stalemated in the interwar period.[5]

---

2   Terry N. Clark. "The Structure and Functions of a Research Institute: The *Année Sociologique,*" *Archives Européennes de Sociologie* IX (1968) pp. 72-91.

3   See Philippe Besnard, ed., *The Sociological Domain. The Durkheimians and the founding of French Sociology.* Cambridge: Cambridge University Press; Paris: Editions de la Maison des Sciences de l'Homme, 1983.

4   In the mid-1930s, the *Année* became differentiated into five "series," known collectively as *Annales Sociologiques*, each having an editorial committee.

5   Of course, many Durkheimians survived the First World War – in fact, the last of the contributors to the first series of the *Année*, Georges Davy, passed away as late as 1976 – and unlike other schools drawn to a strong personality (like the Saint-Simonians, the Freudians, and the Marxists), the death of Durkheim was not followed by factional splits and conflicts over interpreting what the master had taught. Yet, no one stepped forth who could combine Durkheim's role as theoretician and intellectual leader.

The third component of Durkheim's life project immerses us in the sociohistorical situation of the Third Republic and takes us into the sector of ideology and partisanship. This French regime, threatened with abortion at its start in the 1870s, was marked with political instability, like its two republican predecessors.[6] Modern France, from 1789 until today, seems to oscillate between the poles of republicanism and caesarism, punctuated with relatively brief but intense civil or near-civil wars. The French sociological tradition begun by Saint-Simon, followed by Comte, Le Play, and Durkheim, has a common denominator in its repugnance of political upheavals, of group struggles for power, of chicanery and civil strife. The tradition, in contradistinction to Marxist sociology, is to make sociology a healing and stabilizing science, one that will find a viable basis for restoring social consensus and for enhancing societal integration, with a particular concern for the integration of the working class in the social body.[7] This tradition seems, ultimately, to underscore the importance of morality as the cornerstone of social peace and justice. Thus, Saint-Simon, that fabulous visionary of modern society, saw at the end of a meteoric life that the industrial structure was incomplete without a normative component, and he wrote *The New Christianity* to establish the morality appropriate for the new dawning social order. The assessment that the social order needs an integrating morality to complement economic life is a key aspect of nineteenth century French social thought, particularly of the liberal left.[8]

Since morality figures prominently in Durkheim's writings, his sociological orientation has been characterized in some quarters as conservative.[9] Yet Durkheim was a trusted civil servant of the republican regime, which gave him the appropriate accolade of Chevalier de la Légion d'Honneur in 1907; he never frequented conservative circles and instead belonged to liberal voluntary associations (such as the Ligue des Droits de l'Homme). Moreover, it may be said that his most challenging assignment was to develop a scientifically grounded morality which would supersede once and for all the traditional Christian morality and the authority of the Catholic Church which constituted a basic rallying point for every right-wing political movement that contested the legitimacy of the Third

---

6   Turnover in cabinet ministries was notoriously high throughout the Third Republic. A "Président du Conseil" – equivalent of prime minister – who survived as head of government for two years or more was a distinct rarity.

7   On common denominators between Le Play (1806-1882) and Durkheim, see the insightful article by Michel Dion, "Sociologie et idéologie dominante dans l'œuvre de F. Le Play et Emile Durkheim," *La Pensée*, 158 (August 1971): 55-68.

8   The three major sources of liberal left thinking in the Third Republic of Durkheim are republicanism, democratic socialism (exemplified by Jean Jaurés, A. Millerand, and Albert Thomas), and Freemasonry.

9   Lewis A. Coser, "Durkheim's Conservatism and its Implications for his Sociological Theory," in Kurt H. Wolff, ed., *Emile Durkheim 1858-1917* (Columbus: Ohio State University Press, 1960) pp. 211-32; Robert A. Nisbet, "Social Milieu and Sources," in Robert A. Nisbet, ed., *Emile Durkheim* (Englewood Cliffs, N. J.: Prentice-Hall, 1965).

Republic. Consequently, the culmination of Durkheim's life project would entail providing France, as prototypical of modern society, with a civil religion which would be in accordance with the nature of things.

In this respect, Durkheim was the heir to a twofold patrimony. First, in carrying out this project he would assist in completing the Principles of 1789, which are those of modern liberal democracy. Durkheim viewed the French Revolution not as a calamity (the conservative outlook on this event), nor as a sham illusion (the radical outlook), but rather as a great promise lacking completion. The Revolution had installed a secularized religion complete with a cult,[10] but this had not taken root, essentially because of its imposition on society from above rather than its correspondence to felt collective religious needs. In an extensive review early in his career, Durkheim expressed the importance of sociology's concern for the Principles of 1789:

> What are the destinies of the revolutionary religion? What will it become?... There is indeed no question which should attract more the attention of legislators and statesmen: do not all the difficulties in which nations find themselves at the present time stem from the difficulty in adapting the traditional structure of societies to these new and unconscious aspirations which have been tormenting societies for a century?[11]

Second, Durkheim was in this respect also heir to Comte's positivistic legacy. Comtean positivism was more than a cognitive mapping of the world via the "positive" sciences. It was also intended as the formulation of a new world order, a rational, scientifically based "religion of mankind," complete with a calendar and the cult of the Great Being, which is mankind or human society writ large. The French Revolution and Comte, thus, were inspirational sources in the background of Durkheim's project to give sociology an ultimate pragmatic justification: sociology would uncover the appropriate integrative force for a secularized but moral social order. Consequently, the quest for a civil religion has to be kept in mind as one major factor if we are to make sense as to why Durkheim and so many of his ablest lieutenants devoted so much time and effort to the careful study of religious phenomena.[12] Such an effort would otherwise appear incongruous with

---

10   Albert Mathiez, *La Théophilanthropie et le culte décadaire* (Paris: Alcan, 1903); Albert Mathiez, *Contributions à l'histoire religieuse de la Révolution française* (Paris: Alcan, 1906). See in this volume my essay "Durkheim, Mathiez and the French Revolution: The Political Context of a Sociological Classic."

11   "The Principles of 1789 and Sociology," in Edward Tiryakian, ed., *The Phenomenon of Sociology* (New York: Appleton-Century-Crofts, 1971) p. 43. This was first published in *Revue de l'Enseignement* in 1890.

12   In his detailed examination of the *Année* published under Durkheim's editorship, Nandan found that out of a total of 2,073 reviews appearing in the twelve volumes, "Religious Sociology" constituted the single largest category, with total of 581, or 28 percent, of the

the Durkheimians' sympathies for laicization, liberal republicanism, Jauressian socialism, and even anticlericalism.[13]

Durkheim's last work, *The Elementary Forms of the Religious Life* (hereafter cited as *The Forms*), while it may be considered the successful completion of Durkheim's sociology, left incomplete his global life project of providing the normative cement for modern secular society. France survived the holocaust of the First World War, and even had come together politically in 1914 with the "union sacré' in a rare moment of moral unification; but the Third Republic, morally shallow though economically sound, could hardly survive the peace that followed. Symbolically, Durkheim's erstwhile popularizer, Célestin Bouglé, who had become Director of the École Normale Supérieure de Paris (the major spawning ground of the Durkheimian school), died as the Germans arrived at the gates of Paris in 1940. The Third Republic toppled over on the battlefield, but it had become inanimate before, perhaps more than anything else because, as Durkheim had surmised, an implosion follows a society which cannot fill its moral vacuum.

So much for an initial approximation of what marks Emile Durkheim in bold relief. Rather than present summaries of his works or a chronological and descriptive development of his sociology, I will structure this chapter in terms of three approaches. The first ingress will be a consideration of his Bordeaux beginnings and the societal context of France at the time. The second approach will be to treat some of the paramount intellectual influences which are reflected in his work and which provide structures to his analysis. The third and closing section will dwell on methodological aspects of Durkheim's sociology: if Durkheim may properly be seen as the monumental modernizer of sociology, it is above all because he provided the discipline with its first comprehensive scientific paradigm, one which entails more than a set of technical recipes but a whole method of approaching social phenomena. Even if he did not achieve the totality of his life project, the establishment of sociology as a rigorous science, with its own domain of inquiry and with an articulation of its major specialty areas, makes the figures of Emile Durkheim unique in the historical development of our discipline.

---

entries. See Yash Nandan, *L'Ecole Durkheimienne et son opus* (Paris: Microéditions du Centre National de la Recherche Scientifique, 1975) p. 121.

13   In 1905, during the public debates over the controversial "loi Combes" (which led to the separation of church and state and the stripping of the Catholic church of its own schools), Durkheim stated at a meeting of the progressive l'Union pour l'Action Morale, "The Church, from a sociological perspective, is a monster." By this he meant that the Catholic church, given its territorial vastness and multiple social constituencies, should have lost its intellectual and moral homogeneity long ago; the proposed legislation, he felt, would have the beneficial effect of stimulating the differentiation of the church. See *Libres Entretiens*, 13:7 (May 1905) pp. 368-370.

I

Among the routine affairs of the Faculty of Letters at the University of Bordeaux in the year 1887 was the election of its new dean from its ranks. Well-liked and highly regarded by his colleagues, Alfred Espinas handily won the administrative nod. Ten years earlier he had created quite a stir by preparing the first doctoral dissertation in sociology, *Les Sociétés Animales*, which audaciously indicated the stimulus of Comtean positivism on the young scholar's approach to sociobiology; the thesis was accepted but only after deletion in the printed version of reference to Comte. In the 1870s the traditionalists still had enough sway in both the intellectual and the political arenas that secular doctrines, such as positivism, were ill viewed in university circles. But in the following decade the political climate in France began to shift leftward, with liberal republicans firmly in the saddle. The liberal left was the descendant of revolutionary Jacobinism: anticlerical, rationalistic, in favor of the centralization of political authority and state intervention (statism). Without too much distortion, one may compare the dominating liberal left of the Third Republic with New Deal Democrats in the United States; more extreme shades of the left in pre-First World War France were represented at different times by radical republicans and socialists of different convictions, such as Gambetta and Clemenceau on the republican left, and Guesde and Jaurès on the socialist side.[14] The major inspirational source and chief theoretician of the French left in the nineteenth century was Pierre-Joseph Proudhon, not Marx, who was to remain relatively insignificant in French socialist circles until the formation of the Communist Party and its takeover of the labor movement and *L'Humanité*. To the right and in opposition to a republican form of government were two major restorationist factions which became increasingly ineffective over time: the monarchists (whose split as to whether an Orleans or a Bourbon heir was the legitimate ruler prevented a restoration in the 1870s when the monarchists had control of parliament) and the Bonapartists. The right and the far left were in common agreement in opposing large-scale capitalism and the foreign policy of imperialistic expansion adopted by the liberals; they occasionally came together on various national issues, but it was not an enduring alliance. The French parliament became a haze and maze of wheelings and dealings under the "opportunists". Ministries would be toppled but the middle-level bureaucracy would carry on, and after 1876 the republican cause was beyond danger of the repeat of a radical-inspired Commune uprising, a Bonapartist coup d'état, or a rural-based restoration.

But this statement is made with the wisdom of historical hindsight. The republican regime was to pass through two severe crises, one of which had no manifest effect on Durkheim, while the other proved to be an unanticipated

---

14   To extend the comparison, Jauressian socialism was structurally along the lines of the ADA (Americans for Democratic Action). wing of the Democratic Party in the United States. Guesdian socialism, directly Marxist in doctrine, was outside the parliamentary pale of party politics.

boon to the fortunes of Durkheim and his school. The first was the abortive coup d'état of General Boulanger who, during Durkheim's first years at Bordeaux, nearly succeeded in seizing power in the French style of the military hero who regenerates his country from civil morass, in a tradition that extends from Joan of Arc through the Napoleons and on to Pétain in 1940 and De Gaulle in 1958. The second crisis, ten years after the Boulanger episode, was, of course, the Dreyfus affair, which brought out all the cracks and cleavages of French society on the eve of the twentieth century. Had the Dreyfusards not won out, the power structure of French higher education would have changed drastically and Durkheim would probably have languished on the banks of the Garonne rather than go on to flourish on the banks of the Seine.

Returning to Espinas, the University of Bordeaux had opened its doors to schoolteachers who needed academic credits to get certified, and Espinas had taken on the charge of offering them a concentrated course on pedagogy. This curricular innovation proved very successful, but also meant that with Espinas assuming full-time administrative responsibilities in 1887-88, there was need to recruit from the outside a suitable replacement. The search did not take long, for Louis Liard, an ex-Bordeaux professor who had recently assumed charge of higher education in the Ministry of Public Education, knew just the right person for the vacancy: a young lycée instructor teaching at Troyes, a person who had just written some brilliant articles on recent trends in German social sciences.[15]

Liard was a progressive, a modernizer who with other liberal intellectuals had arrived at the conclusion that Germany's crushing of France in 1870 was because Germany had modernized its institutions more rapidly than France. In particular, German higher education had become part of the "German miracle" in overtaking France and England – helpless and overrun by Napoleon two generations before, Germany had become the most aggressive, vigorous modern country in the 1870s and 1880s. Behind its technology, its industrial growth, and its organizational discipline was its university system, which fostered new scientific and empirical approaches to the study of almost everything, including history.

One wing of Frenchmen, coming from the eastern region which had suffered the German annexation of Alsace and part of Lorraine, dedicated itself to the restoration of the "lost territories" and to keep firmly implanted in the national vision the plight of that part of the national soil desecrated by German rule. This wing was one important source of French nationalism during the Third Republic.

---

15   Durkheim later acknowledged that his Bordeaux appointment was due to Liard: see his article "L'Etat actuel des études sociologiques en France" (1895) in Emile Durkheim, *Textes* (Paris: Les Editions de Minuit, 1975) comp. Victor Karady, vol. 1, p. 53 (hereafter designated as *Textes*, with appropriate volume following). Liard would be for the rest of Durkheim's career his staunch supporter in the important ministry; older than Durkheim, Liard outlived him. The two pieces that caught Liard's attention were Durkheim's "La science positive de la morale en Allemagne" (1887) in *Textes* I, pp. 267-343, and "La Philosophie dans les universités allemandes" (1887) in *Textes* III, pp. 437-86.

Another wing from the same area had drawn a different lesson, namely that France must in turn modernize in the footsteps of Germany. To modernize entailed to secularize and dislodge Catholic authority from the public sphere, including the educational one (as Bismarck attempted to do with his *Kulturkampf*). The great figure for French domestic modernization was Jules Ferry, a man from the East, twice prime minister, who achieved great renown for his domestic reforms, particularly in educational legislation providing free and compulsory public education, and in giving schoolteachers a decent salary. Like Lyndon Johnson nearly a century later, his important social reforms would be eclipsed by public reaction against his Indochina entanglements.

In the 1880s, then, the French Ministry of Education was a dynamic, reform-minded ministry, similar if one seeks comparison to HEW (Health, Education & Welfare) in the United States in the 1960s and 1970s. Travel awards were made available annually to a select number of very promising young scholars for a semester's study in Germany, so that they could bring back new ideas for renovating the French curriculum and mode of study, particularly in the matter of research. The young lycée teacher whom Liard found well qualified for the Bordeaux vacancy had been the recipient of such a fellowship and had made good use of his time at Marburg, Berlin, and Leipzig, being attracted at the last named to the famous seminar of Wilhelm Wundt. The instructor, born in 1858 in a part of Lorraine that had escaped annexation, was David Emile Durkheim.

In addition to his publications in scholarly journals, Durkheim had other solid credentials. Like other public schoolteachers in France, his folder in the ministry included evaluation by his superiors.[16] Wherever he had been, Durkheim had received favorable recommendations; his teachers seemed to sense that much would be heard from him. And Durkheim was an alumnus of the elite-training École Normale Supérieure (ENS) de Paris, which produced some of the most important cadres of the Third Republic, its crack educators. The ENS came to have strategic importance for the republican regime since the latter saw the schoolroom as the ideal locale to conquer minds to the republican cause and wrestle them away from a traditional mentality).[17] It is with some truth that the Third Republic, assisted by its educational arm of ENS, was to earn the sobriquet of "The Republic of the

---

16   Durkheim's complete life dossier as a civil servant is available at the Archives Nationales in Paris. I have consulted this as well as his dossier in the Archives Départementales de la Gironde at Bordeaux.

17   The republican regime took this as a major domestic and colonial policy. In the latter, much of the ideology of colonization was an extension of the Ferry policy of modernization via secular education. Symbolic of this is the work of Georges Hardy, at the time Inspector of Education in French West Africa, *Une Conquête Morale: L'Enseignement en A.O.F.* (Paris: Armand Colin, 1917). Furthermore, the École William Ponty at Gorée (Senegal), which provided Black French Africa with outstanding cadres and represented the pinnacle of "assimilation" policy, was patterned after the ENS.

Professors," since so many of its major political personalities were academically trained intellectuals).[18]

Examining the dossier, Liard could readily see that Durkheim had done well at the ENS, as may be attested by the summary evaluation prepared shortly after his graduation by the director of the school, no less than the great historian Fustel de Coulanges:

> Excellent student; a very forceful mind both sound and original, with a remarkable maturity. He has a real aptitude for philosophicall studies, especially psychology. His teachers think highly of him. The École Normale has awarded him the Adolphe Gamier prize as the hardest worker and most deserving member of his class ... [19]

One may note that "philosophy" in the French curriculum encompassed not only logic and metaphysics but also whatever might be seen as a source of reflection bearing on the human condition, including the nature of man and society. The stress on philosophy was not unrelated to republican ideology, for philosophy in the Third Republic occupied the privileged seat formerly held by theology. Durkheim was trained as a philosopher, published in leading philosophical journals (*Revue Philosophique, Revue de Métaphysique et de Morale*), participated in the distinguished Société Française de Philosophie (begun in 1901), and was concerned throughout his life with questions of moral philosophy.[20]

The latter was an exceedingly popular subject throughout Durkheim's lifetime; it was not a mere academic topic but one which had ideological significance. An important problem for the Third Republic was that of getting legitimation. If the republic and the social order behind its polity were to become really accepted by Frenchmen, there was need for the state to have a moral authority for, as much as over, its citizens. Everyone saw that the Catholic church had provided the moral authority behind the monarchy, and because of this past association, the church (particularly the higher clergy) could not be entrusted with assisting the republic in its post-1870 nation-building endeavors. Conversely, the republic had as major proponents anticlerical Catholic liberals, Protestants, Jews, and Freemasons.

---

18   See Albert Thibaudet, *La République des Professeurs* (1927; Paris: Editions André Sauret, 1973).

19   Letter dated October 14, 1882, in the Durkheim dossier in the Archives Nationales. Such evaluations were to accumulate with consistency in Durkheim's dossier. Thus, in filing his report on Durkheim for the year 1899-1900, the Rector (chief administrative officer) of Bordeaux answered various categories as follows. Character, behavior and social habits: "Dominant traits: initiative and authority"; Sagacity and judgment: "A remarkably vigorous mind"; Teaching: "A powerful and systematic originality"; Administrative ability: "More of a head of a school (chef d'école) and theoretician than a man of practical details."

20   See Ernest Wallwork, *Durkheim, Morality, and Milieu* (Cambridge: Harvard University Press, 1972); Robert N. Bellah, ed., *Emile Durkheim on Morality and Society* (Chicago: University of Chicago Press, 1973).

The net result was that republican France was eagerly concerned with philosophy, with morality, and with moral education – not from intellectual disinterestedness but from practical considerations of finding a substitute for traditional Christian teachings, so as to legitimate itself and win the broader support of new generations of schoolchildren, wrestling them away from the moral authority of the Catholic church. There were two stark alternatives to finding a new moral cement for society: on the one hand, power without authority could become reality in a one-man takeover, as had befallen the First and Second republics. On the other hand, "power to the people" as a radical populist ideology (advanced on behalf of the Sans-Culottes by Hébert during the Revolution and by Vallès on behalf of the Communards in 1870) conjured the specter of proletarian uprisings, civil disorder, and violent strife. Philosophy, the rational inquiry for cosmic and social order, was thus for the Third Republic the chosen alternative to either lawlessness or traditional dogmatism. Hence, that Durkheim was trained in and that he had taught philosophy since graduating from the École Normale[21] was a further qualification for replacing Espinas in the teaching of pedagogy, for philosophy dealt more with the "real world" and was considered much more significant for affairs of state in 1887 than in our day.

Pedagogy, teaching schoolteachers the principles of education, was thus the basic charge of Durkheim at Bordeaux. What else would he propose to teach, inquired the outgoing dean of the faculty? The young scholar did not hesitate in his reply: "My intention is to give a public course on *Social Science* ... I propose to take as the theme of the course that of *social solidarity* ..."[22]

Emile Durkheim thus became a member of the faculty at Bordeaux in the fall of 1887, got married in October to Louise Julie Dreyfus, and began teaching a special course in "social science." Seven years later Espinas would be called to the Sorbonne, and this would create a vacant professorship. Durkheim's star continued to rise and within ten years of his entry at Bordeaux he, the son of an orthodox rabbi living in humble circumstances,[23] had scaled the academic height of getting created for him the first chair of social science. His father did not live to see Emile's later successes but his mother, Mélanie Isidor Durkheim, must have felt great gratification that her son, the only Jew in his class (1882) at ENS, had

---

21   Durkheim was assigned as his first position after passing the *agrégation* to teach philosophy at the Lycée du Puy; he took up duties there on October 1, 1882, but before the end of the month was assigned to the more important lycée at Sens. In January 1884 he was shifted to St. Quentin, then took a year's leave during 1885-86, and was teaching at Troyes during 1886-87 when he got word of his appointment to Bordeaux as a "chargé de cours" with a salary of 4,000 francs.

22   Undated letter in Durkheim folder, Archives Départementales de la Gironde.

23   There is a letter in Durkheim's Paris dossier dated January 7, 1880, from the Grand Rabbin du Consistoire Central des Israélites de France to the minister of education asking for remission of the 400 francs required for a student's clothing and laundry at the École Normale (during Durkheim's first year there) on the ground that Durkheim's father could ill afford this expense.

become a university professor; she died in 1901, the year before his being named to the Sorbonne. In 1902 history repeated itself: just as in 1887 Durkheim had been called due to a vacancy in pedagogy, so in 1902 Ferdinand Buisson, who had the chair of moral education, received a cabinet appointment in the new Combes government, and Durkheim was brought in from Bordeaux as Buisson's substitute. His rise to the top of academic circles is indicative not only of his own sweeping accomplishments but also of the fact that the Third Republic was very propitious for Jewish intellectuals to distinguish themselves through talent – Durkheim's peer group in this respect included Henri Bergson, Lucien Lévy-Bruhl, Emile Meyerson, Léon Blum, Henri Berr, Léon Brunschvicq, and Xavier Léon, among others, many of whom were of families from Alsace or Lorraine.[24]

It is opportune to consider his initial university teaching, because I find striking how well formed were his sociological ideas at the very start of his appointment, when he was barely thirty years old. I will concentrate on this formative Bordeaux period and forego the more standard coverage of the "later" Durkheim.

His first sociology course dealt, as he had promised, with the theme of social solidarity.[25] His second year he offered "Introduction to the Sociology of the Family," and in his inaugural lecture[26] he advanced a program of study for the

---

24   I bother to make this point because I think Lewis Coser in his otherwise splendid chapter on Durkheim errs in stating "A Sephardic boy could have moved by almost imperceptible steps into the world of French secular culture; an Ashkenazi boy like Durkheim could not" *(Masters of Sociological Thought* [New York: Harcourt Brace Jovanovich, 1977) p. 162). Unlike Germany and Austria, where Simmel and Freud had to contend with anti-Semitism which blocked university appointments, France readily made room for all those willing to serve the republican cause; and moreover, unlike Teutonic countries, the doors of the lodges in France were open to Jews and provided them with significant behind-the-scenes support. See Philippe Bourdrel, *Histoire des Juifs de France* (Paris: Albin Michel, 1974) esp. pp. 162-225. To be sure, anti- Semitism did break out over the Dreyfus affair and had its vocal spokesmen in figures like Drumont and Maurras, but it had no influence inside the government and institutions of higher education, which remained solidly liberal. Perhaps Durkheim was subject to the "ordeal of civility," which is dealt with so sensitively by John M. Cuddihy in a recent work, *The Ordeal of Civility: Freud, Marx, Levi-Strauss, and the Jewish Struggle with Modernity* (New York: Basic Books, 1974) but all my indications are that he stepped with ease from his familial home in Epinal to his academic home in Paris and Bordeaux. If Durkheim, Brunschvicq, Lévy-Bruhl, Berr, and other Jewish intellectuals were such strong proponents of the Third Republic, it is surely in part because its government made them feel it had merited their trust and legitimation by giving full access to talent. All in all, Durkheim's Paris was a time when "the Jewish intelligentsia was truly coming into its own," and Jewish salons of high society flourished, catching the alert attention of Proust (Seth Wolitz, *The Proustian Community,* New York: New York University Press, 1971, pp. 152-53).

25   "Cours de science sociale. Leçon d'ouverture," reproduced in J. C. Filloux, ed., *La science sociale et l'action* (Paris: Presses Universitaires de France, 1970) pp. 77-110.

26   "Introduction à la sociologie de la famille," first published in 1888 and reproduced in *Textes* III, pp. 9-34, from which citations are here taken.

year's subject matter. His summary brings out that the initial problem which frames sociology, the question of social solidarity, is to know "what are the bonds which unite men, that is, what determines the formation of social aggregates."[27]

As would be typical of his later analysis, Durkheim eschewed a psychological answer to the question. There are different kinds of social solidarity, just as there are different kinds of society. Albeit our present incomplete state of scientific knowledge makes any classification somewhat arbitrary, yet two major social types are discernible in all societies, past and present. The former are "amorphous" societies lacking political organization, which range from roving bands of kinsmen up to groups living in urban settlements; the second type is characterized by political organization, or states, which appear with the city and culminate in the large contemporary nations. Each type of society, Durkheim continued, is marked by a different form of social solidarity: one due to the similarity of minds, to the community of ideas and sentiments, while the other arises from the differentiation of functions and the division of labor.[28] Under the influence of the former, individuals fuse into a mass, so to speak, whereas in the case of the latter each has his sphere of action although dependent on the specific contributions of others to the wellbeing of the whole.

Durkheim termed the former "mechanical" and the latter "organic," noting that these should be seen as analytical distinctions, although one predominates in primitive, the other in modern societies. The less extensive society is, the more similarities predominate over differences, the more like-minded individuals are. Conversely, the more extensive society becomes (in population size and in social ties), the greater the competition between individuals for scarce resources, the more necessary is social differentiation for survival. It follows that "the division of labor becomes the primary condition of social equilibrium," and the major factor behind the transformations of social solidarity and behind all of history is thus "the simultaneous growth in the volume and density of societies."[29]

To reiterate, the above propositions were contained in Durkheim's initial course at Bordeaux in 1887-88. It already proposed the conceptualization, even down to the same terms, which would appear in 1893 as his major doctoral

---

27   Ibid., p. 9. This basic theme of sociology is elegantly explored anew in Robert A. Nisbet, *The Social Bond* (New York: Alfred Knopf, 1970). It may be pointed out that the theme of "solidarity" was a cornerstone of republican social doctrine. Its first major exploration was by Henri Marion in *De la Solidarité Morale, Essai de Psychologie Appliquée* (Paris: Germer Bailliere, 1880). Marion's work articulated the republican temper and aspirations so well that a chair in moral education was subsequently created for him at the Sorbonne, the very chair which Durkheim would inherit from Buisson. For further discussion of solidarity as a key Durkheimian theme, see the essay "Durkheim, Solidarity and September 11" in this volume.

28   "Introduction," *Textes* III, p. 10.

29   Ibid. p. 11.

thesis, *The Division of Labor, Essay on the Organization of Advanced Societies*.[30] Durkheim's first year coincided with the publication of Ferdinand Tönnies's *Gemeinschaft und Gesellschaft (Community and Society)*. It is a bit as if Lamarck and Darwin (rather than Darwin and Wallace) had both brought out at the same time their respective theories of evolution, for like Durkheim, Tönnies dealt with two forms of social solidarity. Unlike Durkheim, however, Tönnies downgraded the social solidarity of modern large-scale society, which he saw as the temporary domination of capitalism stamping social relations with a cash nexus, an artificial sort of society unlike the more natural and earlier form of *Gemeinschaft*. Durkheim reviewed Tönnies in 1889[31] and took the occasion to note their agreement as to the nature, significance, and primacy of *Geineinschaft*. But, he went on, the two differed in their evaluation of *Gesellschaft*. Tönnies saw in this type of society the progressive unfolding of individualism, and the society marked by it lacked internal spontaneity. What social life it had came from the external stimulus of the state; it was the kind of society thought of by Jeremy Bentham.[32] For him, Durkheim countered, modern societies have a life as organic and natural as earlier, less extensive societies. Modern and primitive society are two different types but they are types of the same kind. To demonstrate this, Durkheim went on, it would be necessary to write a book, one which would study inductively this modern form of society, that is, by studying the laws and customs associated with this form of societal structure, rather than the typological and deductive manner of German logicians.[33]

I find rather remarkable that this view of Durkheim's, written at the age of 31, is such an accurate announcement of his later work. He did expand his critique of Tönnies into a book, namely the *Division of Labor*, which is more than a rebuttal of Tönnies's view of modern society as *Gesellschaft* since it is also a critique of British utilitarianism associated with Bentham and advanced in sociological form by Herbert Spencer. Note also that he would in his dissertation, as he had proposed in his review, take up the legal system as a major correlate and manifestation of social solidarity, the latter being a primary condition of what might be termed *intersubjectivity*.

There is one more challenge which *Gemeinschaft und Gesellschaft* presented to Durkheim, namely the question of whether modern, large-scale society does have an internal spontaneity, that is, whether it has a genuine social solidarity

---

30   *De la division du travail social. Etude sur l'organisation des sociétés supérieures* (Paris: Félix Alcan, 1893). The English translation by George Simpson is *The Division of Labor in Society* (1933: New York: Free Press, 1966).

31   An English translation of the review is presented by Werner Cahnman, along with the subsequent review of Durkheim's *Division of Labor* by Tönnies. See "Tönnies and Durkheim: An Exchange of Reviews," in Werner J. Cahnman, ed., *Ferdinand Tönnies, A New Evaluation* (Leiden: E. J. Brill, 1973) pp. 239-56).

32   Durkheim in Cahnman, *Ferdinand Tönnies*, p. 246.

33   Ibid., p. 247.

capable of social renovation and regeneration. Tönnies's description of modern society, Durkheim noted, is a rather bleak portrait in terms of the richness of collective life:

> ... the society which Mr. Tönnies describes is the capitalistic society of the socialists; indeed, the author frequently borrows from Marx and Lasalle the dark colors in which he represents that society.[34]

Durkheim saw Tönnies and the socialists in accord that the organization of modern society depends upon the state: the state is responsible for the administration of social life, for the enforcement of contracts and the limitation of individual wills whose unchained desires might, in the absence of genuine ties, result in a war of all against all. What for the German social thinkers – whether radical or moderate socialists – contained capitalism was and could only be state socialism; whether the state was the organ of the proletariat or of the bourgeoisie, the view of society is similar.

Durkheim, it might be noted, was ambivalent toward the state. He did view the central government as having played a liberating role in the historical process, that is, of liberating individuals from the yoke of tradition and ascription.[35] Undoubtedly this had some personal meaning for Durkheim, since it was the regime of the First Republic which had emancipated Jews from the restrictions of the *ancien régime*, as it did other groups such as slaves in the colonies and quasi-serfs at home. But Durkheim was also a follower of de Tocqueville in viewing a healthy democratic organization of society as consisting of viable and multiple intermediate groups between individuals and the state.[36] Individuals as such are not sufficient for social life to have stability and organization; the state qua centralized polity is at least one level removed from the everyday social world so that what it decrees is, in a sense, an external imposition.

I think it is a reasonable extension of his thoughts to suggest that he felt those who place their hopes on the state to organize modern social life fail to realize that the state cannot decree or legislate the affective dimension of social organization, that is, the essential intersubjective affect which binds fellow societal members into solidary unions. Although very much a rationalist in his cognitive orientation to reality, Durkheim, as will be seen in a later section, actually gave a central place in his sociology to the role of affect in social life, including its

---

34   Ibid., p. 245.

35   Much of Durkheim's political sociology, and in particular his discussion of the progressive role of the state in establishing what would today be called civil liberties, will be found in his *Professional Ethics and Civic Morals* (London: Routledge & Kegan Paul, 1957).

36   Compare Alexis de Tocqueville's *The Old Regime and the French Revolution* (1856) and his *Democracy in America* (1832) with Durkheim's *Professional Ethics*, especially chap. 9.

role in regenerating social organization and cohesion. The challenge of providing a different interpretation of modern society than Tönnies had provided with his somber depiction of *Gesellschaft* would be an underlying stimulus in Durkheim's sociological thinking for many years. Durkheim's rebuttal of Tönnies's notion that modern *Gesellschaft*-like society is void of internal spontaneity is contained, I would propose, in *The Elementary Forms of the Religious Life* (1912). That seminal *opus* contains among so many rich ideas the proposition of the autoregeneration of society, of periodic societal effervescence spontaneously recreating the sacred during the course of intense social interaction and thereby rebuilding social organization. May it not be suggested in terms of the present context that if Durkheim chose as source materials for the development of his theory those pertaining to a stateless or acephalous society (the Australian aborigines), this could be an indication of his refusal to see anything religious or mystical in the state, unlike the German tradition which goes back to Hegel for inspiration?

Returning to his second year course, he laid out at the onset what kind of course on the family he would have liked to offer.[37] He would have wanted to focus on the contemporary modern family, the elements which structure it, how the state defines marital and kinship relations, and how the elements of the family function in interrelating its parts; the network of all these relationships comprise family life.[38] But, he added, such an anatomical (or structural) analysis is not an explanation: to explain, one must find the *raison d'etre* behind the relationship. Natural sciences discover the causes underlying relationships by means of experiments, which are unavailable to sociology. But as Claude Bernard indicated long before, Durkheim continued, what is essential in experiments is not the production of artificial phenomena by the researcher but rather the comparison of what is to be explained in different circumstances and in different forms – in other words, what counts in science is to be able to observe a given fact (*le fait étudié*) under varying conditions.[39] Varying the conditions enables the researcher to establish what is essential and what is contingent about a phenomenon; if variant forms of the phenomenon are produced naturally rather than in the laboratory, its comparative study may be termed indirect experimentation.

Unfortunately, Durkheim added, we lack at present systematic and reliable knowledge concerning the different forms of the family. So we must begin our work by classifying and describing major family types, group them in genus and species, and seek to the extent possible to find the causes which have led to their formation and survival.[40] Such a classification of things past will enable us to explain the present, the more comparative research unfolds, because the forms of

---

37   "Introduction à la sociologie de la famille," *Annales de la Faculté des lettres de Bordeaux*, 1888: 257-81.

38   *Textes* III, pp.11-13.

39   Ibid., p. 13.

40   It may be pointed out that taxonomy was a basic aspect of Durkheim's sociological research.

domestic life, even the oldest and most distant from our own mores, have residues in the contemporary family. Higher social forms have evolved out of lower ones, hence the former is a résumé of the latter, after a fashion; the modern family contains the whole historical development of the family.[41]

The comparative analysis of the historical tableau of family development makes it easier to isolate and explain components of the contemporary family than starting our sociological analysis with today's family: by taking history as a whole we can discern individual family species and types easier than if we were to start with the contemporary scene where the threads are intertwined and jumbled up. But, affirmed Durkheim, no matter how far back into the past our analysis will lead, we shall never lose the present from view; even in describing the most elementary forms of the family, the endeavor is to arrive step by step at an explanation of our modern Western family.[42]

Durkheim's approach to explaining domestic life anticipates, to the letter, his procedures *twenty-four years later* in giving a sociological account of religious life. For when in beginning *The Forms* he justifies approaching religion by a study of its very early versions, he announces: "primitive religions do not merely aid us in disengaging the constituent elements of religion; they also have the great advantage that they facilitate the explanation of it."[43] And shortly before that passage he indicates that although what was sought was an understanding of religion today, we must eschew beginning with a preconceived notion of what religion is or with an abstraction from our contemporary situation; rather, "what we must find is a concrete reality, and historical and ethnological observation alone can reveal that to us."[44]

I draw attention to this because of the striking continuity in Durkheim's approach to social phenomena. From the dawn to the dusk of his university teaching and research, he stressed a *comparative* method of analysis, one which sought to understand major facets of contemporary Western society by means of anthropological and historical data. To provide a linkage between these historical and ethnological strata, Durkheim retained an evolutionary position, one wherein the present represents the latest in a series of stages of development.[45]

---

41   *Textes* III, p. 15.

42   Ibid., p. 16.

43   *The Elementary Forms of the Religious Life* (1912; New York: Collier, 1961) p. 19.

44   Ibid., p. 16.

45   For a recent discussion of evolutionary thought in Durkheim, see Roscoe C. Hinkle, "Durkheim's Evolutionary Conception of Social Change," *The Sociological Quarterly* 17 (Summer 1976) pp. 336-46.

It needs to be pointed out that for Durkheim there is not one universal, unilinear evolutionary development, since he invokes the image of evolution as a tree, with multiple societal branchings. His position, I would suggest, is rather similar to that of Max Weber in seeing that civilizations, once formed, have their own internal logic of development.

Unlike earlier social evolutionists as well as many of his contemporaries, Durkheim did not take the last element in the social series – that is, contemporary institutions – to be morally superior to earlier elements. Primitive = inferior and advanced = superior are definitely *not* part of the Durkheimian evolutionary grammar. This is further indicated in the introduction to *The Forms* where he states:

> In reality, then, there are no religions which are false. All are true in their own fashion ... when we turn to primitive religions, it is not with the idea of depreciating religion in general, for these religions are no less respectable than the others. They respond to the same needs, they play the same role, they depend upon the same causes.[46]

Durkheim had from the outset the vision that the vast panorama of social life constitutes, for the sociologist, a unified whole; in other words, for the sociologist interested in explaining modern conditions – whether it be the family, religion, or whatever – the past is prelude to the present, history and ethnology offer data that unlock the meaning of the present.[47] Sociological analysis, then, makes relevant what is distant from our modern society in time and social space.

For Durkheim and his followers who formed the core of the *Année Sociologique* team, historical and ethnological materials, properly utilized, did constitute sociological "empirical data"; this in itself was not a methodological innovation, for Spencer had made use of these in his evolutionary sociology. However, Durkheim was to refine the comparative method by a much greater degree of rigor in the critical analysis of texts, and also by evolving a conceptual frame for the codification of data. Essentially, the framework of the *Année* represented in itself a theoretical conceptualization of the discipline, and from the first volume published in 1898 to the last one published under Durkheim's editorship, in 1913, modifications were made in the conceptualization in light of the data analyzed.[48]

In his "Introduction to the Sociology of the Family," Durkheim expressed himself on other methodological issues which would later guide him. The sociological method is one of induction resting on facts, but facts reported by travelers or temporary observers in a given society may be misleading: social

---

46   *The Forms*, p. 15.

47   At the same time, Durkheim does not have the covert admiration and respect for the past that Comte does.

48   The *Année Sociologique*, viewed as a sociological laboratory or scientific research institute, illustrates the cross-fertilization between theory and research discussed years ago by Robert Merton in chaps. 2 and 3 of his classic *Social Theory and Social Structure* (New York: Free Press, 1949). For a supplementary discussion of this see Jean Carbonnier's review of the volume of Durkheim's writings edited by Jean Duvignaud (*Journal Sociologique* [Paris: Presses Universitaires de France,]), in *L'Année Sociologique* 3e série: 20 (1969) p. 81.

observers see things through their ideological lens, whether of conservatism or radicalism.[49] What sociological analysis seeks to get at is the internal structure of the institution (such as the family), for this is what is of scientific interest, not superficial aspects which may catch the attention of concerned laymen; literary or moral accounts are not sufficiently objective documents. To go from surface, personal impressions of social phenomena to their basic structural aspects, one must find these in

> those ways of acting reinforced by practice which are called customs, law, mores. Here we are dealing not with simple incidents of personal life but with regular and constant practices, residues of collective experiences, fashioned by an entire train of generations.[50]

Anticipating the famous operational definition of social facts he was to offer seven years later in the *Rules of Sociological Method*, Durkheim then proposes that a custom may be recognized in being mandatory for all members of a society: it is a social rule which must be followed and which is endowed with the authority of some sanction. It is the existence of the latter which differentiates custom from simple habits.[51] So recognized, Durkheim adds, customs provide us recognizable facts analogous to those studied by the natural sciences.

Durkheim went on to indicate some of the anthropological and historical sources that can be used in examining the family (Bachofen, Lubbock, MacLennan, Morgan, Maine, Sohm, etc.). He was aware that mores and their further objectification in laws do not reveal all that is crucial about institutional life; legal features may survive by dint of habit and hide the fact that underlying conditions may have changed. So there is a degree of uncertainty and incompleteness about utilizing

---

49   To illustrate this point, Durkheim makes use of the missionary and the socialist, respectively ("Introduction," *Textes* III, p. 17).

50   Ibid., pp.18-19.

51   Ibid., p. 19. In making the important differentiation of two kinds of social action, those that are morally imperative (which he calls "coutumes," or customs) from those that are merely typical or part of everyday life ("simples habitudes"), Durkheim is making the distinction that was the cornerstone of William Graham Sumner's influential conceptual distinction between "mores" and "folkways." Published in 1906, Sumner's *Folkways: A Study of the Sociological Importance of Usages, Manners and Morals* (Boston: Ginn) makes no reference to Durkheim. Reciprocally, the *Année* did not review Sumner's treatise but merely listed it among other titles of new publications in its section "Moral and Juridical Sociology," vol. 11(1906-09) p. 279. The apparent unawareness of Durkheim and Sumner is noteworthy since both shared the same view of sociology as the "science of mores": finding in mores the appropriate domain of sociological investigation which provides sociology with phenomena as natural as those studied by the physical sciences. In fact, each separately proposed that the scientific study of customs, usages, and mores be designated by the name of "ethology."

historical and ethnological sources to get at the dynamics of a social institution such as the family.

But this methodological imprecision will be remedied when the sociologist comes to the contemporary family because she can use demography. Demography enables us to express contemporary incremental changes in social life;[52] unlike the single observer whose perspective may distort reality through his biases, demography embraces the totality of society. Durkheim (who understood demography in the broad sense of social statistics) found in the impersonality of numbers a guarantee of the genuineness and objectivity of the social phenomena they disclose. Statistical data, moreover, make manifest quantitative variations of social phenomena and allow their measurement. It is clear from this early text as well as from all his subsequent endeavors that Durkheim regarded quantitative and qualitative analysis as an integral whole.[53] There is no disjunction in Durkheim between "positivism" and "interpretive" sociology, any more than there is in Max Weber's sociological analysis.

Durkheim's "Introduction to the Sociology of the Family", a course at the beginning of his sociological career in 1888, could be followed by sociologists today and not found seriously outdated in its basic approach. It is a *modern* sociology course, not in terms of factual information about the family, of course, but assuredly modern in terms of its conceptualization, its objectivity, and its comprehensive analysis of this basic social institution.

Durkheim's courses in general were very successful and drew an enthusiastic audience recruited from various faculties, a rather rare occurrence (then as now); his presence helped considerably in making intellectual sparks fly around the university.[54] Within ten years of his arrival he completed his major thesis on the division of labor and his minor (Latin) thesis on Montesquieu, as well as

---

52   "La démographie, en effet, parvient à exprimer presque au jour le jour les mouvements de la vie collective," "Introduction," *Textes* III, p. 23. In the division of labor which characterized the Durkheimian school, it was Maurice Halbwachs (1877-1945) who became the specialist in demography, although Halbwachs treated demography not as an end but as a means to develop the morphological matrix of social psychology. He thus drew inspiration from this early suggestion of Durkheim.

53   Under his editorship, the *Année* published two quantitative monographs in economic sociology: François Simiand, "Essai sur le prix du charbon en France au XIXe siècle," *Année Sociologique* 5 (1900-01), and Hubert Bourgin, "Essai sur une forme d'industrie: la boucherie à Paris au XIXe siècle," *Année Sociologique* 8 (1903-04). Further, as series editor for the Travaux de l'Année Sociologique, Durkheim was responsible for the publication of Halbwachs's doctoral dissertation, *La classe ouvrière et les niveaux de vie* (Paris: Alcan, 1913).

54   Thus, Dean Espinas in his annual report for 1890 wrote with pride to the rector that several students, candidates for the *agrégation* examination in French grammar, had followed the course for candidates in philosophy, and many others were taking the course in psychology, while yet others had elected the one in social science (Durkheim's). At the same time, students in the natural sciences and in law had gotten together to sponsor

the two other studies since become classics, namely *Suicide* and *The Rules of Sociological Method*. It was at Bordeaux where, beginning with Marcel Mauss, the first generation of the Durkheimian school began to gather. Bordeaux upgraded dramatically the caliber of its faculty during Durkheim's years, many of whose colleagues distinguished themselves sufficiently to receive the desired promotion to Paris.[55]

All in all, Louis Liard had been an astute marriage broker in bringing Durkheim to Bordeaux; Durkheim blossomed at the university where he spent half of his academic career and he added great luster to the name of Bordeaux.

II

The second approach to Durkheim will be through selected major influences; these, together with the societal context, provide an important ground for his sociological analysis.

Obviously, Durkheim's self-awareness as a sociologist led him to a certain identification with the recognized founder of sociology, Auguste Comte, who died the year before Durkheim's birth.[56] Comte's influence on Durkheim is present in Durkheim's acceptance of "positivism" understood in a double sense: (a) as the study of social phenomena in the same scientific and objective method as that used by the sciences in approaching the phenomena of nature; and (b) as opposed to the "negativism" of Enlightenment philosophy and its heirs, more critical of existing institutions than advancing new ones.

So, to understand the sociologist in Durkheim one must certainly begin with Comte.[57] And perhaps one should also end with Comte, for the bold thesis in *The Forms* that religion is no more and no less than the mirror of real society and that the divinity is the total society itself, hence that religion is both immanent (a natural phenomenon of society) and transcendent (since religion symbolically depicts the forces of society which transcend individuals and even subgroups of society) – this

---

a social-science colloquium, dealing in particular with political economy. "Rapport du Doyen," Archives Départementales de la Gironde, T108 (1876-95).

55   Besides Espinas and Durkheim, among Durkheim's faculty colleagues who would join the elite ranks at the Sorbonne or tlse College de France were the historians Ernest Denis, Camille Jullian, and philosopher Octave Hamelin, a close friend whom Durkheim refers to in the introduction of *The Forms* as his authority for treating time and space as categories of human understanding. A brief overview of Durkheim's situation at Bordeaux is presented by R. René Lacroze, "Emile Durkheim à Bordeaux," *Actes de l'Académie de Bordeaux*, 4e série: XVII (1960-61). Bordeaux: Hôtel des Sociétés Savantes, 1962.

56   Symbolic of this identification is the photograph of Durkheim taken in 1911 showing in the background a photo having the likeness of Comte. See Georges Davy, *Emile Durkheim* (Paris: Louis-Michaud, n.d. [ca. 1911]) p. 9.

57   After all, Durkheim did declare on a public occasion in 1914: "J'ai souvent reconnu que je relevais de Comte," *Textes* I, p. 68.

thesis is a reformulation of Comte's later years' proposition concerning the Great Being as the self-divinization of society.[58]

A more significant influence, in my judgment, was Henri de Saint-Simon (1760-1825), the brilliant, somewhat eccentric entrepreneur, who among other schemes and projects thought of a science of social phenomena, a science of "social physiology" which would gather scientific knowledge about social life. Such scientific knowledge, he foresaw, would be necessary to end the intellectual and moral chaos evident behind the turmoils of the French Revolution and its aftermath, with political constitution after constitution being drafted in vain by legislators who drew up their plans without knowledge of social conditions. Of various themes in Saint-Simon which find their later expression in Durkheim's writings, that of *crisis* merits special notice. Saint-Simon saw crisis as a moral condition of society in the state of "social disorganization" or destructuration, which is a transitory (albeit traumatic) state occurring between "social organization" and "social reorganization." There is a dissolution of organized knowledge involved in the broader normative crisis. The modern crisis is the latest in the historical process, for there have been other mutations, other disjunctures in the past when one form of social organization has perished and a new one has not yet become institutionalized. Saint Simon was heavily indebted to the analyses of two of his influential contemporary thinkers, Louis de Bonald (1754-1840) and Joseph de Maistre (1753-1821), important but often unrecognized precursors of structural-functional analysis.[59]

Saint-Simon, while influenced by their diagnosis that a moral vacuum underlies social disorganization, did not follow them in seeking in medieval Europe the model of social reconstruction. He sought in the present society the seeds of tomorrow's social order, and in particular found these in the nascent industrial society characterized by the *productivity* of labor and capital. If productivity is the hallmark of industrial society, it signifies that old status distinctions based on ascriptive rank are of no import in relating men to one another. Each will be judged in terms of his contributions to the whole: "From each according to his abilities, to each according to his needs" is the formula of Saint-Simon.

All social classes in modern society[60] derive their social identity in terms of their social function, that is, in terms of their contribution to the societal beehive. And once the industrial order becomes fully institutionalized, so will the belief system of modern society become reorganized in terms of *scientific* knowledge,

---

58   See the insightful discussion provided by Célestin Bouglé, "Auguste Comte et le Grand Être," in his *Cours de Sociologie Générale* (mimeographed; Paris: Centre de Documentation Universitaire, c. 1935) pp. 46-53).

59   Their designation as "reactionaries" places their works on the secular index. But if one can temporarily shelve one's political inclinations, de Bonald's *Du Divorce* (Paris: Adrien Leclere, 1805) has a surprisingly modern systems approach.

60   Saint-Simon's sociological analysis takes as its basic unit that of the social class, rather than the individual. Among other things, he is the pioneer of social stratification.

unified in terms of the knowledge of society and of nature. Every social order, every organized civilization, has an economic and a political integration to which corresponds an appropriate system of knowledge. Scientific knowledge and industry form the coupling of modern society in the same way as did theological knowledge and feudalism for medieval society.

Saint-Simon as a crucial modernizer of social thought, prophet of industrial technocracy, and charismatic head of a sect which was a forerunner of a sociological school, merits extensive treatment on his own in any study of the history of sociological analysis.[61] But it is Saint-Simon's influence on Durkheim which is the present subject of discussion. Durkheim had a thorough familiarity with Saint-Simon's ideas, and one does not find the element of ambivalence present which seems to be the case in his discussions of Comte. Durkheim certainly credited Saint-Simon with being the first to have a clear idea of the science of society.[62] More revealing is the extensive attention devoted to Saint-Simon and his school in Durkheim's course on socialism, which he taught at Bordeaux in 1895-96.[63]

More than half of Durkheim's study of socialism deals exclusively with Saint-Simon's doctrines. He begins by noting that the starting point of Saint-Simon is the notion that every social system represents the application of a system of ideas, which manifests itself in different institutions. A society is above all a community of ideas, of moral ideas linked together by the religion of the people; further, religion and science are not heterogeneous, for religion is popular science

---

61   For a recent perspective, see Robert Alun Jones and Robert W. Anservitz, "Saint-Simon and Saint-Simonism: A Weberian View," *American Journal of Sociology* 80 (March 1975) pp. 1095-1123.

62   "La Sociologie" (1915) in *Textes* I, p. 110.

63   Marcel Mauss put together Durkheim's lecture notes and brought out *Le Socialisme* (Paris:Felix Alcan, 1928). The English translation, with an introduction by Alvin Gouldner, is *Socialism and Saint-Simon* (Yellow Springs, Ohio: The Antioch Press, 1958). Gouldner's comments bear more on differences between Durkheim and Comte than on the relation of Durkheim to Saint- Simon and Saint-Simonism. In the text, I am using the new French edition of *Le Socialisme* (Paris: Presses Universitaires de France, 1971). The preface by Pierre Birnbaum (pp. 5-26) is informative and insightful.

The stimulus for the course was student interest in the national political scene. In 1893 various socialist factions (excepting the Marxist one which refused to stand for election) had gotten a total of 50 parliamentarians elected and became a vigorous opposition bloc, although lacking ideological unity. It was logical for Durkheim to examine socialism as an instance of collective representations since several of his close friends, colleagues, and students (Jaurès, Herr, Mauss, Simiand, Lévy-Bruhl) were involved in the fortunes of socialism. Perhaps Durkheim in treating socialism objectively as a social fact may have intended to demonstrate that the sociological method could yield practical results: in the context of socialism, a rigorous sociological analysis might uncover the bases of unification for the various French socialist factions.

For a scholarly treatment of socialism in France in the 1890s, see Daniel Ligou, *Histoire du Socialisme en France* (1871-1961) (Paris: Presses Universitaires de France, 1962) chap. 4.

(a theme which Durkheim would come back to in *The Forms*). What binds men together in society is a common way of thinking, of representing the world; in every phase of history, men understand the world as a function of their scientific understanding, i.e., of knowledge which is taken to be certain. What unifies all partial understandings into a comprehensive knowledge is philosophy, which synthesizes the knowledge of all specific sciences.[64] Positive philosophy or the philosophy of science is encyclopedic, but unlike the critical philosophy of the Enlightenment, its spirit is one of reconstruction and organization. Such a synthesizing must be done periodically, since the particular sciences are constantly evolving; hence the scientific encyclopedia must be periodically upgraded.

In any case, adds Durkheim in explicating Saint-Simon's *Mémoire sur l'Encyclopédie* (ca. 1810), philosophy has a basic social function. In periods of normalcy, philosophy is the keeper of social consciousness, and in periods of crises – which Saint-Simon saw as an emergent system of beliefs seeking to displace an outmoded one – philosophy has the role of guiding the crystallization of the new. So Saint-Simon's philosophical and sociological studies, continues Durkheim, have the same object; philosophy was a natural complement of Saint-Simon's sociological interests.[65]

Saint-Simon's project for renewing the encyclopedia of science became Durkheim's own project the year after this course, when he began the preparation of the *Année Sociologique*, which in effect would be an evolving encyclopedia of the social sciences. Durkheim could easily identify with Saint-Simon's stress on the unity of philosophical and sociological inquiry, both of which get fuller justification from seeking practical ends of improving social organization. After all, Durkheim never discarded his training in philosophy, which stood him well in directing sociological attention to philosophical issues.

But this just marks the beginning of Durkheim's affinity for, if not identification with, Saint-Simon. Durkheim was giving his course on socialism just a few years after having completed his dissertation.

I suspect that Durkheim had not undertaken to study Saint-Simon carefully while preparing his dissertation, because the latter's name is not to be found therein. It must have struck Durkheim when he did get to delve into Saint-Simon to see the correspondence between his *Division of Labor* and Saint- Simon's *L'Industrie* (ca. 1816-1818). For while Saint-Simon in this early period of his writings was dwelling on how the industrial order would provide a structural basis for the integration of modern society,[66] he also indicated that social organization could not transform itself successfully without a moral transformation. At

---

64   *Le Socialisme*, p. 120. Compare with Durkheim's statement in *The Division of Labor*, p. 364: "Philosophy is the collective conscience of science."

65   *Le Socialisme*, p. 122.

66   Compare with *The Division of Labor*, p. 190: "... we may be permitted to predict...that a day will come when our whole social and political organization will have a base exclusively, or almost exclusively, occupational."

present, the old moral system had been abandoned without a new one accepted in its place, hence the moral crisis of French society.[67] Durkheim also pointed out that Saint-Simon had initially believed that economic self-interest would suffice as a work ethic for the social order, but that he changed his mind. If anything, egoism or self-interest divides men more than it unites them; in fact, self-interest is a passion which, unless restrained, will lead to the dissolution of society rather than to its reinforcement. We need not elaborate how this point coincided with Durkheim's own thinking in both *The Division of Labor* and *Suicide*, with the latter demonstrating in part that egoism is deleterious to individuals as much as to the organized societal community.[68]

Saint-Simon, Durkheim points out, saw that what had contained self-interest or egoism in a previous social order were traditional religious beliefs, which had lost their efficacy. This left society without a viable moral system to complement the socioeconomic structural system. Hence, no matter how well economically organized modern society becomes in an international more than a national social order,[69] this social organization needs a soul, a spirit in the form of common moral beliefs which will provide the moral unity to cement the economic unity.[70] Consequently, the last stage of Saint-Simon's thinking was to turn in *The New Christianity* (ca. 1825) to a consideration of the religion appropriate and necessary for modern society.

It is worth pointing out how similar to Saint-Simon's intellectual odyssey Durkheim's was to be, albeit at the time of *Socialisme* he had just started renewing his interest in religion. The following passage in which Durkheim describes the last turn in Saint-Simon's writings could equally apply to a commentator viewing the apparent change from Durkheim's earlier analysis to its culminating point in *The Forms*:

> When one finds the opponent of the theological system,the founder of positive philosophy, demanding the establishment of a new religion, one is tempted to think that a revolution has taken place in his thinking and that he has abandoned his principles. This hypothesis is made plausible in that the *New Christianity* (1824) is his last work ... This interpretation is false. On the

---

67   *Le Socialisme*, p. 190.

68   Note in particular the second edition of Durkheim's chapter on anomic suicide in *Suicide* (New York: Free Press, 1963) pp. 246-54. In those pregnant pages, Durkheim anticipates notions of relative deprivation and the revolution of rising expectations.

69   Space consideration prevents a discussion of Saint-Simon's views, as presented and commented by Durkheim, concerning the dissolution of national political boundaries by the industrial order at the macro level and the breaking up of inherited private property at the micro level; both of these are necessary, argued Saint-Simon, if the full productive potential of the industrial order is to be realized. These Saint-Simonian themes are echoed in Durkheim's later teachings; for example, see the concluding chapter of *Professional Ethics and Civic Morals*.

70   *Le Socialisme*, p. 207.

contrary, religious preoccupations were very keenly felt by Saint-Simon in all
periods of his intellectual development. ... Consequently, Saint-Simon never
conceived positive and scientific philosophy as exclusive of every religious
system. On the contrary he felt that one led to the other.[71]

It was the social ethic of Christianity which Saint-Simon stressed as the girder for
the emergent industrial order. "Treat every man as your brother" is the Christian
principle of altruism which in leading man to find himself one with others in God
has both a this-worldly emphasis and an important social dimension. Durkheim
points out that although the new religion will have its cult and dogma, it is ethics
which will be its central feature.[72] The new religion, which has an immanent,
even pantheistic basis – for it finds God in everything which is real and does
not find the divine in any extraterrestrial setting or object of belief – has the
task of providing the spiritual bond linking members of human society. It is
religion for Saint Simon (as it will be for Durkheim in *The Forms*) which gives
to society the consciousness of its unity. If God is one with nature, the antithesis
between science and religion disappears, for God is both the object of scientific
investigation and of religious worship.[73]

This attempted reconciliation of science and religion is not only Durkheim's
exposition of Saint-Simon but also will later emerge in *The Forms* as Durkheim's
own intention. Saint-Simon was, I propose, extremely influential for Durkheim
because of the former's perspective on religion which leads to a "rational
justification of an ethics of solidarity," one which would not be an intellectual
construct but would mesh in with major dimensions of modern society: its
industrial economic nature, its democratic and cosmopolitan tendencies, and its
psychological roots in Christianity. The stress on ethics in the last writings of
Saint-Simon, on a morality of altruism, and on the immanence of religion are
features which Durkheim could readily accept.

> In terminating his course, his summary evaluation of Saint-Simon could well
> serve as Durkheim's own epitaph: A mind eminently alive and keen to learn,
> curious about new trends, gifted with a sort of intuitive sympathy whichmade
> him sensitive to all the aspirations of his contemporaries, Saint-Simon succeeded
> in making of his work a sort of synthesis of all the tendencies of his period.[74]

The second major influence on Durkheim is Immanuel Kant, whose imprint left
visible traces not only on Durkheim himself but on practically Durkheim's entire
generation which attended higher education. I have indicated previously that
philosophy for the Third Republic was of crucial significance in developing its

---

71   Ibid., p. 208.
72   Ibid., p. 214.
73   Ibid., p. 218.
74   *Le Socialisme* p. 231.

ideology and its legitimation; Kant, I would argue, was above all other figures the philosopher who provided inspiration and stimulus for this development.

After the philosophical excitement of the Romantic movement (in which may be included Hegel, Lamennais, Schleiermacher, Schopenhauer, and the young Marx), the second half of the nineteenth century was marked by a more sober, rationalistic current. Kant was "rediscovered" as the major figure of modern philosophy, and in France this was particularly the case in republican circles, headed in philosophy by Charles Renouvier (1815-1903), whom Durkheim avidly read as a student, and by Durkheim's own teacher at ENS, Emile Boutroux, the "philosopher of the Third Republic."

We may ask why this affinity between Kant and this regime. First, it will be recalled that one aim of Kant's *Critique of Pure Reason* was to rescue or salvage the certainty of knowledge from Hume's devastating skepticism. For the generation of Europeans who became adults in the mid-nineteenth century, the ascendance of science, particularly the acceptance of evolutionary theory, had shaken to the foundations the certitude of the stability of the world, a certitude formerly given by the religious interpretation of the universe. Between science and between the image of man as an economic actor motivated by economic self-interest, a generation of Europeans had experienced a drastic and traumatic passage "from the absolute to the relative."[75] The following generation – Durkheim's – became aware of the limitations of "relativism"; after the turmoil of the early 1870s, the nascent republican regime and its adherents were searching for an alternative to either moral anarchy[76] or to traditional Catholic morality with its otherworldly orientation.

Kantian philosophy provided an ideal fit on several dimensions. First, Kant's epistemology sought to restore the boundaries of absolute certainty provided by "pure reason." Second, it also had a crucial "practical" side in establishing the moral basis of action, and this without direct appeal to God, which suited ideally the republican temper for a "morale laïque." There is in Kant an expression of this-worldly Protestant asceticism,[77] which resonated very well with the world view of the effective leadership of Republican France. The Kantian themes of the autonomy of the will and "voluntarism," of the "categorical imperative," of the primacy of fulfilling one's "duty" without regard for material interest – these

---

75   I take this phrase from the novel of Maurice Barrès, *Les Déracinés*.

76   Anarchism was a strong, vocal intellectual current for at least the first thirty years of the Third Republic, even if its followers were relatively a very small number. One of its many sources of inspiration was Nietzsche. Among others, one of the first to militate for the rehabilitation of Captain Dreyfus was Bernard Lazare, a major figure in anarchist circles, and through Lazare and Lucien Herr, Durkheim (who, of course, had a strong distaste for anarchism as a doctrine) came to realize what was involved in the Dreyfus affair.

77   In support of this, there is no better authority than Max Weber: see footnote 58, chap. 5, of his famous essay, *The Protestant Ethic and the Spirit of Capitalism*, trans. Talcott Parsons (New York: Charles Scribner's Sons, 1958) p. 270.

and others provided an injunction for a disinterested individualism compatible with a collectivity orientation. Stated differently, neo-Kantism had extraacademic appeal as a secular morality which would both legitimate the republican regime and provide mobilization for the diffusion of a social altruism that would appeal to the growing middle class, the major constituency of the Third Republic.[78]

The preeminence of Kant in the teaching of philosophy in secondary schools during Durkheim's formative years (and for the remainder of the century) is well shown in one of the most important documents about political life in France in this period. This is *The Uprooted*,[79] a political novel by Maurice Barrès, a contemporary (1862-1923) of Durkheim who also grew up in Lorraine (about thirty-five miles away from Durkheim), was exposed to the same secondary school education (at the lycée of Nancy), and who also like Durkheim eventually became an intellectual drawn to Paris. Yet, unlike Durkheim, Barrès became highly critical of secular education, which he saw as an alienating force that "uprooted" students from attachment to national traditions and their native soil, and became an antirepublican nationalist.

Quite early in *The Uprooted* we are informed that, "a resolute Kantian", the philosophy teacher Bouteiller held that "Our mind perceives the world in terms of the categories of space, time, causality."[80] We are also informed that Bouteiller, "after a phase in absolute skepticism... believed with Kant and by appealing to the heart that he could reconstitute for his students the category of morality and an ensemble of certainties."[81] At the end of the academic year, Bouteiller leaves his students with an overview of the most important points made in the course:

> We examined a crucial thought: how Kant ends in an absolute skepticism and then reestablished the principles of certainty by stating: 'A reality exists, it is the moral law ... Remember the principle on which we established all ethics ... It is to act in such a way that our action can serve as a rule [for mankind in general].[82]

This is the message, I suggest, that Durkheim also received in his philosophy course at the lycée. He was not only thoroughly familiar with Kantian philosophy but also seems to have engaged in a lifelong dialogue with Kant whenever he, Durkheim, reflected philosophically. The preoccupation with morality and ethics, with a science of morality, as constitutive features of social life is an indication

---

78   See Jean-Pierre Azéma and Michel Winock, *La IIIe République* (1870-1940) (Paris: Calmann-Lévy, 1970) pp. 105-81, for an excellent discussion of social structure and political orientations in the period 1880-1918.

79   *Les Déracinés* is the first volume of a trilogy entitled *L'Energie Nationale* by Maurice Barrès, published in 1897. I will refer to it in the edition *L'Oeuvre de Maurice Barrès* (Paris: Au Club de l'Honnête Homme, 1965) vol. 3.

80   *Les Déracinés*, p. 20.

81   Ibid., p. 21.

82   Ibid., pp. 28f.

of Kant's imprint. Just as it may be argued that Marx's sociological analysis is thoroughly grounded in neo-Hegelianism, one may argue that Durkheim's sociological analysis is neo-Kantianism in its philosophical grounding.

For Kant, there is a reality to morality which goes beyond the individual and which makes moral action binding on the individual; this is an a priori condition, yet Kant does not derive morality from God. Durkheim readily accepts the Kantian a priori as transcendental structure given to the faculty of understanding but modifies the source of the a priori so as to validate these structures of reason. The transcendental source of the a priori of moral action, Durkheim proposes,[83] is society, whose existence is both anterior and posterior to that of any of its members. A moral fact (a societal norm) has two important attributes which give this phenomenon a specificity in regard to other behavioral rules of conduct. One of these is that it is binding on individuals, an attribute Durkheim takes from Kant.[84] To be sure, Durkheim then adds that Kant did not mention the second characteristic, namely that a moral action is desirable, a good thing for the individual to perform. Moral actions, like religious actions, Durkheim argues, have the twofold quality of being obligatory and desirable.

Durkheim's pronouncement on moral action is a condensation of materials he presented in his frequently given course, "Science of Education." One need only examine the first part of the posthumous publication stemming from the course, *Moral Education*,[85] to see how Kantian is the core of Durkheim's approach to morality. Durkheim does fault Kant for not being unaware that morality, being related to society in its very essence, will show variability in time and space, since different societies and different historical periods in the same society call for different contents of morality. (Recall that for Kant an action is moral only when it can be made into a universal rule of conduct for mankind, irrespective of where and when). This said, Durkheim's argument in favor of moral relativism is one which should not be magnified. If different moral systems are appropriate for different societies, it is also the case that Durkheim felt there was one appropriate morality corresponding to the social organization of a given society at a given stage of its development.

Nowhere that I know of does Durkheim propose that different social strata, different social groups in the same society, may have different and appropriate moral codes of conduct hermetically sealed off from one another. This would have been tantamount to admitting that *anomie* was the normal and appropriate condition of

---

83   See, for example, his 1906 communication before the French Philosophical Society, "The Determination of Moral Facts," in Emile Durkheim, *Sociology and Philosophy* (1924; New York: Free Press, 1974) pp. 35-62.

84   Ibid., p. 36.

85   *L'Education Morale* (Paris: Félix Alcan, 1925, 1938). An English edition with a new introduction by Everett K. Wilson is available as *Moral Education, A Study in the Theory and Application of the Sociology of Education* (New York: Free Press, 1973).

modern society. If anomie,[86] taken in the sense of conflicting multiple normative paradigms present in the same society, is treated as a normal rather than as a transient pathological aberration of social organization, then what hope is there for national unity and the existence of a societal community? The societal community may evolve rather than stay fixed, leading to the evolution of moral representations, but Durkheim's social realism is anchored on the tenet that there is a societal community[87] beneath or behind all external or institutionalized aspects of social life.

Durkheim's realism can thus align itself with Kantian critical realism, which while making place for subjectivity (since the world is made intelligible by a priori structures of mind or consciousness) retains the facticity of a world that transcends the individual. For both Kant and Durkheim, morality is not the diminution of individual freedom in the face of transcendence; it is its very assertion.[88] In brief, Kantian moral philosophy, rationalistic to the core, must be seen as the guiding philosophical orientation for much of Durkheim's concerns as a sociologist and as an educator. Among these concerns were the form and emphases of secular education so as to promote civic consciousness, social solidarity, and commitment to democratic and republican institutions.

Durkheim also found in Kant a major epistemological stimulus and challenge. Kant's theory of knowledge gives centrality to the categories of mind which, so to speak, "program" our perception of the outer world. Durkheim could not accept that the categories – space, time, causality, totality, etc. – were rooted in the individual, that is, that they were functions of the individual mind. At the same time, Durkheim readily accepted Kant's positing of necessary a priori structures which render the world orderly. In effect, Durkheim sociologized the Kantian categories

---

86   The state of anomie was a major preoccupation of Durkheim in his studies *which precede the Dreyfus affair.* The resolution of that crisis and the subsequent strong ministries of Waldeck-Rousseau and Emile Combes may have cleared the air of competing political paradigms, so to speak: "the morale laïque" and the republican cause had a decisive victory. Whether or not this accounts for it, Durkheim no longer used the term "anomie" after the turn of the century.

87   I take the notion of "societal community" from Talcott Parsons, since it is highly applicable to Durkheim's analysis of society. As Parsons expresses it: The core structure of a society I will call the societal community. More specifically at different levels of evolution, it is called tribe, or "the people,"... or, for the modern world, nation. It is the collective structure in which members are united or, in some sense, associated. Its most important property is the kind and level of solidarity – in Durkheim's sense – which characterizes the relations between its members (Talcott Parsons, "Social Systems," *International Encyclopedia of the Social Sciences*, [New York: Macmillan and Free Press, 1968] vol. 15, p. 461).

88   "The capacity for containing our inclinations, for restraining ourselves – the ability that we acquire in the school of moral discipline – is the indispensable condition for the emergence of reflective, individual will. The rule, because it teaches us to restrain and master ourselves, is a means of emancipation and freedom," *Moral Education*, pp. 48-49.

of understanding by arguing, in a seminal article published with Mauss,[89] that the very structures of logical thought are indeed a priori because they are collective, i.e., societal representations. In other words, Durkheim indicated in *Primitive Classification* that the cognitive mapping of the world is not a function of the individual mind but is rather rooted in a deeper substratum, social organization itself, or at least in the organization and adaptation of a given societal collectivity to its environment. *To understand the structure of a collectivity's classification of the world is, in effect, to understand its rules or principles of social organization.* This may well be considered as one of Durkheim's greatest insights and discoveries.[90]

It anticipates current research of the "ethnomethodological" school in sociology,[91] whose practitioners seem unaware of the implications of Durkheim's later analysis for phenomenological sociology, namely *Primitive Classification* and *The Forms*, which gives a sociological translation of Kantian theory of knowledge by grounding collective representations in the religious consciousness of the collectivity. Durkheim's "sociologism"[92] in this respect amounts to no less than an epistemological revolution from the traditional philosophical perspective that knowledge is a function of the individual knower, since Durkheim posits that knowledge is a function of a priori structures which are societal in origin and imparted to the individual in the socialization process. Hence, Durkheim is very far away from a caricatured image of him as the "positivist" of *Suicide* who naively relies on official statistics to explain an "objective" reality.

I will not dwell long on other figures in this context of influences on Durkheim, particularly since he was such a great synthesizer and incorporated into his sociology strands from diverse currents and disciplines. Nonetheless, Saint-Simon and Kant hold a unique status in providing the key to the unity of sociology and philosophy in Durkheim's overall world view. To be sure, some "lesser" influences need to be recognized: for example, Fustel de Coulanges, Durkheim's history teacher at ENS, whose *Ancient City* undoubtedly sensitized Durkheim to both the importance of historical analysis for the sociological understanding of modern society and to the significance of religion as an institutional structure underlying evolving forms of social organization. Durkheim in the preface to the very first volume of the *Année*

---

89   "De quelques formes primitives de classification. Contribution à l'étude des représentations collectives," *L'Année Sociologique* 6 (1901-02) pp. 1-72. English trans. with an introduction by Rodney Needham, *Primitive Classification*, (London: Cohen and West, 1963).

90   See Mary Douglas, *Implicit Meanings* (London and Boston: Routledge & Kegan Paul, 1975) p. 204.

91   See Harold Garfinkel, *Studies in Ethnomethodology* (Englewood Cliffs, N.J.: Prentice-Hall, 1967); Paul Filmer et al., *New Directions in Sociological Theory* (London: Collier-Macmillan, 1972); Roy Turner, ed., *Ethnomethodology* (Baltimore, Md.: Penguin Books, 1974); Aaron V. Cicourel, "Ethnomethodology," in his *Cognitive Sociology* (New York: Free Press 1974) pp. 99-140.

92   For a brief exposition, see my *Sociologism and Existentialism* (Englewood Cliffs, N.J.: Prentice-Hall, 1962).

Sociologique stresses the need for the rapprochement of sociology and history and invokes Fustel de Coulanges's name to recall that the latter held that true sociology is history; nothing is less debatable, adds Durkheim approvingly yet relishing the last word, provided that history be done sociologically.[93]

Mention should equally be made of German social scientists, particularly Wundt and Schaeffle, both of whom he met on his visit of 1885-86; the "German influence" on Durkheim, while helpful at the beginning of his career would later cause him some moments of anguish.[94] Later on, British social scientists, particularly those interested in the scientific study of "primitive religion," provided Durkheim with new perspectives and new sources of sociologically relevant data – here mention need be made of McLennan, Frazer, and above all, that remarkable Scottish scholar, W. Robertson Smith.[95] One could extend this list considerably, but I will terminate by mentioning just one more group of influences on Durkheim, namely his own students. There was a greater degree of collaboration between members of the school, such as joint essays and monographs, including joint authorship involving Durkheim, than the prevailing norm of "rugged individualism" elsewhere in the French university setting. Marcel Mauss, Henri Hubert, François Simiand, Maurice Halbwachs, Paul Lapie, Paul Fauconnet, Georges Davy, and Robert Hertz

---

93   "Préface," *Année Sociologique* 1 (1896-1897) pp. ii-iii. For perceptive comments in this context, see Robert N. Bellah, "Durkheim and History," *American Sociological Review* 24 (August 1959) pp. 447-61; Robert Nisbet, *The Sociology of Emile Durkheim* (New York: Oxford University Press, 1974), pp. 258-60. An excellent coverage of the relation of the study of history to Durkheimian sociology, including some of its major figures other than Durkheim, is that of Robert Leroux, *Histoire et Sociologie en France* (Paris: Presses Universitaires de France, 1998).

94   Writing in 1902, Durkheim mentioned that he owed much to the Germans, but five years later, when the Kaiser's policies had turned French public opinion against almost anything coming from across the Rhine, Durkheim defended himself from the accusations of Monsignor Deploige that he was one of those introducing into the Sorbonne German propaganda camouflaged as "sociology" (see *Textes* I, pp. 400-07, for Durkheim's declarations). During the First World War, a French senator on the occasion of a discussion on German espionage made an allegation of Durkheim as a Sorbonne representative of the German "Kriegsministerium"; outraged, Louis Liard as Vice Rector of the Academy of Paris set the wheels in motion which led to the public rectification of this slander (Durkheim dossier in the Archives Nationales, letter of Liard dated March 27, 1916). I mention this since the German influence on Durkheim had political as well as intellectual ramifications.

95   For an excellent presentation of Smith and his influence on Durkheim's sociology of religion, see Thomas O. Beidelman, *W. Robertson Smith and the Sociological Study of Religion* (Chicago: University of Chicago Press, 1974). The reading of Smith's *Lectures on the Religion of the Semites* marked a turning point for Durkheim, not only because it suggested to him where one might go to find one of the main roots and foundations of Western religion and civilization, but also, I venture to say, because it enabled Durkheim to rediscover his own roots in orthodox Judaism with its rich symbolism and rituals. Smith's *Lectures* may have been as pregnant for Durkheim as Baxter and Bunyan had been for Weber.

were among those of the first and second generation of his students who not only got their inspiration from Durkheim but who also provided him with important intellectual feedback as he evolved his sociological analysis.

III

Viewed as a whole set of interrelated professional activities,[96] Durkheim's sociological work or project amounts to nothing less than devising what the late philosopher of science Imre Lakatos termed "a scientific research program"[97] (hereafter designated as SRP). One can talk of an SRP as having three major parts: (1) a "hard core" comprised of what Lakatos terms "metaphysical beliefs"; (2) an intermediary "protective belt" of positive and negative heuristics; and (3) outlying theories for subdisciplines which make empirical statements, predictions, and interpretations of differentiated sectors of the real world. Theories have linkage to one another in terms of "adherence to metaphysical beliefs, a priori and hence irrefutable articles of faith, which, together with methodological rules contained in positive and negative heuristics, form the hard-core of the SRP".[98]

It may be argued that Durkheim advanced an early formulation of a scientific research program (SRP) for sociology from the onset of his university career. His initial courses at Bordeaux, as I have indicated earlier, clearly manifest that he had already formulated in his mind what needed to be done for sociology to become a scientific discipline; this initial vision got progressive refinement over the years, particularly as he attracted an actual school of students and colleagues who became, in effect, a scientific research team. In this vein, one may think of his dissertation, *The Division of Labor*, as providing an announcement of the SRP, of its logic of

---

96   The major sociological activities of Durkheim were: (1) author of pioneering sociological investigations in such fields as industrial sociology (*Division of Labor*), deviance (*Suicide*), methodology (*Rules*), sociology of knowledge (*Primitive Classification, Forms*), sociology of education (*L'Evolution pédagogique en France*), etc.; (2) university professor offering first courses in sociology at university level and director of graduate training; (3) editor of the *Année* and series editor of its later "Travaux"; in effect, his editorial work was that of a laboratory director, enabling younger members of his team to get professional recognition and advancement as a result of publishing in a scholarly, high-quality series; and (4) a propagandizer for giving sociology legitimation in academic and intellectual circles by virtue of his participation in other learned societies and journals.

97   Imre Lakatos and Alan Musgrave, eds., *Criticism and the Growth of Knowledge* (London: Cambridge University Press, 1974) pp. 91-196. My attention to Lakatos has been drawn as a result of a remarkable study which demonstrates his applicability to the development of economics: Joseph V. Remenyi, "Core-Demi-Core Interaction in Economics" (mimeographed, Ph.D. thesis, Durham, N.C.: Duke University, 1976). I consider the conceptualization of Lakatos and Remenyi very heuristic for treating the Durkheimian school as a whole, but to do justice to it would require a separate exposition.

98   Remenyi, "Core-Demi-Core Interaction," p. 38.

inquiry, and of its purpose. It contains "metaphysical beliefs" or what I prefer to call "presuppositions" and it advances a theory which Durkheim will subject to falsification. Durkheim's preface makes clear what is the goal of the investigation.[99] If solidarity is a central fact of social life, a social fact par excellence, it nonetheless cannot be studied directly (for subjective and intersubjective dispositions are not physical conditions); hence the need to operationalize solidarity so that it can be studied in its overt manifestations.[100] Consequently, Durkheim spends the first chapter of his dissertation outlining both his method of investigation and the theory which will be subject to falsification: given that systems of law may be taken as externalizations of the inner core of social reality (solidarity), it is predicted that as the inner core undergoes qualitative changes from "mechanical" to "organic" solidarity, there should be manifest shifts in the ratio of types of legal systems (chiefly civil and criminal law) as a proportion of the total legal corpus. There is no need here to go over the substance of the *Division of Labor* which follows the initial chapter; however since I am using this work as illustrative of Durkheim's SRP, let me dwell on it long enough to point out that it contains both positive and negative heuristics.

As Remenyi points out, the negative heuristics of any SRP make clear "the irrefutable metaphysical propositions of the programme,"[101] and thereby indicate what is legitimate and what is illegitimate in the way of scientific explanation. Durkheim does not make it explicit, but his chief negative heuristic is that the division of labor because it is a social fact cannot be accounted for in terms of the spontaneous economic exchanges between individuals; Spencer's accounting of the division of labor is the major target of Durkheim's criticism in chapter 7 of his treatise, and Spencer is for Durkheim representative of those seeking to explain social phenomena in terms of individuals rather than in terms of social structure. Durkheim makes very clear his opposition to an exchange model of society which would reduce social reality to individuals exchanging goods and facilities with one another:

> The division of labor does not present individuals to one another, but social functions.[102]

---

99   "This book is pre-eminently an attempt to treat the facts of the moral life according to the method of the positive sciences," *Division of Labor*, p. 32.

100   "... solidarity ... is a social fact we can know only through the intermediary of social effects," *Division of Labor*, p. 67.

101   Remenyi, "Core-Demi-Core Interaction," p. 39.

102   *Division of Labor*, p. 407. Needless to say, Spencerian sociology may seem outmoded today but the exchange model keeps surfacing, in such figures as George Homans, Peter Blau, Erving Goffman, and Claude Levi-Strauss. Of course, Mauss's *The Gift* is an exchange model, one which may be viewed as exemplifying Durkheimian structural-functional analysis: economic exchanges are analyzed in terms of underlying normative, societal structures and in terms of their further consequences for social organization; the

While *The Division of Labor* does have a methodology which distinguishes this early study, it is, of course, in Durkheim's following volume, *The Rules of Sociological Method*,[103] that he provides his audience with a comprehensive set of negative and positive heuristics. In effect, this was the first primer of "how-to-do sociology," and therefore of cardinal importance in the further articulation of his SRP. It made known to would-be researchers of social phenomena how to approach "social facts," how to recognize them, and how to go about explaining them. Providing a certain standardization of operating procedures is certainly basic to the institutionalization and rationalization of a scientific discipline; Durkheim's *Rules* furnished this to members of his "research team," and it also furnished a certain *tone* to sociological research which "modernized" sociology. By tone I mean the objectivity and rigor of analysis which is to be found in all of the works of the Durkheimians, even when they are dealing with topics of contemporary social concern. In part, this tone, which might be termed "scientific asceticism," follows from an important negative heuristic of the *Rules*, namely that when dealing with social phenomena we must bracket common sense or laymen's understandings of the phenomena being investigated: as Durkheim states it, "All preconceptions must be eradicated."[104]

After this negative heuristic, Durkheim proposes what is essentially a major positive one, namely that in beginning an investigation of social facts, the investigator must articulate an operational definition of what is to be investigated.[105] This is a positive heuristic in the sense that it leads to the externalization of the

---

obligatory aspects of gift-giving, gift-receiving, gift-exchanging cannot be deduced from the volition of the specific actors.

These aspects of the exchange are part of the psychosocial dimensions of role relationships and in turn are part of "the total social phenomenon." I mention this because Mauss's study, an exemplar in its own right of structural-functional analysis and prototypical of sociological exchange models, may also be seen as based or derived from *The Division of Labor*. Hence, rather than being treated in itself, it should be seen as one implementation of Durkheim's SRP. *The Gift* was first published in French in 1925, in *l'Année Sociologique*, 2e ser., vol. 1(1923-1924) pp. 30-186. The English edition (full title: *The Gift: Forms and Function of Exchange In Archaic Societies*) was published by Free Press, New York, 1954.

103 *The Rules of Sociological Method* (1895, French; New York: Free Press, 1950).

104 *Rules*, p. 31. Durkheim suggests in so many words this is a negative heuristic when he comments "As it happens, this first rule for sociology is entirely negative. It teaches the sociologist to escape the realm of lay ideas and to turn his attention towards facts..." *Rules*, p. 34. I use the word "bracket" to suggest a similarity in Durkheim's procedure and that of Husserl's phenomenological method, both of which I consider to deal fundamentally with the analysis of structures.

105 "In order to be objective, the definition must obviously deal with phenomena not as ideas but in terms of their inherent properties," *Rules*, p. 35. This aspect of his methodological principles was followed by Durkheim in all his sociological studies (on suicide, religion, socialism, etc.).

research program, that is, it leads to framing of theories which can make predictive statements or propositions that can be used to codify and interpret empirical social phenomena.

This by no means does justice to the *Rules* but may suffice to give the reader an indication of where this work stands in the totality of Durkheim's sociological analysis. It has not been uniformly accepted by sociologists and even in Durkheim's day it met with considerable objections and misunderstandings. It is for all that a key to understanding the logic of inquiry which runs throughout Durkheim's "empirical" studies (*Division of Labor, Suicide, The Forms*). It also served to orient the researchers of the *Année Sociologique* into producing an organized sociological research marked by the structural differentiation of subdisciplines from the central Durkheimian "hard core."[106]

For the remainder of this section I would like to discuss various elements of the "hard core" of Durkheim's sociology, that is, of the manifold yet interrelated set of presuppositions he entertains. Since these are often interrelated with theoretical propositions about how the social world operates, this discussion will enable us to approach some of the fundamental aspects of Durkheim's sociology we have not yet covered; at the same time, we need ground further Durkheim's analysis in the sociohistorical context of his situation.

Unlike Marxism, which presupposes that the social order is real but built out of exploitative relationships, hence fundamentally an abomination, Durkheimian sociologism presupposes that the social order is more in the nature of a social body (a metaphor probably suggested to him by Schaeffle). A slight modification of the traditional dictum "*mens sano in corpore sana*" results in what might well be taken as a basic Durkheimian perspective on the relation of individual to society: "a healthy mind in a healthy society." That is, for individuals to be truly free from the constraints of physical and biological nature so as to be fully functioning persons, they need to find themselves in a well-organized society. Social rules and discipline are part and parcel of social organization, for Durkheim, and social organization, far from being *alienative*, is integrative and congenial to mental health. In brief, social health and mental health intertwine and are contingent upon a well-regulated (i.e., normatively ordered) society. This presupposition of Durkheim's is certainly what much of the analysis and argumentation of *Suicide* is all about.

Durkheim's view of society in this respect may be linked with Claude Bernard's famous concept of the *milieu interne* as the key to the physiological organization of complex living organisms. It is the *milieu interne* – the blood system and its related fluids – which through its various functions, including the keeping of a constant

---

106   In his own research, Remenyi has found it useful to modify the Lakatos conceptualization of the SRP by introducing the notion of "demi-core," which pertains to the presuppositions of a subdiscipline derived from the structural differentiation of the "hard core" of the discipline as a whole. This applies not only to his study of the development of economics but also to the development of sociology in the Durkheimian school.

internal temperature, enables complex organisms to improve their adaptability to the external environment and develop. Society is the *milieu interne* of human beings, and this in a double sense: (a) relative to the physical environment, society is a mediating system which enables us to sustain adaptation to nature; and (b) the social environment is also internalized by the individual in the socialization process, becoming the human component of the self, so to speak. Socialization for Durkheim is a learning process, chiefly one of learning the normative structures of the social environment."[107] Because of this internalization of society, which Durkheim treats as the reality behind the universal notion of the "soul," the "body-soul" dualism is an apprehension of reality which is borne out by sociological reflection.[108] But society exists not only in our minds: It also has an objective existence, in the form of institutions and their embodiments (legal systems, market systems, etc.).

Far from seeing organized society as being fundamentally immoral, Durkheim presupposes its essential moral nature; in fact, morality and society are coextensive. Social life and social organization are made possible and reflect normative arrangements. Social institutions are aggregates of these normative arrangements, which are both prescriptive and proscriptive and which cross-cut social strata. Whatever its institutional arrangement and whatever its developmental stage, the social order as such is a real moral phenomenon.[109] We cannot say that everything we find in the social world today is moral, but that is not the same as the contention that morality lies outside social structures and social organization.

For Durkheim, then, morality is a social phenomenon and social phenomena have an intrinsic moral component; of course, as a corollary, what is immoral – that is, what strikes us as against the norms and standards or morality – is also a social phenomenon. Morality is not an intrinsic attribute of things, but a quality of behavior, of social action; morality refers to moral *action*, rather than being just an individual attitude or a state of mind. What is at the heart of the notion of social order is a moral or normative ordering of interpersonal conduct. Durkheim's

---

107   "The air of education is, precisely, the socialization of the human being," *Rules*, p. 6.

108   Durkheim's discussion of self, individuality, and personality – in a sense, a formulation of his microsociology – is largely developed in a late essay (1914), available in English as "The Dualism of Human Nature," in Wolff, *Emile Durkheim*, pp. 325-40. Durkheim's conception of the dual aspects of the self and the two modes of consciousness arising from this (i.e., individual and collective or social consciousness) is structurally similar to George H. Mead's duality of the self, since the "I" has its base in the biological system and the "me" or "generalized other" develops from the internalization of the societal community. Although cognizant of Comte, Mead seemed to have little exposure to Durkheim and was probably unacquainted with Durkheim's 1914 essay.

109   There is a twofold aspect to "moral": it should be taken as both that which is ethical or normative *and* that which is nonmaterial, i.e., psychological. To reiterate, for Durkheim, social life is psychological in the sense of being intersubjective, hence his willingness to state that sociology is a social psychology.

analysis antedates current "role theory" or "role analysis," but certainly current microsociological perspective on the role is that of a social structure linking two or more actors in terms of reciprocal normative expectations which frame or "define the situation." This perspective is a continuation of the Durkheimian presupposition of the normative or moral basis of the social order.

Similarly, although Durkheim does not use the contemporary term "deviance," he certainly takes "crime" or "criminal behavior" to be intrinsically a social phenomenon, even "an integral part of all healthy societies."[110] Criminal behavior is negative moral behavior, but such behavior is normal to society in the sense that it is the laws of society, or the collective sentiments behind the laws, which provide the bounds of behavior; without such boundaries there would be neither moral nor immoral behavior. To be sure, Durkheim also advances two other pertinent propositions, which derive from the basic presupposition, namely that punishment is also a normal phenomenon of society and that criminality may have abnormal aspects, "when its rate is unusually high."[111] If morality (and immorality) are social phenomena, it follows that different societies will have different definitions of morality and immorality, and it also follows that the normative system and the system of penal sanctions of a given society are not static but are subject to evolutionary change as the social organization alters over time.

Durkheim's analysis not only postulates the essential nexus between morality and society, but also takes as a central presupposition that society is itself a reality sui generis. At the heart of this social realism is his notion that when individuals interact, the association generates ties or bonds (such as social institutions and social roles) which are real and which cannot be deduced from the property of the individuals. The whole is greater than the sum of its parts albeit the whole would not be without its parts: Durkheim did assert the latter, it should be kept in mind, as for example when he affirmed that society would not be without the individual, "the ultimate element of groups."[112] Still, Durkheim's sociology gives greater weight to the distinctness of social reality, which he saw as both transcendental to any given individual, yet immanent in the natural world, that is, not a "divine creation" nor an instrument of a divine will. Social reality, then, is both constituted by and constitutive of social interaction. The interaction process is not only generative of social reality but, under certain conditions, it is also regenerative of the social order: the latter contains Durkheim's theory of religion and social change, which shall be mentioned later.

Durkheim treats social reality as multilayered, extending on a continuum of innermost spontaneity and effervescence (from which core stem collective currents of enthusiasm, panic, pessimism, etc.) to progressively more institutionalized expressions of collective endeavors; thus, at the outermost layers are objectified

---

110   *Rules*, p. 67. See also Durkheim's "Deux Lois de l'Evolution Pénale," *Année Sociologique* 4 (1899-1900) pp. 65-95.

111   *Rules*, p. 66.

112   "Le Dualisme," in Wolff, *Emile Durkheim*, p. 206.

cultural artifacts, from law courts to courtyards."[113] From the inner to the outer, from the center to the periphery, social life represents expressions of aggregated human consciousness or "conscience collective."[114] Durkheim is a dualist in regard to consciousness, since one source of consciousness is the individual (the body), while the other is the social; it might be pointed out that this twofold subjectivity is disclosed in ordinary language, since the subjective mode contains both the singular "I" and the plural "we." Further, consciousness is cognitive and affective, and social reality as a network of intersubjective consciousness may be thought of as hyperspiritual reality.[115]

Durkheim means here that if human consciousness is a spiritual activity which produces ideational representations, then the consciousness of the whole (of social life) is hyperspiritual in the sense of being vaster and distinct from the individual psychic life, from the limited consciousness of any one individual. Psychic life, or consciousness, is cognitive in the sense that we map the outer world in terms of representations, conceptualizations, classifications of the external phenomena we encounter. A second core aspect of consciousness is that it is characterized by *affective elements*, that is, feelings and sentiments. Among these, Durkheim will give stress to the sentiment of "solidarity," which for him is a normal or natural sentiment, not one "alien" to human nature. In terms of the broader aspects of this discussion, what should be emphasized is that although Durkheim's own attitude toward the world was certainly rationalistic, he very much recognized the fundamental affectivity, or what I would like to call the *sentience,* of social being.

This undercurrent of affectivity is a theme to be found in various of Durkheim's writings. We find it in *Suicide*, particularly in book III, chapter 1, where Durkheim speaks of "collective tendencies or passions" as "forces *sui generis*."[116] Some of these collective sentiments or feelings become institutionalized; others resist the frames of institutionalization but are no less efficacious in manifesting themselves as social forces upon individuals – whether we are talking about patriotism, humanitarianism, stock market mania or depression (bull- and bear-market mentality), or even "suicidogenetic currents." Everyday social life may be structured by articulated laws, by more informal precepts and rules of conduct, by moral principles which are still vaguer in terms of being rendered explicit in language but

> beneath all these maxims are actual, living sentiments, summed up by these formulae but only as in a superficial envelope. The formulae would awake no

---

113   *Rules*, chap. 1. The examples suggested are my own.

114   For Durkheim's theory of mind, memory, and consciousness, see his "Individual and Collective Representations," in Durkheim, *Sociology and Philosophy* (New York: Free Press, 1974), pp. 1-34.

115   Ibid., p. 34.

116   *Suicide*, p. 307.

echo if they did not correspond to definite emotions and impressions scattered through society.[117]

So we can say that Durkheim sees the real depth layer (or its innermost core) of society as an intense foyer of affectivity: this is the heart of social life. Mediating between this foyer and the external physical environment is the system of collective representations, which not only represents the environment to men, but which also reflects the organization of the collectivity. How we view the world, in other words, is not simply what is given to us in perception but is also a reflection of our internal organization; and Durkheim, to reiterate, will interpret Kantian categories sociologically, so that the cognitive ordering of the world will be ingeniously reinterpreted as reflecting the underlying social ordering of the world. In terms of the present discussion what is particularly of interest is that Durkheim finds the ties which bind or connect things are not only social in basis but also essentially affective. Passages in the seminal essay *Primitive Classification* are particularly instructive of his perspective:

> It is thus states of the collective mind which give birth to these groupings, and these states moreover are manifestly affective ... it is this emotional value of notions which plays the preponderant part in the manner in which ideas are connected or separated ... This is how it happens that things change their nature, in a way, from society to society; it is because they affect the sentiments of groups differently.[118]

Of course, Durkheim's perspective on society as a foyer of feelings and affectivity, which are at any period in different forms of institutionalization, reaches its most dramatic expression in *The Elementary Forms of the Religious Life*. The title could have just as easily read *The Fundamental Forms of Social Life*, for while manifestly a sociological exegesis of the ethnography of Australian aborigines, it is closer to being a general treatise on social structure and social change.

First, in terms of social structure, Durkheim extends the direction of his earlier essays, notably *Primitive Classification* and "De la définition des phénomènes religieux,"[119] to view collective sentiments as becoming embodied in symbols. Not lifeless symbols of intellectual construction such as "$x=f(y)$," but collective representations which designate and represent affective states – emblems, flags, religious creeds, prayers, and the like. Symbols and sentiments, as fundamental features of the societal community, are seen by Durkheim to be in a dialectical relationship:

---

117   Ibid., p. 315.

118   *Primitive Classification*, pp. 85-86.

119   "De la définition des phénomènes religieux," *L'Année Sociologique* 2 (1897-98) pp. 1-28.

the emblem is not merely a convenient process for clarifying the sentiment society has of itself; it also serves to create this sentiment; it is one of its constituent elements[120]

Symbols, sentiments, and social life are thus closely intertwined. Social life, Durkheim argues, "is made possible only by a vast symbolism,"[121] and without symbols, "social sentiments could have only a precarious existence."[122] Symbols, understood as collective representations, are externalizations or vehicles which represent intersubjective feelings or collective sentiments. They represent them to later generations as well as to the generation of the collectivity whose interaction has given rise to these sentiments. Symbols therefore perpetuate the social order, for in the collective songs we sing on social occasions, the prayers we recite in unison, the national anthem we rise to hear, the initiation ceremonies we partake in, the "private jokes" we share with the group, the particular handshake of a group – these and myriads of others continue and reinforce the social solidarity.

A noteworthy sentiment or attitude, which for Durkheim is of immense importance since it is the ultimate foundation of group identity, is the religious sentiment, manifest in the feeling of the *sacred*. Durkheim entertains that human consciousness differentiates the world into two categories, the category of entities which are *sacred* and those which are *profane*. Durkheim's notion of *sacred* is strikingly similar to Weber's notion of *charisma*; the recipient of the attitude for Weber is a person and for Durkheim it is more in the nature of symbols or entities, such as the totem, but the attitude is the same. Basically, toward sacred entities we take an expressive orientation, we treat sacred things as ends in themselves, whereas toward profane things we take an instrumental or utilitarian orientation – that is, profane things are means and not ends of action.

Durkheim very clearly suggests, in chapter 7, book II, of *The Forms*, that social life has two main polar modes of activity; economic life and religious life. We may view the poles as standing on an affective continuum, with quality and quantity both being operative. Economic life is dull, monotonous: "it is generally of a very mediocre intensity," and it exercises centrifugal forces on the societal community which results "in making its life uniform, languishing, and dull."[123] The religious life, generated by the coming together of the collectivity, in a ceremonial and dramatic occasion, is an entirely different sort of affect; it is a *festival*, a period of *enthusiasm*. Collective sentiments of stimulation become magnified in the effervescence, the mundane world is transformed into an extraordinary world, one

---

120   *The Forms*, p. 262.

121   Ibid., p. 264.

122   Ibid., p. 262.

123   Ibid., p. 246. In *Rules* (p. 114) Durkheim suggests that it even has a divisive element: "... purely economic relations leave men *estranged* from one another..." (emphasis mine).

wherein individual boundaries break down, solidarity reaches a crescendo, in the process of which even antinomian behavior may take place.[124]

One may ask whether Durkheim's analysis is intended to go beyond the situation of primitive society, and the answer has to be in the affirmative. The year before the publication of *The Forms*, Durkheim presented at the Fourth International Congress of Philosophy a very well-received communication: "Value Judgments and Judgments of Reality."[125] Besides advancing the argument that society itself is the source of values, reflected in value judgments (whether they be aesthetic, religious, political, or economic in kind), Durkheim went on to propose that values reflect ideals generated by society. It is not the routinized, institutionalized, boundary-maintaining society he has in mind (the one appropriately analyzed as a system of organs or structures and their functions).[126] Rather, it is those extraordinary circumstances and periods that mobilize the whole of the societal community, which gathers together in "moments of effervescence." It is during those moments of dramatically intense interaction, moments of collective ecstasy it might be said, that the societal community generates or regenerates its ideals. Durkheim mentions such moments as "movements of collective enthusiasm" of the twelfth and thirteenth centuries (which led to the European student population coming in droves to the University of Paris), the Renaissance and the Reformation, the French Revolution, and the great socialist agitations of the nineteenth century. At the peak of these periods, which are crisis periods for the societal community, there is a sharp qualitative and quantitative upgrading in the nature of social interaction; social distance breaks down, people exchange ideas, feel part of a whole, and forget their banal and selfish personal preoccupations. At the peak of these periods people live in the ideal, they live out the ideal collectively, in unison. And afterward – for such periods of crisis and enthusiasm cannot be sustained – collective memories of these events may take the form of festivals, national holidays, and the like, which provide the occasion for the societal community to relive, at least in partial intensity, the great periods of social ideals.[127]

Durkheim does not mention, in this suggestive model, is what may have been his own experiences. He would have been present, in all likelihood, or at

---

124   *The Forms*, p. 247.

125   First published in 1911, and reproduced in *Sociology and Philosophy*, pp. 80-97. It might be mentioned that at this Bologna Congress were such outstanding figures of the intellectual world as Bergson, Mach, Lévy-Bruhl, Michels, Ortega y Gasset, H. Poincaré, Steiner, and Windelband, among others. Durkheim had not attended the Third International Congress held at Heidelberg in 1908; Max Weber had attended that one but was not present at Bologna.

126   *Sociology and Philosophy*, pp. 90-91.

127   Ibid., p. 92. For a fascinating sociological presentation of the Paris May 1968 "events" which illustrates this discussion, see Alfred Willener, *The Action-Image of Society* (London: Tavistock, 1970).

least read about, the extravagant evening of May 31, 1885, when Victor Hugo's body was displayed at the Arch of Triumph; the next day the body of the poet, who had become a national symbol, collective representation of republican and humanitarian ideals, was taken on a triumphant day-long procession for a final burial in the Pantheon. Maurice Barrès, in *The Uprooted*, provides a description of that "happening," and between the Parisian populace of 1885 and the Australian aborigines interacting when a corroboree takes place (as described in the ethnographic accounts of Howitt, and Spencer and Gillen, which Durkheim used in his analysis of *The Forms*) the distance of civilization breaks down and we are confronted with a structurally similar scene of collective behavior:

> ... among this crowd hardly conscious of itself, some see glory and shiver with excitement; others, feeling death, hasten to live; others yet, elbowed by hobnobbing with their coreligionists, seek to fraternize. Better yet, they unify, this fantastic mixture of enthusiasts and profligates, of simpletons and good people, organizing themselves in a single formidable being ...[128]

And Durkheim was also witness some years later to another period of collective effervescence, namely the upheavals of the Dreyfus affair in 1898-99 when Paris in particular was the scene of wild brawls and dramatic street demonstrations between the Dreyfusards and the anti-Dreyfusards; one important function of these demonstrations was to provide solidarity within different factions of each camp. For Durkheim and the Durkheimians, vanguards of the Dreyfusard movement, the "Affaire" had the serendipity of giving them greater legitimation in academic ranks. The common political struggle against the right led intellectuals such as Lucien Herr, Seignobos, Lavisse, Andler, Landon, and others who had previously had strong reservations about the Durkheimian emphasis upon the primacy of the social over the individual, upon the salience of the "conscience collective,' and other parts of his "sociologism," to reconsider their distrust and opposition to sociology. After all, participation in the same political movement and adherence to the same cause can make for bonds of solidarity which override intellectual divergences.[129] And so, when Durkheim years later reflected upon the integrative function of religion vis-à-vis the societal community, it might be kept in mind that he would have experienced on at least two momentous occasions the generation and regeneration of affective ties of solidarity bringing to the fore the consciousness of belonging to a powerful societal community. Each occasion was a secular event

---

128 Barrès, *Les Déracinés*, p. 333.

129 For an insider's perspective on the rapprochement of the Durkheimians and their university colleagues, stemming from the "affaire," see Célestin Bouglé, "L'Année Sociologique," in *Pages Libres* 353 (October 5, 1907) esp. p. 347.

which nevertheless for its participants took on aspects of a religious gathering, a sacred occasion.[130]

Consequently, *The Forms* may be considered both a seminal study in the sociology of religion and also perhaps a prolegomenon of a religious sociology, that is, of a sociology seeking to formulate the religious parameters necessary for modern society. Durkheim has been aptly termed "the theologian of civil religion" by Bellah;[131] what should be understood as entailed in this designation is that Durkheim (unlike many theologians) did not belittle the affective dimension of the religious life, which he saw in his later years to be the fundamental structure of the societal community, including that of modern society.[132] Durkheim in his Bordeaux period had concentrated on demonstrating that social life is nothing if it isn't a moral reality; that an amoral or anomic society is one that breeds anarchy.[133] He had terminated his study on the division of labor by affirming that the malaise of the time is not due to intellectual criticism of the moral code of society (as conservatives alleged), but to that code having lost its meaning due to changes in the organization and the characteristics of the societal community. Sociology has the urgent task, nay the duty, of discovering the appropriate morality for modern society.[134] Durkheim advanced his analysis further in *Suicide* by showing how a phenomenon as seemingly irrational and individualistic as suicide had in fact

---

130   The Dreyfus affair was, for the opposite camps, a sacred combat between two polar sets of ideals. As to the Victor Hugo "happening," it should be recalled that Hugo remained anticlerical to his deathbed and that the Pantheon, where he was buried, became a sort of symbolic Valhalla of the Third Republic.

131   Bellah, *Emile Durkheim on Morality and Society*, p. xvii. It is because of Bellah's perceptive writings that I have come to realize the nexus between Durkheim's overall sociology and the theme of civil religion. See also Ruth A. Wallace, "A Source of Civil Religion: Emile Durkheim" (mimeographed; paper presented at the 1975 meeting of the Society for the Scientific Study of Religion).

132   Recall that in *The Forms* Durkheim takes religion to be "the serious life" (la vie sérieuse). However much of Durkheim's social realism has points in common with Marx's social realism, they ultimately stand in naked contrast as to what constitutes the infrastructure of social reality. For Durkheim, particularly the Durkheim of *The Forms*, it is in the religious life that the infrastructure of the societal community is to be found; the "deep structure" of social organization and societal change is to be found in the complexity of religion and its symbolism. For Marx, needless to say, the "serious life" is generated by socioeconomic relationships. Where Durkheim finds the infrastructure, there Marx finds the superstructure.

133   At the very time that Durkheim was publishing *The Division of Labor* and *Suicide*, which give a prominent place to *anomie* as the pathological condition of social organization, France was rocked by a wave of violent *anarchism*. One may see a certain overlap between the two, since anomie and anarchy involve the repudiation or a breakdown of the regulations of social life.

134   "In short, our first duty is to make a moral code for ourselves," *The Division of Labor*, p. 409.

irreducible sociological dimensions; when analyzed sociologically, differentials in suicide rates bear out moral aspects of the social milieu.[135]

The Forms should be seen as an extension of his analysis, linking morality, the affective grounding of the societal community, and religion; rather than a changing orientation in Durkheim's presuppositions, it is more in the nature of what Lakatos terms a "progressive problem-shift,"[136] which adds to the heuristic power of Durkheim's fundamental SRP. It is in this work that Durkheim outlines a theory of social change stemming from the moral regeneration of the societal community and expressed in some forms of collective behavior (which is hyperaffective, it may be said). The notion of "crisis" is still present in *The Forms*, but there is a shift of emphasis. For whereas before "the Affaire" there is a certain ominous or pessimistic ring to Durkheim's use of "crisis," a sense of spiritual malaise and social pathology, after the Dreyfus affair was resolved in the triumph of secular republicanism over traditionalism, the notion of "crisis" in Durkheim's analysis becomes more associated with a spring thawing than with an approaching winter. The crisis of the Dreyfus events brought to a head various sores and accumulated tensions, although it left unresolved other aspects of "the social question," such as the relation between the working class and the new industrial bourgeoisie. Under the Combes ministry, the republican goal of the secularization of education was decisively implemented, and as further consequences of the resolution of the crisis, higher education reforms were adopted in 1902,[137] which in part were beneficial to Durkheim's advancement.

Thus, the period of the Dreyfus affair was not so much a period of crisis in a negative sense as a "crucial period" (to borrow the expression of Georges Balandier). It was a period of passionate rhetoric, of violent agitation in which the two great moieties of French society – the left and the right – polarized, clashed headlong, and one emerged as the dominant faction for the remainder of the Third Republic. Such a period of effervescence may be thought of as a "moment of truth" for modern society, and it heightened Durkheim's awareness of the affective and

---

135   As an exemplar paradigm of modern sociological research, *Suicide* needs no introduction. Less obvious is that it constitutes a key part of the Durkheimian "manifesto" establishing the claims of sociology as an autonomous science. As any manifesto, consequently, it has a polemical aspect. It is patently against physical anthropology and biological racism. *Suicide* also contains an attack that Durkheim carried on for years against Gabriel Tarde (even after the latter's death) for his explanation of social behavior in terms of an individualistic microsociology; chap. 5 by its very title, "Imitation," makes clear who is the intended target of his criticisms. This was frankly recognized by one of Durkheim's ablest lieutenants, François Simiand, appraising *Suicide* in his "L'Année Sociologique 1897," *Revue de Métaphysique et de Morale* 6 (1898) pp. 608-53.

136   Lakatos and Musgrave, eds, *Criticism and the Growth of Knowledge*, p. 137. For a concise description of "progressive" and "degenerative" problem shifts, see Remenyi, "Core-Demi-Core Interaction," p. 40.

137   See Viviane Isambert-Jamati, "Une réforme des lycées et collèges. Essai d'analyse de la réforme de 1902," *Année Sociologique*, 3e série: 20 (1969) pp. 9-60.

symbolic dimensions of collective life, which bridge "modern" and "pre-modern" society. Extraordinary moments in collective life, such as those Durkheim would have witnessed in 1885 and 1898-99, would be experienced by a later French generation in May 1968, by an American generation in November 1968, by a Quebec generation in October 1970. In these and other instances, subjacent societal crises would erupt in an "event" whose significance for posterity all would feel, and whose meaning would be multivalent, so that in the words of sociologist Fernand Dumont, reflecting on his own society's critical days, "One event became an extraordinary symbol."[138]

In *The Forms*, then, "crisis" has become more of a catharsis, therapeutic for societal renovation and regeneration. That the Australian aborigines need periodic ritual gathering and effervescence to experience the intensity of religious life, and thereby to reaffirm both the identity of the societal community and the validity of its normative structures which guide everyday life, is a rather easy lesson to draw from an initial reading of *The Forms*. That modern society is also subject to the same phenomenon of periodic regeneration in crucial situations, that modern society also needs to and does experience on rare but vital occasions its "moment of truth," is a subtler lesson which is nevertheless Durkheim's intention to convey.[139]

One may say that the *Année Sociologique* group formed a microcosm of the vaster regenerated social world which Durkheim prophetically envisaged in closing his great study of religion and society. The group met as a body in Durkheim's home on the occasion of the tenth anniversary of the *Année*, and after the holocaust of the war, the remnant of the group had ceremonial or ritual occasions in the form of monthly dinner meetings, which we may see as symbolic communal feasts. This professional group, the *Année* team, was, in effect, Durkheim's own chapel. Relationships in the group exemplified that egalitarianism based on merit which Bouglé saw as the principle of justice of modern society. A common cause, that of sociology as a science, unified the group and generated the energy and devotion for the prolific professional activities of the Durkheimians; it was, so to speak, a sociological cooperative.

The cooperative was formed before the Dreyfus affair but it was that crisis – really one of a civil war – which unified the bonds of the Durkheimian band. The First World War was one of the great moral tragedies of mankind's history, but in

---

138   Fernand Dumont, *The Vigil of Quebec* (Toronto and Buffalo: University of Toronto Press, 1974) p. 98.

139   "There can be no society which does not feel the need of upholding and reaffirming at regular intervals the collective sentiments and the collective ideals which make it its unity and its personality ... the old gods are growing old or already dead, and others are yet not born ... But this state of incertitude and confused agitation cannot last for ever. A day will come when our societies will know again those hours of creative effervescence, in the course of which new ideas arise and new formulae are found which serve for a while as a guide to humanity ..." *The Forms*, p. 475.

the midst of it, Durkheim saw an outcome which might be taken as a postscript to his earlier major studies. Writing to his friend Xavier Leon in March 1915, Durkheim assessed the national situation:

> Events have shown there still is a rich vitality in our country; the latter is worth much more than those who represent and direct it. When a strong sentiment unites it, the country demonstrates its energy. What we shall have to watch over when peace returns is to keep this moral thrust. It will not be easy, for all the mediocre parties will fall upon their prey. Salvation lies in socialism casting aside its outdated formulae or in a new socialism forming itself which would take anew the French tradition. I see so clearly what this could be![140]

So the war could have been a period of collective effervescence, a crucial period of destructuration and regeneration. Durkheim did participate in the war effort – his only son's death was an ultimate cause of Durkheim's own death in November 1917, a year before the armistice; Durkheim was also hyperactive in that period, much as he had been during the Dreyfus crisis nearly twenty years earlier. He served on various faculty committees to mobilize public opinion both in France and abroad in neutral countries (including the United States) on the side of the Allies, and among his so-called "war pamphlets," his essay "Germany Above All"[141] is an analysis of German value-orientations and national character through the use of German writings, notably those of Treitschke, whom Durkheim treated as a sort of collective representation of the spirit of imperial Germany. I draw attention to this seldom-studied writing of Durkheim because however much Durkheim had strong personal feelings – shall we say, existential concerns – about the subject, the analysis is still marked by the same objective approach to social facts which constituted a cardinal precept of Durkheim's methodology. Moreover, this little essay is also an innovative use in the study of "national character," and antedated by thirty years similar attempts during the Second World War of American social scientists (such as Ruth Benedict in *The Chrysanthemum and the Sword*) to decipher the cultural code of the wartime foe through the use of the latter's own writings. So, to the last, Durkheim stuck to the canons of his methodological principles.

To speculate on what would have happened to Durkheim had he survived the war and what would have happened to sociology if the Durkheimian school had not been decimated is a tempting invitation to engage in daydreaming. Unfortunately – or fortunately – it has no place in an essay designed to present actual features of Durkheim's sociological oeuvre. Perhaps after we have become thoroughly familiar with his writings and after we relate structural features of our own intellectual and societal situation to his own, then can we begin to reformulate what has to be done for sociology to renovate the Durkheimian

---

140 Letter of March 30, 1915, to Xavier Léon, in *Textes* II, p. 478.
141 *"Germany Above All"*: *German Mentality and the War* (Paris: Armand Colin, 1915).

project. Moralist, philosopher, even visionary, but above all a sociological scholar and teacher par excellence, Durkheim is an appropriate role model for those seeking to identify with the best that sociology has to offer. Appreciative of the contributions of the society of yesterday and sensitive to the needs of the society of the present, he was dedicated to the positive task of articulating the social order of tomorrow. Son of the Grand Rabbin des Vosges, Emile Durkheim found his roots in becoming the "grand rabbin" of modern sociology.

Chapter 2
On Discovering Durkheim[1]

Durkheim buffs the world over – and they seem to be a growing legion – will rejoice at the publication of this three-volume set; this is undoubtedly one of the most important publication events of the decade for sociologists having more than a passing interest in the figure who, after all, secured the foundations of modern sociology. Durkheim's fame, renown, even notoriety, essentially rest upon four major books, easily available in translation *(The Division of Labor, Suicide, The Rules,* and *The Elementary Forms)*; several courses that be gave have posthumously been published as books and for the most part are readily accessible also. But there is a much larger output of his writings, which while assuredly of lesser importance than the "big four" sociological symphonies he composed are nevertheless significant in a number of ways; as early drafts or sketches for the later, more polished., mature works; as preliminary and necessary scaffolding for Durkheim's sociological enterprise; as lad of debates he was engaging in with both academic end extra-academic audiences; and lastly, as personal documents which reveal something of the "inner man," whose outer self so totally identified with sociology that Durkheim the total man has yet to be discovered. Victor Karady, research associate of the French Centre National de la Recherche Scientifique, has combed high and low to put together in these volumes writings of Durkheim which are not available in book form; left out are Durkheim's essays and extended book reviews which he published in *l'Année Sociologique*, because these have been available in a single volume, *Journal Sociologique*, compiled by Jean Duvignaud.[2] The result is an outstanding labor of love and a real service to the profession, since it places at our disposal writings published in journals and annuals which at best only a handful of libraries and collections in the United States have; moreover, there are also unpublished items – such as letters – that have previously not appeared in print.

In *Volume 1* (which Karady has designated by the thematic title of *Elements of a Social Theory*), most of the writings deal with Durkheim's delineations of sociology as a discipline. These include the analytical differentiation of sociology from other social sciences, the relation of sociology to still other disciplines such as philosophy and history, and the state of sociology in France. An important

---

1   Review essay of Textes, by Emile Durkheim. Volume I: Eléments d'une Théorie Sociale. Volume 2: Religion, Morale, Anomie. Volume 3: Fonctions Sociales et Institutions. Presentation by Victor Karady, Paris; Editions de Minuit, 1975. Published in Contemporary Sociology, 6, 1 (January 1977).

2   Emile Durkheim, *Journal Sociologique*, introd. J. Duvignaud, Paris: PUF, 1969.

section of this volume, Chapter 3, is devoted to writings of Durkheim, done in his early formative period, which pertain to social science studies in Germany. Of particular interest are the two major articles that Durkheim published in *La Revue philosophique* in the 1880s following his study tour in Germany; one can see from these and other items the important stimulus of Wilhelm Wundt and Albert Schaeffle, in particular, on the young but already intellectually mature Durkheim. Wundt's laboratory and comparative studies of folkways and mores may well have served Durkheim later as the inspiration for the *Année Sociologique*. Also in this section are to be found his comments on Toennies's *Gemeinschaft und Gesellschaft*, which Durkheim reviewed in 1889; the review (p. 390) hints at the need for a book which would provide a thorough critique of Toennies's thesis concerning the evolutionary aspects of modern society, from organic to mechanical solidarity. That critique, of course, became Durkheim's doctoral dissertation four years later, and in *Volume 2*, Karady has appropriately included the extensive portion of the introduction to the first edition (which is the appendix to the Simpson translation of *The Division of Labor*). However fruitful Durkheim's early contacts with German social thought were, they also made Durkheim suspect in some conservative circles as being unduly under German influence; his letters on the subject (pp. 400-407), indicate how rankled he was at the unfairness of the accusations. The volume's concluding section or "annex" has various materials, which, though not sociological, present us with a spectrum of his concerns. They range from his first writing (1883), an address to the graduating class at the Lycée de Sens (which this reviewer had the pleasure of discovering in the archives of Durkheim's hometown of Épinal and which is now available in English in Robert N. Bellah, ed., *Emile Durkheim on Morality and Society)*, to one of his last written items: a description of the history and structure of life at the University of Paris. The latter is part of a collective work that was designed during the war to make the United States have greater familiarity, understanding, and sympathy for France. Durkheim's piece is not only highly informative but also is part of his "war effort" for France, alongside his more partisan tracts written to persuade international public opinion of the rightfulness of the French cause against Germany (his two major pamphlets, written in 1915, are not reprinted in the present set). Also included in this section are writings which take us deeply into the "inner man," namely four necrological notices Durkheim wrote about persons very close to him: his dearest friend at the École Normale, Victor Hommay; Octave Hamelin, a philosopher of great promise and one of Durkheim's closest colleagues at Bordeaux; Robert Hertz, one of the greatest of the great team Durkheim had organized in pre-war France; and André Durkheim, his only son, killed, like Hertz, during World War I. The notices that Durkheim wrote are not maudlin; they tell us about the essence of each unfortunate victim, but they also indicate that Durkheim was as full of deep feelings as he was of profound thoughts.

Volume 2: Religion, Morale, Anomie takes us to what we may regard as the core contributions of Durkheim to sociology, namely the elucidation and conceptualization of the moral dimensions of the social order (including its threatened dissolution or destruction in the phenomena of anomie). Well in advance of the 1912 publication of *The Elementary Forms*, Durkheim gave repeated attention to the relation of religion to society. The volume opens with a letter written in 1889 in which Durkheim suggests that while religiosity is very diffuse and complex, it is not an individual creation; he also states that myths and rituals are interrelated components of any religion. Reports by observers of Durkheim's conferences and lectures on religion are also made available in this volume. This includes a very extensive summary (pp. 65-122) of a course Durkheim taught in 1906-07 on the origins of religion, wherein he developed the structures for his later crowning achievement, *The Elementary Forms of the Religious Life*. But in addition to the scholarly writings on the structure and origin of religious life, there are also materials Durkheim wrote or presented in public debates on the future of religion in modern society, on the separation of church and state, and other related topics. Other writings of Durkheim to be found in this volume pertain to various aspects of "anomie and social health," including pieces on divorce, illegitimacy, and sexual education; yet another major section presents various of Durkheim's approaches to morality, which of course he wished to develop into an objective, scientific field of investigation inasmuch as Durkheim approached it as a social phenomenon.

The "annex" of this volume, like the preceding one, is extremely rewarding in uncovering dimensions of Durkheim the person. Victor Karady has managed to gather nearly one hundred pages of letters Durkheim wrote. The largest set (pp. 389-439) was made available to the editor by the daughter of Célestin Bouglé, one of the initial collaborators of the *Année Soclologique* who eventually became Director of the École Normale. The entire correspondence was written while Durkheim was at Bordeaux, during the years 1896-1902, and certainly informs us of the toils involved in the early years of the *Année Sociologique*. Other letters in this section are to François Simiand, Octave Hamelin, Louis Havet, and Xavier Léon, the latter being the enterprising young publisher of *La Revue de Métaphysique et de Morale* and founder of the French Society of Philosophy. A close friendship developed between the two, which one can follow through the letters.

The third volume (*Social Functions and Institutions*) presents us with Durkheim's writings on a variety of institutional structures and practices, notably marriage and kinship (this includes his inaugural lecture of the course on the family he taught in his second year at Bordeaux, pp. 9-34), the polity, law, and jurisprudence. The closing section presents diverse materials on pedagogy and the university teaching of philosophy in France and Germany. In lieu of an "annex," Karady has provided us with a fifty-page bibliography of primary sources thoughtfully categorized and arranged by year of publication. I should add at this point that, unlike too many French scholarly publications, Karady fortunately provides in this and in each of the other two volumes a useful summary, as well as a name and a subject index.

I trust that from what I have said, readers of this review will feel prompted to have their libraries acquire this major collection of Durkheim materials. Perhaps some altruistic soul will feel the call to translate these volumes so as to broaden further the American readership. Durkheim's *Textes* make for amply rewarding reading by filling in some of the lacunae of the man and his works; they will remain required readings for some time to come.

Chapter 3
Emile Durkheim and Social Change[1]

One may look in vain in Durkheim's oeuvre for an explicit discussion of social change, to be found neither in his major texts nor as a rubric in the twelve *Année Sociologique* volumes published in his lifetime. *Social change* does not figure in Durkheim's major divisions of sociology (1978a:83). Yet, like the Scarlet Pimpernel, it is here, it is there, it is everywhere. No consideration of Durkheim can be considered complete without taking into account his immanent social realism: societal systems structurally change from within, ultimately from qualitative and quantitative changes in social interaction (a presupposition widely shared with Marx and Weber, albeit for different primary factors). This seeming paradox can be best understood if one takes into account that the nineteenth century which provided the context for Durkheim was the modern period's crucible of enormous economic, political, cultural and technological transformations of the social order, with Durkheim's predecessors and contemporaries all seeking to ascertain the major features, causes and outcomes of the transformation. If Durkheim did not write explicitly about social change, he and his immediate followers (the "Durkheimians" who will be briefly mentioned in this entry) were indeed very cognizant and attentive to addressing social change. This was at least partially recognized long ago by Robert Bellah in a seminal article (1960) pointing to the significance of history in Durkheim's epistemological and substantive thought.

Ultimately, following the general dictum of Durkheim that to explain social facts one must seek recourse to social facts, to account for social change one needs to consider changes in the thickness or density of social interaction in time and space (i.e., in the frequency and extent of social interaction). This paramount focus is to be found in at least three major works where social change takes on different manifestations.

As Lukes noted in his landmark intellectual biography (1977:167), Durkheim proposed in his doctoral dissertation *The Division of Labor in Society* a misunderstood theory of social change invoking a morphological key variable: an increase in the "moral" or "dynamic density" of society. The division of labor and its concomitant "organic solidarity" are advanced by demographic factors of population increase in urban areas and by technological factors of increased means of communication and transportation. This perspective has been at the core of much of the initial modernization theory of the 1950s and 1960s stressing structural differentiation as change internal to social systems. As such, Durkheim's

---

1   Published in George Ritzer, ed., *The Blackwell Encyclopedia of Sociology*, vol. III, pp. 1261-64. Malden, MA and Oxford: Blackwell 2007.

theory of societal change as structural differentiation is not altogether novel, since elements of it are to be found in Spencer. However, Durkheim not only proposed the mechanisms of change but also the problematic of the (normative) integration of societal systems in the wake of structural differentiation. This of course involves the question of *anomie* in the modern social order, which will not be treated in this article.

Much of the treatment of long-term social change in Durkheim as well as other social scientists of the nineteenth and early twentieth centuries rests on the evolutionary paradigm. An understanding of the contemporary present forms of society and their interrelationships was viewed in the optic of biological evolution, by tracing the development of origins from simpler to more complex forms of social organization: the more complex, the more organized a social species, the more advanced it is in the evolutionary ladder. While Durkheim analyzed social change in such evolutionary terms (Durkheim 1978b:154), he rejected a linear view of the succession of societies (and of institutions), and even more, of Social Darwinism which lent itself to colonialism and imperialism in justifying the rule of "advanced" societies over those seen to be more "primitive."

Durkheim's deployment of an evolutionary perspective, utilizing historical data, is evidenced in his various analyses of long-term institutional change. Among these may be mentioned his study of (1) the evolution of penal institutions, formulated in terms of laws of quantitative and qualitative changes in punishment (1978b); (2) the evolution of individualism in its interrelation with the evolution of the State and political society (1957); and (3) the evolution of the institution closest to Durkheim's heart, higher education (1977). The last named represents his most elaborate tracing of the development of an institution critical to modernity, written at a time when France in a period of turmoil and uncertainty (1977:7) was grappling with the course to take in educational reforms.

Durkheim maintained in positivist fashion that secondary education needed a sound theoretical foundation based upon knowledge of how educational theory and its applications developed over time. The strengths and weaknesses of these theories in different epochs should be uncovered so as to inform policy makers and public opinion and connect proposed legislation and decrees with reality. We need not detail the evolutionary historical path Durkheim drew in going back to the origins of modern education to Rome as the initial starting point of modern higher education, and then following it forward at various stages. It is a richly textured organizational analysis of the emergent university system seeking to cull what features in an evolutionary perspective appear to have lasting merit and hence deserving to be part of the contemporary educational system, and which do not and should be discarded (1977:160).

His rejection of linear progress in evolutionary change is manifest in Durkheim redressing the negative image of the Middle Ages (as an era of coarseness, harsh discipline, and little educational merit of the Scholastics); instead, he argued, this was a dynamic setting for educational development bringing forth virtually from scratch "the most powerful and comprehensive academic organism which history has ever known," (1977:160). On the other hand, later educational systems had shortcomings: the early Renaissance with its overwhelming stress on classical education and self-centeredness, or the later Renaissance, with Jesuits in charge who made discipline and control more important than students exploring and discovering on their own.

Durkheim's study of the evolution of education, and in particular of the university system is still of twofold merit, besides an important congruence between Durkheim and his great contemporary educator, John Dewey, with whom he shared the view that educational reforms should promote and facilitate the development and creativity of the student. First, because *The Evolution of Educational Thought* (*L'Évolution Pédagogique en France*) documents that at different periods of modernity, the university and secondary education have felt the need to reinvent themselves. Durkheim's study presents here comparative materials that may provide a perspective for the twenty-first century, where higher education is subject to new challenges (multiculturalism, new fiscal constraints, etc.). Second, because it lays to rest the criticism that the functionalist mode of analyzing complex modern social institutions does not address the question of social change.

There is a third sort of social change in Durkheim's work, one which has as focus short-term, intensive transformation of the social whole. Some elements of the analysis in *The Elementary Forms of Religious Life* (1995) are surprisingly similar to the analysis of long-term structural differentiation in Durkheim's first period; yet, the accent is on what may be termed "de-differentiation" rather than "differentiation." In common with *The Division of Labor*, written 20 years earlier, Durkheim posits that increased interaction and the density of actors interacting, in a concentrated time and place, underlie changes in social consciousness. Brought about by religious rituals in the case of the Australian aborigines or by extraordinary events as in the case of the all-night meeting of the French National Assembly in August 1789, or by similar "effervescent social milieux" in our own times from Managua and Tehran in 1979 to Eastern Europe in November 1989 (Tiryakian 1995), what is at stake is the renovation of collective solidarity at a critical moment.

Durkheim sees such extraordinary moments of interactive intensity unparalleled in ordinary quotidian life. They are moments of destructuration or de-differentiation, moments of collective enthusiasm, attended by a collapse of hierarchical status distinction and even, on occasion, of antinomian behavior. While Durkheim drew his theory of the genesis of the sacred in the extraordinary interaction setting involving the whole social group, he also pointed out that social life oscillates between two poles: colorful, festive periods of "hyperexcitement" and periods of "secular activity" of "utter colorlessness" (Durkheim 1995:221). Short-term intensive change gives way to "normalcy." In modern society, the contrast, as Durkheim noted, is more muted, although the need for periodic assemblies and reaffirmation of collective sentiments remains.

Several of Durkheim's collaborators dealt with social change, some with traditional and some with modern society. As an instance of the former, Mauss and Beuchat, in advance of *The Elementary Forms*, published a monograph on the social life of the Eskimo in two major seasonal cycles, winter and summer (Mauss and Beuchat 1979). A study in social morphology, they analyzed variations in social organization and density of interaction. In the summer, the group is disbanded and the cultural life which integrates Eskimo society is at a minimum, as individual families are on their own. In the winter, they come together, and cultural life is thick with the renovation of "a genuine community of ideas and material interests" (Mauss and Beuchat 1979:76). Quantitative changes in interaction produce qualitative changes of increased group solidarity and consciousness, sometimes even leading to sexual license. Finding similar seasonal patterns in other North American native settings, Mauss and Beuchat proposed a general law: social life goes through cycles (phases) of increased and decreased intensity, of activity and rest, of dispersion and concentration, at the individual and collective levels (Mauss and Beuchat 1979:79). Essentially, changes in the cultural life of a group correlate with changes in the form of a group.

François Simiand, a collaborator of the *Année Sociologique* who, with Maurice Halbwachs, was in charge of the major rubric "Economic Sociology", also developed a long-term, cyclical view of change, one applied to economic cycles (1932). After extensive historical studies of the movements of prices, wages, economic production and other indices of economic life, Simiand proposed that there are fluctuations with two major cycles: a cycle of general expansion – the major A-cycle – and one of contraction –the major B-cycle. Writing in a period of global economic crisis, Simiand analyzed it as the early phase of a B-cycle and criticized patchwork economic solutions that failed to realize the complex set of factors that make up economic life, including as a critical variable the social psychological reality of confidence or trust in economic conditions (1932:113). The reality of economic progress, economic development, Simiand argued, is A + B, and mistaken are those theories or models of society that ignore fluctuations and believe they can organize a static economy. There is no general panacea for economic ills, but various options are present which require knowledge of previous economic conditions in periods of transition from A to B or B to A.

Simiand's two phases have been utilized in World Systems theory which has developed cycles complementing long-term (secular) growth of global capitalism (Hopkins and Wallerstein 1982:107). However, more attention has been paid to a Russian contemporary of Simiand, Nikolai Kondratieff, whose theories of alternating "long waves" of expansion and contraction did not fit in the Soviet model of a planned economy. A comparative assessment of Simiand and Kondratieff would provide an important chapter in the history of political economy.

References

Bellah, Robert N. 1960, "Durkheim and History," *American Sociological Review*, 24(4): 447-61.

Durkheim, Emile 1957, *Professional Ethics and Civic Morals*. London: Routledge & Kegan Paul.

—. 1977 1938, *The Evolution of Educational Thought: Lectures on the Formation and Development of Secondary Education in France*, Peter Collins, trans. London: Routledge & Kegan Paul.

—. 1978 (1899-1900), "Two Laws of Penal Evolution," pp. 153-80 in Traugott, *Emile Durkheim on Institutional Analysis*.

—. 1995 1912, *The Elementary Forms of Religious Life*, Karen E. Fields, trans. New York: Free Press.

Hopkins, Terence and Immanuel Wallerstein (1982), "Cyclical Rhythms and Secular Trends of the Capitalist World-Economy," pp. 104-42 in Terence Hopkins, Immanuel Wallerstein and Associates, *World-Systems Analysis: Theory and Methodology*. Beverly Hills, CA and London: Sage.

Lukes, Steven 1977, *Emile Durkheim. His Life and Work: A Historical and Critical Study*. Harmondsworth, Middlesex (UK) and New York: Penguin.

Mauss, Marcel and Henri Beuchat 1979, 1904-05, *Seasonal Variations of the Eskimo: A Study in Social Morphology*. James Fox, trans. London: Routledge & Kegan Paul.

Simiand, François 1932, *Les Fluctuations économiques à longue période et la crise_mondiale*. Paris: Félix Alcan.

Tiryakian, Edward A. 1995, "Collective Effervescence, Social Change and Charisma: Durkheim, Weber and 1989," *International Sociology* 10 (September): 269-81.

Traugott, Mark, ed. 1978, *Emile Durkheim on Institutional Analysis*. Chicago and London: University of Chicago Press.

Chapter 4

Durkheim and Husserl: A Comparison of The Spirit of Positivism and The Spirit of Phenomenology[1]

I

… Whereas barely a decade ago sociological positivism had such a monopoly in the methodology of empirical research that most practicing sociologists in the United States would have tended to equate them as identical, today there is an increasing awareness of meaningful alternative methodologies which are actively competing for attention and professional recognition. Among these alternatives, phenomenological sociology as such is gaining increased visibility.[2]

Before proceeding further, we may point out that the expression "phenomenological sociology" carries with it a certain ambiguity as to its referent(s), an ambiguity which is also the case for "positivistic sociology," which I shall be dealing with later in the body of my exposition. If we use "phenomenological" in a very broad sense as pertaining to the subjective or "inner" aspect of social reality, that is, to an elucidation of the subjective meaning component of social situations and social structures, then we must recognize that there have been various spokesmen for phenomenological sociology, many of whom are not readily thought of as "phenomenological" sociologists: such diverse figures as Max Weber, Talcott Parsons, Pitirim Sorokin, Florian Znaniecki, Robert McIver, Georges Gurvitch, and Erving Goffman come to mind. If we use "phenomenological" in a more restricted sense as pertaining to a demonstrable nexus and identification with the formulator of modern philosophical phenomenology, then the circle becomes more restricted. In the contemporary situation, the circle would seem to have as its nucleus those whose affiliation with Husserl is chiefly through Alfred Schutz, and here we would find Maurice Natanson, Harold Garfinkel, Peter Berger, and Thomas Luckmann. Several contemporary figures have been students of Schutz, some have been students of these students, and yet others have gotten their phenomenological perspective through other sources than Schutz. Since I do not

1   Originally published in Joseph Bien, ed., *Phenomenology and the Social Sciences: A Dialogue*. The Hague, Boston, and London: Martinus Nijhoff, 1978, pp. 20-43.

2   See, for example, George Psathas, ed., *Phenomenological Sociology: Issues and Applications* (New York: John Wiley and Sons, 1973); Paul Filmer, Michael Philipson, David Silverman, and David Walsh, *New Directions in Sociological Theory* (London Collier/Macmillan, 1973).

mean to provide an inventory of names, there is no need to mention many other contemporary figures who might constitute the "phenomenological school" in sociology.[3]

Certainly there is need for a systematic historical and structural delineation of the development of phenomenological sociology, along the lines of Herbert Spiegelberg's excellent study of phenomenology and psychology.[4] Such an assessment would have to go beyond a chronology and a categorization; it would need to clarify internal relations of phenomenological sociology. For example, what is the relation of today's generation of phenomenological sociologists to those of the first generation, the contemporaries of Husserl such as Mannheim and Scheler? Is it the "Americanization" of phenomenological sociology in the post World War II period that accounts for the present micro- and ahistorical tendency, whereas the direction of phenomenological sociology in pre-war Europe under Scheler, Mannheim, and Gurvitch had a pronounced macro-historical emphasis? This seems to be the case, but if so, is phenomenological sociology itself a cultural phenomenon rather than a general methodology of cultural phenomena? At another level of assessment, how does phenomenological sociology relate to other stances in opposition to positivistic sociology, such as so-called "reflexive sociology" or even "critical" sociology (in the vein of Alvin Gouldner's 1970 *The Coming Crisis of Western Sociology*)? Where do they come together (is it again in Hegel?) and where do they part ways?

No matter how amorphous the boundaries of "phenomenological sociology" are, those who identify themselves with this stance have as a common front an opposition to the dominant methodology of positivism. Their critique has various facets, and a brief exposition will suffice. The positivistic orientation takes for granted, or as a given, an objective world out-there constituted by an invariant, determinate (and determinable) set of objective relationships. It is a set that can be adequately represented by formal, quantitative formulae, obtained by elaborate inductions from empirical facts and observations which are ascertained by increasingly precise and reliable measurements. The guiding techniques for this cognitive mastering of the workings of the social world are provided by the recipes of "statistical inference." Although improvements in sociological knowledge ("harder data," more powerful techniques of analysis, etc.) may lead to new "paths" besides the well-trodden one of statistical analysis, all positivistic roads lead to the same heaven: the grasping of the determinate, objective forces which produce, independently of observers, an objective social reality. This is the great beatific

---

3   Nicholas C. Mullins provides a fairly extensive Inventory (subject to some sins of omission and commission) in his Chapter "Ethnomethodology" in his volume *Theories and Theory Groups in Contemporary American Sociology* (New York: Harper and Row, 1973), pp.183-212.

4   Herbert Spiegelberg, *Phenomenology in Psychology and Psychiatry* (Evanston: Northwestern University Press, 1972).

vision of the positivistic sociologists ... a vision which for phenomenological sociology is a pathetic delusion.

It is a delusion because the world does not exist independently of our perception of it; a delusion because the social world is constituted by multiple realities of consciousness, rather than being an unproblematic unitary entity; a delusion because the objective depictions of the positivists are intellectual abstractions which are not validated by the world of experience; a delusion because social reality is an emergent process of intersubjective interactions which relate to a texture of meanings (tacit and explicit) that is always present but undetectable by objective or quantitative procedures. In brief, the phenomenological critique essentially amounts to a condemnation of the naïveté of positivism for the latter's unawareness and neglect of the *validity* of its finding.

II

What I propose to do in this chapter is to get a certain "historical" perspective on the contemporary controversy between phenomenological and positivistic sociology by means of returning to their sources of inspiration, to their respective "spirit." For this purpose I take as their respective foundations arid fountains of inspiration the thoughts of Emile Durkheim and Edmund Husserl. Durkheim and Husserl did not originate the tradition of positivistic sociology and that of phenomenological philosophy, respectively. However, each is recognized in contemporary circles as the figure who articulated for modern times the paradigmatic structure of the respective intellectual tradition, who imparted a new vitality to that tradition, and whose intellectual leadership produced, inspired, and guided new generations of students into broadening the areas of inquiry in the horizon of their respective paradigm of investigation.

For heuristic purpose, I wish to concentrate on the relation of their respective last work, namely *The Elementary Forms of the Religious Life* and *The Crisis of the European Sciences and Transcendental Phenomenology*.[5] I will do this for several reasons, but foremost because I see these works as a coming-together in certain crucial respects of two master theorists. In a sense Durkheim and Husserl had commonality in their beginnings: they were born a year apart (Durkheim in 1858, Husserl in 1859), which means that for about six decades they shared a common European history. They also shared in their formative years, though not at the same time, the same teacher, Wilhelm Wundt (and his famous seminar at Leipzig), the founder of experimental psychology (although both Durkheim and Husserl came

---

5   Emile Durkheim, *The Elementary Forms of the Religious Life* (1912), trans. Joseph Swain (New York: Collier Books, 1961); Edmund Husserl, *The Crisis of the European Sciences and Transcendental Phenomenology*, trans. David Carr (Evanston: Northwestern University Press, 1970). Hereafter these will be cited as *The Elementary Forms*, and *The Crisis*, and references will be given to their respective English edition.

to reject "psychologism" as an accounting of the phenomenal world). But these common "beginnings" have something accidental about them.

On the other hand, the "essentials" in comparing their standpoint, and through this obtaining a perspective on the relationship of phenomenology and sociology beyond what Merleau-Ponty has already indicated,[6] may be more adequately discovered by examining their culminating works, the end-point of their life task as formulators of modern sociology and modern phenomenology, respectively. It is in the last work of Durkheim and Husserl that their initial vision of their intellectual mission reaches full fruition: the actualization of the possibilities of sociology and of phenomenology attains in *The Elementary Forms* and in *The Crisis* the culmination of the *telos* that structured their antecedent explorations. Why a comparison of their last works may be even more apposite for us today, whether we be sociologists or philosophers, is that each work is not simply an "end-point," a conclusion of an intellectual career; each work also has the significance of a new beginning, so that in a sense all their previous writings may be thought of as a prefiguration of the new beginnings, of the New Dawn for sociology and philosophy, announced in *The Elementary Forms* and in *The Crisis*. Beyond that, their respective last work, taken together, have a contemporary timeliness for us to fathom our own world situation, or at least the situation of Western Civilization in the world.

III

In approaching the last work of Durkheim and of Husserl, respectively, it may be noted that some commentators have treated each work as a "break" or as a discontinuity with earlier writings. So, in the case of Durkheim's *Elementary Forms* we have the following considerations which might seem to indicate a discontinuity, if not a reversal, with his previous undertakings. To summarize the arguments, first, here is a sociologist whose previous major works dealt with structural aspects of modernization and modernity, who now seems to leave the domain of modern society for an extensive and prolonged examination of Australian totemism and aboriginal social organization. Second, here we have Durkheim the formulator of sociological positivism who seems to abandon positivism in favor of a transcendental idealism concerning the nature of society, who leaves the realm of objectively documented facts given in statistical data in favor of a structural-functional analysis of religious symbols and experiences! And as to Husserl's *Crisis*, here is the philosopher of radical subjectivity, the philosopher of solitude,[7] not just plunging himself into the lifeworld of intersubjectivity but at the

---

6   Maurice Merleau-Possty, "The Philosopher and Sociology," in *Signs*, trans. Richard C. McCleary (Evanston: Northwestern University Press, 1964), pp. 98-113.

7   Thus did not Husserl say "Autonomous philosophy ... comes into being in the solitary and radical attempt of the philosophising individual to account and to be accountable

same time engaging phenomenology in a bold grasp of history, and in fact doing less than a radical interpretation of the historically manifested essence of Western civilization!

Are we then dealing with the paradox of Durkheim, a founder of modern sociology, turning his back on Western, modern society and on positivism, and on the other side, Husserl turning his back on descriptive phenomenology and its quest for apodictic knowledge, which surely cannot be established by the contingencies of history? Should we consequently treat *The Elementary Forms* and *The Crisis* as perhaps interesting detours if not outright deviations from their authors' preceding investigations?

I think not. Having no pretension of being a Husserlian scholar, I gladly accept the independently arrived at judgment of two authorities on Husserl that there is no essential continuity between *The Crisis* and the anterior phenomenology of Husserl. I have in mind the penetrating studies of Husserl done by Paul Ricoeur and Maurice Natanson.[8] As to Durkheim's *Elementary Forms,* I feel better qualified to assert that it has a fundamental continuity with the development of Durkheim's thoughts; in fact, in some respects, it is the culmination of themes he had broached in his earliest essays.[9] In particular, Durkheim had in 1886 outlined the profound interrelationship and interdependence of religion, morality, and social organization, and these themes are the contextual background of his "middle period," the period of his most pronounced "positivistic" investigations. The background comes to the fore in *The Elementary Forms*, which should be properly seen as much more than a study of the social structures of religion: it is an investigation into the essential structures of social consciousness. This culminating work of Durkheim places his "positivism" in a new light, one which enables us to rethink the controversy between phenomenological philosophy and positivistic sociology.

So much by way of a prologue. Bearing in mind that the reader should not expect an exegesis of the contents of the respective works, let us consider whether a dialogue emerges out of the comparison of *The Elementary Forms* and *The Crisis.*

---

only to himself"? Later in the same text, the theme of the solitary ego, detached from his fellow men, is further accentuated, for "Due to this epoché, human solitude has been transformed into transcendental solitude." These citations come from his 1931 Berlin lecture, "Phenomenology and Anthropology," reprinted In Roderick M. Chisholm, ed., *Realism and The Background of Phenomenology* (New York: Free Press, 1960), pp. 133, 135, respectively.

8   Paul Ricoeur, *Husserl, An Analysis of His Phenomenology*, trans, Edward G. Ballard and Lester E. Embree (Evanston: Northwestern University Press, 1967); Maurice Natanson, *Edmund Husserl: Philosopher of Infinite Tasks* (Evanston: Northwestern University, 1973).

9   "Les études de Science Sociale," *Revue Philosophique*, 22 (1886), pp. 61-80; "La Philosophie dans les universités Allemandes," *Revue Internationale de l'Enseignement,*13 (1887), pp. 313-38, 423-440.

IV

Husserl in his essay "Phenomenology and Anthropology"[10] had prepared an overture to his later momentous *Crisis* by suggesting what he intended phenomenology to be. It is worthwhile to dwell on some points of this 1930 essay which heralds his culminating philosophical endeavor. He tells us that phenomenology is a "hermeneutic of the life of consciousness," and adds in the same paragraph, "Rather than 'interrogate' nature, as Bacon recommended, we must, therefore, interrogate consciousness or the transcendental ego in order to force it to betray its secrets" (p. 140). Further on in his essay, Husserl observes:

> Starting out from myself as ego constituting existential meaning.I reach the transcendental others, who are my peers, and at the same time the entire open, infinite transcendental intersubjective realm. In this transcendental community the world as "objective" and as the same for everybody is constituted.[11]

And Husserl concludes his essay by declaring:

> If one has understood our aims ... one can no longer doubt that there is only one ultimate philosophy, only one kind of ultimate science, the science inseparable from transcendental phenomenology's method of exploring origins.[12]

Now here we have three themes which announce the coming *Crisis* and which place in relief essential aspects of the thrust of phenomenology. First, phenomenology seeks the truth of the world by deciphering consciousness rather than by deciphering the mysteries of bio-physical "nature"; this statement of Husserl points to the naïveté of empiricism which assumes that the truth of the world, its foundation, lies in an *objective* realm of nature. The second theme prefigures the re-emergence of the phenomenologist from his solitary explorations into the communal world, much in the fashion of Plato's figure in The Republic who leaves the shadowy cave of darkness but then reenters it after having been illuminated in order to inform his fellow men of true knowledge of reality.[13] And in *The Crisis* the nexus

---

10   In Roderick M. Chisholm, op. cit.

11   Ibid., p. 141.

12   Ibid., p. 142.

13   Not only do I find a strong affinity between Husserl and Plato concerning the doctrine of essences, which might make us consider Husserl a neo-Platonist, but also a case might be made for both as participating in that esoteric tradition of Western civilization (as manifested in *The Republic's* allegory of the cave). Although I lack evidence as to whether Husserl was in fact an adept of a school of esotericism, there are passages in *The Crisis*, for example, Part III A, sections 39-41, which are remarkably akin to the language of esotericism, such as theosophy or anthroposophy. For materials on the esoteric, see my volume, *On the Margin of the Visible* (New York: Wiley and Sons, 1974).

between transcendental phenomenology and the European community as a global, historical phenomenon, will become a major probe of Husserl's analysis. Finally, the concluding theme stresses what is distinctive and radical about phenomenology as a philosophical method, namely, it is a method of exploring origins.

What does exploring origins mean? It means to get to the ground of phenomena, to the roots, to that which makes possible the appearance of things as phenomena. Now there is involved an interrelated task: on the one hand, to get to the origins entails going back in the historical or temporal process, back to the historical seedbed of the visible phenomenon which is before our consciousness. On the other hand, to go to the origins is not only an historical task but also a structural task, that is, a task of discovering the fundamental structures which ground the phenomenon that we are concerned with. So, we now see phenomenological analysis as entailing *a structural as well as an historical analysis*.

We can now understand why Husserl's phenomenology was not only a method entailing both eidetic and transcendental reductions, but more important in this context, why *The Crisis* is the appropriate culmination of Husserl's entire phenomenological investigations. Why appropriate? Because the phenomenon that is the appropriate subject matter of transcendental phenomenology is the phenomenon of Western civilization, which is not an "objective," "natural" object that can be understood by empiricism or by historicism, but a global, historical, spiritual phenomenon, a phenomenon of intersubjective consciousness. It is a phenomenon that has a unity and whose historicity has a *telos*: Husserl will find as the essential theme of Western civilization (or "Europe") that of *rationalism*. This is the core structure of the historical emergence of Western civilization, and what underlies the profound malaise of our century, will add Husserl, is the destructuration of rationalism.[14] Husserl's *Crisis* is both a phenomenological analysis and a diagnosis of the "crisis" of the modern world; it is, as he suggests, a thoroughgoing radical critique of what underlies the crisis. And here we have yet to recognize the full import of Husserl's declaration:

---

14   "In order to be able to comprehend the disarray of the present crisis," we had to work out *the concept of Europe as the historical teleology of the infinite goals of reason*; we had to show how the European world was born out of ideas of reason, i.e., out of the spirit of philosophy. The 'crisis' could then become distinguishable as the apparent failure of rationalism," (*The Crisis*, p. 299, emphasis in the original).

Although the present essay is limited to a dialogue between Husserl and Durkheim, it would be germane to consider here the convergence between Husserl and Max Weber. More, than Durkheim, Weber saw the unfolding of rationalism as the central theme of the modernization of Western civilization, and like Husserl, Weber perceived the tragic exhaustion of the spirit of rationalism as having the gravest implications for the future of Europe.

> I would like to think that I, the supposed reactionary, am far more radical and
> far more revolutionary than those who, in their words proclaim themselves so
> radical today.[15]

It is only by going to the origins, to the roots, to the depth structures of consciousness,
that one can be truly radical; by going below the surface of phenomena one ascends
or transcends the place of mundanity. The *epoché* ("bracketing the world") had
provided Husserl with the means of liberating the philosopher from the natural
attitude. In *The Crisis* this liberating heuristic device will permit Husserl to
grasp the sense of the "crisis" of Europe as the alienation of rationalism from its
existential roots in transcendental consciousness. He will see this alienation as
involving philosophy falsely identifying itself with the positive sciences, leading
to a fundamental crisis in epistemology, a crisis in the grounding of knowledge.

So much for a preliminary view of Husserl's *Crisis* and its background. Let
me pause further consideration of Husserl until we discuss how Durkheim's
Elementary Forms complements *The Crisis*, or more broadly, how Durkheim's
stance in approaching sociologically the phenomenon of the religious life
converges with Husserl's phenomenological endeavors. What is it that Durkheim
has in mind in analyzing in that work the most primitive religion he knew of, that
of totemism?[16]

To be sure, as he tells us at the very beginning of his introduction, he will
seek in studying totemism to deepen our understanding of an essential feature of
humanity, namely "the religious nature of man."[17] But the horizon of Durkheim's
research project is wider than this, for as he adds a few pages later:

> ... the study of religious phenomena gives a means of renewing the problems
> which, up to the present, have only been discussed among philosophers.[18]

This statement gives an inkling of the relevance of his study for phenomenology as
philosophy. What is the fundamental problem of philosophy if not the grounds of
knowledge? Is this not the central theme of Husserl's *Crisis* which is posed in the
beginning of Part I, where Husserl sees the original establishment of philosophy
in the Greek awareness of reason, of *episteme* as opposed to (unreflective) *doxa*?
Here philosophy in its origins "conceives of and takes as its task the exalted idea
of universal knowledge concerning the totality of what is."[19]

---

15   *The Crisis*, p.290.

16   To be sure, several scholars have criticized Durkheim for taking Australian
totemism as the simplest, i.e., most primitive, religion , this controversy is of no relevance
to the present discussion.

17   *The Elementary Forms*, p. 13.

18   Ibid., p. 21.

19   *The Crisis*, p. 13.

Durkheim wrote *The Elementary Forms* after having conducted a preliminary investigation (with Marcel Mauss) concerning the fundamental forms or categories of knowledge.[20] He had in his formative years received a thorough exposure to philosophy, and was an active member of the French Society of Philosophy. We may say that Durkheim and Husserl came to their respective last works with a felt concern to ground the structural foundations of knowledge; why each felt the pressing need to ground knowledge apodictically will be discussed shortly. But that Durkheim in *The Elementary Forms* was returning to philosophy, or to its renewal, and this in terms of the central theme of knowledge is self-evident in his very introduction. There he indicates his concern with accounting for the fundamental categories of the understanding (time, space, cause, etc.) as structures which are collective representations (i.e., which in effect are the structures of the lived world). He further adds, "This hypothesis, once admitted, the problem of knowledge is posed in new terms."[21]

So it is with the structures and the ground of knowledge that Durkheim and Husserl are concerned with, and in fact, it is with renovating the traditional notions of knowledge that is at the heart of both *The Elementary Forms* and *The Crisis*. Moreover, just as Husserl's radicalism entails a phenomenologicai investigation of origins, so also does Durkheim take sociological investigation as a going to beginnings. In taking the categorizations of knowledge to the setting of the most primitive society, he is surely going as much to the structural grounds of knowledge as was Husserl by taking it back to the early Greek apprehension of *episteme*, wherein Husserl found the original unity of science and philosophy, the unity of knowledge contained in philosophy *as* science. Durkheim in *The Elementary Forms* takes us to the beginnings and finds in his "primitive" data ideas which "while being of religious origin, still remain at the foundation of human intelligence."[22] Just how radical this exploration is can further be appreciated if we take cognizance of the fact that in Durkheim's days the prevailing opinion was that "primitives" or those living in non- Western societies were considered to have a very different and inferior mentality than the modem mind. There is thus an added audacity in Durkheim's last work to go to the roots of the social world by going back to "primitive" Australian society. But why is this search for beginnings common to both Durkheim and Husserl? Asking this brings to view a fundamental concern of Durkheim's positivism and Husserl's phenomenology, namely their awareness of a deep-seated crisis in contemporary society.

Husserl's diagnosis of the crisis of Europe goes beneath the political and economic turmoil of the 1930s, the period in which he prepared *The Crisis*. He finds it a crisis at the heart of the *telos* of Europe, which *telos* he saw as the unfolding of *rationalism*. What underlies the crisis for Husserl involves (a) the separation of

---

20   Emile Durkheim and Marcel Mauss, *Primitive Classfication*, trans., Rodney Needham (Chicago: University of Chicago Press, 1963).

21   *The Elementary Forms*, p. 25.

22   Ibid., p. 33.

science from its original philosophical conception, (b) philosophy losing its own identity in identifying itself with the model of the natural sciences, and (c) the separation of nature from the spiritual life of the psyche or soul. Not only has there been a separation of science from philosophy, but with it a separation of one science into compartmentalized sciences. This fragmentation of knowledge from "the intuitive surrounding world of life, pregiven as existing for all in common,"[23] is the product of "objectivism" and positivism, whose very overt successes mask modern science's epistemological shallowness.

To accentuate the point, Husserl invokes Helmholtz' image of Plane-beings "who have no idea of the dimension of depth, in which their plane-world is a mere projection."[24] All activities of science in the modern world take place on the "plane." Positive science ignores and dismisses its own foundations, the substratum of the "life-world" which will have to be discovered by transcendental phenomenology, for the ground of the plane-world lies in "transcendental consciousness." And Part II of *The Crisis* prepares the way for the task of restoring the unity of science and philosophy by liberating the idea of unity which has been deformed by positivism and objectivism; objectivism has objectified the *Lebenswelt* into an objective, mathematical world rendition of nature, a model first conceived by Galileo.[25]

In the historical process of objectification of the world, that is the transformation of the world by modern science from an existential, pretheoretical life-world into one which conforms to the hypothesis of a mathematical nature, Husserl notes that psychology (stemming from the influence of Wundt?) has lost the sense of the psyche, of the soul. For him, modern psychology is not the science of the psyche but rather of an objectified ego, which far from being the true ground of knowledge has become an object of knowledge, like other scientific objects. Hence Husserl's rejection of psychologism, as part of his general critique of positivism.

But then, are not Husserl and Durkheim poles apart? If one is the champion of phenomenology, which has as one of its fundamental tasks the liberation of man in the phenomenological attitude from the prejudices and philosophical naïveté of the positive sciences,[26] and the other the champion of sociological positivism, does this not, once-and-for-all occasion end any real possibility of a dialogue? Perhaps, and then again, perhaps not.

Durkheim's "positivism" is a good deal more complex than its contemporary image (just as Husserl's phenomenology is also "multivalent, so to say). True, Durkheim participated in the general scientific ethos of the second-half of the 19th century, including the commitment to a universally valid scientific method in observing, measuring, analyzing, and reporting objectively the "facts," i.e., the

---

23   *The Crisis*, p, 121.

24   Ibid., p. 119.

25   "One can truly say that the idea of nature as a really self-enclosed world of bodies first emerges with Galileo," ibid., p.60.

26   I base this interpretation of the task of phenomenology on materials in *The Crisis* p. 59.

facticity of the science-specific domain of phenomena. In this restricted sense, Durkheim's positivistic sociology and Husserl's phenomenology have little in common. But Durkheim's "positivism" has another tradition feeding into his formulations, one which transcends the tradition of the natural sciences. That one is the primary sociological tradition of positivism, which has as the key figure Auguste Comte, although this tradition began with Saint-Simon (Comte's mentor) and also owes much to Comte's contemporary, LePlay (the founder of comparative empirical research in sociology). Let me briefly remark on Comte, who after all not only coined the term "sociology but also "positivism." Comte understood by "positivism" firstly the positive knowledge obtained by science, in contradistinction to the knowledge obtained in two earlier evolutionary forms of mankind's mentality, namely "metaphysical" and "theological" knowledge – and in passing, we might point out that Husserl himself seems to have an emergent perspective on knowledge which is, at least the way I look at it, structurally similar to Comte.[27]

Secondly, and even more important, Comte took "positive knowledge" to be the opposite of the "negativism" of the *philosophes* (the leading intellectuals) of the eighteenth century, of the negative, critical spirit whose analysis helped to undermine the organic unity of man and society by dissolving in critical ideas the essential unity of knowledge. For Comte there was no question of restoring the social order of the *ancien régime*; yet, the political malaise of modern society was a surface symptom of the fragmentation of knowledge. Political divisions and cleavages reflected this condition of crisis of modern Europe, and positivism was intended not only as the synthesis of knowledge but, in fact, as providing the basis of a new synthesis for the social order by providing the ground for its restructuration. The later Comte, as we know, saw in "positivism" more than a new cognitive system of knowledge which would unify society; he also saw it as a religion, a religion grounded not in revelation but in sociological observations. Sociological positivism, in Comte, is animated then by a motivation of social

---

27   The relevant materials here are to be found in Husserl's "Vienna Lecture" (1935), included in *The Crisis* as Appendix I, pp. 269-299. The first mentality, common to all mankind, Husserl calls the "religio-mythical attitude"; it is geared essentially to practical ends. With the pre-Socratics in the seventh century B.C., there arises a distinctively new world attitude which will differentiate Europe from other civilizations radically. That is the "theoretical attitude" which itself undergoes evolution, and in the process, it transforms the "whole praxis of human existence" (*The Crisis*, p. 287).

    The late phase of the "theoretical attitude" might be seen as Comte's "positivistic attitude," but the third attitude Husserl has in mind, namely the emergent, "phenomenological attitude", is from another consideration similar to what Comte had in mind. Namely, for Comte the "positivist attitude," that of science, would not be complete until the establishment of a science of society, that is, a science of the most complex domain of reality, social (or intersubjective) consciousness. Furthermore, is not for Husserl transcendental phenomenology a rigorous science of consciousness whose ultimate endeavor is the accounting of intersubjective consciousness?

reconstruction, and by a concern with the spiritual crisis of modern Europe that leads it to probe beneath the surface, beneath the "objective" appearance of Europe to its spiritual depths.[28]

Durkheim was the heir of Comte's positivism, although he rejected certain features of Comte's over-all system, for example, Comte's monistic evolutionary principle of the "law of three stages." Nevertheless, the spirit of Comte's positivism underlies Durkheim's task in developing sociology. Further, the spirit of this sociological positivism has two aspects which are highly germane for our discussion. First, sociological positivism goes beyond the mere scientific inquiry of the social world; it seeks a new moral basis for the modern social order, one which will reconcile social cleavages by providing the religion appropriate for integrating the constituent parts of society. Second, Comte's positivism (and that of Durkheim) repudiates the attempt to reduce the specificity of the *socius* to a mathematical and physicalistic interpretation of nature. For Comte "science" is fundamentally a human activity, one which emerges in the historical process, and it might be said that the development of science is for Comte a stochastic process. This implies that although the emergence of a new science, such as biology, is contingent on the anterior development of previous sciences, each science is a new level of knowledge since its phenomenon has a complexity irreducible to the previous level of development. Sociology deals with a reality, that of "social existence" (the expression is formulated by Comte in his *Système de politique positive*, II, Chapter 6) which cannot be reduced to biological/physiological existence, much less to the reality of chemical or physical being. It is a reality of intersubjective consciousness, manifested in what Comte terms human "consensus," differentiating human society from animal society by its spontaneous and volitional elements.

Having said that Durkheim accepted the patrimony of Comte's sociology, we need to amplify this observation for a proper consideration of the full significance of *The Elementary Forms*. That aspect of Comte's sense of sociological positivism as the repudiation of physicalistic reductionism of social reality is clearly to be found in Durkheim's famous anterior methodological work, *The Rules of the Sociological Method*, where in his preface to the first edition Durkheim had announced a theme that runs throughout his treatise:

> Just as the idealists separate the psychological from the biological realm, so we separate the psychological from the social; like them, we refuse to explain the complex in terms of the simple.[29]

---

28   For a recent succinct overview of the dimensions of Comte's positivism, see Pierre Arnaud, *Sociologie de Comte* (Paris: Presses Universitaires de France, 1969).

29   Emile Durkheim, *The Rules of the Sociological Method* (New York: Free Press, 1950), p. xxxix. This is reaffirmed in his conclusion "Sociology, then, is not an auxiliary of any other science; it is itself a distinct and autonomous science, and the feeling of the

I have also indicated that the spirit of Comte's positivism has a second dimension, namely the quest for restructuring the moral substratum of modern society; this is emphasized or accentuated by Comte's intention for positivism to be the new religion of humanity. To be sure, Comte sought a "secular" or what might even be termed a "civil religion," but nevertheless, a religion, and for Comte, positivism had a trinitarian basis albeit not that of Christianity.[30]

Durkheim, to reiterate, had expressed in his first sociological articles an interest in religion's relation to society. In *The Elementary Forms* this interest becomes paramount, as over the years Durkheim had come to accept that every society's existence tends to be organized around a core set of religious beliefs and practices: these *are* the elementary or fundamental forms of social life. Modern society is characterized by a heterogeneity of groups and by a division of labor which render social organization more complex than those of "traditional" society. Yet, however arduous the task, sociology must seek to find the religion and normative ensemble appropriate for the ideals, aspirations, and cohesion of the modern social order. This is the unstated quest of *The Elementary Forms*.

Moreover, Durkheim in this work also seeks to reconcile the fragmentation if not the opposition between science, religion, and philosophy. Thus, in his concluding chapter, Durkheim proposes:

> ... the realities to which religious speculation is then applied are the same as those which later serve as the object of reflection for philosophers: they are nature, man, and society ... Religion sets itself to translate these realities into an intelligible language which does not differ in nature from that employed by science ... We have even seen that the essential ideas of scientific logic are of religious origin.[31]

We can see from this argument that Durkheim's positivism does not "surrender" social reality (which is inextricably related to the religious life) to a naturalism or a physicalistic conception of nature, but rather, like Husserl, he sees science as grounded in the activities of intersubjective consciousness. To make a further comparison between them in terms of their last work, Husserl's phenomenological-psychological *epoché* enables us to proceed from "the external attitude" of empiricism and psychologism to the "inner perception" of structures.[32] Husserl takes us to fundamental and universal structure of the life-world, which he views as transcendental consciousness; it is the source of consciousness, the pure consciousness which underlies all specific projects, all intentional aspects

---

specificity of social reality is indeed so necessary to the sociologist that only distinctly sociological training can prepare bins to grasp social facts intelligently" (ibid., p. 145).

30   Comte's formula for positivism as the religion of humanity was: "Love as its principle; Order as its basis; Progress as its goal."

31   *The Elementary Forms*, p. 477.

32   See the crucial discussion in *The Crisis*, Part III B, esp. pp. 247-50.

of psychic experience. But has not Durkheim similarly located the ground of consciousness in the transcendental aspects of society, in its religious life, when he declares in his conclusion:

> ... the collective consciousness is the highest form of the psychic life, since it is *the consciousness of consciousness* ("une conscience des consciences")[33]

Husserl and Durkheim have traveled different paths, and yet have come in their respective last work to the same cross-road; phenomenology and sociology come to a meeting on the cross-road of transcendental consciousness. Their respective discovering of this structure of structures gives a fuller sense to their intellectual endeavors when we take into account their respective sensitivity to the crisis of Europe, a crisis that stems from losing sight of the transcendental ground of our civilization.

In brief, then, Husserl's and Durkheim's last work are both explorations of origins and both go from the exteriority of the world to its interiority in transcendental consciousness. In this respect, their endeavor bears a striking resemblance with modem figures of esotericism such as Rudolph Steiner and René Guénon,[34] who also sought to recover the truly spiritual dimension of man which has been blocked from view by the prejudices of objectivist science, of mathematical natural science which abstracts subjectivity out of existence.[35] It should be borne in mind that Husserl and Durkheim do not reject "science" any more than they reject "rationality," for surely both saw themselves as "rationalists." What each rejected in his own way were the imperialistic claims of mathematical natural science reducing the reality of the life-world to an "object" reality, one in which the depth of experience, of meaning, of subjectivity has been shallowed out of existence.

V

My remarks in the preceding pages point to the rapprochement between Husserl's phenomenology and Durkheim's sociology, yet I have also suggested there exists an area of disagreement, which now deserves to be acknowledged. Let me term

---

33   *The Elementary Forms*, p. 492, emphasis mine.

34   Rudolf Steiner, *The Stages of Higher Knowledge* (New York: Anthroposophic Press, 1967), and *Macrocosm and Microcosm* (London: Rudolf Steiner Press, 1968); René Guénon, *The Reign of Quantity and the Signs of the Times* (Baltimore: Penguin Books, 1972).

35   "Someone who is raised on natural science takes it for granted that everything merely subjective must be excluded and that the natural-scientific method, exhibiting itself in subjective manners of representation, determines objectivity," Husserl, *The Crisis*, p. 295.

this a disagreement as to the ontological nature of consciousness. However radical Husserl saw his philosophy in terms of the corpus of philosophy, there is one limitation of his radicality, or in other words, there is one presupposition, one pre-reflexive "given" that he shared in common with his fellow philosophers (from Socrates through Kant). That is the following: subjectivity and its activities of consciousness are grounded in the individual *cogito*. For Durkheim, on the other hand, consciousness has two irreducible constitutive modes, those of the individual *and* those of the collectivity. Durkhem views our knowledge of the world, our representations of reality, in terms of which we experience the world, as a dual product of individual and collective consciousness, without one being more fundamental than the other. Man qua social human being is *homo duplex*.[36]

Consequently, although *The Crisis* shows an increasing awareness of intersubjectivity and of community, Husserl's transcendental grounds of worldhood remains an I-pole at its core, whereas Durkheim's transcendental grounds of worldhood emphasizes its We-pole. Durkheim could not accept the following declarations of Husserl:

> This individual psychology must, then, be the foundation for a sociology and likewise for a science of objectified spirit (of cultural things) ...[37]

> Human beings are external to one another, they are separated realities, and so their psychic interiors are also separated. Internal psychology can thus be only individual psychology of individual souls ...[38]

Have we then traveled all this way only to reach an impasse between Husserl's phenomenology and Durkheim's positivism? I would like to propose the dialogue has just begun. Just as currency tends to become debased in the modern world, so do words become debased as they become popular. The word "dialogue" is no exception. To have efficacy, a dialogue should start with an awareness on the parts of the conversants of their initial premises, which entails an agreement as to where they disagree. If disagreement is "masked," dialogue may be rewarding social "small talk" but not an intellectually rewarding discourse. So, a dialogue between Husserl and Durkheim must entail an awareness of their differences as to the ontological nature of consciousness, albeit it must also entail an awareness that for both the life-world is constituted by consciousness. That the dialogue has just begun is also indicated by the unfinished nature of their respective last work.

---

36 Durkheim treated this in one of his last articles, "Le Dualisme de la Nature Humaine et set conditions Sociales," *Scientia*, x. (1914), pp. 206-21. An English Translation of this important sequel to *The Elementary Forms* appears in Kurt H. Wolff, ed., *Emile Durkheim 1858-1917* (Columbus: Ohio State University Press, 1960), pp. 325-340. The reader will find in Husserl's *The Crisis*, pp. 229ff., a complementary discussion of the self's dualism.

37 *The Crisis*, p. 220.

38 Ibid., p. 247.

As the reader of *The Crisis* will know, Husserl achieved in this work only parts of his intended reconstruction, or reformulation of philosophy.[39] *The Elementary Forms* seems more conclusive, yet I would argue that it is a prolegomenon. To what? To a sociological formulation of the religious life appropriate for the ideals and actualities of modern society, one which would give society a firm anchor to withstand the twin tendencies of nihilism and totalitarianism.[40]

Although far from being an apologist for traditional religion, Durkheim was more worried about the dissolution of intermediary groups between the individual and the State than he was about the dangers of religion in secular society. That is, I would suggest, he saw as part of the crisis of modern society the tendency of polarization between radical individualism, or nihilism, and Statism. He had in earlier works given attention to restructuring professional groups as buffers, but ultimately saw that these by themselves are not sufficient. Hence my argument that *The Elementary Forms* is as much an introduction as Husserl's *Crisis* is one. In the case of the first, it may be viewed as an introduction to religious sociology whose starting point is the sociology of religion – that is to a sociology bold enough to help society formulate its necessary religious (and ethical) structure, which is needed to overcome the anomie or spiritual malaise of the modern world. For sociologists in their sociologizing to seek the spiritual reconstruction of the society in which they live, is this not the spirit of Durkheim's positivism echoing the spirit of Husserl's phenomenology:

> In *our* philosophizing, then – how can we avoid it? – we are *functionaries of mankind*. The quite personal responsibility of our own true being as philosophers, our inner personal vocation, bears within itself at the same time the responsibility for the true being of mankind.[41]

Arguably, then, there is not an impasse between Husserl and Durkheim, although neither is there a fusion of the two. I think there is ground for a fruitful dialogue. If sociology can profit from this dialogue by enriching its method in terms of the riches of the phenomenological method, let me also add that phenomenology has something to learn from Durkheim's positivism, and specifically from a thorough consideration of *The Elementary Forms*. Husserl's phenomenology of consciousness, if it limits itself, even in its transcendental aspects, to the solitary ego as the primary soil of consciousness, cannot adequately account for the moral and religious dimensions and structures of consciousness; yet, these are cardinal

---

39   In this context, see Appendix X of *The Crisis* for Fink's outline of what Husserl bad envisaged (pp. 597-400).

40   One must read Durkheim's Leçons *de Sociologie, Physique des Moeurs et du Droit* (Paris: Presses Universitaires de France, 5950), esp. pp. 52-130, for a background discussion of this point. The English edition is *Professional Ethics and Civic Morals*, trans., Cornelis Brookfield (London: Routledge and Kegan Paul, 1957).

41   *The Crisis*, p. 17. Emphasis in the original.

aspects of human experience, however varied the contents of the experience may be. Durkheim's *Elementary Forms* has brought out in full relief these modes of consciousness as structures of the life-world. His theorizing is an integral aspect of his reformulation of the theory of knowledge, which well merits serious attention by phenomenology since its core concern is also an epistemological one.

VI

We have examined in the course of this essay aspects of Husserl and Durkheim whose respective last work, *The Crisis* and *The Elementary Forms of the Religious Life* is truly seminal and truly radical, for philosophy and for sociology. We have done this in the context of a comparison of the guiding "spirit" of phenomenology and that of sociology. We have sought to bring them together, to indicate they have a common meeting ground, although this will not blur their standpoint.

In this exposition, the reader may have begun to wonder about his/her anterior image of "positivism." I think it appropriate in this conclusion to state as a paradox that "there is positivism and positivism," or to put it in a less ambiguous way, Durkheim's positivism is perhaps more divergent from contemporary sociological positivism than it is divergent from Husserl's phenomenology. How so?

A succinct overview of contemporary positivism is contained in Abraham Kaplan's article on the subject in the *International Encyclopedia of the Social Sciences*.[42] Kaplan mentions two forms of positivism, that of the nineteenth century, associated with Comte, and that of the twentieth century, formulated first by the Vienna Circle (Carnap, Neurath, Feigl), somewhat later in Berlin (Reichenbach), and later still in the 1930s at Chicago (following an exodus from Austria and Germany). It is this form of positivism, which we may call *logico-mathematical positivism*, that has come to be tacitly accepted as to what sociological positivism is all about. This contemporary form of positivism is in its spirit analytical and reductionist. Let us consider what its major components are.

The thrust of logical positivism is linguistic analysis, and involved in this is a reduction of philosophical activity to an analysis of language; *meaning* is reduced to rules of language. And there is one language which seems to be given primacy, namely mathematical language. Hence, modern positivism seeks the linguistic formalization of the world into mathematical language, whose structure is seen as the logic of scientific inquiry. Whether by induction or by deduction, the end sought is the reduction of world phenomena to mathematical language. This form of positivism, this pursuit, has come to characterize today's positivistic sociology which tacitly seeks the mathematization of social reality, whether we see it in its labels of "theory-construction," "axiomatization," or other labels. There is an echo in this of Comte's original vision of the unity of scientific knowledge, which

---

42   Abraham Kaplan, "Positivism," *International Encylopedia of the Social Sciences*, vol. 12 (New York: Macmillan and The Free Press, 1968), pp. 389-395.

he saw as a new synthesis of science and philosophy. Nonetheless it is an inversion of the vision, for neither Comte nor Durkheim for one minute believed in the reduction of social phenomena to the model of natural sciences, much less to their being expressed in formal or mathematical expressions.

Husserl's objection to positivism, to its imperialistic claims, is well-founded. He undoubtedly would repudiate the positivist conception that

> Philosophy is not a doctrine embodying 'wisdom' – it is an activity; it is neither a theory nor a way of life but rather a way of analyzing what is said in the course of living or in theorizing about life.[43]

Husserl would object to this, for logical positivism does not address itself to the life-world but to a lifeless world, the world of intellectual, logical, mathematical abstractions. Philosophy, or philosophy of science, in this positivistic framework is not a critique of science; it has renounced its mission and its end purpose, its *telos*. And if Husserl would repudiate this positivistic conception, so also would Durkheim deny this as being in accordance with his awareness of positivism. Yes, of course, Durkheim believed that one could study objectively social phenomena, and when he said the sociological attitude must treat these phenomena as "things," he clearly meant not that social phenomena are to be treated as if they were in the same domain as physical "entities". Rather, they must be approached free from the prejudices of the natural attitude which makes naive assumptions as to how social phenomena are constituted. Hence his injunction "all preconceptions must be eradicated"[44] is of the same methodological import as Husserl's dictum, "to the things themselves;" in both, there is an emphasis on the *epoché*, the bracketing of the natural attitude if we are to go behind appearances to the ground of reality. Both Husserl and Durkheim would agree, I believe, with Phillipson's apt comments:

> Mathematization may appear elegant but it obscures the problems of meaning and language and thus mystifies the events the sociologist is trying to understand. The formal elegance of mathematics is a stark contrast to the social realities of the lived world.[45]

The life-world, the everyday social world, does have regularities and "typifications" (to borrow from Schutz) which may even be expressed in mathematical relationships. Certainly, Durkheim's famous positivistic monograph, *Suicide*, is a demonstration that even such a seemingly individual act as "suicide" is a phenomenon having a sociocultural context whose objective manifestations may

---

43   Kaplan, *op. cit.,* p. 389.

44   *Rules of the Sociologcal Method*, p. 51.

45   Michael Phillipson, "Phenomenological Philosophy and Sociology," in Paul Filmer, et al., op. cit, p. 145.

be approximated in statistical relationships. But even in this monograph, to say nothing of the later *Elementary Forms*, Durkheim went on to explore the layers of meaning-structures that are constitutive of this phenomenon. Suicide, like religious activity, like crime, like altruism is a phenomenon of the life-world; in this sense they all are "natural" phenomena, but they are not phenomena that can be interpreted or explained in terms of a natural science model of physical nature. They are phenomena of intersubjectivity ... just as the natural science model(s) of physical nature are themselves not objective entities but essentially phenomena of intersubjectivity.

To summarize this chapter, I propose that the respective last work of Emile Durkheim and of Edmund Husserl discloses a similar spirit in their endeavor. Both Husserl and Durkheim should be seen as striving for a rigorous foundation of knowledge, a foundation far more rigorous than that provided by today's prevailing definition of "positivism." Husserl's phenomenology and Durkheim's sociology are complementary in seeking to restore the fundamental unity of philosophy and science in the original Greek apprehension of *theoria*. If we, the successors of Husserl and Durkheim, have understood their spirit, then our own immediate task becomes clear: to begin anew the dialogue between genuine philosophy and genuine sociology, a dialogue whose intentionality is not idle academic talk but is to restore speech to a deaf-and-dumb civilization suffering a paralysis of *ratio*. Working together, philosophy and sociology can assist Western civilization in renovating its *telos* of rationalism, which Husserl aptly saw as

ratio in the constant movement of self-elucidation.[46]

---

46   *The Crisis*, p. 338.

Chapter 5

Durkheim, Mathiez, and the French Revolution: The Political Context of a Sociological Classic[1]

This chapter has a dual purpose. First, on the eve of the bicentennial of a major watershed of modern history, the French Revolution, we wish to propose that Emile Durkheim may be recognized as truly a "grandson of the Revolution." Second, we will bring out an important albeit neglected aspect of Durkheim's classic *The Elementary Forms of the Religious Life,* a work which has been analyzed and scrutinized by a host of contemporary sociologists, yet none of these apparently has paid attention to a major reference for Durkheim's *magnum opus.* In bringing this to light, we consider materials that go beyond an excursion in the history of sociology to a consideration of the problematics of "reading a classic" as well as those relating sociology to the discipline of history.

I Recent readings of *The Elementary Forms*

Unlike Marx and Weber who have over the years *become* sociologists, or at least who have been increasingly viewed as theorists of modern society by sociologists, Durkheim from the very beginning of his academic career to this day has always been thought of as a primary figure of the discipline. One work of his, however, has had its ups and downs in sociological visibility, namely *The Elementary Forms of the Religious Life* (1965), his last, most ambitious, and longest work. The first of the quaternate of his major studies to be translated into English, in the midst of World War I, for half a century or so it gathered dust on the sociological shelf, albeit Parsons (1937) did devote a chapter to it; he saw it as containing both an epistemological break from Durkheim's earlier positivism as well as an inchoate cyclical theory of social change (1937: 450). Perhaps because of its focus on the structures and functions of the religious life in societies studied by ethnographers, *The Elementary Forms* until the mid-1960s or so was much more a significant work for anthropologists (and after World War II particularly for those associated with E. E. Evans-Pritchard at Oxford) than for sociologists, who avidly read the more "positivistic" monographs: *The Division of Labor, Rules of Sociological Method,* and, of course, that exemplar of theory and research, *Suicide.*

---

1   First published in the *European Journal of Sociology*, 29 (1988): 373-96.

In the past quarter of a century, however, the benign neglect of *The Elementary Forms* has been rectified, and it has become, if anything, the *primus inter pares* of his writings. In itself this constitutes a phenomenon that merits broader attention than can be given to it by the scope of this chapter. At least in passing I would like to suggest that it is in this time period that the sociology of religion has become an important specialty area of its own, spurred on by the writings of Bellah (1970, 1975), Berger (1967, 1969), Robertson (1970), B. Wilson (1973, 1982), Wuthnow (1976), Yinger (1970), and many others. It is also in this time period that the broader societal context of modernity has provided the religious life with a relevance it seemed to lack previously: the complex phenomena of the "counterculture" of the late 1960s and early 1970s (Leventman 1982; Yinger 1982), the new religious movements (Glock and Bellah 1976; Robbins and Anthony 1978; Wilson 1981) and, lastly, the political force of religious institutions in a wide array of settings, from the United States to Iran, Nicaragua, Poland, and the Philippines (Liebman and Wuthnow 1983; Tiryakian 1987; Wald 1987). Both the sociological and the societal contexts, then, have provided greater "relevancy" to Durkheim's last major work.

In fact, the past two decades are witness to a number of important sociological studies and "revisits" of *The Elementary Forms,* beginning with the important place given to it by Lukes (1972) in his own "classic" study of Durkheim. Thus, beyond the magisterial but conventional approach to it *qua* sociology of religion by Pickering (1984), Parsons (1978) reread it as a bold sociological conceptualization of the human condition, Lacroix (1981) as an important *political* study of the foundations of power and authority, and Tiryakian (1981) as an endeavor to establish the foundations of a new "depth sociology."

Complementing the above and other recent analyses that locate Durkheim's sociology of religion in relation to the totality of his *oeuvre* (e.g., Alexander 1982; Fenton 1984; Giddens 1978; Nisbet 1974; Thompson 1982), an equally original if not radical methodological approach to *The Elementary Forms* is found in a series of writings by Jones (1977; 1983; 1986a; 1986b; Jones and Vogt 1984). Following the lead of Quentin Skinner in raising the issue of the problematics in the history of political theory of "understanding a classic," such as Hobbes' *Leviathan,* Jones utilized *The Elementary Forms* as a demonstration of the extent to which "presentism" in sociology obfuscates the real or true meaning of the text in question.

Typically, in Jones' judgment, what is involved in doing the history of sociology is a blurring of the distinction between seeking to explicate the past to establish continuities and cumulativeness with the present, and explicating the past in its fullness for its own sake. This distinction between the "history" and "systematics" of sociological theory was clearly articulated by Merton (1967), for whom much of what passes as "theory" is more "history" than "systematics." In his first article, Jones found Merton wanting in specifying the characteristics of an "authentic history of sociological theory" (1977: 291). Leaving aside "systematics" as the goal of research on a classic, Jones first criticized contemporary interpreters of

The Elementary Forms (presumably the line of criticism can be extended to any other "sociological classic," whether *The Division of Labor, The Protestant Ethic and the Spirit of Capitalism,* or whatever) for trying to "explain" a classic either in terms of how it relates to or is incorporated in or anticipates later theoretical conceptions *or* in terms of antecedent "influences" on the classic in question. Essentially, as Jones argued for *The Elementary Forms,* to understand properly a classic sociological text, one must put aside one's presuppositions and tacit causal framework, *and recover the author's own intentions in the intellectual context and controversies of his time* (1977: 297). The thoughts expressed in the classic will then be recovered as "social actions" of the actor, with the classic essentially a response to actions (texts) of his contemporaries. Although Jones does not put it this way, his methodological proposal is to "recover" a text whose very familiarity to later readers clouds its meaning precisely because it has become embedded with later theories and presuppositions of subsequent interpreters and theorists.

If Jones stops short of asking for a "deconstruction" of *The Elementary Forms,* he proceeds to demonstrate what he later termed "the new history of sociology" (1983) by a careful examination of the intellectual and theological context which may be said to have "influenced" Durkheim's study of religion and society, particularly the writings of Robertson Smith and Frazer. Extending the discussion of the context of *The Elementary Forms,* Jones and Vogt, in introducing Durkheim's participation in a session of the French Society of Philosophy (a sort of "author meets the critic" session having as theme "The religious problem and the dualism of human nature"), comment as follows:

> [...] it is clear that Durkheim's 'problem of religion' will be fully illuminated only for those willing to study the larger context of religious ideas – especially Liberal Protestantism[2] and Roman Catholicism – quite beyond 'Durkheimian sociology' itself (1984: 57).

Jones' endeavor is sound in cautioning us against a premature abstracting of the contents of *The Elementary Forms* from its context and from the intentions of its author. Nevertheless, the "new history of sociology" itself merits caution before it is accepted as the proper hermeneutics of the history of sociology. First, Stephen Turner in his cogent critique of Jones (1983) has pointed out that the intentions of major classical sociological figures, such as Durkheim and Weber, in their social actions (i.e., writing of texts) had broader aims of establishing "disciplined

---

2   As Nielsen has clearly shown recently (1987) the figure of Sabatier, a forceful spokesman for the liberal Protestant perspective in the latter half of nineteenth-century France, was equally part of the controversial context of religion and society for Durkheim and his followers. Linking Sabatier with Spencer, a major *bête noire*, Durkheim in a footnote readily dismissed their 'speculations' about the emergent future of religion being found in the 'privatization' of individual cults (Durkheim 1965: 61).

sociological discourse," or establishing new paradigmatic frames of sociological inquiry. These larger concerns may be lost sight of if we limit the context of inquiry to intellectual controversies with contemporaries. Turner also notes that "contextualism," presumably the opposite of "presentism" or a "Whiggish" interpretation of a theory classic, itself *"requires* many of the interpretive practices which the partisans of contextualism polemically object to" (1983: 287).

In addition, it may be argued that the very designation of a work in sociology as a "classic" is itself problematic in a sociology of knowledge perspective. Although the matter cannot be pursued here, we have alluded above to the phenomenon that *The Elementary Forms* has greatly gained in stature and prominence in the eyes of the sociological profession in recent decades. On the other hand, other works (for example, *The Social System, The Mind and Society, Social and Cultural Dynamics*) – if not other authors – which by an intellectually objective yard-stick are as impressive as other works by the same author or as other works considered "classics" at the time, have become forgotten or considered unessential in the formation of sociologists and for the development of contemporary sociological theory. In brief, "classic" is not a once-for-all qualifier or "ascribed status" but rather a social categorization which is dynamic and which must ultimately pass the acid test of relevance to contemporaries. These include historians of sociology no less than those who seek to develop and further sociological theory around interpretations of both "past" and "present" objects of sociological relevance.

If we accept that 'understanding' a classic entails relating it to the actor's contemporaries and to its context, the question of the actor's intentions in bringing out his work cannot *a priori* be limited to knowledge of the immediate intellectual context of the work. Upon first reading *The Elementary Forms,* the salient context appears to be that of *anthropological* studies of religion, and the "contemporaries" of significance are indeed Robertson Smith, Frazer, Spencer and Gillen, etc. A second intellectual context is readily discernible, namely the *philosophical* one of epistemology, with its "Introduction" and "Conclusion" pointing to the social grounding of the Kantian categories of understanding. This intention of Durkheim has also been noted by various scholars (e.g., Parsons 1937, 1978; Needham 1963; Lukes 1972; Giddens 1978; Tiryakian 1978; Alexander 1982, etc.).

More complex and harder to specify, yet very much part of the background of any seminal social science treatise, is the societal context. *The Elementary Forms* in this vein appeared in a pre-war period of tremendous cultural efflorescence if not outright *revolutions* in the arts and sciences (from the theory of relativity and psychoanalysis to cubism and the atonal scale) and continuing ferment, decadence and innovations in popular culture (Weber 1986). It was also a period of "advanced capitalism" with giant trusts and cartels carving economic empires that matched the global political ones. Politically, the left (republicans and democratic socialists) had emerged triumphant from the outcome of the Dreyfus affair, and the major social victories of the left were educational reforms and the separation of church and state, achieved in successive legislations in 1901, 1904, and 1905 that basically secularized school and society (Ozouf 1982).

Yet, although the "nationalists" who championed the church, the military, and the traditional economic sector had lost political control, the period in which *The Elementary Forms* was written was marked by an upsurge of neo-conservative "patriotism" throughout the political spectrum (Weber 1959), stimulated by growing conflict between Germany and France over North Africa. The newly secularized school and university system gave an important place to patriotism, which the republicans hoped would bring about the reconciliation of generations and the unity of the country (Ozouf 1982: 113). Patriotism was an important theme found in courses and instructions, running from physical exercises and group singing to geography and, above all, the discipline of history which was given a pre-eminent place in the curriculum as "the privileged school of the national sentiment" (Ozouf 1982: 113). Within the broad context, Durkheim had acceded to the highest rung of the academic ladder, a chaired professorship at the Sorbonne. As is well known (Lukes 1972, Clark 1973), Durkheim and his *Année* team were early adherents of the Dreyfus cause and the famous manifesto of Zola, which as Levy has recently noted, signaled the coming of age of the modern French *intelligentsia*. For them,

> The sacred principles of 1789, a vague social republicanism shading into outright collectivism, and an underlying spiritual high-mindedness defined the boundaries of the signatories' worldview. Honest work, anticlericalism, and a secularization of daily life were their principles, usually joined with membership in the Freemasonry (Levy 1987: 159).[3]

We shall return later to the question of how *The Elementary Forms* relates to its societal context, and ultimately what the relevance of this classic is to our own situation. The next section will examine the bearing of the French Revolution on Durkheim's analysis of primitive religion.

---

3   Although we have found no record of Durkheim's membership in Freemasonry, his relation to the lodges was undoubtedly cordial; he was, for example, brought in to the Sorbonne as replacement for Buisson when the latter, one of the many Freemasons in the cabinet of Emile Combes (who was forced to resign in 1905 because of scandals involving the access of the lodges to personal information on army and other government officials), became Minister of Education. Buisson obviously thought highly of Durkheim, and later had Durkheim as contributor and even co-author with him in articles published in Buisson's influential *New Dictionary of Pedagogy and Primary Instruction* (Lukes 1972: 583). On at least two occasions, once at Bordeaux and once in Paris, Durkheim was an appreciated guest speaker in lodges. The theme of solidarity which is so basic in Durkheim's conception of human nature and which corresponds to the collectivism noted by Levy (1987) was the sociological expression of the social doctrine of solidarism expressed by an eminent Freemason and leading political figure, Léon Bourgeois (1902). On Freemasonry and the Third Republic, see Headings (1949) and Faucher and Ricker (1967).

II From Durkheim to Mathiez to Durkheim

In a work which boldly synthesizes a great deal of literature pertaining to anthropological studies and controversies concerning the nature and origins of religion, and which also touches upon a variety of psychological and philosophical issues pertaining to human cognitive development, it is easy to overlook what may seem to be an anomalous reference to the French Revolution. In the concluding Chapter on the origins of totemic beliefs in quasi-divine beings, Durkheim advances his sociologistic argument that society is both the moral authority and the force behind representations that actors make of the sacred. He then brings in the French Revolution by noting the phenomenon of the assembling of the Estates on August 4, 1789, when in the course of the evening there was a voting away of the traditional privileges that had characterized the feudal aspects of the *Ancien Régime* (Durkheim 1965: 240). This "vivifying action of society" can produce acts of "sacrifice and abnegation" which individuals would not do on their own. Durkheim continues with the well-known discussion of "the general effervescence [...] characteristic of revolutionary or creative epochs" that can transform "the most mediocre and inoffensive bourgeois," leading the person to acts of either heroism or barbarism, as took place in the French Revolution (1965: 241f). A few pages later, Durkheim expands on the human environment being differentiated in human consciousness into sacred and profane things, with society having the ability to make ordinary things and agents into those considered sacred by actors. All societies, traditional and modern, have principles of interdiction, of what cannot be touched,[4] without this being considered a sacrilege.

This observation of Durkheim, which follows a reference to the notion of *mana* found in Melanesia and Polynesia (1965: 244), is then succeeded by mention of the French Revolution illustrating the "aptitude of society for setting itself up as a god or for creating gods" in sacralizing such things as "Fatherland, Liberty, Reason," and establishing its own religion that had its own "dogmas, altars, and feasts" (ibid. 244f). If these did not last, adds Durkheim, it is because "patriotic enthusiasm" waned, a point he repeated about the French Revolution in the conclusion of *The Elementary Forms* where he notes that the cycle of holidays that had been established to rejuvenate the revolutionary principles had not lasted once the revolutionary faith itself went by the board (ibid.: 476).

The passages pertaining to the French Revolution are nugatory in terms of the totality of *The Elementary Forms*,[5] albeit accompanied by suggestive remarks

---

4   Interdictions may be thought of as the "negative heuristics" of the cultural code viewed as a vast "scientific research program" (Lakatos 1970).

5   There is one writing of Durkheim that deals expressly with the French Revolution; his extensive review (1971) of Ferneuil's *Les Principes de 1789 et la science sociale*, a book published during the centennial celebration. Durkheim's review is noteworthy in two respects. First, he treats the Principles as articles of revolutionary faith to be analyzed as a social fact; in doing so, he proposes that if they continue to be believed in, one must

Durkheim makes which will be examined in a later section. A major question involved in the understanding of this classic is how fortuitous the reference to the French Revolution is; to deal with this we must consider what other commentators have glossed over, namely the sources used by Durkheim.

In drawing upon the French Revolution to illustrate a dramatic historical instance of society sacralizing itself, crucial for his argument that religious sentiment is produced and reproduced by the assembly of the collectivity, Durkheim cites (1965: 245, n. 15-20) two works of Albert Mathiez, *Les Origines des cultes révolutionnaires (1789-1792)* (1904) and *La Théophilanthropie et la culte décadaire* (1903).[6] They deal with the attempts of the French Revolution to set up new secular religious cults as deliberate substitutes for traditional Catholicism. Since these works were presumably read in their entirety by Durkheim, and since Mathiez and his doctoral committee of distinguished historians (Croiset, Aulard, Denis, Seignobos, Michel, Rambaud) were university contemporaries of Durkheim, it is important to consider these works at some length. In doing so, it will be indicated that Durkheim influenced Mathiez *no less than Mathiez may have influenced Durkheim.* Moreover, the civil religion formulated by the founders of *Theophilanthropy,* the central focus of Mathiez' major thesis, is one that bears a striking affinity with Durkheim's own conceptions of the morality and religion necessary for modern society (Bellah 1973).

---

seek to understand the underlying change that has occurred in modern Western society in order to establish the destiny of "revolutionary religion" (1971; 43). Second, his tacit sociology of knowledge perspective in dealing objectively with the tenets of the French Revolution laid the groundwork for his later studies of ideology, such as socialism (1958) and the German mentality (1915). As will be discussed shortly, the Principles were the core belief systems of "the revolutionary religion" but the latter also contained important organizational structures and rituals. Since Rousseau was perhaps the most important philosophical influence on the framers of the Principles, Durkheim's exegesis and balanced critique of *The Social Contract,* and the attention he gives to Rousseau's stress on civil religion in his study (1960), may be included in works of his pertaining to the French Revolution. Obviously, his output on the topic is meager, and this is echoed by the relative dearth of works in political sociology reviewed in the *Année Sociologique.* Yet our present reading of Durkheim is in agreement with Lacroix's thesis that "even when Durkheim does not deal with specific political institutions [...] he is always concerned with the political aspect" (Lacroix 1981: 304).

6   These represented the "minor" and "major" theses presented by Mathiez as requisites for a university career. Mathiez (1874-1932) quickly established himself as a leading historian, indeed the first specialist, of the French Revolution (see Friguglietti 1974). However, Mathiez' political orientation was much further to the left than his teacher Aulard, symbolized in Mathiez espousing Robespierre as the real hero of the French Revolution rather than Danton (championed by Aulard and the republican regime), whom Mathiez associated with the corruption of the parliamentary system, and thereby a symbol of a decadent bourgeois social order (Gérard 1970; 78). As a consequence, Aulard kept out Mathiez from the ranks of the Sorbonne faculty.

In dealing with the early revolutionary cults of Reason and the Supreme Being, Mathiez acknowledged the debt to his teacher Aulard for having pointed out that patriotism was at the heart of revolutionary religion. More important for our purpose, Mathiez in his introduction credits Durkheim's 1899 essay "On the definition of religious phenomena" (1975) for the conceptualization necessary to treat the religion of the Revolution as a real one. A key point of Durkheim cited by Mathiez (Mathiez 1904: 11) is that the notion of God or the divinity is not a necessary feature of religion. What characterizes religious phenomena – beliefs and cult practices alike – is their obligatory nature because they are held in common; thus, Mathiez cites Durkheim further, "the homeland (la patrie), the French Revolution [...] are for us sacred" (Mathiez 1904: 11; Durkheim, 1975: 20).

Mathiez then says that he added to Durkheim's definition some of his own characteristics of religion: (a) in its formative period, a religious phenomenon is attended by "a general heightening of feelings" (une surexcitation générale de la sensibilité), (b) new religious beliefs become concretized in material objects which for the believers are both emblems as rallying signs and efficacious talismans, while the material symbols of other cults are destroyed in rage, (c) those who do not share the new faith nor the cult's symbols are placed outside the pale of the community (1904: 12).

It is important to note that what Mathiez added to Durkheim's definition would become incorporated in *The Elementary Forms* not only in the discussion of "patriotic enthusiasm" and other references to the French Revolution taken from Mathiez (1965: 245) but elsewhere in the pregnant passages of Book II, chapter 7, where Durkheim, in reference to totemic religion, talks about "enthusiasm," "effervescence", and "violent heightening (violente surexcitation) of physical and mental life" as well as "emblematic symbols" that are "useful as a rallying-centre" for the collectivity (ibid. 1912: 245-265). Likewise, Mathiez's statement (prophetic in the light of later events of the century) that the revolutionary religion is not as burned out as contemporaries think and that "revolutionary cults could well reappear one day in new guises" (ibid. 14) finds a striking echo in the second section of the concluding Chapter of *The Elementary Forms*. There, in a passage that also bears affinity with Weber's conclusion in *The Protestant Ethic* about the "great rebirth of old ideas and ideals" (Weber, 1958: 182), Durkheim exclaims:

> A day will come when our societies will know again those hours of creative effervescence, in the course of which new ideas arise [...] We have already seen how the French Revolution established a whole cycle of holidays to keep the principles with which it was inspired in a state of perpetual youth [...] But, though the work miscarried, it enables us to imagine what might have happened in other conditions (Durkheim 1965: 475f).

To conclude this section, if it was a bold gesture for a young historian to make use of a sociological conceptualization, so conversely was it bold for Durkheim to bring in the French Revolution's religious side in discussing predominantly staid ethnographic materials of Australian totemic religion. Were we to stop at this point, however, we would have little else than an interesting footnote on the construction of a sociological classic, one where a young scholar in one discipline borrows conceptual tools from an established figure in another discipline, who some years later utilizes the younger scholar's materials to fashion an enduring masterpiece.

Yet, Durkheim's conclusion points to something besides his having completed a comparative study of the fundamental forms of religious life (as an ingress to the fundamental forms of social organization) and even besides his radical sociological epistemology. It points to his broader interest in social regeneration and the potentiality and potency of a secular religion to bring this about.[7] To link this with the initial claim of this essay that Durkheim be recognized as a "grandson of the French Revolution," an important complement to his spiritual heritage as a "son of a rabbi" (Filloux 1976), there is need to examine aspects of the religious culture of the French Revolution. This will be undertaken in the following section by drawing upon materials found in Mathiez as well as later studies.

III Revolutionary religion and festivals

Among other features of the French Revolution that gives it such sociological salience in the comparative study of societal transformations is the conscious endeavor of its leaders to transform overnight the cultural basis of society. This undertaking had a wide variety of manifestations: changing titles of address that had reflected hierarchical differentiation to the egalitarian *citoyen*; restructuring the administration of "natural" regions into departments; emancipating minorities such as women and Jews from traditional ascriptive ties; even doing away with the Gregorian calendar in favor of one that started its year I on September 22, 1792, gave seasonal names for each month so as to indicate a renewed linkage of society with nature, and had a ten-day week with the tenth day (*décadi*) replacing Sunday as the day of rest.[8] Our focus here is on one feature of the vast cultural

---

7   The immediate global setting might have well served Durkheim as a comparative laboratory since the same year as *The Elementary Forms* was published; revolutions broke out in China and Mexico, and the year he died was of course marked by the one Russia. In spite of the profusions of revolutions in this century, the comparative study of revolutionary religion has received little attention from social scientists, one exception being the important historical study of Billington (1980).

8   Zerubavel (1982) has drawn attention to social functions of replacing calendars in the formation of group boundaries and identity. For a greater discussion of the French republican calendar, see Aulard and Zerubavel (1977). The republican calendar, which

overhauling; revolutionary religion and its festivals as means of a "transfer of sacrality" (Ozouf 1976) involving attempts to set up a new secular religion that would legitimate and renew commitment to the new social order, and thereby neutralize the emotive underpinnings of the old order.

This topic, which has had renewed interest in recent years (Ozouf 1976, 1984, 1985; Ehrard and Viallaneix 1977; Hunt 1984), was opened by the historical studies of Mathiez and his teacher Aulard. Its interest to Durkheim was likely more than the passing scholarly reference to the French Revolution given in *The Elementary Forms*: it was, ultimately, in some significant political and cultural factors that France in the first decade of the twentieth century had in common with France in the last decade of the eighteenth. Basically, the situation was similar regarding the problem of institutionalizing and revitalizing a civil religion in a modern secular state. Grappling with the problem of the relations between religion and polity, including the kind and limits of secularization optimal for the state, was an acute problem for Durkheim and his contemporaries no less than for the French revolutionaries. Since it is also a growing source of conflict in our societies (school prayer, Christmas crèches, etc.), the historical materials on revolutionary religion and festivals are pertinent for a broad sociological perspective on modernity.

Borrowing Durkheim's definition of religious phenomena, Mathiez saw an underlying unity to succeeding aspects of French revolutionary religion.[9] In the work dealing with the origins and early phase of revolutionary cults (to the end of 1792), Mathiez discussed the inception and structure of the civil religion. Its ideology owed much to Rousseau's notion in his *Social Contract* of civil religion replacing Catholicism in a future society: the law promulgated by the modern state as an expression of the general will must rest on civil religion to be knowingly and freely accepted by the people (Mathiez 1904: 59). A part of the revolutionary credo was that the human condition may be indefinitely improved by changing the social body, which is instrumental to human happiness; the state cannot be indifferent to religion for it is "constituted by philosophers as the supreme guardian of religion" and has "a moral mission to accomplish" (ibid. 54).

Mathiez then examined the early manifestations of the charisma of the revolutionary setting that later scholars have noted in examining a host of millenarian and "revitalization" movements in diverse settings (e.g., Adas

---

lasted until 1805, was designed to provide the temporal framework of a new national identity and thereby to complete the transfer of authority from church and monarchy to the secular state. The ten-day week did not survive the Revolution but the metric system, also part of the cultural ideology, did.

9   Although different revolutionary cults had different clienteles with different class participation and different degrees of secular orientation (from the outright atheism of the Worship of Reason to the more modulated deism of the Cult of the Supreme Being), still there is ground to speak of the civil religion of the French Revolution, however differentiated it became. Ozouf (1976: 35-37) traces different interpretations on the unity of revolutionary festivals and essentially follows Mathiez.

1987; Cohn 1961; Hill 1972; Knox 1961). At the start of 1789 the convocation of the Estates General took place as the populace awaited "a miracle" with the deputies seen as "artisans of this miracle" charged with the "mission of operating a regeneration of the human species in its entirety" (Mathiez 1904: 20). A new revolutionary symbolism developed spontaneously which freely borrowed from various traditions (classical antiquity, Freemasonry, popular Christianity) cultural symbols and artifacts of collective identity including the Phrygian cap and its *cocarde,* trees of Liberty (from the American Revolution), patriotic altars, and the Tables of Human Rights and of the Constitution (the 'Principles' as the new Mosaic tables). The revolutionary religion, then, was the cultural arm of the French Revolution. In seeking to create new institutions and a new sense of collective identity based on popular sovereignty, the revolutionary leaders gave heed to the actual mobilization of the population to provide regime support and commitment. Hence, a major feature of revolutionary or civil religion was the significance of ritualized public gatherings of various sorts, ranging from solemn ceremonies of oath-taking around a Liberty tree (Hunt 1984: 27) to joyous celebrations of events and symbols of the Revolution as harbinger of a new social order, and also including gatherings around "the holy guillotine" to witness the destruction of enemies of the Revolution. The materials that Mathiez and contemporary scholars such as Hunt and Ozouf have brought to light testify to the acumen and sophistication of the revolutionary leaders in their awareness of techniques and functions of cultural manipulation. This is clearly shown in the emphasis given to national festivals. These began early with the festival of the Federation on July 14, 1790, followed a year later with the carrying of the ashes of Voltaire to the Panthéon in an elaborate pageantry designed by the artist David to imitate the funerary celebration of heroes in Greece and Rome.[10] Other festivals followed such as the Festival of Liberty and Reason, held at Notre-Dame-de-Paris that was renamed "the Temple of Reason," and the Robespierre-inspired Festival of the Supreme Being held at the Tuileries in 1794, the year that saw the peak popular participation of national festivals (Soboul 1977: 5).

The social philosophy, if not ideology, of the national festivals received elaborate attention very early. As Mathiez noted, the new civil constitution would be completed by civic ceremonies which would in effect be a "school of patriotism" and hold in abeyance the more virulent atheism of the ultra-Left (1904: 77). Thus, Mirabeau, the eloquent orator of the National Assembly, saw national festivals as

---

10   This ritualized burial was meant as an alternative to the traditional Catholic burial which reinforced the authority of the clergy in the eyes of the masses. Nearly a century later, in 1885, the all-night transfer to the Panthéon of the ashes of Victor Hugo, a collective representation of nineteenth-century Republican ideals, was an immense similar popular gathering. The televised funeral procession and burial of President Kennedy in 1963 was used effectively in reaffirming collective identity and public renewal of commitment to liberal ideals in a moment of political crisis. These are instances in modern society of what Durkheim termed *piacular* rituals (1965: 434ff).

having an integrative function that would dissolve social divisions and distrust between citizens, and renew their ties in common as they had in antiquity; he proposed four yearly civic festivals at the time of equinoxes and solstices, four military festivals, and finally July 14th as the celebration of Federation.[11] Mirabeau was one of several revolutionary figures who gave important attention to festivals and civic celebrations.

In the first year of the Republic (1792), Lanthenas proposed a series of civic conferences that would reach the masses, evolve into religious ceremonies, and form a "universal church" instrumental for the regeneration of society (Mathiez 1904: 105f). Also that year Condorcet presented a report to the Assembly calling for civic celebrations and public conferences that would teach civic virtues and keep the masses away from "witches and miracle-tellers," an obvious reference to the clergy (ibid. 130). In June 1792 the deputy Gohier called for civic ceremonials involving all major events of the life cycle done before an altar of the Homeland in every commune. He suggested these public spectacles would touch the sentiments of those gathered and this would provide occasions to "imprint them, if we may speak thusly, with a civic tinge" (ibid. i33f).

One other ideologue of national festivals discussed by Mathiez of interest here is Poyet, an architect of Paris, who prepared in 1792 a *Plan for a national circus and annual festivals*. He argued that public festivals foster a feeling of general well-being and love for public prosperity. Moreover, in words that bear a striking resemblance to Durkheim's description of the rise of religious sentiment in the gatherings of Australian aborigines (1965: 246f), Poyet wrote about these festivals: "In the midst of large assemblies, citizens unite, evaluate each other, know one another, a common benevolence rouses them, the imagination is exalted, courage waxes [...]" (Mathiez 1904: 132).

Mathiez concluded his study of the origins of the religion of the French Revolution by noting that beneath its diverse manifestations, it was a religion of patriotism that was being fashioned. The various plans of public conferences and festivals were treated as important means of mobilization of the population around the project for a civic-religious institution that would function to defend and provide commitment to the new polity. Mathiez saw these collective gatherings as so many "religious assemblies" where the crowds came to "commune with the Homeland," in effect, a secularization of the Eucharist.

The relation of state and religion in the French Revolution was complex and ambiguous. Early on, the overthrowing of the old order led logically to

---

11 Of Mirabeau's proposal, July 14th is the one that is still celebrated in France as a national holiday. But it is interesting to note, following Ozouf, that it was only in 1880 that it became the national holiday after the republicans won the majority in the elections of 1879 and needed a symbol for the new thrust of the Third Republic. As Ozouf makes clear (1984: 128-133) there was a bitter division as to which possible date would be the most appropriate, and even the date of July 14 is ambiguous as to whether it refers to the violence of 1789 or to the more joyous and conciliatory Federation Festival of 1790.

casting aside its bases of legitimation; this involved the gradual separation of church and state. But to disestablish the Roman Catholic Church as *the* sacralizing agency of temporal authority and further to abolish Catholic rituals from everyday life, as took place in the mid-1790s at the peak of revolutionary agitation, raised new problems. As various members of the revolutionary intelligentsia surmised, doing away with the old religion created a void, a loss of communal meaning of the world. The consequences of the absence of public rituals might well lead to personal anomie, to public immorality, or equally bad from their perspective, to a new Catholicism rising from its ashes (Ozouf 1976: 322f). Separation of church and state meant at first the *neutrality* of the state toward all religions, that is, an acceptance of *pluralism.* However, partly because of the fear that in a state of neutrality the Catholic church might regroup its strength in villages and the countryside, partly because the very model of the virtuous republic led the republicans back to the classical state of Greece and Rome with one civil religion, the question of what religion was appropriate to the modern state far from being closed took on new urgency. This urgency was compounded by the political instability at the helm as one leader after another fell from grace. *This situation paralleled strikingly the situation of the Third Republic, including the abrupt falls of governments that Durkheim was close to ideologically – those of Ferry, Waldeck-Rousseau, and Combes, in particular.*

It is pertinent to examine the other work of Mathiez, which gave major attention to a new secular religion that for a brief while seemed to be *the* appropriate civil religion of republican France. In that work Durkheim may have found if not the inspiration at least a confirmation of the implicit political project of the scientific (sociological) articulation of a civil religion, the inspiration for which went back to Rousseau. This project of the revolutionary religion, which in the 1790s was dramatically articulated in the new religion of Theophilanthropy, may be thought of as transmitted to the first sociological "sons" of the Revolution: Saint-Simon and Comte (in their writings on the new Christianity and on the religion of humanity), and later to the "grandson" in *The Elementary Forms.*

IV Theophilanthropy

In *La Théophilanthropie et le culte décadaire, 1796-1801*, also cited in *The Elementary Forms,* Mathiez examined the revolutionary cults which appeared in the second, post-Robespierre phase of the Revolution. The early expectations of the regeneration of society with new laws and new institutions had begun to fade and the public stopped believing in "the virtue of its representatives" (Mathiez 1903: 36f). The Revolution , begun as a great revitalization movement, was itself in need of revitalization. It was in this "liminal period" (Turner 1969), when, so to speak, the routinization of the revolutionary charisma was at stake, that a new syncretic religious movement emerged which eventually took the name of Theophilanthropy.

To reiterate, if the revolutionaries gave a great deal of attention to religion and morality as basic to a social order, for them the problem was how to wean the masses away and keep them away from Catholicism. This entailed how to develop a revolutionary religion whose tenets and practices would provide necessary support for new republican institutions. Mathiez examined the various attempts of the mid-1790s to articulate and organize new religious cults that would revive patriotism. For instance, as proposed in 1796 by Benoist-Lamothe in the city of Sens (which was to become a stronghold of theophilanthropy and where by coincidence Durkheim was to begin his teaching career), the "social cult" would defend the revolutionary society from Catholicism, preach solidarity, and introduce greater equality in the distribution of wealth. As Comte would later espouse in his universal calendar to replace the Catholic calendar venerating saints, Benoist-Lamothe saw the cult as paying homage to the great benefactors of humanity: Brutus, Socrates, Jesus, Rousseau, etc. (1903: 57-64).

In the same year the Freemason Chemin-Dupontes brought out a handbook for the organization of a "rational and civic cult" that was first entitled *Handbook of Theoanthropophiles (Manuel des théoanthropophiles)* and which later was changed to *Théophilanthropie*. The handbook had two parts, the first dealing with doctrines, dogmas and morality; the second with the organization of the cult and with its rituals of worship. As Mathiez notes, the dogmas and the ethical precepts stressed as their essential justification the social utility of the new religion, that is, the interest of society above all (1903: 93f).

The cult might have remained obscure except for the activities of an intellectual politician, La Revellière-Lépeaux, who delivered a major speech (later printed) on the 12th of Floréal, year V, entitled "Reflections on the cult, on civil ceremonies, and on national festivals" *(Réflexions sur le culte, sur les cérémonies civiles et sur les fêtes nationales)*. He followed this up with an essay the following year on how to organize mass participation at national festivals. These remarkable documents received a good deal of attention by his contemporaries as well as by Mathiez (1903) and more recent historians of the cultural aspect of the French Revolution (Grange 1977; Ozouf 1976: 322ff). Some discussion of their contents are in order since they are interesting formulations of the nature of civil religion in modern society and also since their orientation resembles so much everything known about Durkheim's own outlook.

La Revellière-Lépeaux strongly urged on fellow members of the Directory of the Convention (the ruling body of the Revolution after the reaction of Thermidor) the need for a major renewal of national festivals. The republican ideal of the regeneration of the French people and humanity in general required a recasting of both religious and political institutions; this called for a new moral unity of the French people, a unity that might be brought about by national festivals, civil ceremonies, and a "rational" religious cult without the dogmas and hierarchy of Catholicism (Mathiez 1903: 144-47).

The French Revolution in its basic ideology rejected all transcendental authority, that is, authority which was not "in nature." But the secular morality of the Enlightenment, the hedonistic doctrine of utilitarianism, could not be effective, argued La Revellière-Lépeaux, for it lacked popular appeal. A completely secularized state would have the problem of the basis of civic morals, of the voluntary acceptance of state authority and devotion to patriotism which are key aspects of regime support (Grange 1977: 496). La Revellière-Lépeaux advocated the adoption of a civil religion which would have just two basic dogmas (the immortality of the soul, and the existence of God) and though it would not be the established religion, it would be favored by the government (Mathiez 1903: 149). For it to have mass appeal, the austerity of its teachings and of its temples stripped of all the holy images of a Catholic church (Ozouf 1976: 326) needed to be complemented by elaborate outdoor festivals and ceremonies that would play on the senses of spectators, especially those of sight and hearing. The secular ideals of liberty, equality, patriotism (essentially, the sacred elements of the new social order) needed to be felt in collective gatherings, hence the astute attention that La Revellière-Lépeaux gave to the latter in his handbook on national festivals. Religious rituals, properly organized, would be conducive to generating powerful emotions, as he stated in terms that might have been written by Durkheim: "The gathering together of a large number of persons moved by the same feelings, all expressing themselves at the same time and in the same way, has an irresistible power on the minds" (Grange 1977: 497).

Festivals, as rituals of the civil religion, could be organized so as to induce "emotions of an extraordinary intensity." The number of participants, the space where the festivals were held (Ozouf 1976, Chapter 6), and the lengthy duration of the spectacle were carefully intended to generate mass emotions. Ingeniously, La Revellière-Lépeaux planned to divide the huge audiences (well over a hundred thousand) into sections, each having a leader and each with a chorus and an orchestra that coordinated the section with what was happening at the main altar. All voices would unite at the beginning and at the end, singing the same hymns (Grange 1977: 498-501).

The proposals of La Revellière-Lépeaux got increased attention, albeit after much discussion the revolutionary legislature turned down a proposal to establish it as the civil religion of France (Mathiez 1903: 165). Lasting five years, longer than other revolutionary cults, it was particularly favored by "enlightened bourgeois" and intellectuals, especially among Freemasons and liberal Protestants (*ibid.* 708). As Ozouf more recently noted, the appeal to these groups was that the revolutionary festivals sought to bring about the unity of religion and science, with the temple of worship being the conjunction of "astronomy and civil religion" (Ozouf 1976: 335).

After his extensive discussion of the emergence, spread and even internal dissension within theophilanthropy, Mathiez provided an evaluation of this revolutionary cult. Its leaders were committed to the democratic ideals of a people rationally governing themselves. This called for a new religious cult which would be at the basis of the moral unity of France (Mathiez 1903: 705). To complete the revolution, minds must be cast in a new mold, and for that, the public must be instructed in civic morality; ultimately, as Siauve had stated it, theophilanthropic assemblies were really schooling for civic morality (ibid. 292f).

Mathiez saw this emphasis upon morality and public education as a legacy of theophilanthropy. Republican education during the French. Revolution was undertaken by the revolutionary cults and their organization of national festivals; in our day, he noted, this is done by secular instruction, adult education, public conferences, and the like (ibid. 707). The major difference, he added, was that the revolutionaries freely borrowed elements from different traditions, from Catholicism as well as Rousseau and Freemasonry, and unlike the present setting, they were not repelled by religious forms for they felt that no society was possible without religion (ibid.).

V Conclusions

The central argument of this essay has been that a comprehensive understanding of a sociological classic requires grounding the text not only in the immediate intellectual debates of the day but in the broader societal and cultural context in which it was fashioned. The latter requires as much a "thick description" as the manifest intellectual context. I have sought to illustrate this with the case of *The Elementary Forms of the Religious Life,* an understanding of which may be enhanced by viewing this sociological classic as a continuation of the conscious attempts in the French Revolution to formulate and enact a civil religion. This underscores Prager's recent assertion that "Durkheim's writings [...] are preeminently political" (1986: 3). The themes of the regeneration of society, of the importance of civic morals, of instructing the public in putting the good of society ahead of individual interest are ones that link Durkheim to the French Revolution. In fact, one might almost think of him as a sort of latter-day "theophilanthropist," particularly since he came from the eastern France where the cult of theophilanthropy had its greatest number of adherents, including in Epinal, Durkheim's home town (Mathiez 1903: 307, 347).

The question of the appropriate religion and civic morality necessary for the revitalization of the republic was as acute to the Third Republic as to the First, as discussed earlier. These were major problems for Durkheim as they had been for his spiritual Jacobin ancestors. At stake was the question of the unity of France, how long it could remain "one and indivisible." The festivals of civil religion, secular rituals of coming together, were viewed as important means of unification, and the revolutionaries gave a great deal of care and serious study of comparative aspects of the religious life to devise effective festivals. Ozouf, in examining the writings of La Revellière-Lépeaux, Benoist-Lamothe, and others, is struck by their research on festivals and rituals of primitive tribes as well as religious life in antiquity being a "rudimentary anthropology" (Ozouf 1976; 336). Their concern, she suggests, was to abstract out what is fundamental to religion,, in the hope of getting to the original cult: "What the men of the Revolution sought is really the identity of the essence of religions as evidence for the identity of mankind" (ibid.).

That concern and that intention can be viewed as framing the investigation of Durkheim into the fundamentals of the religious life. Furthermore, the concern of the revolutionaries for national unity and their belief in the essential oneness of humanity were also a patrimony of the Principles of 1789 evidenced in Durkheim's sociology: the absence of attention to class conflict and class divisions is not based on conservative values as much as on the liberal endeavor of the French Revolution to rebuild one, homogeneous nation. The French Revolution was not completed in its lifetime and the Third Republic, especially after 1880 when the republican left took over, sought to continue the work of societal transformation. Secularization or the "transfer of sacrality" to civil institutions was a basic endeavor, and the crucial institution of the Third Republic was that of education. Meyer (1977) has discussed its crucial *legitimating effects* at the societal level, such as nation-building and citizenship, in validating both elites and citizens. In France this was clearly felt as the liberal left, of which Durkheim and his associates were an important part, saw the school as the battleground where the continuing struggle of the Revolution to dechristianize France was carried out.

The men of the Third Republic saw that the First Republic had not completed its task because the educational understructure was undeveloped in the 1790s. Consequently, they gave priority to educational reform and expansion, particularly under the vigorous leadership of Jules Ferry as Minister of Public Schooling in the 1880s. The year he was forced to resign as Prime Minister because of military setbacks in colonizing Indochina (a fate that bears a parallel with Lyndon Johnson in 1968), the cornerstone of the "new" Sorbonne was laid. The institution that would be the bastion of the intelligentsia of the Third Republic, including Durkheim, was inaugurated on August 1889, at the centennial celebration of the French Revolution with the rector of the university proclaiming: "The principles of 1789 have become the charter of civilized nations" (Gérard 1970).

To understand the broader context of Durkheim's seminal study of "primitive" religion, one has to see the socio-political context, which includes both the legacy of 1789 (the secular principles of the Rights of Man and the unfinished revolution) as well as the situation of France during the Third Republic. Indeed, the attention that Durkheim gives to the French Revolution in *The Elementary Forms* is itself part of the recurrent significance of the French Revolution to the Third Republic.

Gérard has noted how the French Revolution kept its actuality and virtue for the liberal republican regime of the Third Republic, threatened domestically by the right or on its frontiers by military tyrannies or totalitarian states (1970: 65). The Republican Left during the 1880s saw the coming centennial of the French Revolution as an occasion to regroup its factions by having the "shining spirit of the French Revolution" penetrate every small town (Gérard 1970: 67). They also penetrated higher education, since in 1885 Aulard was appointed to the newly created chair of the History of the French Revolution at the Sorbonne, giving the Revolution an important academic dignity, while placing its interpretation in trusted liberal republican hands.

Hobsbawm in his insightful discussion of the "invention of tradition" has discussed how the tradition of 1789 played a vital role for the Third Republic in fending off "both socialism and the right" (1983: 270). The Third Republic did not begin the invention of the revolutionary tradition of 1789 – that can be traced back to at least Michelet with his nationalist and populist depiction of the spontaneity of the glorious uprising of 1789. Even before Michelet, the "invention of tradition" took place in early nineteenth-century histories and conspirational accounts of the Revolution, and before those it might be said that the endeavors to revive the revolutionary faith by leaders of the cults and rituals studied by Mathiez were themselves – only five or six years after 1789 – the beginnings of the "invention of the revolutionary tradition."

For the Third Republic, then, the French Revolution carried an immensely powerful mystique, a "demiurgic Grand Temps" (Rearick 1977: 449) of glorious acts and heroic giants. It could be celebrated either in official circles and state-sanctioned ceremonies, as the centennial festival of 1889, or by critics to the left of the regime as a condemnation of a decadent social order. The latter is illustrated by the popular theater addressed to a working class audience, in particular that of Romain Rolland:

> Rolland designed *Le 14 Juillet* to be so unequivocally pro-Revolution that it passes on the burdens and joys of the great Revolution to the audience of 1902, who, inspired by the spectacle of collective emancipation, are to complete the work interrupted in 1794 (Fisher 1977: 471).

Did Durkheim see Rolland's *Le 14 Juillet* or Rolland's *Danton* that were performed about ten years before *The Elementary Forms*? That is a moot question but we may think of Durkheim and his *Année Sociologique* entourage as "supporters of the popular theatre movement [...] fired by an idealistic attempt to harmonize the collective vitalism of the masses and the rationalism of the Enlightenment" (Fisher, 1977: 490). Rolland's *Le 14 Juillet* ending with "'a spontaneous People's Festival; violence gives way to bacchanalian song, dance and procession" (Fisher: 473) is not far removed from the corrobori of the Australian primitives discussed by Durkheim.

The theme of ritual gatherings, of the *fête,* celebrating and restoring the unity of society, is a powerful theme for the Third Republic, for Durkheim no less than for Rolland no less than for all republicans (Rearick 1977); in this they were true to the "tradition" of the First Republic. The occasions were not always joyful, since Rearick has mentioned that *fêtes funèbres* were also important ritual occasions for the nation to come together – witness the spectacular funeral in 1885 of Victor Hugo, "a giant of thought and democratic faith" (Rearick 1977: 447). Rereading *The Elementary Forms* in the light of this broader context of the Third Republic and its attachment to the French Revolution, one gets an added dimension in sizing up Durkheim's seminal study of "primitive" religion. For the major structures of religion he analyzes – beliefs and rituals, the latter differentiated into "positive rites" (joyful feasts) and "piacular rites" (sad celebrations) – echo and parallel the major structures of republican civil religion: the Rights of Man (beliefs) and its rituals, including imposing state funerals (piacular rites).

Luke has recently (1987) drawn attention to the overlooked question of the revitalization of civil religions which are themselves subject to secularization. His discussion is based on contemporary Marxist-Leninist regimes, but the problem is surely pertinent to France in the 1790s and early 1900s. La Revellière-Lépeaux's theophilanthropy in the later years of the First Republic and Durkheim's analysis of religion and society in the mature years of the Third Republic have a common concern in laying the foundation for a viable republican civil religion which would both provide national solidarity and prevent backsliding to the Catholic Church. Both La Revellière-Lépeaux and Durkheim addressed themselves to what Hoffmann sees as one of the great dramas of French history, namely, how does one establish (or regenerate) the French nation? How does one create the modern citizen out of the diversity of the past (Hoffmann 1987: 152)? The religious assembly in *The Elementary Forms* is a unification of individuals and at the same time a revival of the collectivity.[12]

Such a reading of *The Elementary Forms* as sketched out in this essay offers us other materials for reflection. The first bears on the relation of sociology to history. Many years ago Bellah (1959) alerted us to the historical dimension of Durkheim's writings. In recent years, we have had increasing contacts between historians and sociologists, more methodological reflections about the interchange between the two, more forays into the historical realm by sociologists and more forays into social science conceptualizations by historians wishing to break from traditional molds of historiography (Furet 1982; Lefebvre 1971; Le Goff and Nara 1985; Skocpol 1984; Tilly 1981).

Welcome as this effort of interdisciplinary exchange is in comparison to narrow compartimentalization, the discussions still manifest a certain tension and distrust of the limits of explanation that one discipline can offer the other. In this respect they echo the debates between sociologists and historians at the turn of the century, for example, as Lefebvre notes (1971: 301) between the eminent historian Seignobos and the rising Durkheimian star, Simiand (1985).

More telling, in this context, is the rather cool evaluation of Mathiez's dissertation given to it by Marcel Mauss (Durkheim's nephew and leading associate) in the next issue of the *Année sociologique*. Mauss agreed with Mathiez that the revolutionary festivals as social gatherings had generated symbols and a certain mystique, with some symbols becoming sacred. However, he commented,

---

12 The problem of unification and regeneration of the republican ideals and virtues also applied to the American situation. See the materials provided by Perry Miller concerning religious revivals which became seen in the 1830s as a great hope "that the civil institutions of our country will be perpetuated" (1965: 69).

they were transitory, created and organized by ideologues, and therefore they were "religious phenomena without being religions" (Mauss 1905: 297). Furthermore, Mauss found that, although the historian had dug up a mass of interesting facts about the religious cults, he did not provide an explanation of why revolutionary phenomena took on a religious aspect, nor did Mathiez inform in what sense theophilanthropy, as a religion of the State and of Reason, was something novel, when its ideas were those of the *philosophes* and its rituals those of Catholicism and Freemasonry (*ibid.*). In brief, this study was not even half-way sociological (*ibid.*). That review cooled off Mathiez from further interchanges with sociology and the year after the publication of *The Elementary Forms* he published a caustic critique of a study by an associate of Durkheim (Hubert Bourgin) on the meat industry during the French Revolution in which Mathiez remarked: "History is for him only the humble servant of sociology according to Saint Durkheim" (Friguglietti 1974: 6of, n. 61).

In a sense we might wind up by saying that the interchange between sociology and history and the task of an appropriate civil religion, both of which figure in the Durkheim-Mathiez materials we have examined, are of contemporary concern as important "unfinished business," one of academic relevance, but the other, pertaining to the question of civil religion and morality in modern society, of greater societal relevance. The French Revolutionaries who, like the theophilanthropists, spent so much time on planning and organizing national festivals as means of building up national solidarity and patriotism would no doubt have felt at home in New York in July 1986 at the festival of the Statue of Liberty, the gift of the Third Republic (and its eminent Freemason sculptor, Bartholdi) to the American people. It was a spectacular national festival of American civil religion, just as earlier the 1984 Olympic games took on the aura of an American national pageant.

One should also retain that republican contemporaries, no less than their spiritual ancestors of the First Republic, felt some urgency in finding (even if finding might include "inventing") an appropriate civil religion and a civic morality to restore societal unity and renovate abiding commitment to democratic institutions. After the severe erosion of confidence in America in the morality of "insiders" in the public and the financial sectors, stemming from Watergate, Irangate, and the economic scandals of Wall Street, the ultimate sociological concern of Durkheim as suggested in this essay is one that should be seen as of contemporary relevance. A sober lesson to be gleaned from the societal contexts of France and the United States is that costly staged festivals and other rituals of civil religion are by themselves no guarantors that civic morality will be maintained or renovated as "habits of the heart."

References

Adas, Michael 1987, *Prophets of Rebellion: Millenarian Protest Movements Against the European Colonial Order*. Cambridge and New York: Cambridge University Press.

Alexander, Jeffrey 1982, *Theoretical Logic in Sociology*, vol. II: *The Antimonies of Classical Thought: Marx and Durkheim*. Berkeley and Los Angeles: University of California Press.

Aulard, Alphonse 1927, *Christianity and the French Revolution*. London: Ernest Benn Ltd.

Bellah, Robert N. 1959, "Durkheim and History." *American Sociological Review* XXIV (August): 447-465.

—.1970, *Beyond Belief: Essays on Religion in a Post-Traditional World*. New York: Harper and Row.

—.1973, "Introduction." pp. ix-lv in Emile Durkheim, *On Morality and Society*. Chicago: University of Chicago Press.

—.1975, *The Broken Covenant: American Civil Religion in Time of Trial*. New York: Seabury Press.

Berger, Peter 1967, *The Sacred Canopy: Elements of a Sociological Theory of Religion*. Garden City, N. Y.: Doubleday.

—.1969, *Rumor of Angels: Modern Society and the Rediscovery of the Supernatural*. Garden City, N. Y.: Doubleday.

Billington, James H. 1980, *Fire in the Minds of Men, Origins of the Revolutionary Faith*. New York: Basic Books.

Bourgeois, Léon 1902, *Solidarité 3*. Paris: Colin.

Clark, Terry N. 1973, *Prophets and Patrons: The French University and the Emergence of the Social Sciences*. Cambridge, MA: Harvard University Press.

Cohn, Norman 1961, *The Pursuit of the Millennium: Revolutionary Messianism in Medieval and Reformation Europe*. New York: Harper.

Durkheim, Emile 1915, *"Germany Above All": German Mentality and the War*. Paris Colin. Also published in French that year.

—.1958, *Socialism and Saint-Simon*. Yellow Springs, Ohio: Antioch Press. First published posthumously in French in 1928 by Marcel Mauss; new French edition 1971.

—.1960, *Montesquieu and Rousseau: Forerunners of Sociology*. Ann Arbor, Michigan: University of Michigan Press. Essay on Rousseau first published posthumously in 1918.

—.1965, *The Elementary Forms of the Religious Life*. New York: Free Press. First published in French in 1912.

—.1971, "The Principles of 1789 and Sociology," pp. 37-43 in E. A. Tiryakian (ed.), *The Phenomenon of Sociology*. New York: Appleton-Century-Crofts.

—.1975, "On the Definition of Religious Phenomena," pp. 74-99 in W.S.F. Pickering (ed.), *Durkheim on Religion*. London and Boston: Routledge and Kegan Paul. First published in French in 1899.

Ehrard, Jean and Paul Viallaneix (eds) 1977, *Les fêtes de la Révolution*. Paris: Société des études robespierristes.

Faucher, Jean-André and Achille Ricker 1967, *Histoire de la Franc-Maçonnerie en France*. Paris: Nouvelles éditions latines.

Fenton, Steve C. 1984, *Durkheim and Modern Sociology*. New York and Cambridge: Cambridge University Press.

Filloux, Jean-Claude 1976, "Il ne faut pas oublier que je suis fils de rabbin." *Revue française de sociologie*. XVII (April-June), 259-266 (special issue on Durkheim).

Fisher, David James 1977, "The Origins of French Popular Theatre." *Journal of Contemporary History*. XII, 461-467.

Friguglietti, James 1974, *Albert Mathiez, historien révolutionnaire (1874-1932)*. Paris: Société des études robespierristes.

Furet, François 1982, *L'Atelier de l'histoire*. Paris: Flammarion.

Gérard, Alice 1970, *La Révolution française, mythes et interprétations (1789-1970)*. Paris: Flammarion.

Giddens, Anthony. 1978, *Emile Durkheim*. Harmondsworth, England and New York: Penguin.

Glock, Charles Y. and Robert N. Bellah (eds) (1976), *The New Religious Consciousness*. Berkeley and Los Angeles: University of California Press.

Grange, Henri 1977, La Revellière-Lépeaux, théoricien de la Fête Nationale. 1797. pp. 493-502 in Jean Ehrard and Paul Viallaneix (eds), *Les fêtes de la Révolution, op. cit*.

Gréard, Octave 1900, Untitled speech inaugurating the New Sorbonne in collection *Discours aux étudiants*. Paris: Colin.

Headings, Mildred J. 1949, *French Freemasonry Under the Third Republic*. Johns Hopkins University Studies in History and Political Science, vol. LXVI, no. 1. Baltimore, MD: Johns Hopkins University Press.

Hill, Christopher 1972, *The World Turned Upside Down. Radical Ideas During the English Revolution*. New York: Viking.

Hobsbawm, Eric 1983, "Mass-Producing Traditions: Europe 1870-1914." in Eric Hobsbawm and Terence Ranger (eds). *The Invention of Tradition*. Cambridge and New York: Cambridge University Press.

Hoffmann, Stanley 1987, "A Note on the French Revolution and the Language of Violence." *Daedalus*. CXVI (Spring), 149-156.

Hughey, Michael W. 1983, *Civil Religion and Moral Order: Theoretical and Historical Dimensions*. Westport, Connecticut: Greenwood.

Hunt, Lynn 1984, *Politics, Culture, and Class in the French Revolution*. Berkeley and Los Angeles, University of California Press.

Jones, Robert Alun 1977, "On Understanding a Sociological Classic." *American Journal of Sociology*. LXXXIII (September), 279-319.

—.1983, "The New History of Sociology." *Annual Review of Sociology*. IX, 447-469.

—.1986a, *Emile Durkheim: An Introduction to Four Major Works*. Beverley Hills and London: Sage.

—.1986b, "Durkheim, Frazer, and Smith: The Role of Analogies and Exemplars in the Development of Durkheim's Sociology of Religion. *American Journal of Sociology*. LXXXXII (November), 596-627.

Jones, Robert Alun and W. Paul Vogt 1984, "Durkheim's Defense of *Les Formes élémentares de la vie religieuse*." In Henrika Kurlick and Elizabeth Long (eds), *Knowledge and Society: Studies in the Sociology of Culture Past and Present*. V, 45-62.

Knox, Ronald A. 1961, *Enthusiasm: A Chapter in the History of Religion*. New York: Galaxy/Oxford.

Lacroix, Bernard 1981, *Durkheim et le politique*. Paris: Presses de la Fondation nationale des sciences politiques; Montréal: Presses de l'Université de Montréal.

Lakatos, Imre 1970, "Falsification and the Methodology of Scientific Research Programmes." pp. 91-166 in Imre Lakatos and Alan Musgrave (eds), *Criticism and the Growth of Knowledge*. London and New York: Cambridge University Press.

Lefebvre, Georges 1971, *La naissance de l'historiographie moderne*. Paris: Flammerion.

Le Goff, Jacques and Pierre Nora (eds). 1985, *Constructing the Past: Essays in Historical Methodology*. Cambridge and New York: Cambridge University Press; Paris: éditions de la Maison des sciences de l'homme. Translated selections of *Faire de l'histoire*, 3 vols., 1974.

Leventman, Seymour (ed.), 1982, *Counterculture and Social Transformation* Springfield, Ill.: Charles C. Thomas.

Levy, Carl 1987, "Socialism and the Educated Middle Classes in Western Europe: 1870-1914." pp. 154-191 in Ron Everman, L. G. Svensson and T. Soderqvist (eds). *Intellectuals, Universities, and the State in Western Modern Societies*. Berkeley/Los Angeles/London: University of California Press.

Liebman, Robert C. and Robert Wuthnow 1983, *The New Christian Right*. New York: Aldine.

Luke, Thomas W. 1987, "Civil Religion and Secularization: Ideological Revitalization in Post-Revolutionary Communist Systems." *Sociological Forum* II (Winter), 108-134.

Lukes, Steven 1972, *Emile Durkheim, His Life and Work*. New York: Harper and Row.

Mathiez, Albert. 1903. *La Théophilanthropie et le culte décadaire 1796-1801. Essai sur l'histoire religieuse de la Révolution*. Paris: Alcan.

—.1904, *Les Origines des cultes révolutionnaires 1789-1792*. Paris: Société Nouvelle de librairie et d'édition.

Mauss, Marcel 1905, Review of Mathiez (1903). *L'Année Sociologique* VIII, 296-298.

Merton, Robert K. 1967, "On the History and Systematics of Sociological Theory." pp. 1-37 in R.K. Merton, *On Theoretical Sociology*. New York: Free Press.

Meyer, John W. 1977, "The Effects of Education as an Institution." *American Journal of Sociology*. LXXXIII (July), 55-77.

Miller, Perry 1965, *The Life of the Mind in America*. New York: Harcourt, Brace, and World.

Needham, Rodney 1963, "Introduction to Emile Durkheim and Marcel Mauss, *Primitive Classification*, transl. and edited by Rodney Needham. London: Cohen, and West. First published in French in 1903.

Nielsen, Donald A. 1987, "Auguste Sabatier and the Durkheimians on the Scientific Study of Religion." *Sociological Analysis* XLVII (Winter), 283-301.

Nisbet, Robert A. 1974, *Emile Durkheim*. New York/Oxford.

Ozouf, Mona (1976), *La Fête révolutionnaire 1789-1799*. Paris: Gallimard.

—.1982, *L'Église et la République 1871-1914*. Paris: editions Cana/Jean Offredo.

—.1984, *L'École de la France. Essais sur la Révolution, l'Utopie et l'Enseignement*. Paris: Gallimard.

—.1985, "The Festival in the French Revolution." pp. 181-197 in Jacques Le Goff and Pierre Nora (eds), *Constructing the Past, op. cit.*

Parsons, Talcott 1937, *The Structure of Social Action*. New York: McGraw-Hill. Reissued in 1949.

—.1978, "Durkheim on Religion Revisited: Another Look at *The Elementary Forms of the Religious Life*." pp. 213-232 in T. Parsons, *Action Theory and the Human Condition*. New York: Free Press.

Pickering, W. S. F. 1984, *Durkheim's Sociology of Religion*. London and Boston: Routledge and Kegan Paul.

Prager, Jeffrey 1986, "Rhetoric, Symbol, and Solidarity. A Durkheimian Contribution to Political Sociology." Paper presented at the Annual Meeting of the American Sociological Association. New York.

Rearick, Charles 1977, "Festivals in Modern France: The Experience of the Third Republic. *Journal of Contemporary History* XII, 435-460.

Robbins, Thomas and Dick Anthony 1978, "New Religious Movements and the Social System. *Annual Review of Social Sciences of Religion* 11: 1-27.

Robertson, Roland 1974, *The Sociological Interpretation of Religion*. Oxford: Basil Blackwell.

Robison, Georgia 1938, *Revelliére-Lépeaux, Citizen Director, 1753-1824*. New York: Columbia University Press.

Simiand, François "Historical Method and Social Science." *Review* IX (Fall), 162-213. 1903.

Skocpol, Theda (ed.). 1984, *Vision and Method in Historical Sociology*. Cambridge/London/New York: Cambridge University Press.

Soboul, Albert 1977, "Préambule" (Introduction). pp. 2-7 in Jean Ehrard and P. Viallaneix (eds), *Les fêtes de la Révolution, op cit.*

Thompson, Kenneth 1982, *Emile Durkheim.* New York: Tavistock/Ellis Horwood.

Tilly, Charles 1981 *As Sociology Meets History.* New York: Academic Press.

Tiryakian, Edward A. 1978 "Emile Durkheim." pp. 187-236 in Tom Bottomore and Robert Nisbet (eds.), *A History of Sociological Analysis.* New York: Basic Books.

—.1981, "Durkheim's *Elementary Forms* as 'Revelation.' pp. 114-135 in Buford Rhea (ed.), *The Future of the Sociological Classics.* London and Boston: George Allen and Unwin.

—.1988, "From Durkheim to Managua: Revolutions as Religious Revivals." in Jeffrey C. Alexander (ed.), *Durkheimian Sociology.* New York: Cambridge University Press.

Turner, Stephen 1983, "Contextualism and the Interpretation of the Classical Sociological Texts." *Knowledge and Society: Studies in the Sociology of Culture Past and Present* IV, 273-291.

Turner, Victor W. 1969, *The Ritual Process: Structure and Anti-Structure.* Chicago: Aldine.

Wald, Kenneth D. 1987, *Religion and Politics in the United States.* New York: St. Martin's Press.

Weber, Eugen 1959, *The Nationalist Revival in France, 1905-1914.* Berkeley and Los Angeles: University of California Press.

—.1986, *France Fin de Siècle.* Cambridge, MA: Belknap/Harvard University Press.

Weber, Max 1958, *The Protestant Ethic and the Spirit of Capitalism.* New York: Charles Scribner's Sons. First published in German, 1904-1905.

Wilson, Bryan 1973, *Magic and the Millennium: A Sociological Study of Religious Movements of Protest Among Tribal and Third World Peoples.* New York: Harper and Row.

—.(ed.). 1981, *The Social Impact of New Religious Movements.* New York: Rose of Sharon Press.

—.1982, *Religion in Sociological Perspective.* New York: Oxford University Press.

Wuthnow, Robert 1976, *The Consciousness Reformation.* Berkeley: University of California Press.

Yinger, J. Milton 1970, *The Scientific Study of Religion.* New York: Macmillan.

—.*Countercultures: The Promise and Peril of a World Turned Upside Down.* New York: Free Press.

Zerubavel, Eviatar 1977, "The French Republican Calendar: A Case Study in the Sociology of Time." *American Sociological Review* XLII (December), 868-877.

—.1982, "Calendars and Group Identity." *American Sociological Review* XLVII (April), 284-289.

Chapter 6
Situating Durkheim's Sociology of Work[1]

Introduction

Work has had a core meaning for the human condition since, it may be said metaphorically, the expulsion of Adam and Eve forced mankind to work for a living rather than enjoy the fruits of Eden; to return to an Eden free from toil and living there in innocence have fed at various times utopian dreams. Paradise, however different in Christian conceptions and those of other communities of faith, is anything but a *workshop*: it is a place exempt from work, at least in popular imagery.

The *meaning* of work differs significantly for major figures who analyzed the foundations of the modern social order. Although my focus in this paper is a discussion of how Durkheim analyzed work, it may be well to contrast briefly the central meaning of work for Durkheim with the positions of other classic figures, in particular Marx and Weber, I will then discuss elements of the sociohistorical setting of Durkheim's most important treatise on work and continue with major themes of his enduring classic, *La Division du Travail Social* (hereafter in this essay, *DT*).[2] In a concluding section, I will briefly relate this classic to our own period, including what is the meaning of work today to ordinary people, at least as obtained in extensive survey research, something neglected by classic authors.

1 Durkheim's Peer Group on Work

The transformation of the modern social order entailed a radical change in the nature of work at the core of social organization. To have an initial perspective on Durkheim's contribution, it might be heuristic to compare his approach to what might be viewed as his peer group among classical authors – not necessarily his contemporaries but in any case major authors who saw in work or the division of labor a key entry into analyzing modernity. I do this in terms of "optimists" and "pessimists".

---

1   Translated and adapted from "Le Travail chez Émile Durkheim," pp. 229-50 in Daniel Mercure, ed., Les Classiques et le Travail. Québec, Canada: Les Presses de l'Université Laval, 2003.

2   My citations in this paper are taken from the 1902 French edition, hence the abbbreviation. Available in English is The Division of Labor in Society, with an introduction by Lewis A. Coser and translated by W.D. Halls, New York: Free Press 1997.

The optimists: Smith and Saint-Simon

At the beginning of the modern social order, roughly 250 years ago,[3] Adam Smith, in his immensely influential *The Wealth of Nations* (1776), saw in the division of labor the engine of economic development and progress; it was for him a master theme of human social evolution, interrelated with technology and commerce. The general optimistic tone of Smith was continued by Saint-Simon, the great visionary of the industrial order,[4] whom Durkheim held in high regard (in higher regard, probably than he held Comte) as "having founded both positivist philosophy and sociology," (Gouldner 1958:ix).[5] Although he did not focus on industrial *work* as such,[6] Saint-Simon took the industrial order as a totality liberating men from the shackles of the feudal order; when institutionalized – an *industrial revolution* more lasting than *political* ones – the industrial system based on productivity and merit would replace outworn privileges and the social anarchy characteristic of periods of transition. Though Saint-Simon was more concerned with industrial innovators, and hence with the elite of the new social order, he also showed sympathetic compassion for those he addressed as "proletariat" – those who want to work but cannot find work, the unemployed.

The pessimists: Marx and Weber

The meaning of work for Marx (himself an unemployed intellectual most of his life in exile) was very negative. The industrial revolution had in effect provided chains for the masses of industrial worker, since workers could control neither the processes of production nor the prices of the commodities they produce; modern (factory) work is alienative and dehumanizing. If modern work has a redeeming feature it is that it places in the same alienating work situation a vast and growing

---

3   I think there is much merit in the insightful interpretations of such keen observers of modernity as the British Martin Albrow (1996) and the American Francis Fukuyama (1999) that we are on the threshold, if we have not already crossed it, of a very different social order from the one of the modern industrial order with its nation-state polity. This is not the occasion to elaborate such a discussion.

4   See for example, Henri Saint-Simon, *Du Système Industriel* (On the Industrial System), Paris : Chez Antoine-Augustin Renouard, 1821).

5   Gouldner in his introduction to Socialism and Saint-Simon posits that Durkheim sought to synthesize two major competing theoretical social systems at turn-of-the century: Marxism and Comteianism: "a compromise which leads him back to Saint-Simonian formulations which had influenced both Marx and Comte," (1958:xvii). In Durkheim's own inner circle, most of whom would have been drawn to Saint-Simon's brand of democratic socialism, Célestin Bouglé edited in 1924 a collection of Saint-Simon texts with an important commentary (Doctrine de Saint-Simon, nouvelle éd, Paris: M. Rivière).

6   Broadly speaking, Saint-Simon took the useful work of the scientist, the artist and the craftsman as making genuine contributions to human happiness, unlike the non-work of the feudal elite, lawyers included.(see Bouglé, 1924: 115f).

myriad of workers, stripped of property and human dignity. The realization of their situation is propitious for a mass movement of liberation (insurrection?). Marx's pessimism about working conditions becoming increasingly exploitative under a capitalist regime, which is the crux of the modern social order, does have a brief and sociologically undeveloped vision of a post-capitalist society. In that idyllic vision, as Louis Dumont (1983) has elegantly discussed Marx in the context of the Western ideology of *individualism*, man would now be free to enjoy life as a totality, including, presumably doing some work that he (and she?) enjoys. But Marx gave little attention to his New Jerusalem, and much more to the modern wasteland of alienation.

To categorize Weber as a "pessimist" in the present discussion must be done with caution, because there are important elements of his masterly survey of the dynamics of Western civilization that are, if anything, optimistic. The famous "Protestant ethic" thesis of Weber, which needs not be reiterated here (Freund 1969, 1990), essentially sees human work, even "ordinary" work when done with devotion and steadfastness, as redemptive, that is, as a worldly instrument of salvation. To Luther's epochal break with ecclesiastical authority by declaring "each man his own priest", the Calvinist/Puritan found in the "calling" a redemptive meaning, which when aggregated and institutionalized significantly contributed to (but was not *the* cause) of modernity. So why the pessimism? It is found in the conclusion of *The Protestant Ethic and the Spirit of Capitalism:* "The Puritan wanted to work in a calling; we are forced to do so" (Weber 1976: 181). The redemptive value of work introduced by worldly asceticism has been eroded and corroded by commodification, perhaps even truer a century after Weber wrote "material goods have gained an increasing and finally an inexorable power over the lives of men as at not previous period in history," (1976: *ibid*). Weber came to North America in 1904 and saw a vibrant society, which still manifested the Protestant ethic in full bloom, but he felt it would be only a matter of time before, it too, would lose that special quality, and thereby take the United States in the same course as had befallen Europe (Weber 1946: 302-22).

2 Durkheim's Analysis of Work

Where does Durkheim stand regarding the meaning of work? I would characterize him as a *social realist*: he accepts the reality and significance of the growth in the division of labor as a long-term structural change. There are two approaches in *DT* that operate at different levels, and which make it hard to categorize Durkheim as either a "pessimist" or as an "optimist". The first two books of *DT* looks at work at the system level, that is, what are the functions and causes of the division of labor for society; there really is not much concern for the individual worker as a unit of analysis. It is when after a thorough discussion of the structure and dynamics of social organization as a function of changing modes of solidarity, and ultimately, of changing demographic conditions (the increase in the volume and density of populations), that Durkheim turns his attention to the plight of workers in situations of "abnormal" or "pathological" forms of the division of labor. In other words, the first and major part of the treatise is the social meaning of work for society, the whole; the second part gives greater weight to the worker, to the pathologies of the work situation for workers. Obviously, in the "normal" instance of the well-functioning of the division of labor, the work situation will prove fulfilling in an echo of Saint-Simon's "from each according to his capabilities, to each according to his needs".[7] It is clear that Durkheim's treatise gives paramount attention, not to the meaning of work for the *individual* worker, but rather to the bearing of the division of labor as an *aggregate* on social integration.

The Division of Labor, Forms of Solidarity and Anomie

There are several ways of considering De La Division du Travail Social (The Division of Labor in Society). Very broadly, it may be viewed as a first version of a scientific research program (as conceived in the philosophy of science by Lakatos 1970[8]) in formulating the major lines of inquiry and Durkheim's overriding preoccupations: the empirical and comparative analysis of the structures and functions of the social order in modern society, as well as the sources of disorder.[9] Underlying this is also a moral engagement: to reconstruct on a sound basis the social order best suited for modern times. Grosso modo, Durkheim's oeuvre, from beginning to end, is to promote sociology in placing it in charge, through its empirical knowledge, of societal reform.

Given that in the course of evolution, the largest sector of society has become that of the economy, it is of the utmost importance for the new sociology to study the economic sector in its functioning, not as economists would with their abstract models of homo economicus but as sociologists concerned with social cohesion in everyday life. We will note that for Durkheim, social cohesion, a moral phenomenon in human society, gravitate around two poles to which two concepts apply: solidarity and anomie. Furthermore, solidarity in his analysis takes two major forms: mechanical solidarity and organic solidarity. Where do

---

7   Ultimately behind Durkheim and Saint-Simon there is Plato's Republic where the division of labor is the primary vehicle of social organization according to capabilities of individuals assigned to different "work stations", so to speak.

8   For a fuller discussion of Lakatos and the concept of a scientific research program in Durkheim, see my discussion in the essay "Emile Durkheim's matrix" in this volume.

9   To complement his research program, Durkheim published two years after *The Division of Labor* his methodological treatise, *Les Règles de la Méthode Sociologique*. Current editions of the latter are in French, with an Introduction by Jean-Michel Berthelot, Paris: Flammarion, 1988, and in English, *The Rules of Sociological Method*, trans. by S.A. Solovay and J.H. Mueller, edited by George E.G. Catlin, New York: Free Press, 1962.

these key concepts come from? From two intellectual stimuli, one in Germany, one in France.

In 1889 Durkheim wrote a review essay of the famous thesis of Ferdinand Tönnies, Gemeinschaft und Gesellschaft. Abhandlung des Communismus und des Socialismus als empirische Culturformen.[10] In the state of Gemeinschaft or community, Durkheim noted (1975a [1889] 1: 384), "there is an absolute unity which excludes the differentiation of its members; it is the family which is its most perfect form." And Durkheim added, "it is an organic group." Later in his review he echoes this saying "while the composition of Gemeinschaft was organic, that of Gesellschaft is mechanical," (ibid., p. 387).

Durkheim well accepted the evolution of society proposed by Tönnies: from Gemeinschaft as a "community of souvenirs and of occupations" emerged brotherhoods (confréries), along with political, economic and religious corporations. All these groups, noted Durkheim in reading Tönnies, are not individual efforts (des volontés individuelles) since their lives are regulated by customs, practices, traditions. One must wait, his review continues, until the coming of Gesellschaft with a much larger social body in the large modern cities for the coming of individualism, industry, and cosmopolitanism. Further, this large-scale transformation of society is drawn in "somber colors" by Marx and Lasalle,[11] as well as by Tönnies, added Durkheim (and he could have equally mentioned Simmel).

Nevertheless, Durkheim diverged from Tönnies in the interpretation of Gesellschaft by inverting the concepts of "mechanical" and "organic" solidarity. He refused to accept that a progressive development of individualism perforce atomizes contemporary society to make the latter only a "mechanical aggregate".[12] Durkheim concluded his review essay in accepting a certain challenge: to show that the life of large social groupings today has also an internal organic dimension, as natural as the small villages of Tönnies' childhood.

Lastly, Durkheim, writing in 1889, announced what in fact he was to elaborate as his own thesis in 1893: "To prove [the organic dimension of modern society], one would require a book, since I can only formulate a proposition ... The only way to reach this conclusion would be ... to study Gesellschaft by means of the legal system and the habits (moeurs) which are peculiar to it and which adorn its

---

10   Ferdinand Tönnies (1855-1936) published his seminal Gemeinschaft and Gesellschaft (commonly translated as Community and Society) in 1887. He became the first and long-lasting president of the German Society for Sociology (1909-1933), to which also belonged from the start Weber, Simmel and Sombart.

11   Ferdinand Lasalle (1825-1864) was the founder of the German Democratic Socialist Party and an advocate of state socialism to promote from above the situation of the proletariat.

12   Indeed, a few years after this review and arising from the Dreyfus affair, Durkheim even grudgingly recognized the cult of the individual as having a central place in modern secular religion (Durkheim 1973 [1898]).

structure," (ibid., p. 390). When Durkheim did present his doctoral thesis four years later, he placed the accent on the internal solidarity of modern society, on solidarity now treated as organic from the interaction of each in the social division of labor which has above everything a normative dimension. And, as he had earlier proposed, Durkheim made use of the legal system – a system of regulations external to the individual – to have an indicator of the prominence of one kind of solidarity over another. The further one advances in the historical process, the more one should observe increase in "cooperative" law; the further one goes back, the greater "repressive" (or criminal) law. The former, in Durkheim's argument in Book One of DT, is used as an index of organic solidarity, the latter as an index of mechanical solidarity. Durkheim's critique of Tönnies thus was an important point of departure for his own theory that the "normal" in modern society is an "organic" cohesion allowing where the diversity of talents can freely find space in an increasingly advanced division of labor.

If the pair of solidarities and the historical changes in their part of the total provides a sociological perspective on the bases of integration in modern society, where does Durkheim get the notion of anomie?

As shown by Marco Orrù (1987), the concept was not invented by Durkheim. It certainly had an ancient lineage in Hebraic and Greek thought as the unjust transgression of a divine order. But in modern times, a contemporary of Durkheim, Jean Marie Guyau, had published in 1887 a sociological perspective of the history of religions, L'Irréligion de l'avenir, étude sociologique (an English translation, The non-religion of the future, a sociological study, was published in 1897). That study (which went through many editions) gave a major role to anomie, not as a pathological but rather as a positive condition of morality, as allowing a voluntary choice of moral judgment precisely because there is no transcendental order.

In 1888 Durkheim wrote a lengthy review of this work (Orrù: 104f) and found Guyau's analysis important to study the development of both religion and society. But just as he did with the concepts of Tönnies, Durkheim changed the value of *anomie*. In his 1893 preface to *The Division of Labor in Society*, Durkheim negated the interpretation of Guyau and adopted a position similar to the ancient Hebraic and Greek perspective: *anomie* is not the foundation of morality but on the contrary "a contradiction of all morality." Further, in the preface to the later second edition, Durkheim squarely indicated the gravity of present day society: "We insist again and again … on the condition of juridical and moral anomie in which economic life is found today," (DT: ii).

For Durkheim, anomie has two sociological aspects. At the macro level, it is an abnormal condition of deregulation making for a precarious life together (for example, the loss of trust in the other, class warfare, and civil war). At the micro level, work and organic solidarity lose their meaning, and instead of expanding men's horizon, industrial work can lead to degrading human nature. In Book Three of his doctoral thesis, Durkheim provides an in depth analysis of anomie as the opposite condition of solidarity, yet equally important for sociology to study, as is pathology for the study of physiology (DT: 343).

Solidarity and *anomie* are key levers that open up Durkheim's perspective on the centrality of work in modern society. Neither is the conceptual abstraction of "armchair speculation"; rather, it is a pair drawn by Durkheim from a period of social life in France that only a century's perspective makes it initially appear carefree, part of the long 19th century of peace and progress.[13] The following offers a contrasting retrospective:

> 1892 is a year which does not offer the best souvenirs in the history of France. Hardly had Boulangisme gone away, the country became mired in affairs. The political sector was splashed with the scandals of Panama ... The social climate was no longer tranquil, and the miners' strike broke out at Carmaux ... Anarchists were making their bombs ... The only consolation for advocates of the regime, (Pope) Leo XIII advocated support to the Republic (Freon 1992).[14]

The period of heavy industrialization and rapid economic growth that took place in the waning decades of the nineteenth century brought significant benefits in standards of living, to be sure. It also carried social costs and new forms of social conflict. Durkheim's doctoral dissertation first appeared in a period of both new abundance for an industrial bourgeoisie but also of anguish for the less fortunate and social marginals (those depicted, say, in the novels of Zola). It was a period of *deregulation*, the weakening of traditional rules of the game – economic rules and moral rules.

One manifestation of the consequences of economic deregulation and the socioeconomic conflicts generated was *anarchism*, that took forms of violent labor agitations and political assassinations in France (President Sadi Carnot in 1894) and also in the United States (the Haymarket riot of 1886; the assassination of President McKinley in 1901). It is clear, in the Preface to the second edition of *DT*, that anarchism and anomie are for Durkheim part of the same ensemble of profoundly disturbed societal conditions. In contrast, the *virtual* tendency of regulated social life is agreeable and conducive to solidarity and self-development:

> Collective life (la vie commune) is attractive while at the same time coercive. Undoubtedly, constraint is necessary for man to exceed himself. (*DT*: xvii).

---

13   For a parallel discussion, see Tiryakian 2005.

14   In this citation, "Boulangisme" was a short-lived right-wing movement of General Georges Boulanger (1837-1891) which drew enough popular support that it almost succeeded in a coup d'état in 1889; the Panama Canal Company scandal in 1892-93 was the most notorious corruption of high officials in the nineteenth Century, easily comparable to the S&L and Enron debacles in the United States in recent years; Carmaux was a small village in southern France that became the scene of a major labor unrest in 1892 in what had been a seemingly tranquil company town; Leo XIII made a major accommodation of the Church of Rome with modernity, including recognition of a secular republican regime and the issuance of a landmark social encyclical, Rerum Novarum (1891).

On the same page, Durkheim compares this state of normalcy with the pathological condition of the deregulated work situation, a situation nefarious for both society and the individual:

> Anarchy[15] is painful for man. He himself suffers from the gnawing and disorders which happen every time that inter-individual relations lack regulatory influence. It isn't good for man to live thus on a war footing amidst his immediate companions (*DT*: *ibid.*).

Perhaps drawing an inspiration from Claude Bernard and Louis Pasteur to make sociology a healing science, perhaps drawing an inspiration from Comte to have sociology useful for social policy makers, Durkheim in both *DT* and in *Suicide* (published in 1897, before the second edition of *DT*) proposed the renovation of the *corporation* as an intermediary structure between the state and society. Drawing on the monumental studies of Emile Levasseur,[16] Durkheim valued these professional work associations (guilds) that had provided a code of ethics and a corporate identity to artisans and professionals from Roman times down to the Revolution (Levasseur 1900-01 [1859]; 1903-04 [1867]). In abolishing corporations as part of the revolutionary overthrow of all constraints on the liberty of individuals,[17] the "baby was thrown out with the bath", so to speak, in this instance, economic life was deregulated, allowing for rapacious economic appetites, greed, and workers being pitted against owners, against each other, and against civil authorities.

The deregulation of economic life is the condition of economic anarchism, anomie, as brutal and violent in its manner as political anarchism. There is no moral discipline which regulates employees-manager relations or the relation between competitors. *Caveat emptor* is a precept of the market place, void of legal character. Since modern society has increasingly taken the ethos of an economic, industrial [or to bring Durkheim to our situation, *post-industrial*] order, a very large segment of social life is void of a normative regulatory mechanism. Absent a moral force that constrains individual appetites, a Hobbesian state will come to be. And since economic life is the predominant feature of modern society, said Durkheim in a period when the 40-hour week was only a dream of the future, this means that the majority of people live the greatest part of their lives in a work situation devoid of morality. Without recourse to survey data or field data as how workers experience the work situation, Durkheim viewed this as a sham freedom, for equitable freedom is predicated on the respect of the rights of

---

15   Note that Durkheim uses this term, not anomie.

16   The leading French economic historian of both the Second Empire and the Third Republic and professor at the Collège de France.

17   Recall that at its peak, the revolutionary enthusiasm also did away with slavery and accepted divorce (to free women form the bondage of marriage). The subsequent reactionary regime of Louis XVIII and Charles X restored slavery and nullified divorce, but did not restore corporations and their traditional privileges.

others, in accordance with social rules of conduct, which is what morality is all about. Although Durkheim is not explicit on this, he views work as meaningful and satisfying when it is done in a regulated, normative milieu in solidarity with others. I don't think that Durkheim would think of regulated work as being "fun", but he would think of it as a satisfying, even necessary, component of the "human condition".

But how to return to a state of normalcy, given the anomic conditions of the present industrial order? That is where the past may provide a useful model in the corporation:

> ... the corporation is the natural milieu in which morality and professional obligations must develop (*DT*: xx).[18]

To be sure, acknowledged Durkheim, it cannot be the same structure as the corporations or guilds of the *ancien régime*; if the French Revolution could abolish them easily, it is because they had outlived their usefulness and their localization made them vulnerable as economic life went beyond the local and regional to the national level of heavy industry (*DT*: xxvi f). The new corporations must amplify their scope and their organizational structure to become national. They are not only regulative foyers of the work situation but also serve other functions. The social group anchored in the work situation is a moral authority which is also a source of warmth and sympathy that curbs selfishness. What was nascent in the corporations of the past will become emergent in those of the future:

> The corporations of the future will have an even greater complexity of features as their scope widens (DT: xxx).

What would those functions be? To provide mutual aid to its members (as in benevolent societies), but also educational, artistic and other leisure activities.[19] Even, proposes Durkheim, the corporation can become a new basis of political life, since in the past it was at the basis of the urban commune. Without mentioning Saint-Simon who had a vision of a reorganized European Parliament (1925) with industries as the political unit, Durkheim suggested that the renovated corporation might come to function as a basic political unit of the modern State.

Durkheim did not articulate how the renovation of corporations was to be undertaken; practical details should be worked out by policy makers, not by sociologists (*DT*: xxvii). He did not elaborate further his discussion and he even

---

18 Durkheim was later to give courses on this topic with notes which were posthumously published and translated into English (Durkheim 1983). For a discussion, see Cladis (1992).

19 Although Durkheim well qualifies as a "workaholic", he understood the limits of "all work and no play": "it seems in the nature of things that this noble form of play and recreation develops alongside la vie sérieuse," (DT:xxxi).

warned that the corporative structure would not be a panacea for all of society's problems, because the crisis of our age does not come from a single cause (*DT*: xxiv). Indeed, what he was to undertake beyond his *thèse d'état* was a multidimensional investigation of the renewal of modern society, one that ultimately would lead him beyond the work situation to coming to grips sociologically with religion as an institution. Religion in France, mainly Catholicism, had been banished from the public sphere by republican legislation from the bitterly anticlerical ministries of Waldeck-Rousseau and the ex-priest Emile Combes (Daniel-Rops 1964). Fervent republican as he was, Durkheim realized that the occupational sphere was insufficient to fill the void of religion as a buttress of civic morality.[20] Consequently, on the heels of the secularization (*laïcisation*) policy of the State, he turned his energy in the last decade of his career to deeper structures of the social order: religion and morality. After dealing with the first in his seminal *The Elementary Forms of the Religious Life* (1912), he began the even more ambitious *La Morale* (1975b) but that work was never completed.

3 *The Division of Labor* in Retrospect

I have argued that Durkheim's *DT* is, given the title, paradoxically *not* primarily a study in the sociology of work. It is about many important things, like establishing Durkheim's vision of sociology against competing perspectives, such as the individualistic perspectives of Tarde and especially Spencer. It provides important empirical materials for the important advocates of *solidarisme*, like Léon Bourgeois, who sought to steer the republican regime between the Scylla of economic liberalism and the Charybdis of socialism. It is, in retrospective, not so much an advocacy of corporatism as one of social democracy, as may be noted in a passage that might well have been written (or cited) by John Rawls (if not by Proudhon or Marx):

> The task for the most advanced societies is thus … a work of justice … [Our ideal] is to place always more equity in our social relations so as to assure the free display of all socially useful forces (*DT: 381*).

---

20   In the conclusion of DT he had stated "Law and morality are the totality of ties which bind us to one another and to society" ("Le droit et la morale, c'est l'ensemble des liens qui nous attachent les uns aux autres et à la société,") (DT: 393), But in 1912 he moved religion to the center of solidarity, as expressed in Durkheim's famous definition: "A religion is a unified system of beliefs and practices… uniting in a single moral community called a Church all those adhering to it," (Durkheim 1912: 65). The problem of modernity, which Durkheim posed but did not resolve in The Elementary Forms, is: what is the socially appropriate form, in terms of beliefs and practices, for religion in a complex, diverse, pluralist society?

Durkheim in this and related studies (1950) argued that the division of labor based on organic solidarity functions best when inequalities, other than intrinsic skills, are minimized, in the market place as well as in the work situation. In a direct echo from Saint-Simon, Durkheim went so far as to argue that the reduction of inequalities and the fullness of the sentiment of sympathy for others could not be completed without eliminating the transmission of property from parents to children (1950: 254-59).

So undoubtedly *DT* is a rich study at many layers: as a sociological inquiry into factors of human social evolution, as a methodological contribution to social indicators (since Durkheim takes changes in the legal corpus as an indicator of changes in the predominant form of social solidarity), as an early formulation of a scientific research program defining basic assumptions regarding the nature of society as *sui generis* , and even in proposing remedies for social ills, as an initial social philosophy. All these aspects and the clarity of Durkheim's arguments justify this being taken as an enduring – if not as *the first* – sociological classic that continues to attract attention around the world.

But this said, *DT* is not primarily about conditions of work, the workplace, and workers themselves. Émile Levasseur, as cited earlier, published numerous first-rate historical and descriptive studies on the work situation in France and the United States (1898, 1900-1901, 1903, 1904, 1907). Durkheim relied on Levasseur for historical sources, but it was to his own younger collaborators of the *Année Sociologique*, that central vehicle of Durkheimian collaborative research, that he turned to develop the nascent field of economic sociology. There were among the brilliant "Pléiade" that gathered around Durkheim (Nandan 1977) two who were given major responsibility to cover the sociology of economic life in the important "5e Section: Sociologie Économique".

From the first volume that appeared in 1898, the 5e Section, was entrusted to François Simiand, later shared with Maurice Halbwachs. Both combined expertise in statistics with economic sociology. Simiand, who eventually became Professor at the Collège de France, wrote extensively on varied socioeconomic subjects, from the wages of coal miners (1904) to broad economic cycles (1932). In the last volume of *L'Année* published in Durkheim's lifetime (volume 12, 1909-1912), Maurice Halbwachs began a brilliant sociological career as a reviewer in this section. An early translator of Weber into French, a pioneer in French demographic studies (who gave a course at the University of Chicago on demography in the early 1930s), Halbwachs has become better known better known to American sociologists for his work on memory (1975). Still, Halbwachs's early studies (1970; 1933) were important contributions to economic sociology, relating empirical research to the study of money, of unemployment, and to the social psychology of social classes and the situation and needs of workers. In a sense, then, one can consider the 5e Section as an extension of Durkheim's dissertation. Taken together, the 5e section and its sub-headings are frames for a still elusive economic sociology and the sociology of work, as indicated in the citation at the start of this article.

Epilogue: *Preface to a Third Edition*

It might be appropriate to mark the 100th anniversary (1902-2002) of the second edition of *DT,* the one for which Durkheim wrote an important new preface, to conduct a bit of a mental experiment. What features of the post World War II world might Durkheim take notice of were he to update a new edition of his pre-World War I classic? What, then, might be empirical elements for a *preface to the third edition*? To list a few, and invite readers to supply additional ones, let me mention some outside and some inside France.

1. Since the theme of *organic solidarity*, and the conditions for the flourishing *or* inhibiting of it is a paramount concern in *DT*, Durkheim could not fail to notice the very appropriation of the term in the revolutionary trade union workers' movement in Poland. *Solidarność*, which formally came into being at the beginning of the 1980s, was indeed a movement of "organic solidarity" which embraced all sectors of the economy, and in fact became a movement of national solidarity that startled the world as a grass-roots resistance to the communist regime (Touraine *et. al.*: 1982). Whereas workers' movements in earlier periods were directed against the oppression of capitalist regimes, *Solidarność* was a courageous display of resistance to the authority of the communist State.

2. Durkheim would also note that "solidarity" has had earlier in the present decade a political rebirth in France, in the form of the establishment of an important new cabinet ministry, the *Ministère de l'emploi et de la solidarité.*[21] It has important functions relating to providing the social integration of immigrants, improving working conditions, and leading the fight against racial discrimination. When Minister Elisabeth Guigou addressed the French National Assembly in December 2001, the focus was on the legislation to modernize solidarity (*Projet de loi de modernisation sociale*):

> If the Government wished to place together different measures of this project under this title, it is because it considers they all contribute to modernizing our work legislation and the solidarity of our society ... to modernize solidarity is equally to come to the assistance of those who need society.[22]

Equalizing the life chances of foreigners and ethnic immigrants in the work place would certainly have endeared this ministry to Durkheim; moreover, given his active participation as a *Dreyfusard* in the fight against bigotry, he would have certainly have applauded the Ministry being a prime mover in the struggle against

---

21   With a slightly different name – Ministère de l'Emploi et de la Solidarité Sociale – this ministry with the same basic functions exists in the Quebec government.

22   www.travail.gouv.fr/actualites/declaration/dagenda.asp?id=264.

racial discrimination being declared early in 2002 by the Jospin government the "Grande Cause Nationale".[23]

3. Outside of France, Durkheim would certainly note how the division of labor has taken on a transnational dimension as an aspect of *globalization*. Of course, an international division of labor may be derived from the complex trade routes connecting East and West possibly two millennia ago, and in Durkheim's lifetime globalization rose sharply in terms of global trade, facilitated by interactive empires, new modes of transportation, and general political stability between 1870 and 1914. However, it is only recently that an elaborate, rationalized global system of production and distribution has become part of the world economic system, for example in "global commodity chains" in the apparel and other consumer industries (Gereffi and Korzeniewicz 1994).

The extension of the division of labor beyond national borders would not bother Durkheim, for his basic model of social change could factor in globalization as a logical development of a "civilization of organic solidarity".[24] But for this to become a structural condition of global integration, Durkheim would probably voice concern about major regional inequalities separating rich nations from poor nations (Bradshaw and Wallace 1996); and he might well take note of movements of protest against the IMF, World Bank and other agencies, which indicate that the international division of labor is presently not based on equitable distribution and production facilities (Stiglitz 2002; Broad 2002).

4. Finally, since this essay started by raising the question of the meaning of work, Durkheim might find considerable interest in the cross-national survey data on work that was conducted in over 40 countries about ten years ago.[25] Durkheim, as a comparativist, would have noted national variations as well as data on France itself.

When respondents were asked whether work is important in their lives (V4), 61% of French answered it was, those on the political right higher (65%) than those on the left (53%), and about the same for men (62%) as for women (61%). The figures are about the same for the United States (62%) with a higher figure for the right (63%) than the left (57%). Canada had a somewhat smaller overall figure (59%), but West Germany had a much less figure (35% of total, 40% men, 30% women), with a somewhat higher level of important accorded by those who identify politically on the right (37%) than those on the left (30%).

---

23   That later in 2002 the socialists lost both the May presidential and the June assembly elections would have worried Durkheim, since the Ministry and its authority was to a large extent the creation of the democratic left. Its fortunes with a new market-friendly right-wing government are not assured.

24   I am indebted to Shmuel N. Eisenstadt for this concept.

25   All materials here are taken from tables reported in Inglehart, Basañez and Moreno (1998). Since page numbers are not provided in this volume, I indicate the reference with the table number.

Why do people work? In response to this question and when given as a choice "working for a living is a necessity. I wouldn't work if I didn't have to," (V 120), 22% of the French agreed with this (19% of men, 24% of women; 25% of those identifying with the left, 18% with the right). In West Germany, 15% of the sample mentioned this factor of necessity, while the United States had the highest incidence of all the countries with 34%; on the other hand, another "Protestant" country, the Netherlands, was near the bottom with only 7% mentioning this factor.

The last item that Durkheim (and Weber) might ponder over regarding the meaning of work today was another response to the general question of why do people work (V122). The option presented here was "I enjoy my work; it's the most important thing in my life." If we accept the centrality of occupation in providing identity and solidarity in the modern world, the results of the survey give pause for thought. For the world sample as a whole (n=43 countries), 14% agreed with this option (16% men, 12% women). Canada and the United States are similar (16%) in being slightly above the world average.

Perhaps surprising is how few Germans and Frenchmen respond positively to this option. In Germany, only 8% of the sample cited this (10% of those on the right, 5% of those on the left). But what would surely chagrin and greatly concern Durkheim is that only 4% of the French total (6% of men, 2% of women; 2% of those 16-29 and 2% of those 30-49, while 7% of those over 50 years) agreed, with no split between left and right! Such a low figure, if the data are valid, is an indicator of *anomie* in the work place.

Durkheim, just as he sought to make sense of the statistical tables on suicide furnished him by Tarde, would find in the survey data materials to be reworked, especially on the section on pathological aspects of the division of labor. But he would not necessarily take a pessimistic view of work, of the meaning of work, and of the division of labor in our own day. Durkheim would find in the four instances I have suggested, and in additional instances that others might adduce (foremost in all likelihood the increased participation of women at all levels of the labor force), plenty of materials for a new preface to a new edition of *La Division du Travail Social*. He might well in closing this preface warn us that the climate of deregulation which has swept market economies and formerly planned economies is far from the panacea envisioned by liberal economics and that in fact the human costs of deregulation have even more problematized the meaning of work than a century ago when he wrote about *anomie*. He could only point to the social costs of deregulation, the growing inequalities within advanced societies and between "North" and "South", and the increase in violence in developing societies. And after enunciating that, then, perhaps extending a challenge to Weber, we might expect him to tell us

"And now, let's get to work!"

References

Albrow, Martin *The Global Age: state and society beyond modernity*, Stanford: Stanford University Press, 1996.

Besnard, Philippe Massimo Borlandi, et Paul Vogt, eds., *Division du Travail et Lien Social*, Paris: Presses Universitaires de France, 1993.

Bouglé, Célestin ed. *L'Œuvre d'Henri de Saint-Simon*, Paris: Félix Alcan, 1925.

Bourgeois, Léon et Afred Croiset *Essai d'une Philosophie de La Solidarité*, Paris: Félix Alcan, 1907.

Bradshaw, York and Michael Wallace *Global Inequalities*. Thousand Oaks, CA and London: Pine Forge Press 1996.

Broad, Robin ed. *Global Backlash. Citizen Initiatives for a Just World Economy*. Lanham, MD: Rowman & Littlefield, 2002.

Cladis, Mark S. *A Communitarian Defense of Liberalism. Emile Durkheim and Contemporary Social Theory*. Stanford: Stanford University Press. 1992.

Daniel-Rops, Henri *L'Église des Révolutions: Un Combat pour Dieu*. Paris: Fayard, 1964.

Dumont, Louis *Essais sur l'individualisme: une perspective anthropologique sur l'idéologie moderne*. Paris: Seuil, 1983.

Durkheim, Émile *De la Division du Travail Social*. 2e ed. Paris: Félix Alcan, 1902.

—. *Les Formes Élémentaires de la Vie Religieuse*. Paris: Alcan 1912.

—. *Leçons de Sociologie. Physique des mœurs et du droit*. Paris: Presses Universitaires de France, 1950. Translated by Cornelia Brookfield as *Professional Ethics and Civic Morals*, Westport, CT: Greenwood Press, 1983.

—."*Individualism and the Intellectuals*,", trans. Mark Traugott, in Robert N. Bellah, ed., *Emile Durkheim on Morality and Society*. Chicago and London: University of Chicago Press, 1973.

—. "Théories Allemandes de la Société," *textes 1. éléments d'une théorie sociale*, Victor Karady, ed., Paris: Editions de Minuit, 1975a, pp. 344-99.

—. "Introduction à la morale," in Durkheim, *textes: 2. religion, morale, anomie*, Victor Karady, ed., Paris: Editions de Minuit, 1975b (1917), pp. 313-31.

Féron, Bernard "Le choléra envahit l'Empire des tsars", *Le Monde,* 17/18 mai 1992, p. 2.

Freund, Julien *Max Weber*. Paris: Presses Universitaires de France, 1969.

—. *Études sur Max Weber*, Genève: Droz, 1990.

Fukuyama, Francis *The Great Disruption: human nature and the reconstitution of the social order*, New York: Free Press, 1999.

Gereffi, Gary and Miguel Korzeniewicz (eds.) *Commodity Chains and Global Capitalism*. Westport, CT: Greenwood Press, 1994.

Gouldner, Alvin "Introduction," to Emile Durkheim, *Socialism and Saint-Simon*, Yellow Springs, Ohio: The Antioch Press, 1958, pp. v-xxix.

Halbwachs, Maurice *La classe ouvrière et les niveaux de vie: Recherches sur la hiérarchie des besoins dans les sociétés industrielles contemporaines: thèse pour le doctorat présentée à la Faculté des Lettres de l'Université de Paris*, Paris & New York: Gordon & Breach, 1970 (1912).

—. *L'Évolution des besoins dans les classes ouvrières*. Paris: Alcan, 1933.

—. *Collective Memory*, New York: Harper, 1975 (1950).

Inglehart, Ronald, Miguel Basañez and Alejandro Moreno, *Human Values and Beliefs a Cross-Cultural Sourcebook. Political, Religious, Sexual and Economic Norms in 43 Societies. Findings from the 1990-1993 World Values Survey,* Ann Arbor, MI: University of Michigan Press, 1998.

Lakatos, Imre "Falsification and the Methodology of Scientific Research Programmes," in Imre Lakatos and Alan Musgrave, eds, *Criticism and the Growth of Knowledge.* Cambridge: Cambridge University Press, 1970.

Levasseur, Émile *L'Ouvrier Américain. L'ouvrier au travail. L'ouvrier chez lui. Les Questions Ouvrières,* en 2 tomes. Paris: Librairie de la Société du Receuil Général des Lois et des Arrêts, 1898.

— *Histoire des classes ouvrières en France depuis la conquête de Jules César jusqu'à la Révolution.* Paris: Guillaumin, 1859. Second edition, 1900-1901 entitled: *Histoire des classes ouvrières et de l'industrie en France avant 1789.*

—. *Histoire des Classes Ouvrières et de l'Industrie en France de 1780 à 1870.* Paris: Arthur Rousseau. T. 1 1903, T. 2 1904.

—. *Questions Ouvrières et Industrielles en France sous la Troisième République* Paris: Arthur Rousseau, 1907.

Nandan, Yash *The Durkheimian School: a systematic and comprehensive bibliography,* Westport, CT: Greenwood Press, 1977.

Orrù, Marco *Anomie. History and Meanings.* Boston: Allen & Unwin, 1987.

Policar, Alain "Sociologie et morale: la philosophie de la solidarité de Célestin Bouglé", *Recherches Sociologiques*, 1997, 2: 85-110.

Saint-Simon, Henri *De la réorganisation de la société européennes* Paris: Les Presses françaises, 1925 (1814).

Segrestin, Denis "Sociologie du Travail," in Raymond Boudon, et. al., *Dictionnaire de la Sociologie*, Paris: Larousse, 1990, pp. 199-201.

Simiand, François *Le salaire des ouvriers des mines de charbon en France. Contribution à la théorie économique du salaire.* Paris: Société Nouvelle, 1903.

—. *Les fluctuations économiques à longue période et la crise mondiale.* Paris: Félix Alcan, 1932.

Stiglitz, Joseph A. *Globalization and Its Discontents.* New York: W.W. Norton, 2002.

Tiryakian, Edward A. "Durkheim, Solidarity, and September 11," pp. 305-21 in Jeffrey Alexander and Philip Smith, eds, *The Cambridge Companion to Durkheim.* Cambridge: Cambridge University Press, 2005.

Touraine, Alain, F. Dubet, M. Wievorka et J. Strzelecki, *Solidarité*, Paris: Arthème Fayard, 1982.

Chapter 7
Durkheim, Solidarity and September 11[1]

Introduction

Jeffrey Alexander (1987) has vigorously defended the centrality of the classics in the social sciences in opposition to a more "natural science" optic regarding the progress of a scientific discipline. It is part of the training of sociologists to internalize the classics (Alexander 1987: 20) as much as they internalize the methods and rules of evidence required to established empirical facts, which are the "stuff" of the natural sciences. The classics, thus, provide frames for finding, sensing, mapping the major dimensions of the social order (Wrong 1994).

To add to Alexander's discussion, I suggest that we see a two-way interaction between the classics and our contemporary situation. On the one hand, the classics are heuristic in sensitizing us to a broader view and broader search of social structures and patterns in our contemporary social world. They provide us with a "perspective" which may be otherwise missing simply because we may be so immersed in our situation as to be, in a certain sense, myopic of broader operative features. On the other hand, our contemporary situation may bring to light elements or dimensions that undergird the classic text, helping to understand (that is, to stand under) the text, ultimately, to bring out features of the text that may have remained obscure. Thus, to bring out a new understanding of our contemporary situation, to make sense of what might be otherwise an unwieldy set of data, and to make new sense of an accepted text is really a dialectical process of theorizing, from the past to the present and from the present to the past.

These remarks may be exemplified by taking as an ingress a well-trodden classic of Durkheim, *The Division of Labor in Society*. It was his doctoral dissertation, which unlike almost any doctoral dissertation that comes to mind, went through several editions in his lifetime and beyond,[2] and English translations of which have been widely available since 1933.[3] Further, to mark its centennial

---

1   Published in Jeffrey Alexander and Philip Smith, eds, *Cambridge Companion of Durkheim*. Cambridge and New York: Cambridge University Press, 2005.
2   The second edition (1902), published nearly ten years after the initial defense and therefore after two other classical treatises (*Suicide* and *Rules of the Sociological Method*), has the most important additions, notably a new introduction advocating the modernization of corporatism.
3   The George Simpson translation of 1933 did yeoman's duty for half a century, being replaced by the Halls translation of 1984, currently in paperback edition (Halls 1997).

in the preceding decade, collective works appeared on both sides of the Atlantic (Besnard et al. 1993; Tiryakian 1994).

In standard theory courses, students (at least in theory) become well-versed in certain themes which justify the classical status of this text: (1) That *The Division of Labor* was a devastating critique of utilitarian thought in arguing for the social embeddedness of economic institutions (Durkheim's refutation of Herbert Spencer's liberal individualism). (2) That the work provides a broad frame for the evolution of society from "simple, segmented" society organized by kin-based clans to increasingly more complex, more differentiated societies functionally integrated, i.e., made cohesive, by the division of labor that is at its most complex form in the modern industrial order. (3) That Durkheim made an ingenious use of the legal code to examine shifting proportions or the relative weight of restitutive (or civil) law that regulates relations between individual actors) and criminal law where the offense is against the State, which stands for the entire collectivity[4] (4) That Durkheim's functional analysis of modern society as an evolving, adaptive totality is tempered by a jarring analysis of the pathologies of the industrial order, making anomie a problematic condition of modernity. Durkheim sought a structural remedy for a structural malaise, namely the renovation of professional associations, something akin to craft unions but in a more corporatist image than the British trade union. (5) That Durkheim made use of a major conceptual dichotomy: mechanical and organic solidarity which is one of many such dichotomous pairing in classical sociology, along with Gemeinschaft and Gesellschaft,[5] capitalist and socialist, primary and secondary groups, "I" and "me", and so on.

"Mechanical" for Durkheim is the condition typical of early, segmentary, relatively homogeneous society when sentiments and beliefs are shared in common, where individuation is minimal and collective thinking is maximal; "organic" is the condition that becomes prevalent with demographic increases in the population producing a more differentiated population that becomes interdependent with an increase in the division of labor. Functional instead of kin relations become salient in establishing social cohesion via thick layers of functional interdependence, and for Durkheim, the modern division of labor tends to become a moral force in providing for social cohesion and allowing individualism to flourish, since our

---

4   Given Durkheim's argument that one cannot get directly at social bonds or social relationships, his invoking an objective social fact like the corpus of the legal code and changes over time in it, this was a pioneering effort in developing social indicators (Land 2000).

5   Durkheim in the course of his fellowship study of German social scientists had come across Tönnies and published in 1889 a review of *Gemeinschaft und Gesellschaft* that had appeared two years earlier. The review gives the reader a good view of the treatise, and faults the author for an undocumented bias shown towards the small-scale, traditional society of the *Gemeinschaft* kind. Durkheim closes by affirming that modern complex society is also "organic" but that a book examining the evolution of *Gesellschaft* through laws and customs would be necessary to demonstrate this (Durkheim 1975: 390). Neither the review nor the treatise itself used "solidarity".

individuality is given so many options in the modern occupational structure. Other themes might be adduced but it would not serve the purpose of this essay to draw them out.

It is the last named theme above that retains attention. As the editors of one the commemorative works laconically stated it, "the notions of 'mechanical solidarity' and 'organic solidarity' are undoubtedly what one retains of *The Division of Labor in Society* when one has forgotten everything else (or when one has learned little from it)." (Besnard et al.1993: 3).

The objective of this essay is to take this very old familiar pair of concepts and apply it to a totally new setting, that of post-September 11. My argument here is that "mechanical" and "organic solidarity" have had and continue to have new manifestations in America and globally. I also wish to take what happened, or rather some of the consequences of the aftermath of September 11,[6] to link us back to Durkheim's societal setting, something which exegetes of classics frequently neglect. In sum, it is the *actuality* of the classic that I hope will emerge from this study. That seems to me the way to make students feel that a classic text is, in keeping with this volume's title, a *companion*.

II

If Durkheim never defines "solidarity" [see the excellent overview of Durkheim in Bellah (1973)], this should not be construed as an intentional theoretical disregard on his part. The question of solidarity was close to his preoccupations both as a sociologist and as an active member of French society during his whole lifetime. It went well beyond his explicit treatment of "mechanical" and "organic solidarity", even if he discarded this pair of concepts after the dissertation. The preoccupation with "solidarity" can be discerned in his two following substantive studies, *Suicide* and *The Elementary Forms of the Religious Life* (hereafter, *Elementary Forms*). While displaying his sociological virtuosity of analysis, close to the surface of each is Durkheim pointing to the significance of the social ties of solidarity , in giving meaning to the life of social actors, in renovating and providing a foyer for social ideals and values. At the core of his message is this: solidarity, our

---

6 Consequences of a world historical event such as "September 11" continue to unfold in the historical process. In this instance, the counteractions of the American government together with the domestic and international repercussions of the terrorist attack on New York and Washington, will continue to unfold for an indefinite period. This is accentuated by a declared "war on terrorism" having no territorial boundary.

However, the implicit time frame for this essay is narrower: my focus is the reactions to the September 11 morning attacks from that fateful morning to the beginning of the American bombardment of Taliban Afghanistan a month later. Following Van Gennep and Victor Turner, this was essentially a "liminal period", in this case, between "normalcy" and "wartime".

attachment and ties to others,[7] is the founding, the source of morality (Miller 1996: 150; Jones 2001: 97).

If we bring together Durkheim's discussion of "organic solidarity" as an aspect of modernity with his discussion of types of suicide, we can draw as an inference what sort of solidarity he saw early in his career as desirable for individuals and for modern society. It is a rich network of social ties, beyond the kinship network, that are freely entered into and developed by social actors; such social ties are both pleasurable and are also sources of obligations voluntarily accepted. The relations I have with my co-workers [to invoke Benedict Anderson, with not only my fellow workers here-and-now but also with my "imagined community" (Anderson 1991)] are, in Durkheim's treatment of *Suicide*, anchors without which individuals may drift into the *néant* of egoistic or anomic suicide. To be sure, the social ties, in the form of normative demands of the group for its survival, even at the expense of the individual actor, may be more *chains* than anchor. This extreme form of solidarity has its pathological instance in "altruistic"suicide: the latter might be viewed as prototypical of the small tight-knit group of "mechanical solidarity".[8]

Solidarity is equally an important underlying aspect of his later *magnus opus, The Elementary Forms of Religious Life*. Recall that in his definitional gambit of the phenomenon, he underscores not only the twin components of the sacred (beliefs and practices set apart) but also that these are constitutive of *"one single moral community called a Church, all those who adhere to them"*. To make sure the reader does not miss the emphasis, Durkheim adds in the next breath, "The second element thus holds a place in my definition that is no less essential than the first. In showing that the idea of religion is inseparable from the idea of a Church, it conveys the notion that religion must be an eminently collective thing," (Durkheim 1995: 44).

If a major aspect of his monumental study is, broadly speaking, to establish the sociology of knowledge by an in-depth analysis of primitive totemism, the concern with the real social world of the modern present is never far away. In the concluding chapter he evokes the collective enthusiasm of the French Revolution and anticipates "hours of creative effervescence during which new ideals will again spring forth" (1995: 429); his following discussion arguing for a new symbiosis of religion and science – with the authority of science as unquestioned, to be sure – situates him as an advocate of a sociologically enriched "Project of the Enlightenment".[9] One can read Elementary Forms as a sociological critique

---

7   Sociologically, "others", following Comte, would be not only those of our generation but also those of previous and future generations.

8   Although Durkheim's own treatment of "altruistic suicide" suggests it is a form associated with archaic or pre-modern forms of organization, this does not mean they have disappeared from the contemporary scene. I have discussed this in reference to the plethora of "suicide-bombers" (Tiryakian 2002).

9   I follow Holub's discussion of Habermas taking that "project", identical with the project of modernity, as both promoting the rationalization of the spheres of science and

of reason, and it is that. For the present discussion, solidarity is an important part of that critique. The cognitive development of mankind, rationication, thinking and acting morally – all these aspects of a higher, impersonal life that can be attained by individuals and which Kant, the philosopher of the Enlightenment had grasped – could not take place without solidarity. Or as Durkheim stated it,

> Collective thought is possible only through the coming together of individuals ... The realm of impersonal aims and truths cannot be realized except through the collaboration of individual wills and sensibilities. (1995: 447).

While *Elementary Forms* is undoubtedly a seminal work, in the context of discussing solidarity I do not read it as anything final. Turning to religion as a social phenomenon intimately connected to the deep structures of society, Durkheim was pointing to the incompleteness of "organic solidarity" in the occupational sphere in providing for moral integration of modern society. Even if the "pathologies" of the modern division of labor were substantially reduced – for example, by minimizing social inequalities that prevent some from participating in the labor market to the fuller extent of their ability – would this suffice? Durkheim , sociologist and moralist, was looking for broader bases than professional and occupational associations, which after all are still in the realm of the *profane*, however that profane is enriched beyond the interests of the market place. The religious life tapped at aspects of the *sacred*, especially beliefs and rituals in Bellah (1973), which, free of coercion, bind together an entire society.

The question that remains when one finishes *Elementary Forms* is: can the moments of "collective effervescence" regenerative of societal solidarity occur in the modern world, and under what circumstances? For a believer in democracy like Durkheim, it might well be the historic night of August 4, 1789 when the National Constituent Assembly eliminated feudal privileges, paving the way for the egalitarian ideals of the Rights of Man. [10] It would *not* have been, for Durkheim,

---

morality (and also of art) and releasing "the creative potentials of each of these domains" (Holub 1991: 136). The "Project of the Enlightenment" as seeking an accumulation of positive knowledge of the spheres of science, religion and the aesthetic to provide a richer and more fully rational organization of the "life-world" is a key theme in Habermas (1989).

10   See the poignant passage in the Conclusion of *The Forms* (1995: 429f). Alternatively, Durkheim might have evoked the solidarity generated at the spectacular mass funeral procession to the Pantheon of Victor Hugo, poet, national hero and icon of democratic republicanism, in 1885; or perhaps, to the effervescence aroused in the confrontations between the Dreyfussards and the anti-Dreyfussards in Paris in the late 1890s at the time of the retrial of Captain Dreyfuss. More modern settings of collective effervescence that would have drawn Durkheim's sociological attention as sites of possible progressive renewal of collective ideals and aspirations could well include, appropriately enough, the *Solidarność* movement in Gdansk and elsewhere in Poland in 1980-81, and, in his own Sorbonne backyard, the student movement of May 1968. Since Durkheim gave

Berlin in February 1933 and the burning of the Reichstag, but in retrospect, modernity gives no assurance as to which or some other form of effervescence might take place. In the few years that remained to Durkheim after *The Forms*, there was an unexpected "happening" that relates to and even completes his quest for solidarity albeit he did not write a monograph about it. But before presenting it, *and relating this to "September 11"*, we need to contextualize Durkheim's treatment of solidarity.

III

However much we see today Durkheim as a "theorist" of society, which indeed he was, we need keep in mind that he was very much a social actor of turn-of-century France, interested in questions and problems of his day, as any contemporary sociologist might well be, however the settings may differ. Durkheim was not the only one who made much of the question of solidarity; other prominent figures addressed the very same theme, so much so that it might almost be considered the key social philosophy of the Third Republic in the 1890s and first decade of the new century. Moreover, it has continued to have appeal in France today.[11]

Around the turn of the last century, the political figure (head of the centrist l0 Radical-Socialist Party), and future Nobel Peace Prize winner Léon Bourgeois articulated the idea of solidarity as social justice in economic exchanges, without which violence and frustration ensues. The same year as the publication of Durkheim's revised edition of *The Division of Labor*, Bourgeois mentioned in his preface to the third edition that "solidarity" had become tantamount to "fraternity" in the republican discourse (1902:6). Cognizant of the need to rise above political cleavages and acrimony between liberal economists and socialists, Bourgeois saw appeal to solidarity as establishing common social bonds between contentious factions. He proposed that solidarity

> is the study of the exact causes, of the conditions and the limits of this solidarity, which only can give the measure of the rights and obligations of each towards all and of all towards each, and which will assure the scientific and moral conclusions of the social problem. (Bourgeois 1902: 15).

---

year-long courses on "pragmatism" and "socialism" in response to students' interest in these movements, one can envision Durkheim giving a course on the student movement in the wake of 1968.

11   Since 1997 solidarity has entered into official governmental recognition as a cabinet position in the important *Ministère de l'Emploi et de la Solidarité,* charged among other tasks with caring for the unemployed and with fighting racial and ethnic discrimination.

The above might well be taken as a mission statement for Durkheim's mature conception of sociology. And it is hard to say that it is not Durkheim writing some pages later,

> Let us not be surprised if at present all our institutions, all legislation is questioned. The moral and social malaise from which we suffer is but the clash between certain political, economic and social institutions and the moral ideas that the progress of human thoughthave slowly transformed (Bourgeois 1902: 77).

As social philosophy, then, solidarism[12] sought a union of morality and the social sciences in refashioning the social world, an extension of the democratic ideas of the Enlightenment. At the prestigious *Ecole des Hautes Etudes Sociales* during the academic year 1901-02 Bourgeois and Dean of the Faculty Alfred Croiset organized a series of colloquia in Paris on the theme of solidarity, with a volume of proceedings appearing a few years later (Bourgeois and Croiset 1907). The speakers were a distinguished group of public figures, including Durkheim's teacher and influential philosopher Emile Boutroux, Ferdinand Buisson at the University of Paris (whose chair Durkheim occupied in 1906 when Buisson became a cabinet minister), Xavier Léon (director of the *Revue de Métaphysique et de Morale* in which Durkheim published some key essays) and other intellectual notables.

For whatever reason, Durkheim does not appear to have given a colloquium on the topic, since he was not in the list of volume contributors. Yet the volume has clear reference to sociology. Croiset in his preface indicated that solidarity "is a socialist idea drawn from the nineteenth Century which takes society, the collectivity... as a special object of study... that becomes sociology," (Bourgeois and Croiset 1907: viii). And in his presentation, Alphonse Darlu (who taught Marcel Proust in his philosophy course at the *Lycée Condorcet*) pointed out that as the guiding principle of contemporary philosophy "the idea of solidarity is a social idea, one can even say a sociological one," (Bourgeois and Croiset: 129).

While approving that solidarity is a new, positive ethical doctrine that encourages social activism, Darlu went on to question those strict sociologists like *Espinas and Durkheim* who take society to be an end in itself (Bourgeois and Croiset 1907: 129n, my emphasis). Darlu, Bourgeois, and the others in this volume took their distance from an overdetermination of morality by sociology, at least in their upholding of the individual as both a social agent and as an autonomous moral agent. Still, there was a lot of consensual overlap between them and Durkheim, especially if one were to compare these to either liberal economic individualism, on the one hand, or the Marxist collectivism, on the other.

---

12   In the mainstream of social democratic thought, I would argue that *solidarism*, which may sound quaint to contemporary ears, is very proximate to Amitai Etzioni's *communitarianism* (Etzioni 2000) and Anthony Gidden's *Third Way* (1998).

In the background of the salient discourse of solidarity, I would propose, were some harsh social realities of France, some peculiar to the country, some shared with other advanced industrial societies. However prosperous and affluent France had become at century's end with industrialization, the image of *La Belle Époque* that we may gather from movies about the period or a hurried look at the exuberant art of Impressionism and post-Impressionism is misleading. There were severe political and cultural strains and widening socioeconomic inequalities:

> At the beginning of the 20th Century, France seemed not only divided, but threatened with internal conflicts, some of which had already erupted. It was at the same time a prosperous country ... but also [one] of the excluded (Félix 1991: 166).

> Whatever else it was, the Belle Epoque was a fine time for ferments, flare-ups, disorders, rampages, riots, turbulence,tumults, barricades, and bloodshed. (Weber 1986: 128).

In retrospect, the most patent but not sole social conflict of the period was the trial in the 1890s of a Jewish military captain accused and convicted of passing defense secrets to Germany. The ensuing "Dreyfus affair" rocked France and pointed to various fault lines, with massive street demonstrations and ultimate polarization that brought to a head simmering boils between various social factions. Many of the military high command had Catholic loyalties that clashed with the republican regime's anticlerical outlook (especially regarding control over education), while republicans were nervous that another military coup might take place like the aborted one by General Boulanger in the preceding decade.[13] Ultimately, Dreyfus was shown to have been framed and finally released; although his vindication was a triumph for the civilian republican regime and particularly for the academic intellectuals of the left, the political scars were not healed for the remaining years of the Third Republic.[14]

However gripping and ultimately a triumph for liberal democracy was the Dreyfus affair, there were other serious cleavages in the social fabric. If Durkheim talked about *anarchy* in the same breath as *anomie* in the preface to the second edition (1997: xxxiii), it was a reflection of the real presence in France and other

---

13   It might be noted that three quarters of a century after Boulanger another military coup in France was narrowly averted at the end of the Algerian War when De Gaulle came out of retirement in time to lead the country out of the morass of the Fourth Republic and into a more modernized Fifth Repbulic.

14   Hubert Bourgin, an alumnus of the prestigious École Normale Supérieure and who in his younger years had been a member of the *Année Sociologique* team, bitterly complained in his memoirs of the politicization of French higher education, especially at the hands of "philosophers of anarchy". He does, however, provide an intimate and respectful look at Durkheim (Bourgin 1938).

countries such as Spain and Russia of anarchism as a movement of individual terrorist acts, a cult of violence. The cult appealed to avant-garde artists – much as it seemingly does today to "punk" and other artists – and in its more extreme forms translated into assassinations of heads of state, including President Carnot of France and President McKinley of the United States.[15]

Anarchism/anomie fed on severe economic malaise, ranging from a variety of financial scandals and stock swindles, to serious discontent in the working class and marginalized agricultural producers; class divisions hardened with the syndicalist movement and following violent strikes, the formation the militant *Confédération Générale du Travail* (CGT) in 1895, and subsequently the launching of the Socialist Party in 1905 headed by Jean Jaurès (Félix 1991: 165). The latter had cordial ties with Durkheim as a fellow *Normalien* and as a fellow militant on behalf of exonerating Dreyfus.

Internal conflicts and growing external conflicts with Germany[16] were very much part of the pre-war scene in France. French political life reflected this, with a polarization between those favoring taking a hard line against Germany and those seeking accommodation in order to attend to internal social (especially labor) problems. Ultimately, what came to dominate the scene were the war clouds. In July 1914 Jaurès got the Socialist Party to accept staging a general strike against war and sought a repeal of the military draft; two weeks later he was assassinated by a young fanatic who felt Jaurès was a traitor, playing in the hands of Germany (Favier 1987: 1025). This and the war on France declared by Germany at the beginning of August marked a new type of solidarity, one that was not analyzed in *The Division of Labor*, but one which Durkheim was to experience along with his fellow citizens, *national solidarity*. I draw attention to it not only because it is an additional dimension of the concept of solidarity in relation to Durkheim's France but also because the circumstances of its manifestation in 1914 have some interesting structural similarities with the post September 11 United States.

IV

The assassination on July 31, 1914, of Jean Jaurès, the charismatic socialist leader who had earlier that month got at the Socialist Party Congress a motion passed to have a general strike in opposition to any war, was followed by Germany's

---

15   For a succinct discussion, see "anarchism," *Encyclopedia Brittanica Online.* <http:search.eb.com/bol/topic?eu=127633&sctn=6>.

16   The conflict with Germany was twofold: conservatives in France were bent on restoring the "lost territories" of Alsace and Lorraine which Germany had taken as an outcome of its victorious war in 1870, and a new German imperialism sought claims to Morocco, which France considered under its sphere of influence.

declaration of war on France the following Monday.[17] The twin attacks produced an unprecedented wave of solidarity that adds an important chapter to Durkheim's analysis of social integration. On Tuesday morning, August 4th, the public funeral of Jaurès drew a large, emotional, bipartisan crowd. The secretary of the CGT, Léon Jouhaux, who shortly before advocated opposition to war and the three-year draft, announced he was in total support of resisting the aggressors; the president of the Chamber of Deputies declared that foes and friends alike of Jaurès had been struck by the assassination: there were no longer foes in France, only Frenchmen "ready to make sacrifices for the holiest of causes: the salvation of civilization," (Fèlix 1991: 10). And the grand climax of that day was a presidential message read to the hushed Chamber of Deputies that afternoon, a message that read in part

> France represents again today before the world freedom, justice and reason...
> She will be heroically defended by all its sons for whom in front of the enemy
> nothing will break the sacred union (Félix 1991: 171).[18]

A "collective effervescence" ensued, in the Chamber and in the country in general. In the Chamber, after the message closing with "Lift up your hearts and vive la France!", the legislators in a heightened state of emotion fell into each other's arms, including two on opposite sides of the bench who had not spoken to each other in over 40 years (Félix, ibid). Across the country the center of republican France was joined in the union sacrée with the marginals of the periphery: pacifists, revolutionary syndicalists, farmers, and even the staunch foe of the regime, priests, 5000 of whom were killed in World War I out of 45000 drafted (Félix 1991: 174). Durkheim had, of course, not anticipated the conditions that gave rise to national solidarity, nor in the brief time that remained to him did he have the leisure and the occasion to theorize this extraordinary and rare form of solidarity. Durkheim himself, like all his countrymen, whether of the left, the center, or the right, religious or secular, experienced national solidarity. Too old to volunteer, he used his talents as an intellectual to assist the war effort in writing pieces destined to influence a yet neutral America as to where lay the aggression behind the greatest bloodshed in history (Durkheim 1915; Durkheim and Denis 1915).

---

17   For a detailed chronology of the ante bellum period and thereafter, see Favier (1987).

18   In his presidential memoirs, Poincaré relates the pregnant phrase *union sacrée* to the ancient Greeks opting to die together in indissoluble friendship to defend the Temple of Delphi (1927: 541).

V

Fast forward to September 2001. The United States had less than a year before engaged in one of the most acrimonious presidential election recorded, with just about half of the voters feeling they had been cheated by a judicial but not judicious decision of the Supreme Court. The outgoing administration, despite notable domestic achievements, had been tainted by ethical and other breaches of conduct. The racial gulf between whites and blacks, despite all the socioeconomic improvement of African-Americans stemming from the civil rights movement, was still patent. Republicans and Democrats sought to wrestle control of the other chamber, one hanging on to the House, the other with the help of a defection having barely gained control of the Senate. And after what seemed in retrospect the good times of the 1990s, the country (along with the world economy) was in an economic downturn with significant layoffs in employment. I bring this out to suggest that, structurally speaking, *the United States on the eve of September 11 was similar to the situation of France in 1914.*

The startling attack on the World Trade Center and the Pentagon produced, to be sure, enormous damages, physical and psychological. But, for the purpose of this paper, it also produced a massive national solidarity. The president of the United States, George W. Bush, became transfigured from a minority president to a wartime leader with the highest public opinion support recorded in American poll history. The theme of national unity from the start was recurrent in speeches made by the White House, similar to the messages of Poincaré to the Chamber of Deputies and to his countrymen. The following are illustrative:[19]

> This is a day when all Americans from every walk of life unite in our resolve for justice and peace. (September 11, address to the Nation).

> Today, we feel what Franklin Roosevelt called the warm courage of national unity. This is a unity of every faith, and every background. (September 14, remarks at National Day of Prayer and Remembrance).

> All of America was touched on the evening of the tragedy to see Republicans and Democrats joined together on the steps of this Capitol, singing "God Bless America." (September 20, address to a joint session of Congress).

And just as the president of the Chamber of Deputies in 1914 appealed to national unity for the holiest of causes, the salvation of civilization, so "civilization", previously tarnished by academic controversies around multiculturalism (Taylor and Gutman 1994; Jopke and Lukes 1999), was extolled as that separating good from evil, the just from evildoers:

---

19   All the following may be located at http://web.archive.org/web/20010911-20011201*/www.whitehouse.gov/

> Civilized people around the world denounce the evildoers who devised and
> executed these terrible attacks (September 13 Proclamation of a National Day of
> Prayer and Remembrance).

> This is not, however, just America's fight ... This is the world's fight. This is
> civilization's fight. This is the fight of all who believe in progress and pluralism,
> tolerance and freedom ... The civilized world is rallying to America's side.
> (September 20. Address to a joint session of Congress.)

In the aftermath of September 11, President Bush may be taken as a "collective
representation", to use Durkheimian terminology, of American sentiments of
national solidarity combined with the desire for resistance and retaliation to
perceived wanton aggression. The solidarity was enhanced by nationwide sharing
of heroes – the firefighters and police who gave their lives to rescue lives at "ground
zero" in New York City—and by symbols of oneness: the ubiquitous display of the
American flag, the singing of "God bless America", and so on.[20]

National solidarity, however, is insufficient to broaden our conceptual horizon.
In recognition of the profound interlacing of the world from various processes of
globalization, it is relevant to view "September 11" as having generated *global
solidarity*. Because of television, to paraphrase Gitlin (1980), literally "the whole
world was watching" when the second plane, United flight 175, rammed into the
second World Trade Center tower. The devastating attack on a pillar of modernity
did produce on a global basis an unprecedented feeling of horror and sympathy.
When President Bush proclaimed on September 13 that the following day be a
National Day of Prayer and Remembrance and asked the American people to
mark the day at noontime with memorial services, he did not anticipate that this
would be observed in other countries, Western and non-Western. Remarking on
this outpouring of solidarity, he later told Congress

> I want to thank the world for its outpouring of support. America will never forget
> the sounds of our National Anthem playing at Buckingham Palace, on the streets
> of Paris, and at Berlin's Brandenburg Gate.
>   We will not forget South Korean children gathering to pray outside our
> embassy in Seoul, or the prayers of sympathy offered at a mosque in Cairo ...
> (September 20, Address to a joint session of Congress).

Of course, in the same address, the President not only humbly acknowledged his
country receiving global solidarity, he also forcefully requested it:

---

20   I have discussed elsewhere (Tiryakian 2005) related aspects of September 11 in
terms of Durkheim's *Elementary Forms*.

Every nation, in every region, now has a decision to make, either you are with us, or you are with terrorists. From this day forward, any nation that continues to harbor or support terrorism will be regarded by the United States as a hostile regime.

VI

"September 11" offers supplementary materials for the pertinence of "mechanical" and "organic", not as static but as dynamic concepts of modernity. Recall that in *The Division of Labor* (Book One, chapter two) Durkheim broaches the discussion of mechanical solidarity by discussing the strong collective feelings generated in reaction to a crime:

> As for the social character of the reaction, this derives from the social nature of the sentiments offended. Because these are to be found in every individual consciousness the wrong done arouses among all who witness it or who know of its existence the same indignation. All are affected by it; consequently everyone stiffens himself against the attack. (Durkheim 1997: 57).

One can venture that far from "mechanical solidarity" being peculiar to pre-modern, pre-industrial society,[21] it was certainly reactivated in the United States during and after September 11. All segments of the population, all regions of the country felt the attack on the World Trade Center and on the Pentagon was an attack against the American people, a crime of violence which made all segments realize what they shared as Americans. The American flag became a renewed symbol of collective identity, displayed in churches, on lapels, on cars; the pledge of allegiance to it, which had been contested by some organizations, reentered the public sphere. This renewed mechanical solidarity was carried out by very much in a religious framework that underlies Durkheim's *Elementary Forms*: beliefs and rituals reaffirming the sacredness of the collectivity (and the presidential addresses are replete with religious imagery, including invoking a "crusade" against the criminal terrorists in the world).

Of course, there is a dark side to mechanical solidarity. For in highlighting what the collectivity has in common with each other in the way of beliefs and practices, it may set up compartments that lead to the exclusion of those who are deemed outsiders. For many years, the United States had had violent confrontations outside its borders with Arabic/Islamic nations (notably Libya, Sudan, Iraq, Iran) and the theme of an Islamic "jihad" against the West had gained currency (Barber 1996; Huntington 1996). The attack on the United States and the pointing of finger

---

21   Elsewhere (Tiryakian 1994) I have alluded to the lure of mechanical solidarity in modern society at various levels, for example in invoking ethnic, racial or gender solidarity.

to an Islamic-inspired terrorist organization could easily have provoked a mass vengeance on the Arab-Islamic population in the United States. A heightened emphasis of being a "we" can generate an equally strong vilification of a "they" as outsiders, perhaps even more so in a Puritan culture which tends to differentiate between "saints" and the "wretched". The actions of the government toward the Muslim-Arab population in the United States has been equivocal. On the one hand, there has been by both the public and the private sector (especially the churches) professions and actions of inclusion toward Islam as a "peaceful" religion that is a valued part of American religious pluralism.[22] On the other hand, government surveillance of persons of Arabic names and descent, including students in the United States from Arabic countries has been widely reported.

Finally, one other dimension of September 11 that merits attention is an *enhanced organic solidarity*. It may be seen as global solidarity at the micro level. Let me cite from personal experience. Shortly after September 11, I received e-mails from sociologists I know around the world, from such countries as France, Germany, Macedonia, Italy, Japan and China, among others. They were spontaneously expressing messages of condolence, sympathy, and solidarity with our entire nation, and they saw me as a nexus to the American people because we were fellow sociologists. I have checked with colleagues in other disciplines and found that the same phenomenon has happened to them, namely, spontaneous messages of support and sympathy from their counterpart around the world. I don't know whether Durkheim in August 1914 received telegrams from American sociologists when France was overrun by Germany. I am sure he would have seen these messages as an important extension of his concept of organic solidarity as a reflection of globalization, and Durkheim would surely have been interested in making a comparative study of these e-mails of solidarity as important new "social facts" of our advanced modernity.

The expression of ties of solidarity, whether mechanical, organic, national or global, in line with Durkheim's seminal analysis, is basic to social integration. There are two sides to this, a dualism rooted in the human social condition. One aspect is that solidarity is an *expressive* relationship between social actors, an expression of a deep togetherness, of a shared, intrinsically shared "we". As discussed above in relation to September 11, this aspect is powerful in dissolving the social compartments that separate actors in the everyday life. The other aspect is that expressing solidarity may also cloak an *instrumental* utilization of others: asking others to make sacrifices since we are *together* may be to promote *my* rather than *our* ends.

---

22   It is interesting to note two months after September 11 the U.S. Postal service issued a 33-cent stamp commemorating in *Arabic calligraphy* the Islamic Eid festivals in honor of Ramadan. American bombardment of the Taliban in Afghanistan were not suspended during Ramadan, however.

References

Alexander, Jeffrey 1987. "The Centrality of the Classics," pp. 11-57 in Anthony Giddens and Jonathan H.Turner, eds. *Social Theory Today*. Stanford: Stanford University Press.

Barber, Benjamin R. 1996. *Jihad vs. McWorld. How Globalism and Tribalism are Reshaping the World*. New York: Times Books.

Bellah, Robert N. 1973. "Introduction," pp. ix-lv to *Emile Durkheim, On Morality and Society*. Chicago: University of Chicago Press. Heritage of Sociology series.

Besnard, Philippe, Massimo Borlandi et Paul Vogt 1993. *Division du Travail et Lien Social. La thèse de Durkheim un siècle après*. Paris: Presses Universitaires de France.

Bourgeois, Léon. 1902. *Solidarité,* 3rd ed. Paris: Librairie Armand Colin.

Bourgeois, Léon et Alfred Croiset (eds) *Essai d'une philosophie de la Solidarité*, 2nd ed. Paris: Félix Alcan.

Bourgin, Hubert 1938. *De Jaurès à Léon Blum. L'École Normale et la Politique.* Paris: Arthème Fayard.

Daniel-Rops, Henri 1966 (1963). *A Fight for God* 1870-1939, J. Warrington, trans. London: J.M. Dent & Sons; New York: E. P. Dutton.

Durkheim, Emile 1915. *"Germany above All": German Mentality and War*. Paris: A. Colin.

—. 1975. (1889). "Communauté et Société selon Tönnies." pp. 383-90 in Durkheim, Textes. 1. *Èléments d'une théorie sociale*, Victor Karady, ed. Paris: Editions de Minuit.

—. 1997 (1893). *The Division of Labor in Society*. W.D. Halls, trans., with an Introduction by Lewis Coser. New York: Free Press/ Simon & Schuster

—. 1995 (1912). *The Elementary Forms of the Religious Life*, translated and edited by Karen. E. Fields. New York: Free Press.

Durkheim, Emile and E. Denis 1915. *Who Wanted War? The Origins of the War According to Diplomatic Documents*, A.M. Wilson-Garinei, trans. Paris: A. Colin.

Etzioni, Amitai 2000. *The Third Way to a Good Society*. London: Demos.

Favier, Jean, et al. 1987. *Chronique de la France et des Français*. Paris: Larousse/ Editions Jacques Legrand.

Félix, Christian 1991. *Alsace-Lorraine et Union Sacrée*. Ecully (France): Horvath.

Giddens, Anthony 1998. *The Third Way: the Renewal of Social Democracy*. Cambridge: Polity Press; Malden, MA: Blackwell Publishers.

Gitlin, Todd 1980. *The Whole World is Watching: Mass Media in the Making and Unmaking of the New Left*. Berkeley: University of California Press.

Holub, Robert C. 1991. *Jürgen Habermas. Critic in the Public Sphere*. London & New York: Routledge.

Huntington, Samuel P. 1996. *The Clash of Civilizations and the Remaking of World Order*. New York: Simon & Schuster.

Jones, Susan Stedman 2001. *Durkheim Reconsidered*. Malden, MA: Blackwell.

Joppke, Christian and Steven Lukes 1999. *Multicultural Questions*. Oxford: Oxford University Press.

Land, Kenneth C. 2000. "Social Indicators." pp. 2682-90 in *Encyclopedia of Sociology*, rev. ed., Edgar F. Borgatta and Rhonda V. Montgomery, eds. New York: Macmillan.

Miller, W. Watts 1996. *Durkheim, Morals and Modernity*. Montreal & Kingston: McGill-Queen's University Press.

Poincaré, Raymond 1927. *Au service de la France*. v. IV: *L'Union Sacrée 1914*. Paris: Plon.

Taylor, Charles and Amy Gutman, eds 1994. *Multiculturalism*. Princeton: Princeton University Press.

Tiryakian, Edward A., ed. 1994. "The 100th Anniversary of Durkheim's *Division of Labor in Society" Sociological Forum*, 9, no. 1 (March).

—. 2005. "Three Levels of Teaching Durkheim," in Terry F. Godlove, ed., *Teaching Durkheim on Religion*. New York: Oxford University Press.

Weber, Eugen 1959. *The Nationalist Revival in France*, 1905-1914. Berkeley: University of California Press.

—. 1986. *France, Fin de Siècle*. Cambridge, MA & London: Belknap/Harvard University Press.

Wrong, Dennis H. 1994. *The Problem of Order: what unites and divides society*. New York: Free Press.

PART 2
Durkheim and Cultural Change

Chapter 8

Contextualizing the Emergence of Modern Sociology: The Durkheimian School in Search of Bygone Society[1]

... religious, judicial, moral and economic facts should be treated consistent with their nature, i.e. as social facts. To either describe or explain them, they have to be contextualized within a certain social milieu, a certain type of society, and it is in the specific characters of this type that one seeks the determinant causes of the phenomenon under consideration. Emile Durkheim, Preface to *L'Année sociologique* II 1897–1898, p. 11.

For several decades, sociology has become a topic of study for sociologists of knowledge.[2] This, together with the renewal of a sociological interest for historical studies on the one hand and for Emile Durkheim[3] on the other, seems to weigh in favor of a detailed examination of the socio-intellectual community which formed around its leader and remained in the avant-garde of French sociology 40 years.[4] A fruitful way of approaching the Durkheimian School would be to treat it in a

---

1   Revised version of "L'École Durkheimienne à la recherche du temps perdu: La sociologie naissante et son milieu culturel,", *Cahiers Internationaux de Sociologie*, 66 (Janvier-Juin 1979): 97-114.

2   Robert Friedrichs, *A Sociology of Sociology*, New York, Free Press, 1970; Alvin Gouldner, *The Coming Crisis of Western Sociology*, New York, Basic Books, 1970; Edward Tiryakian (ed.), *The Phenomenon of Sociology*, New York, Appleton-Century-Crofts, 1971; Larry T. and Janice M. Reynolds (eds.), *The Sociology of Sociology*, New York, McKay, 1970.

3   Dominick La Capra, *Emile Durkheim*, Ithaca, NY, Cornell University Press, 1972; Ernest Wallwork, *Durkheim*, Cambridge, Harvard University Press, 1972; Steven Lukes, *Emile Durkheim, His Life and Work*, New York, Harper & Row, 1972; and the collective work *Regarding Durkheim*, special number of the *Revue française de Sociologie*, 17, April-June 1976; the thesis of Yash Nandan, *The Durkheimian School and its Work*, Paris, Microeditions du CNRS, 1975 and the bibliography by the same author, *The Durkheimian School*, Westport, Conn., Greenwood Press, 1977. This School is the subject of a special number in the *Revue française de Sociologie*, "Les Durkheimiens", January-March 1979, vol 20 (1).

4   For an important collective volume published subsequently to the present article, which covers some of the ground here, see Philippe Besnard, ed. *The Sociological Domain. The Durkheimians and the founding of French sociology.* Cambridge and New York:

Durkheimian fashion, i.e. as a social phenomenon, hence the lead citation of this article.

To examine this School as a social phenomenon means that it will not suffice merely to analyze its role in the history of sociological thought. Neither will it suffice to understand how the central ideas of the Durkheiminan paradigm and the formulation which its leader gave them in his writings and teachings, have been used by members of his entourage in their research, their dissertations, their monographs, their courses, etc. It goes without saying that this is a critical task in the presentation of the unity and the specificity of the School. However, the links, which form the structure of a school[5] bring out levels other than the obviously intellectual ones. As Durkheim recognized, the construction of a social fact must be viewed through its social context. This precept, or rule, corresponds to the precept in gestalt psychology of *form,* in which a perceived object is seen as a totality in the intrinsic relationship of the figure and its background. In other words, a social phenomenon is framed by its social context.

A sociological analysis of the Durkheimian School must therefore take into account the creation and development of this School in the context of its societal environment, the French Third Republic (1871-1940) since the existence of the School coincided with the struggles, victories and decline of the latter. Conversely, we could well imagine the School as a door opening to the "total societal phenomenon" (to adapt a key concept from Marcel Mauss's *The Gift*) of French society during the Third Republic, thereby via this specific phenomenon accessing the economic, political, and cultural dimensions of society as a whole. More broadly, this may well be then the ultimate justification for sociology: viewing sociology as a subject of sociological research could open a new approach to its societal context, while at the same time the study of the societal context is necessary to highlight the structures of sociology. This would be an important contribution to a "reflexive sociology". But *which* "social context" should be chosen to understand the Durkheimian group in a sociological way is a complex question, since there are, in fact, multiple contexts.

Multiple Contexts of the School: Academic, Economic and Political

Firstly, the professional context, which may be called, in the tradition of Claude Bernard, the "internal context" (*milieu interne*). We might therefore examine the Durkheimians in the context of the different dimensions of the university

---

Cambridge University Press; Paris: Editions de la Maison des Sciences de l'Homme, 1983.

5   See my study, The Significance of Schools in the Development of Sociology, pp. 211-33 in William E. Snizek, Michael K Miller and Ellsworth R Fuhrman (eds), *Contemporary Issues in Theory and Research: A Metasociological Perspective*, Westport, Conn, Greenwood Press, 1979.

and intellectual environment: the modernization of French academia during the 1880s and 1890s;[6] the academic structures which provided openings for the Durkheimians (e.g., Section V of the École Pratique des Hautes Etudes en Sciences Sociales, EPHESS); the École Normale Supérieure, which after it was joined with the Sorbonne in 1904 became an important recruitment center for Durkheimians.[7] Also part of this context were the journals and their editors which provided a forum for the School such as the *Revue de Métaphysique et de Morale*, with Xavier Léon who, furthermore, played an important role in the creation of the French Philosophical Society, in which Durkheim and several of his colleagues, such as Parodi and Bouglé, participated; and equally supportive was Félix Alcan the publisher who introduced and supported *L'Année sociologique*).[8]

Furthermore, to account for the spread, if not near hegemony, of Durkheimian ideas in secondary education (including elite *lycées*) during the 1920s, we should signal the number of important administrative positions occupied by Durkheimians (e.g. Lapie, Bouglé and Davy) in higher education.[9] In this regard, one also has to take into consideration the relationship between Durkheimians and competing academic social philosophies (for example, sociologists of the Le Play school or the group led by René Worms). We might even ask if the well-known intellectual conflict between Durkheim and Tarde (methodological realism vs. nominalism), no matter how well articulated, doesn't cloak an aspect of academic politics and turf.[10] While Durkheim was well established at the Sorbonne with a strategic link

---

6   For a broad coverage of the changing institutional framework for scientific research and teaching (in which the Durkheimian school may be located), see Robert Fox and George Weisz, eds, *The Organization of Science and Technology in France, 1808-1914*, Cambridge and New York: Cambridge University Press, 1980.

7   Although we follow an accepted usage in speaking of a *Durkheimian School*, it might well be noted that there was a differentiation, as in the case of other major social science schools, between "core" members having extensive interaction with Durkheim and more "peripheral" ones. For a network presentation see Philippe Besnard, "The *Année Sociologique* team," p. 27 in Besnard, ed., *op. cit*; see also Yash Nandan's elaborate differentiation in his *The Durkheimian School. A Systematic and Comprehensive Bibliography*, Westport, CT: Greenwood Press, 1977.

8   Félix Alcan's publishing house before World War I was for the publication of Durkheimian sociology what Jerry Kaplan's *Free Press* was for the publication of Parsons's sociological writings after World War II. Alcan subsequently became part of today's Presses Universitaires de France.

9   Of particular relevance are two pieces in the Besnard volume, *The Sociological Domain*: Roger Geiger, "Durkheimian sociology under attack: the controversy over sociology in the Ecoles Normales Primaires," pp. 120-136 and Mohamed Cherkaoui, "Education and social mobility: Paul Lapie's pathbreaking work," pp. 217-30.

10   See the excellent study by Victor Karady, "Innovation, Institutionalisation of innovation and the Birth of Sociology in France", mimeograph, AP of CNRS, no 6348, 1974; also, T. N. Clark, *Prophets and Patrons*, Cambridge, Mass, Harvard University Press 1973.

to the Ecole Normale Supérieure at the Rue d'Ulm, Tarde and Izoulet, other critics of Durkheim, were professors at the prestigious Collège de France, as was Bergson, whose vitalistic approach to morality and religion clashed with Durkheim's.[11]

It would also be necessary to examine the relationship between the Durkheimian School and a larger academic environment outside of France (for example, the reception granted to Durkheimians in the UK and particularly at Oxford in social anthropology). All these factors among others are relevant to the relationship between this School and its broad *academic environment*.[12]

A broader contextual brushwork should deal with the *external environment of political economy*. Consistent with our usual view of modern society, we could raise the two principal aspects, which are inter-connected, of French society: the socio-economic structures which dominated industrial development during the second half of the 19th century (which Marxists consider as the setting of "advanced capitalism"); and the underlying ideology comprised of a social laissez-faire philosophy and utilitarianism, which was one of the principal targets of Durkheim and his group. In this regard, the *socio-economic environment* is important for an understanding not only of *The Division of Labor in Society* as a comprehensive analysis of the ills and remedy for socioeconomic *anomie*, but also of research led by members of the Durkheimian team who had specialized in economic studies. They were critical of laissez-faire capitalism, which they accused of destroying the social fabric: the most recognized names are those of Simiand, Halbwachs and Hubert Bourgin.[13]

Secondly, and equally important, is the *sociopolitical environment*. The Durkheimian School was characterized by its commitment to science and objectivity, as its professional and scientific works show; but it was as well a group of sociologists committed to the interests of and service to a republican France and its ideals. Durkheim had been trained by the generation of progressive republicans like Jules Ferry and Léon Gambetta. He was a close friend of Jean Jaurès, the charismatic and political socialist leader, an activist in the peace movement and an inspiration to the young Durkheimians among others. The Durkheimians for the most part belonged to the center left; they were closely associated with the

---

11   See the comments of D. Draghicesco in *The Socialist Movement*, 22, July-Dec 1907, pp. 266-269. In condemning the determinism and rationalism, which the Durkheimians apply to social sciences, he praises Bergsonian philosophy: "Moral philosophy, recently perverted by the inflexible rationalism of M. Durkheim, will find its way and true methods..." (p. 267).

12   For an excellent study see Terry N. Clark, *Prophets and Patrons. The French university and the emergence of the social sciences.* Cambridge, MA: Harvard University Press, 1973.

13   See for example, François Simiand, *Les fluctuations économiques à longue période et la crise mondiale.* Paris: Alcan, 1932; Maurice Halbwachs, *Les expropriations et le prix des terrains à Paris,* 2nd ed. Paris: Presses Universitaires de France, 1928; Hubert Bourgin, *Les Systèmes Socialistes.* Paris: G. Doin, éditeur, 1923.

Radical Party and the democrat Socialists such as Millerand and Albert Thomas.[14] Their public positions during the Dreyfus Affair to a large extent brought them the respect of colleagues who had remained skeptical concerning "sociologism" (e.g. Lucien Herr, the librarian "gatekeeper" at the *Ecole Normale Supérieure*).[15]

Undoubtedly their circles and networks in French political life contributed later to their rise in the academic and administrative hierarchies of the Ministry of National Education. The Durkheimians were so closely identified with the political regime of the Third Republic, and above all its progressive but not Marxist wing, that they were attacked not just by the traditionalists on the right (whose sympathies were with Maurras' *l'Action française* and with the Catholic Church, which was conservative at this time), but also by a Marxist like Paul Nizan in *The Watchdogs* (1932), a tract whose tone brings to mind that of Gouldner, forty years later, in mocking Parsons in *The Coming Crisis of Sociology*.

The political environment, as complex as it was, turns out to be particularly germane in situating the Durkheimian School. Its members were without any doubt very talented social scientists, whose sociological studies can still be profitably read today. Still, the background isn't complete without taking into account that their socio-political views and political networks in government facilitated the institutionalization of sociology as an autonomous discipline in French education.

The Artistic Environment

Beyond the above contextual layers, I wish to relate the Durkheimian School with another extra-academic environment: the French *cultural environment* at the time when the School was at its peak. My thesis is that *there exists a notable affinity between avant-garde art and the Durkheimian School*, albeit there were not, as far as I am aware, any continuous contacts between the Group and the artists of the Parisian avant-garde.[16]

---

14   After World War I, however, some of the Durkheimians, like Georges and Hubert Bourgin became nationalists on the right.

15   See D. Lindenberg and P. A. Meyer, *Lucien Herr, Socialism and its Destiny*, Paris, Calmann-Lévy, 1977, p. 149.

16   Let us signal some possible intermediaries. The first would be Bernard Lazare, anarchist, friend of Lucien Herr and of Léon Blum, and a contributor to the literary *Revue blanche* of Natanson. He had made a habit of visiting avant-garde circles prior to his premature death in 1903. Lazare was an important anticonformist figure in the 1890s whose early study of anti-semitism, which seemed to put the blame on Jews as much as on others, gave way with the Dreyfus affair to his becoming an early French recruit of Zionism. The second intermediary would be Romain Rolland, novelist, dramatist, art critic and as well graduate of the elite École Normale Supérieure (1886-1889). Starting in 1895, he taught an art history class at the ENS, and later, organized a section on music at the École des Hautes Études Sociales.

My analysis has been stimulated by a provocative study of Robert Nisbet, *Sociology as an Art Form*, in which the author states that "sociology and art are intimately linked."[17] He posits there is an essential unity among creative spirits, whether in art or in sociology, and that both of these show similarities of style and means in their depictions of nineteenth century social reality. In particular, Nisbet developed the notion that the frequency of landscape themes in sociological writings depicts reality in a way comparable to that of artists in their portraits and landscapes. This is my starting point in exploring certain important preoccupations of the Durhkeimians, which will be better understood, I believe, if they are viewed as the preoccupations shared with avant-garde artists and writers.

The Arts in the *Année Sociologique*

To begin with, let's consider how the Durkheimian School treated the arts as a subject of sociological interest. Table 8.1 shows the position dedicated to arts in volumes of *l'Année sociologique* during the period when Durkheim himself was its editor.

This table requires certain clarification. In the first place, one has to note that the rubric "*Sociologie esthétique*" (Sociology of aesthetics) appeared in the third volume of the residual 7th section ("*Divers*"). It remained there during the entire first series of *l'Année*. As a sign of where it stood in the priority of fields of sociological investigation, Durkheim himself only once in the entire series had an entry in this section (volume V, p. 592) with two brief reviews of works relating art to the sociology of work. Further, the number of pages covered by this rubric was minimal compared to the total length of each volume. The arts, just like popular culture and folklore which I have discussed elsewhere,[18] was not one of the major preoccupations of the most active members of the group; nevertheless, one of its more distant contributors, Charles Lalo, did become a specialist in the sociology of the arts.[19]

I venture that L. Herr himself had simultaneous contacts with avant-garde art and avant-garde social science. However they diverged in other political respects, Durkheim worked closely with these figures in taking, along with Herr, leadership of the Dreyfusard movement seeking the liberation and rehabilitation of Captain Alfred Dreyfus.

17   New York, Oxford University Press, 1976, p.4.

18   *Popular culture and folklore in classic sociology*, Round table of the Association internationale des Sociologues de Langue Française, held at Mount Orford (Québec), in October 1977. For a more extensive discussion, see François Isambert, "At the frontier of folklore and sociology: Hubert, Hertz and Czarnowski, founders of a sociology of folk religion," pp. 152-76 in Philippe Besnard, ed., *The Sociological Domain. The Durkheimians and the founding of French Sociology*. New York: Cambridge University Press; Paris: Editions de la Maison des Sciences de l'Homme, 1983.

19   For a bibliography of the writings of Charles Lalo, see Yash Nandan, *The Durkheimian School: A Systematic and Comprehensive Bibliography*, Westport, Conn.

Table 8.1 The Arts in the *Année Sociologique* under Durkheim's Editorship

Volume	Year	Rubric (section and sub-section)	Pages	Reviewers of works
I	1896-97	None		
II	1897-98	None		
III	1898-99	7.1 Sociologie Esthétique	575-83	Hubert, Parodi
IV	1899-1900	7.1 Sociologie Esthétique	584-93	Hubert, Parodi, Richard
V	1900-01	7.1 Sociologie Esthétique	577-93	Hubert, Cl. E. Maître, Stickney, Durkheim, Parodi
VI	1901-02	7.1 L'Esthétique	560-67	Hubert, Mauss
VII	1902-03	7.1 Sociologie Esthétique	666-75	Lalo, Hubert, Mauss
VIII	1903-04	7.1 Sociologie Esthétique	629-38	Hubert, Reynier, Beuchat, Bouglé, Biancourt
IX	1904-05	7.1 Sociologie Esthétique	588-92	Hubert, Chaillié
X	1905-06	7.1 Sociologie Esthétique	656-59	Hubert
XI	1906-09	7.1 Sociologie Esthétique	774-89	Mauss, Hubert, Lafitte
XII	1909-12	7.1 Sociologie Esthétique	840-49	Gelly, Hubert, J. Marx

The table shows that Henri Hubert was the major contributor in this area, the only one whose name shows up in each of the 10 volumes with this rubric. Multiple comments drawn from this rubric show to what extent Hubert and his friend Marcel Mauss felt the importance of the arts for sociology. In the fifth volume of *l'Année*, in which one can find the only "Introduction" dedicated by the editors to "Sociology of aesthetics", Hubert indicates how sociology should tackle the question of art:

> We are not claiming to explain art, even less so to diligently weigh the respective parts of the individual and society in the production of works of art ... From our point of view, the study of art could well be divided between technology and the study of the phenomena of representation ... In a general theory of collective representations, art should without any doubt hold a significant place ...   it is

Greenwood Press, 1977, pp. 316 and following.

clear as well that one could analyze particularly well the sentient and affective elements of what is represented"[20]

In one of his rare entries under this rubric, Marcel Mauss brought forth suggestive propositions in the course of a critique of the book by W. E. Roth, *Games, Sports and Amusements*:

> "If *l'Année sociologique* ... was concerned with a sociology of today which one could consider complete, then the work of Mr. Roth should be considered above all as a contribution to aesthetics. We are speaking of aesthetics approached from a broad perspective, including decorative arts (*les arts d'agrément*) together with the *beaux-arts*, as opposed to the arts of mass production or merely technical, which arise from technological input. But neither the studies of our colleagues in sociology, nor our own, are advanced enough to tackle a theory of such an eminently social phenomenon as games"[21]

Still, as further indicated by Table 1, it might be noted that the rubric of the arts acted as a stepping stone for the new members of the School. It was in this way that Parodi, Lalo, Maître, Reynier, Beuchat, Bianconi, Gelly and Jean Marx made their initial contribution to *L'Année* providing entries under this rubric. With the exception of Hubert and Charles Lalo, who contributed only one review (in volume 7) yet went on to make sociology and the arts his major academic field,[22] their interest in this area seems transitory; it was connected with their training. This is unfortunate, since it would seem that the Durkheimian School did not draw on Lalo to propose a comprehensive theoretical analysis of the arts compared with those of social structures and social changes. Even today, the arts, just like popular culture, remain rather exotic for sociology on both sides of the Atlantic, judging by their benign neglect, for example as a rubric or subject matter in the *Annual Review of Sociology*. It would be worthwhile to comb the *Année* analyses, which appeared under this rubric; they did range far and wide covering works in English, German, Italian, as well as French, ranging from the origins of art and poetry to African poetry, South African art and Greek tragedy. One might well find in these critical reviews certain insights quite likely to put a sociology of art in a better theoretical standing than it enjoys today.

---

20   *Année sociologique*, V (1900-1901) p. 577.

21   *Année sociologique*, VII (1902-1903), p. 666.

22   See for example, *L'art et la vie sociale*, Paris: G. Doin, 1921, and "A Structural Classification of the Fine Arts," special issue of *The Journal of Aesthetics and Art Criticism*, 11, 4 (June 1953): 307-23.

The Broader French Cultural Milieu

The period during the end of the 1880s (more precisely, from 1885 to 1890) was as rich for the early Durkheimian School as for the French cultural milieu. It was around 1885-1886 that Durkheim, energized by his trip to Germany and his meeting with sociologists like Wundt and Schaeffle, really became aware of his vocation as a sociologist.[23] In May 1885 Victor Hugo, perhaps *the* republican icon, died, an event of tremendous importance: the grandiose national funeral ceremonies in honor of the deceased poet and writer who was buried in the Pantheon, were a critical moment for the cultural circles, a death and renaissance of immense proportions for the Third Republic.

> In the years following the funeral of Hugo in 1885, all the arts took a new direction, as if they had been awaiting a sign ... they liberated themselves from the influences of the 19th century to react instead to the initial stirrings coming from the 20th century. In all the arts, 1885 was the moment starting when one has to take into consideration the meaning of the word "modern"[24]

On September 18, 1886, Jean Moréas, the Greek-born poet, published his literary manifesto, "Symbolism" in *Le Figaro*. He contended that this movement marked a renaissance of French literature and a return to more ancient and fundamental forms of language.[25] Symbolism, introduced by Baudelaire and enriched by Verlaine, Mallarmé, Rimbaud, and, in Belgium, by Maeterlinck, was an avant-garde movement, which took off during the early years of the Durkheimian School. It shared common roots with post-impressionism and expressionism, which had received their inspiration from Van Gogh (who dazzled the artistic scene like a blazing comet at the end of the 1880s) and from Gauguin. These roots were later put to use in Cubism, whose path was cleared by the radical innovations of

---

23   See Steven Lukes, *Emile Durkheim His Life and Work*, New York, Harper & Row, 1972, pp. 66-95. For a "revisionist" view, see Bernard Lacroix, The original vocation of Emile Durkheim, in *The French Sociology Review*, 17, Apr.-June 1976, pp. 213-245, and Social Dynamics and Relative Subordination of Politics according to Emile Durkheim, in *International Sociology Notebooks*, LXII, Jan.-June 1977, pp. 27-44.

24   Roger Shattuck, *The Banquet Years: the Origins of the Avant-Garde in France: 1885 to World War I*, 2nd ed, NY, Vintage Press, 1967, pp. 18 and following. A gripping description of the funeral of Hugo can be found in Maurice Barrès, *Les Déracinés*. I have found germane in Shattuck the suggestion that the collective behavior at the time of this event may well have provided a background to certain key extracts of *Elementary Forms*. See my essay "Emile Durkheim", in Bottomore and Nisbet, *op cit.* [in this volume].

25   "... the good and luxurious and delicious French language pre-dating Vaugelas and the Boileau-Despréaux, the language of François Rabelais and of Philippe de Commines and of Villon...", Jean Moréas, *The First Weapons of Symbolism*, text edited by M. Pakenham, University of Exeter, UK, 1973, p. 32.

Cézanne and brought to maturity with Picasso, Braque, Gris, etc at the same time as the Durkheimian Group was reaching its zenith (1905-1914).[26]

Arguably, a critical break in the representational arts began in the latter half of the 19th Century with Impressionism and the new paradigm introduced by the impressionists or, if one prefers, by their way of seeing and depicting reality.[27] As the secondary literature is vast and as I don't have any claims to expertise in art history, I prefer to cite the penetrating comments of René Huyghe of the French Academy in highlighting the relationship between impressionism and science, above all physics: "Each one can be summarized by the…same principle: rational sensualism … Impressionism … has deferred to science in accepting its primacy, a major preoccupation at the end of the 19th century."[28] Similarly for the Durkheimian School, adopting the scientific method was one of its major preoccupations in order to establish its merit over competitors.

Impressionism and Durkheimian sociology both encountered obstacles and aroused hostility from the fact that the works produced were contrary to what one could call "the natural attitude", as Husserl put it. For Durkheim, the appeal of the scientific method was to demonstrate the reality of "the social fact" as irreducible to individual, biological, or environmental causes, and this generated hostility particularly but not solely in the humanistic disciplines.

In parallel fashion, Huyghe observed that the impressionists aroused anger among the middle classes for having defied conventions of reality, ideas based on inveterate habits, techniques and traditions.[29] The public trusted common sense, but impressionism followed the laws of physics and above all optics. The solid and material reality of the world, the objectivity of its "being-there", so critical for the bourgeois, was put into question by the scientific developments at the end of the nineteenth century, from which came a new understanding of nature and in general reality. Following the formulation of Planck's quantum theory, "matter" was denied its traditional stability and the world might henceforth be seen as a bewildering confluence of turbulent forces in perpetual Brownian motion and stochastic processes. Aristotelian logic and Euclidian geometry no longer provided premises, nor an adequate framework, to situate and describe the familiar world.

---

26   See my companion article, "Avant-Garde Art and Avant-Garde Sociology: "Primitivism" and Durkheim ca. 1905-1913," in this volume.

27   For an informative discussion of the institutional changes in the nineteenth Century French fine art scene that promoted the rebel Impressionists, see Harrison C. White and Cynthia A. White, *Canvasses and Careers. Institutional Change in the French Painting World*, New York, Wiley, 1965.

28   "Shifts in Thought during the Impressionist Era: Painting, Science, Literature, History and Philosophy", in *Impressionism: A Centenary Exhibition*, catalogue, Metropolitan Museum of Art, New York, Special exposition from Dec 12, 1974 through February 10, 1975. The French text is published by the Éditions des Musées nationaux, Paris, 1974. *Op. cit.*, p. 18.

29   *Loc. cit.*

The dissolution, or, in the expression of Georges Gurvitch, the *"destructuration"* of the material world, defined not just the direction taken by the scientific spirit, but also by avant-garde art at the end of the nineteenth century and beginning of twentieth. The impressionists depicted an unstable, evanescent reality on the road to dissolution. That is what for example is notable in the works of Monet, where the solidity of the countryside or the Cathedral of Rouen is dissolved under the effects of light which strikes the surface of objects. After 1886, Van Gogh no longer saw an unmoving landscape; he saw, and felt and painted a world of forces, of movements, of speed, a world in which intense destructuration brought forth a vision in all respects compatible with the one which modern physics was in the process of constructing.

Huyghe raises a last point, which deserves our attention. It is the new critical dimension of time, which impacted the perception of reality at the end of the 19th century. The traditional principles of causality and of generality of scientific laws depended on the repetition of identical effects under identical conditions. But abruptly, time became problematic, a "fourth dimension", important in Einsteinian physics, and equally so for Bergsonian philosophy and for other great philosophies of the 20th century (pragmatism, the theories of Heidegger, Whitehead, G.H. Mead). The dissolution or destructuration of the world was linked to the destructuration of "objective" time.

This new paradigm of reality – evanescent, ambiguous, deliquescent – could not but arouse major doubts, and anxieties as to the nature of identity. Aristotelian logic depends on the principle of identity, but if something is no longer identical to itself, then that logic lacks an ontological foundation. At the level of being, what is to ensure a self identity? Bergsonian philosophy obtained a certain popular following, in part because of its redefinition of reality in terms of time as *duration (durée)*, and also because of the primacy it gave to *conscience* as a foil to the determinism of an external and closed world.

The search of philosophers was shared as well by artists who tried to find not solid matter, but *forms*. They observed the external world in order to find its essential (geometric) forms, which held up appearances; it was cubism that analyzed the internal world in order to identify a series of forms through the flux of memory and consciousness. Artistic attempts such as Expressionism and Impressionism were echoed in the literature of Proust and Joyce.

What relationship do these comments have with the Durkheimian School? I venture that the perception of the ephemeral aspects of reality and the rejection of a solid, objective and material reality by the sciences and by avant-garde art at the end of the nineteenth century are intimately linked to the rapid change and the destructuration of the social world.

One could easily (maybe too easily) express this in terms of changes in technology and social structures, and say that it was advanced capitalism which destroyed the lower middle class, as well as the social and political influence of the traditional aristocracy. Still, there were other considerable cleavages which fissured the social landscape: Republican and Masonic anticlericalism waged a bitter and ultimately successful fight against the Church, seeking the goal proposed during the *Siècle des Lumières: "Ecraser l'Infâme!"* This resulted in the victory of anticlericalism and the secularization of public education under the prime ministry of Emile Combes (1902-1905) and his successor. Other centrifugal forces included: conflicts between traditionalist and modernists politically and academically which tore society apart at the beginning of the 20th century; the weakening of moral consensus and moral criteria during the Belle Époque; the serious demographic disruptions due to the rural exodus and internal migrations following industrialization and intensive urbanization in certain areas; the depopulation and rural and agrarian impoverishment in other areas such as Brittany and Languedoc; and growing acute labor agitation among miners and anarchosyndicalists.

As France was expanding its Asian and African possessions and as the "Metropolis" was developing economically, French society was internally in the public sphere going through a difficult period. To be sure, there was not the explosion of political violence seen in 1830, 1848 and 1870; nevertheless there was a continuous malaise.[30] It culminated in the great crisis of 1898 with the Dreyfus Affair: that notorious crisis with its complex and multiple implications and multi coalitions, to which the observation of one of our Québecois colleagues Fernand Dumont, with respect to the Canadian crisis of 1970, is equally applicable:

> With a tragic suspense, a few individuals for several weeks were able to dominate the attention usually so disperse of society. An event became an extraordinary symbol.[31]

After resolution of the Affair in favor of the Dreyfusards with Durkheimians as activists, there was an opportunity for the reconstruction of a modern and secular society under the aegis of the "Block of the Left" in the National Assembly and among those intellectuals who were their allies in the university system. It was Jean Jaurès, "the Minister of the Word in the Combes cabinet"[32] who acted as a powerful whip and mediator among progressive parliamentarians and university intellectuals. The democratic socialist inspiration of Jaurès to build a new social order, which was rooted in the Principles of 1789, sought to adjust these at the dawn of the twentieth century. After 1898, the landscape became very exhilarating

---

30   David Sumler very convincingly shows that the fragmentation of French society during the Third Republic was not mitigated by institutions favoring integration, such as the national education system or the benevolent associations and organizations who were in a way prolonging it. See: "Subcultural Persistence and Political Cleavage in the Third French Republic", *Comparative Studies in Society and History*, 19, October 1977, pp. 431-453.

31   Fernand Dumont, *La Vigile du Québec*, Montréal, Editions Hurtubise, HMH, 1971, p. 174.

32   Maurice Baumont, *Gloires et tragédies de la IIIe République*, Paris, Hachette, 1956, p. 275.

and exciting, even gratifying for the Durkheimians (after all, their leader entered the Sorbonne in 1902 as the "presumptive" heir of the chair of Ferdinand Buisson), for the socialists and … for avant-garde artists. Each group represented a wave of the future in its own domain.

Nevertheless, it was not a horizon of "greener pastures" and bucolic hills. If 1898 was a year of crisis marked by a civil war without bloodshed, 1905 saw multiple conflicts break out on several fronts, at home and overseas. In that year, the Combes ministry and its successor carried the day and finished the left's great anticlerical program with the voting of a separation of Church and State, which broke the interconnection of secular and religious power in effect since Charlemagne, (with the exception of the period of the French Revolution). That year, by the same token, the shock wave created by the belligerent declaration of the Kaiser at Tangier regarding German intervention in Morocco added to the anxiety brought about by the humiliating defeat imposed on Russia (France's new ally) by the Japanese and the eruption of political disorder in Russia. The combined anxieties and interstate tensions led many to believe that worldwide cataclysms were in the works that could well tip over into a barbarism which would sweep away Western civilization and its culture of liberty.[33]

Furthermore, the scientific community, already quite shaken in 1900 by Max Planck's initial piece of quantum theory on the emission spectrum of black bodies (http://en.wikepedia.org/wiki/Quantum), encountered a new shock in 1905 with the publication of Einstein's general theory of relativity, with even more significant implications. If there was no longer any "standard measure", how could "order and progress" triumph in the universe? The social applications and implications of this theory shattered the very foundation of Western identity, including its values of rationality and objectivity. Thereupon, the famous art Salon of 1905 added yet another shock: the triumph of the "Fauves" (Matisse, Vlaminck, Derain, etc) and of their "savage" use of colors went against the monochromatic world of superficial bourgeois conventions. Fauvism yielded its leading position in 1906-1908 to an even more radical movement: Cubism, perhaps the ultimate consequence of the new direction taken by the arts in the 1880s.

Arguably, then, the Durkheimian School must be understood in the total context of the sociopolitical and sociocultural situation of sociology in France. Having highlighted several of the general traits of the social and cultural landscapes of the School, I now turn to specific cultural themes it expressed.

---

33   For example Charles Péguy was thrown into a violent state of agitation by the Morocco crisis. See Romain Rolland, *Péguy*, vol 1, Paris, Albin Michel, 1944, pp. 97-115. I believe many Americans experienced a similar shock when the Russians launched Sputnik at the end of the 1950s. The Tangier crisis provoked by the Kaiser seeking a German presence on the Moroccan doorstep was perhaps like the Cuban missile crisis for the United States in 1962: violent confrontation was averted at the last minute.

It is true that some of the principal representatives of the Durkheimian School were focusing their research on the modern industrial society (above all Halbwachs, Simiand and Bourgin), but it may well seem paradoxical that the most noteworthy work of this first modern school of sociology dealt with aspects of society which were neither modern, premodern or even "archaic". The principal works of the Durkheimians were above all linked to the domains of religion and morality. We would like to review them briefly.

To begin, those of Durkheim himself. Although his doctoral thesis, *The Division of Labor in Society* made a strong impression on the examining committee and although *Rules of Sociological Method* and *Suicide: A Study in Sociology* are as well "classics" of sociology, it is *The Elementary Forms of Religious Life* on which he worked many years that is today considered his *magnum opus*. It is appropriate therefore to ask why Durkheim, founder of modern sociology and concerned with major problems of modernity, had brought such a great interest in the analysis of religious forms of primitive Australian society. Following our earlier discussion, we would suggest that this preoccupation is linked, or shows an affinity with, the avant-garde movements (first off, Symbolism and then Cubism). It is not stretching things to relate *The Elementary Forms* to a cultural context where the significance of "symbolism" ranged from an intense verbal lyricism to a spiritual challenge,[34] as the sweeping sociological vision of Durkheim formulated in Book II, Section 5 attests:

> Thus, social life, in all its aspects in all moments of its history, is only possible thanks to a grand symbolism[35]

Like the cubists looking for a new foundation of reality among basic geometric forms which produced a superficial reality, Durkheim wanted to penetrate beneath the surface of western social reality, in order to find the obscure underlying but fundamental forms of social existence. It is not so surprising that he found them in religious life.

In 1894-1895, a profound personal experience had redirected him toward the sociological study of religious life. It was then that his nephew, Marcel Mauss, directed his attention to English writings, which examined religion from a scientific and comparative perspective. It was the work of Robertson Smith,[36]

---

34   Shattuck, *op. cit.*, p 18.

35   *The Elementary Forms of Religious Life*, Paris, Félix Alcan, 1912, p. 331. Talcott Parsons does well delineating the critical importance of a sociological analysis of symbolic cultural systems by Durkheim: see his "Emile Durkheim", in *International Encyclopedia of the Social Sciences*, vol. 4, New York, Macmillan & Free Press, 1968, pp. 310-320.

36   For a lucid and penetrating overview of Smith, see, Thomas O. Beideleman, *W. Roberston Smith and the Sociological Study of Religion*, Chicago, University of Chicago Press, 1974.

Lectures on the Religion of the Semites, which markedly impressed Durkheim.[37] I venture that this momentous reading led him to rediscover his own Judaic roots. Furthermore, Durkheim belonged to that generation of Jews strongly integrated and assimilated, above all in Alsace, which Bourdrel has so well described.[38] That generation produced eminent philosophers and writers like Bergson and Lévy-Bruhl and later, Proust, André Maurois, Julien Benda and Léon Brunschwig.

In every society, the intellectual is a personage on the margins, but the one who comes from an ethnic minority is all the more marginal. While he/she believes himself to be assimilated in society at large, he/she runs the risk of finding out his own identity destroyed or put into question by some. In France, Jewish intellectuals went through a critical period in the 1890s, because the Dreyfus Affair set loose a very strong current of anti-Semitism, latent since the Panama Canal Company scandal that had implicated two prominent German Jewish financiers along with high French Government officials. At the same time, Zionism, as a reaction to pogroms of Jews in East Europe in the 1890s, brought forth a challenge to the assimilated French Jews when they heard about the persecution of Jews in Czarist Russia, even as that country entered into an alliance with France. The universe of the assimilated intellectual Jew in France, which seemed so self assured and stable, during the 1880s, was suddenly shaken by the events of the mid 1890s.[39] In this sense, the Durkheimians, or at least several among them, would have felt the same sense of destructuration of the world as did the avant-garde artists.

Reading Roberston Smith gave Durkheim an intellectual and sentimental appreciation for the religion of his father (Rabbi Moïse Durkheim) which he had set aside while pursuing his graduate studies. Smith gave him a privileged access to the richness of rites as essential traits of traditional religion, and his analysis helped to rehabilitate that which, following the extension of industrial and scientific civilization, was regarded as anachronistic, less advanced or sophisticated. Durkheim finding himself in the ambiguous position of being assimilated, while at the same time being "uprooted", like the figures of Barrès,[40] therefore rehabilitated "primitive" forms of religion as essential forms of social life. For a lay intellectual, whether his origins are Christian or Jewish, the rediscovery and revalorization of religious forms (ideal symbolic forms) offered an escape route to the anxieties brought about by the destructuration of the world (social and physical). Because of a growing urbanization and industrialization as well as political cleavages all the more noticeable, social solidarity was becoming ever weaker. Durkheim and

---

37   Stephen Lukes, *Emile Durkheim, His Life and Work.* New York: Harper & Row, 1972, p. 237f.

38   Philippe Bourdrel, *History of the Jews in France*, Paris, Albin Michel, 1974.

39   For an excellent analysis of the French Jewish community at the turn of the century and of the impact of the Dreyfus Affair on its various constituents, see Seth L. Wolitz, *The Proustian Community,* New York, New York University Press, 1971, chap. 5, "The Biographical Perspective: Israel-sur-Seine".

40   Maurice Barrès, *Les Déracinés*, Paris: Plon, 1922.

his team of contributors, above all the young ones he had initiated to sociology, felt an urgent need to find a new epistemological and ontological foundation for the modern social order.

The Durkheimians were not nostalgically seeking a prerepublican regime. As previously noted, politically speaking they were not conservative but rather progressive. However, they were looking for the most ancient roots of social life; the economic reality born of modern civilization was not satisfactory, because they felt it to be unstable and superficial. Their search backward was to find a more authentic blueprint for the progressive society of tomorrow. That is why it seems to me the underlying search of the Durkheim School is parallel to that of Proust's *A la recherche du temps perdu,*[41] in the sense that the implicit or tacit dimension of *L'Année* is comprised of a sociological quest for the Holy Grail, a quest which might well be entitled: *In Search of Lost Society.*

If this argument might seem a bit fanciful, let us recall that the principal work of Marcel Mauss, which he never finished, examines *prayer.* Or that one of the key pieces of collaboration by the members of the School is the essay of Mauss and Hubert, on *sacrifice.* Or that Hubert discovered the archaic world of *magic and heroes,* while his archeological training helped him to rediscover his own distant roots in studying *the Celts.* Or that Marcel Granet had at first proposed studying the notion of *honor* in feudal times in Europe, and that Lucien Herr easily convinced him of the importance of a comparative perspective in studying that same notion in an other feudal system, that of Japan.[42] Or that the major work of Célestin Bouglé in his capacity as a sociologist reviewed *hierarchal structures of traditional society* (the system of castes in India)*,* a subject diametrically opposed to the "egalitarian ideals" of modern society, in favor of which he was ideologically committed. Or that the dissertation of Paul Fauconnet was about *responsibility.* Or that of Georges Davy revolved around *sworn faith (la foi jurée).* Or that among the Durkheimians killed during the First World War before being able to complete their doctoral theses: one can cite Maxime David who was working on the moral concepts of ancient Greece, Jean Reynier who had chosen as his subject "asceticism", and Robert Hertz who was preparing his great work on "sin and its expiation in primitive societies."[43]

---

41   Proust began to prepare for his monumental multi-volume work at about the time Picasso and Braque were launching Cubism, and the first volume of *A la Recherche du Temps Perdu* was published shortly after *Les Formes Elémentaires.*

42   Mrs Marcel Granet confirmed this to me during an interview, which she had the graciousness to accord me on May 24, 1975. This anecdote is repeated by Maurice Freedman in "Introduction" to Marcel Granet, *The Religion of the Chinese People*, New York, Harper & Row, 1975, p.8.

43   Robert Hertz, *Sins and Expiation in Primitive Societies.* Trans and edited by R. Parkin, with preface by W.S.F. Pickering. Oxford: British Centre for Durhkheimian Studies, Institute of Social and Cultural Anthropology, 1994.

One can interpret the choice of these subjects and their treatment in various ways. It is easy (and I submit too simplistic and even deceptive) to attach the label "conservative" to Durkheim and, by necessity to his School.[44] One could, to be sure, conclude that all these themes are products of a Christian or traditional school of sociology. However that is not the case, and there were not many religious believers among the Durkheimians.[45]

I propose that the accent placed by this School on religious and moral structures constitutes a radical attempt to dis-cover in the archaic and the ancient that which is fundamental in societal organization (such as solidarity and the social bond), that which was "lost" (or covered up) in the modern process of civilization.[46] The Durkheimian explorations of the symbolic and moral dimensions of social reality are to be configured in the vast, amorphous cultural movement, which, under the Third Republic was seeking a new understanding of a fragile world of solid appearances on the way to dissolution. The Durkheimians found in "primitive" societies materials which allowed them to draw "fundamental" forms of social reality, exactly in the same way as avant-garde artists (like "primitive artist" le Douanier Rousseau, or in an even more convincing way Picasso, Apollinaire and Modigliani among others) saw in their "primitive depictions": a door leading to fundamental forms of reality.

Just as the avant-garde artists were seeking, at least since the Romantics, to find themselves in their own creativity (that is to say, they were looking to reestablish a broken identity),[47] the Durkheimians looked to find their own roots in exploring the "deep structures" of society.[48]

---

44   As Lewis A. Coser did, "Durkheim's Conservatism and its Implications for his Sociological Theory", in Kurt H Wolff, *Emile Durkheim, 1858-1917*, Columbus Ohio, Ohio State University Press, 1960, pp. 211-232.

45   One of the rare "believers" (*croyants*), Gaston Richard, separated himself from the Durkheimian group because its approach to religion struck him as atheist. This occurred before the publication of *Elementary Forms*, since Richard was no longer a contributor after the 9th volume (1904-1905) of *l'Année*. See Gaston Richard, Dogmatic Atheism in Religious Sociology in *Revue d'Histoire et de Philosophie religieuse*, III, March-April 1923, pp. 125-137, and May-June 1923, pp 229-261.

46   See Bruce Mazlish, *A New Science: the breakdown of connections and the birth of sociology*. New York: Oxford University Press, 1989.

47   For a general sociological perspective, see Harrison White, *Careers and Creativity. Social Forces in the Arts*. Boulder, CO: Westview Press, 1993.

48   It is risky to attribute a motivation, especially unconscious to the Durkheimians. That applies even more so to the critique of Seignobos, by Durkheim. See the famous meeting of May 28, 1908 in *Bulletin de la Société française de Philosophie*, vol. 8, pp. 317-247, whose theme "The Unknown and the Unconscious in History" was the object of a passionate debate.

Apart from the Durkheimians and the avant-garde artists, other groups (for example, the esoteric circles)[49] were also trying to probe reality, but it is not possible here to discuss the influence of all cultural environments bearing on the Durkheimian School. We hope nevertheless that these pages have highlighted an aspect of this School – notably its affinity with the arts and particularly with avant-garde[50] art – which has not yet drawn sufficient attention and which therefore deserves far greater attention in the future. Beyond this, the approach of this paper may be taken as a case study in contextualizing major schools of social thought that have marked the development of disciplines.[51]

---

49   Edward A. Tiryakian, *On the Margin of the Visible*, New York Wiley Interscience, 1974, p. 235.

50   After preparing this article, I came across the article of Christophe Charles, "Field of Literature and Field of Power: Writers and l'Affaire Dreyfus", *Annales (Economies, Sociétés, Civilisations)* 32, March-April 1977, pp. 240-264. This excellent study shows well how the different groups situated themselves vis-à-vis the Affair; it therefore provides a supplemental proof of the affinities between these two groups. Charles notes that both the Durkheimians and the avant-garde symbolists were devoted partisans of Drefyus and that they were living a relationship of "dominated" to "dominating" in the sectors of the *establishment* from they which respectively drew strength.

51   Edward A. Tiryakian, "Sociology, Schools," pp. 9-12 in *International Encyclopedia of the Social Sciences,* William A. Darity, Jr., ed., vol. 8, 2nd edition. Detroit: Macmillan Reference USA, 2008.

Chapter 9

Avant-Garde Art and Avant-Garde Sociology: "Primitivism" and Durkheim ca. 1905-1913[1]

Culture, long a favorite stomping ground of anthropology and the humanities, has in recent decades become "discovered" with gusto by sociology, as a marked "cultural turn" has led to the formation of one of the largest sections of the American Sociological Association, the Section on Culture. As Gabe Ignatow noted in a recent issue of the section's newsletter, Durkheim in *The Elementary Forms of the Religious Life* and elsewhere "developed a 'religious sociology' that is an inspiration for much of contemporary cultural sociology."[2] Yet, however much sociologists have made heuristic and other use of *The Elementary Forms* (hereafter, *The Forms*) in the growth of cultural sociology, it seems to have little significance for those writing in the sociology of art, such as Nisbet, Bourdieu, Luhmann, Alexander, and Zolberg.[3]

There are some exceptions that deserve mention. Jean Duvignaud, whose contributions to cultural sociology have unfortunately gone unnoticed outside the francophone world, found in *The Forms* an important point of departure for access to the creative, dynamic imagination in artistic works. Festivals producing 'an effervescent environment', as discussed by Durkheim, allow artistic forms "to acquire an emotional and affective power" beyond their being only *objets d'art*:

---

1   An early version of this paper was presented at The British Centre for Durkheimian Studies, Maison Française d'Oxford, Oxford (UK), May 15, 1999. My thanks to W.S.F. Pickering, W. Watts-Miller, Mike Gane, and Ken Thompson, in particular, for their initial encouragement in this project and more recently to Patricia Leighten of the Duke Department of Art History for suggestions regarding cubism.

2   Gabe Ignatow, "Locating the Body in Cultural Sociology: Durkheim on 'Organico-Psychic' Phenomena," *Culture*, 21, 3 (Spring 2007), p. 1.

3   Robert Nisbet, *Sociology as an Art Form*, New York: Oxford University Press, 1976; Pierre Bourdieu et Alain Darbel, *L'Amour de l'Art. Les Musées et Leur Public*, Paris: Les Éditions de Minuit, 1966; Niklas Luhmann, *Art as a Social System*, trans. Eva M. Knodt, Stanford: Stanford University Press, 2000; Victoria D. Alexander, *Sociology of the Arts. Exploring Fine and Popular Forms*, New York: Blackwell, 2003; Vera L.Zolberg, *Constructing a Sociology of the Arts,* Cambridge and New York: Cambridge University Press, 1990. Among these, Zolberg is the only who mentions in passing *The Elementary Forms*, in a footnote, but only to say that like other of his works it is part of Durkheim's polemic against psychologistic explanations.

they constitute "immediately communicable *particles of signification*"[4] Drawing
further on Durkheim's analysis of the societal basis of nomenclature (for example,
the categories of genre and class), Duvignaud is impressed with the creative
principle of classification in enabling even illiterate societies through individual
creative artists to cope symbolically with a harsh and demanding environment
(ibid. p. 102). When detached from their existential group setting, these art forms
(in museums or private collections) remain "something signified but without
significance," (ibid*.*). Duvignaud leaves this point of departure for a wide
coverage of art and artistic expression. He views modern societies as providing
new functions for artistic creative innovation, noting in passing

> ... the emergence of 'primitive' rhythms as developed by black Americans,
> which became popular in Europe after the 1914-18, has never been properly
> investigated, although it had profound effects on the individual and on human
> relations in Europe (*ibid.* p. 131).

I will touch later on the points he raises regarding "primitive" rhythms, since that
is a paramount theme I wish to explore in this essay, in particular the linkage it
provides *The Forms* to avant-garde art. Karen Fields in her "Introduction" to her
excellent translation of Durkheim's *magnum opus* suggests in a passing observation
that Durkheim lived in a Paris alive with "experiments in artistic representation"
and at a time ..."Picasso painted his *Demoiselles d'Avignon* in 1907 launching
cubism and therewith, a new vocabulary for the art of the new century."[5] She then
insightfully remarks

> It may turn out that illuminating connections can be drawn between Durkheim's
> transgressing the boundaries between "primitive" and "civilized" in the search
> for a vocabulary suited to comprehending, and then representing, the real
> and Picasso's own encounters with those same boundaries as he reconceived
> perspective (*ibid.*).

Fields does not pursue it further, but this will be a major ingress for our viewing
Picasso/Cubism and Durkheim/The Forms as arriving on the same cultural plane,
though from different points. For the moment, there is a third author who made
even greater use of *The Forms* and Durkheimian sociology in ways which provide
important overlap with our own analysis.

Fuyuki Kurasawa has located an important, even critical focus relating avant-
garde literary intellectuals in interwar France (1919-1939) to the Durkheimians
via their common exploration of *primitivism* (or alternatively, *primitiveness*).

---

4   Jean Duvignaud, *The Sociology of Art*, New York: Harper & Row 1972 (1967).
5   Karen Fields, "Introduction" to Emile Durkheim, *The Elementary Forms of the
Religious Life*, p. xxii.

By way of background to Kurasawa's discussion, we need bring in that in the wake of the calamitous World War I, and its senseless slaughter of millions by means of new murderous technologies, a new avant-garde came on the European scene, first with Dadaism, then into a more full-blown Surrealism headed by André Breton and an intellectual and artistic elite that rallied around him and his 1924 *Manifesto*.[6] The critique of modernity that had begun in the latter part of the Nineteenth Century with Nietzsche as a *vox clamantis* seeking postmodern values affirming life free of a "slave morality", and which questioned the thesis of the age of economic and scientific progress, had generated what in retrospect was labeled as a *fin-de-siècle malaise*. But the dominant cultural and political orientation well into the twentieth century was still a climate of Victorian/ bourgeois progress and contentment with the benefits of a rational civilization buttressed by a set of empires which demonstrated the material and moral worth of Western "humanitarian" domination over the non-West. As will be developed later in this essay, avant-garde movements before World War I (components of which went far back into the nineteenth century) were looking for cultural and political alternatives to industrial, bourgeois, scientific undergirding of the social order and its felt threat to individual freedom of expression. But the real justification for the rejection of the industrial, rationalist social order was brought out by the Great War which spared no one, including intellectuals and artists who died at the front alongside industrial workers, farmers, and clerks. What was the vision of the avant-garde that had survived the European holocaust?

Kurasawa takes as a starting point a pregnant sentence at Durkheim's conclusion of the *Forms*: "… the former gods are growing old or dying, and others have not been born," (Durkheim 1995: 429). This Nietzschean-like judgment and its surrounding analysis of the sacred as a fundamental aspect of social organization would, Kurasawa notes, become a key thread relating the postwar surviving Durkheimians and the French school of sociology and ethnology (including Mauss, Lévy-Bruhl, Griaule) to avant-garde surrealist circles and its offshoot in the *Collège de Sociologie* of brief duration (1937-39).[7] Alongside and overlapping with the surrealists, the names of Roger Bataille, René Caillois, Michel Leiris,

---

6   The *Manifesto of Surrealism* made use of Freud's work on the unconscious and dreams in seeking to capture the dream process by what Breton and his associate Philippe Soupault called automatic or dream writing. As a radical critique of positivism and rational logic, surrealism in Breton's definition was "thought dictated in the absence of all control exerted by reason, and outside all aesthetic or moral preoccupations," http://screensite.org/ courses/Jbutler/T340/Surmanifesto/ManifestoOfSurrealism.htm. The appeal of seeking thought freed from the constraint of reason attracted many of the most prominent literary and artistic figures in the interwar and even yearly postwar years, such as Paul Éluard, Louis Aragon, Antonin Artaud,René Magritte, and Salvador Dali.

7   For fuller discussions of the *Collège* see Denis Hollier, ed., *The Collège de Sociologie 1937-39* (Minneapolis: University of Minnesota Press 1988), and Simonetta Falasca-Zamponi, "A Left Sacred or a Sacred Left? The *Collège de Sociologie*, Fascism, and Political Culture in Interwar France," *South Central Review*, 23.1 (Spring 2006): 40-54.

Jules Monnerot were among the most prominent of the avant-garde of the 1920s and 1930s, many of whom followed courses of Marcel Mauss at the Institute of Ethnology and at the Collège de France. Unlike the pre-war sociologists, the interwar sociologists and ethnologists, with the prodding and encouragement of Mauss, actually went overseas to see life in non-Western settings and to collect themselves artifacts of "primitives", not as some crude or barbaric relic but as something important informing an authentic culture, rich in art and technology.[8]

The manifold appeal of "primitive" societies in its artifacts and thought systems, even in its "primitive mentality" as analyzed by the social philosopher and Durkheimian affiliate Lévy-Bruhl,[9] was to provide a radical critique of European modernity. The latter Durkheimians collaborated in formulating a critical sociology, and Kurasawa proposes: "Inspired by the encounter with cultural otherness, this sense of wonderment constituted a radical decentring of European modernity" (Kurasawa 2003: 8). The "encounter" came in several modes: attending the lecture of Mauss, engaging in anthropological "missions" to Africa and other colonial territories, and viewing and acquiring African art objects.

The identification of the avant-garde radicals – sociologists, ethnologists, and surrealists – with "primitive peoples" had complex bases, but the post-war disillusionment with the bases of European modernity (including bourgeois democracy, rationality and technology) was of paramount significance.[10] To be sure, Kurasawa notes there were intellectual differences within the broad spectrum of social scientists, between those who like Mauss, Leiris and Bouglé wanted to stick to "the perceived epistemological positivism and normative scientism of Durkheim's early work" and those who wanted a more pronounced radical political stance. Nonetheless, Kurasawa emphatically argues

> ... a common theme links all these authors to one another: the invocation of primitiveness as the key cultural motif of a critique of European modernity, or, put differently, a flight from its confines through the exploration of 'primitive' cultures... Primitiveness was thus imagined as a condition in which 'mystical' and 'alogical' thinking prevails over its rationalist brethren...The primitive

---

8   See further in Dumont (1972) and Schlanger (1998).

9   Lucien Lévy-Bruhl (1857-1939), had with *How Natives Think* (1910), *Primitive Mentality (*1922) and *The "Soul" of the Primitive* (1928) enjoyed great success, including English translations. But seeing how Hitler used racist ideology to invoke superior mentalities, he came in his last years to repudiate his earlier analyses.

10   Kurasawa does not consider the cultural disillusionment that also took place in Germany after WWI. Stripped of its colonies, German sociologists and anthropologists did not go overseas to find a "primitive *alter ego*", but equally strong critiques of modernity were formulated, on the one hand by Frankfurt School neo-Marxists (Adorno, Horkheimer, Benjamin, Marcuse and others), and on the other by phenomenological existential philosophy, notably that of Martin Heidegger.

universe was thus portrayed as an enchanted one ... as vibrant because well endowed in collective myths and sacred rituals (*ibid.*p. 10).

In his discussion, Kurasawa implicitly views Durkheim as a sort of "godfather" to the postwar avant-garde setting with his fecund analysis of the sacred, both in its part in society and its genesis. The key phrase, to reiterate, was "the former gods are growing old or dying and others have not been born", which led avant-gardist Roger Caillois, for example, to extol a reinjection of the primitive and its Dionysian-like celebration of the irrational into the excessive, destructive ingredients of the rationalist culture of Europe (*ibid.* p. 16). Further, the *Collège de Sociologie* and its heterogeneous members

> can itself be read as a Durkheimian institution bent on combating anomie ... modeled itself on 'primitive' sacred societies, its meetings acting as catalysts for the release of communal energies.Bataille, Caillois, and their colleagues were self-styled sorcerers'apprentices, shamans who attempted to spread the virus ofcollective effervescence throughout the body social (*ibid.* p.22).

There is merit to Kurasawa's discussion giving centrality to the theme of the *primitive* in connection with Durkheim, avant-gardism and modernity.[11] There is equally need to complement it, which is the major concern of this paper. To do justice to Durkheim, it will be important to go back to the pre-World War I cultural setting, where indeed *primitiveness* (or primitivism) was a major theme of the avant-garde, not as a detached "art-for-art's-sake movement but as a radical movement seeking an overhaul of the structures of European modernity. Durkheim's *Elementary Forms of the Religious Life*, I will argue, was indeed part of the cultural ethos of the avant-garde movement, or at least shared an amazing "elective affinity" with it, albeit Durkheim himself had strong ambivalence toward the "aesthetic" side of life.

The European Efflorescence

Durkheim resettled in Paris in 1902 from Bordeaux, where he had gained attention and admiration for his intellectual prowess in publishing a few years apart *The Division of Labor in Society, Suicide,* and *Rules of Sociological Method*, and also where his strong stand on behalf of Dreyfus and in defense of the secular values of the Third Republic had added to his luster. He arrived on the Paris scene at

---

11   Not taking away anything from his discussion, for the interwar period it might be kept in mind that the Durkheimian legacy of positivism and the separation of judgments of value from judgments of facts was retained in the interwar period by the sociologists of the *Institut Français de Sociologie* and their attempted revival of the *Année Sociologique* which took on in a decentralized form the title of *Annales de Sociologie.*

the beginning of one of the most creative, innovative periods in practically all realms of inquiry, throughout the Western world and certainly including France. He was to contribute to this efflorescence with his own *The Elementary Forms* being published ten years after his arrival, and five years after he became a full professor at the Sorbonne.

The amazing creative burst in the first years of the new century tends to be sandwiched between two negative frames of historical play-back: the fin-de-siècle malaise and Europe on the eve of World War I. But the frame may not fit the historical reality if one considers just a few of the lasting innovative achievements in this condensed period. The vitality of the United States under the reform-minded presidency of Theodore Roosevelt was shown foremost with the technological launches of the automobile age and the aviation age with Henry Ford and the Wright Brothers respectively and the engineering feat of the Panama Canal. Europe underwent a decade of complementary cognitive creativity: Planck and Einstein revolutionizing classical physics with quantum theory and the special and general theories of relativity, the creative ferment in new mathematics with Poincaré, Hilbert, and Whitehead and Russell's *Principia Mathematica,* among others; Husserl's phenomenology with its radical way of looking at how "objects" are constituted subjectively; Freud's probing of the unconscious and his psychoanalytical method.

Not to be neglected are the enormous cultural innovations which transgressed the established canons in the decorative and performing arts as well as in music, for instance, in abstract painting, modern ballet and atonal revolutionary musical compositions. It is in this context of the intense creativity of both avant-garde and revolutionary innovations, highly concentrated for the most past within a ten-year period, that we will treat Durkheim, however initially this seems distant from a customary contextualization of *The Elementary Forms*. Like the innovations of Picasso, Braque, Diaghileff, Stravinsky, and Schoenberg in their respective artistic domain, Durkheim produced a *scandal* in his innovative treatment of the sacred, and a common denominator is their utilization of the "primitive" from African and Oceanic origins.

Durkheim's Ambivalence?

At first glance, the nexus between Durkheim and avant-garde art, much less art in general, is not obvious. *Ambivalence* may be a fair characterization of his orientation to art and aesthetics, one picked up by several commentators.

One indication that he did not consider art or aesthetics to hold much promise for sociological investigation is that it only occupied in his "laboratory", the *Année Sociologique*, residual review entries in the category *"Sociologie Aesthétique"* in the 7th section itself categorized as *"Other" (Divers)*. The only trained specialist in art/aesthetics, Charles Lalo, was tapped only once for a review (in volume 7 appearing in 1904), although he dutifully applied Durkheimian positivism to the study of the science of aesthetics and the fine arts, and was in post-war France Professor of Aesthetics at the Sorbonne.[12]

In contrast to what may well be seen as a "benevolent neglect" of the arts, Durkheim gave much more attention to another ancillary field, comparative linguistics. He found an important collaborator in Antoine Meillet, who had studied under the great Ferdinand Saussure, the founder of modern linguistics. Besides dozens of reviews, Meillet (who would inherit Saussure's chair at the Sorbonne when the latter returned to Switzerland) also published in volume 9 of the *Année* an important original monograph "How Words Change their Meaning" ("*Comment les mots changent de sens*"). That Durkheim thought very highly of linguistics's ties to sociology is further indicated in his training his only son André to become the younger generation's specialist in linguistics, the way Durkheim encouraged young Hertz into the sociology of religion.[13]

In any case, like their intellectual leader, none of the "regulars" or major collaborators of Durkheim seemed to have much professional interest in the arts as a field of research, at least during his lifetime. Later on I will anew make mention of Mauss whose eclecticism regarding technology and magic is seen as a bridge between "high" and "low" culture leading him to a rapprochement with surrealism in the 1920s (Kurasawa 2003; Schlanger 1998: 200).[14] Presently, however, let us consider what recent Durkheimian scholarship has had to say about Durkheim's position on art.

Pickering, who has for years galvanized British sociological interest in Durkheim with the formation of a Durkheim Studies Centre at Oxford, has also emphasized the weakness of the *Année* in not giving greater attention to the arts when Paris was preeminent in the artistic world of painting, poetry, music, literature (Pickering 2000: 43). He sees the ambivalence of Durkheim who on the one hand saw art and play as very much integral to religion, even if in a secondary capacity, but on the other hand had misgivings about aesthetic culture (on which he lectured at Bordeaux) whose imagination, when it is removed from the control of religion

---

12   In his most important work, *L'Art et la Vie Sociale*, he asserted that art has a collective function that will grow in importance as mankind passes through a present crisis of "anarchic individualism" (1921:2). For his extensive publications in the sociology of art and aesthetics, see Nandan 1977, 316-17. Lalo fared better as Mauss assumed charge of the *Année* when it resumed publication briefly in the 1920s, but it was a modest two reviews he provided to the initial volume.

13   And most tragically, both Hertz and young Durkheim perished at the front in the early months of World War I.

14   During Durkheim's lifetime, however, Mauss seems to have kept his interest in the arts under wraps or away from the gaze of his uncle; we take as an indirect piece of evidence for this point is that the volume containing informative letters of Durkheim to Mauss (Durkheim 1998) has no entry on art, much less on the revolutionary avant-garde artists of the period. In the concluding section of this essay, however, I will bring out a datum indicating Mauss's pre-war awareness of a key avant-garde artist, Picasso.

"either disregards or threatens what is sacred to society" (*ibid.,* p. 44).[15] Basically, Pickering considers that art was for Durkheim more in the domain of *la vie légère* than *la vie sérieuse*, the latter being the sphere of the sacred and religion. Whether this neglect stemmed from his family's Jewish cultural background, as Pickering also suggests, or from personality temperament, the fact is that art lacked much appeal for him.

Menger echoed Pickering in the same issue of *Durkheimian Studies* in noting Durkheim's ambivalence. Drawing on Lalo's *L'Art et la vie sociale,* Menger locates art functionally as " the social discipline of luxury" (Menger 2000: 82) and suggests the ambivalence of Durkheim related to art being a problem "for a theory dealing with equilibrium and social regulation" (*ibid.* 81). Like all creative productions of imagination – scientific, intellectual, and technological – art has a role in history reinventing itself. But rather than seeing this in positive terms,[16] Menger considers the more negative side of the ambivalence, tracing it back to Durkheim's critical stance of J-M Guyau, author of both an early work on the sociology of art and the sociologist who had introduced the term "anomie" and given it a positive emphasis in the individuation.[17] Much as Durkheim in the Dreyfus case endorsed the role of public intellectuals and their espousal of "individualism" as a value of modernity, the individualism of the creative artist – and here perhaps what is unstated is not just the work of an artist but also the *lifestyle* of creative artists – is also potentially a destabilizing factor in social equilibrium and its normative grounding (Menger, 2000: 63).[18]

Menger draws attention to Durkheim's related discussions in *The Division of Labor* and *Suicide* wherein aesthetics is viewed as a foil to economic utilitarianism: the notions of *luxury* and ludic recreation take us out of the realm of regulated conduct, enforced by group norms. The imaginative powers, harbored deep inside the self, freed by anomie and imagination in aesthetic activity can become pathological and undermine the social order (Menger, *ibid.,* p.72).[19] The freedom of the artist and artistic individuality are in this consideration a potential source of

---

15   Contemporary controversy over artistic displays in museums of works such as those of photographer Robert Mapplethorpe would illustrate the point.

16   Unlike Hans Joas (echoing Duvignaud's previous emphasis) has done in viewing the creativity of action in Durkheim's religious sociology (Joas 1994).

17   Jean-Marie Guyau, *L'art au point de vue sociologique.* Paris: Alcan 1903, 6th edition, introduction by Alfred Fouillé. The focus is on literary forms, not on representational art. Guyau had previously published *The Non-Religion of the Future*, New York: H. Holt, 1897 (1890), which Durkheim had critiqued at length in the *Revue Philosophique* 23 (1887): 299-311.

18   Throughout the past two centuries, a strong public image of "Bohemian life" and its flouting of the conventions of domesticity has been associated with the creative talent of artistic life.

19   The cultural revolution of the mid-1960s offers a vast terrain to explore this on both sides of the Atlantic. For a vivid discussion of the arts in the French cultural revolution of 1968, see Alfred Willener (1971).

destabilization, of breaking the norms of community institutionalized in the social order and its conventions.

But ambivalence is two-sided, and Menger also considers passages in *The Elementary Forms* which positively evaluated the aesthetic side of rituals as enhancing the moral efficacy of the group. It is in the collective assembly and its rituals generative of enthusiasm that societal ideals are (re)generated, that is, in collective acts of imagination which transvalue the worth of objects. Such "hot periods" in the life of the collectivity are not confined to pre-modern societies but are also found in periods of crises, and Durkheim explicitly mentions the passionate moments of 1789 and might have equally well mentioned the "hot period" of the Dreyfus affair a century later in which he himself participated, a period which saw the challenges and re-creation of the republican ideals.

On a lesser plane than the dramatic creation of ideals instrumental in social change, Menger's discussion is complemented by Durkheim's own observations regarding the positive *recreational* contributions of religion to the quotidian. The religious cult makes us forget the world and its cares and transports us to one where imagination prevails. These elements of the cult entertain and sometimes

> They even go so far as having the outward appearance of recreation. We see those present laughing and openly having fun. (*The Forms*, p. 384).

However stern, somber and even puritanical our image of Durkheim might seem, his discussion shows a broad understanding of the play of art and the aesthetics in the vitality of the sacred:

> Religion would not be religion if there were no place in it... for games, for art, for all that refreshes a spirit worn down by all that is overburdening in day-to-day labor. that which made art makes it a necessity... the cult in itself is aesthetic in some way.

One can sense in his analysis that it is not just the distant Arunta of Australia he is talking about but perhaps of fellow Frenchmen in Paris and Epinal when he further states

> Recreation is one form of the moral remaking that is the primary object of the positive cult. Once we have fulfilled our ritual duties, we return to profane life with more energy and enthusiasm... our own capacities have been replenished through living, for a few moments, a life that is less tense, more at ease, and free. Religion gains thereby an appeal that is not the last of its attractions, (*The Forms*, p. 386).

To be sure, Durkheim does not go overboard on the recreational aspect: "when a rite serves only as entertainment, it is no longer a rite," (*ibid.)* and though aesthetics, art, and religion have overlapping areas in our imaginative faculty, they do exert different influences. Ultimately, "a rite is something other than a game; it belongs to the serious side of life," (*ibid.*). To state the matter perhaps more prosaically, a church service *is* a performance but for its participants it is also *more* than that.

The legacy of Durkheim's perspective on aesthetics including his ambivalence toward art is extended in another piece by Sue Stedman Jones, "Durkheim and Bataille: Constraint, Transgression and the Concept of the Sacred," (Jones 2002). Her focus is on the stimulus of *The Forms* on Georges Bataille, a pre-WWII member of the *Collège de Sociologie*, who later became highly influential in cultural studies with various works interrelating violence, the erotic/pornography and the sacred. Bataille was much indebted in his reading of Durkheim's text, particularly in elaborating the dialectic pair of sacred and profane. Bataille found particularly appealing descriptions of transgressions, rule-breaking and violations of norms of organization in sacred rituals – these are key elements of Durkheim's "dynamogenic theory of society and of religion", captured in the concept of creative "collective effervescence" (Jones 2002: 54). For Bataille, the excess of energy generated in rituals and the sacred, even if or perhaps because of the violence, is not to be feared but to be welcomed: "Life," Jones quotes Bataille, "is in its essence an excess, it is the prodigality of life," (*ibid.*) and she later notes that "exultation in heterological excess is central to the Bataillian vision of the sacred and of cultural renewal," (*ibid.* p. 57). It is not surprising that the explorations of Bataille led him to analyze the appeals of fascism, and to probe the dark forces of the unconscious, for all these are forces of the irrational which society seeks to harness in routinized objects. Bataille dropped Durkheimian anchorage to go on his own experiencing the sacred as "a powerless horror… simultaneously dangerous and of incomparable value," (*ibid.*p. 59) – *very much as Picasso reported his experience encountering "primitive" African art objects at the Trocadero* (infra, p. 197).

Indeed Durkheim did reflect in the Conclusion of *The Forms* on the dual aspects of the society that is idealized in religion. The sacred is not only the good and the beautiful (and as we have just discussed, there is also a place for the ludic in it) but it is also the dark and the ugly, because religion *is* realistic. And Durkheim details this:

> Far from ignoring and disregarding the real society, religion is its image, reflecting all its features, even the most vulgar and repellent (p. 423).

All told, then, a barebones examination of Durkheim on art shows beyond suggestive remarks little that is noteworthy, much less foundational, unlike his major lines of inquiry. To amplify our perspective it may be heuristic to treat *The Elementary Forms of the Religious Life* as being produced in an ethos of avant-gardism that privileged "primitiveness", with overlapping elements common to Durkheim's *Forms* and to sectors in both the decorative arts (painting and sculpture) and the performing arts (ballet, music, theatre). Because of space limitation, we will cover only some aspects of each, chiefly painting and ballet, where there are themes in common with *The Forms*.

What I will take as a lead-in to Durkheim and the avant-garde is a seemingly banal episode, the "revelatory" visit of Picasso to the Trocadero Museum of Ethnography in the spring of 1907 when he encountered what Durkheim noted as the dark side of the sacred and what thrilled Bataille, essentially, the collective, even magical forces of the primitive (Rubin 1994:103-05).

The Primitive in Representational Avant-Garde Art

Pablo Picasso and Georges Braque are the key figures in introducing radical innovations in the pictorial representation of reality, with Picasso's 1907 landmark in modernism that is *Les Demoiselles d'Avignon* (Elderfield 1994). It marked the debut of *analytical Cubism,* presenting an entirely new perspective on objects from that which had prevailed since the Renaissance. The "primitive" was a critical lever that Picasso applied, but although highly innovative, Picasso did not use his artistic imagination to put in place primitiveness *ab novo* on the art scene. It had already been gathering momentum.

"Primitivism", to tack on an ideological note, might well be considered in early twentieth century Europe a broad counter-culture to the dominant orientations and institutions of modernity, rather like the counter-culture of the 1960s. Although elusive and amorphous, the covert ideology sought to bring down the bourgeois social order resting on rationalization, materialism, economic individualism and the market place in which it flourished. And like its later twentieth century off-shoot, the counter-culture of primitivism attacked the established norms of tradition, sought to remake communal ties, found appeal in anarchistic currents and an Archimedean lever in archaic and exotic. The "primitive" served as both a perspective of the pre-modern past and as a resource for the remaking of the future, a lever, in the expression of the avant-garde poet Apollinaire, for "re-ordering the universe," (Leighten 1989: 113). In the pictorial arts, "primitivism" had several components which need brief mention.

In an earlier essay immediately preceding the present one, "The Quest for the Bygone Society, Emergent Sociology and its Cultural Setting" (*supra,* pp. XXX), I invoked *the symbolic movement* in the cultural scene of the arts and literature (Redon, Gauguin, Verlaine, Mallarmé, among many others) and suggested that the emphasis on symbols and rituals of the Durkheimians partook of this ethos.

This has led the noted historian of religion, Ivan Strenski, to think that I was proposing Durkheim and his associates, who wrote monographs on symbolic structures of society, were in accord with their contemporaries who extolled the exotic, the esoteric, the irrational (Strenski 2006: 160). That was not my intention, but the fact remains that the Durkheimians, many the product of the elite Ecole Normale Supérieure and other jewels of French secular higher education, *did* give a prominent place to expressive symbols. The construction and reconstruction of republican France, as I interpret the motivation of Durkheim and his close associates like Mauss, Fauconnet, Hertz, and Hubert, was to understand the scaffold of society, one resting on morality, the sacred and its symbolism. To understand present-day modern France and its institutions, there was not only need to examine scientifically contemporary social organization (as Durkheim, Halbwachs, and Simiand showed the way in various monographs), but also to return to much earlier bases and to alternative, earlier and more fundamental structures or "elementary forms". Their explorations of the symbolic realm and the avant-garde artists at the turn of the century who made extensive use of symbols were part of a general cultural ethos, but ultimately the mission of the Durkheimians was different from the avant-garde artists. Not only were their methods of exploring the "irrational" different, but their objective differed. Ultimately, the Durkheimians sought to energize and reconstruct liberal society; the avant-garde, to deconstruct it.[20] Before validating this contention, however, there is need to follow avant-gardism in the representational arts and its political underpinning that followed the symbolist movement.

Of brief duration (less than ten years) as an avant-garde movement yet relevant for our situating *The Forms* in a broad cultural context is **Fauvism**, which appeared on the French scene at the turn of the century. It is associated with well-known names in painting like Derain, Vlaminck, and Matisse, young painters who created a "scandal" when they exhibited at the prestigeful Salon d'Automne in 1905, a scandal generated by their "wild" use of colors that jarred the senses, as well as by their sensuous deployment of exotic and archaic themes (for example, from ancient Greek vases).[21] Fauvism is a sort of transition in avant-gardism, away from the traditional representations and toward the very radical movement of abstraction that came with Picasso and Braque.

Besides introducing a new vitality to the palette of artists, the Fauvists were also in Paris when different civilizations intersected. Ornamental objects, sometimes with and sometimes without their subjects, from Africa, Oceania, and other distant and exotic lands – now part of overseas colonies and empires – left their native environment and entered that of the *métropole*, in emporiums and ethnographic museums.[22] In France, besides dealers and new collectors (such as Gertrude Stein) of *art nègre* (the generic term used for "primitive" objects from Africa, Melanesia,

---

20   It might be noted, however, that the Cubist movement did find welcomed support from social philosopher Henri Bergson with his espousal of "intuition" and his anti-rationalist philosophy of vitalism critical of "closed systems" of causation. Immensely popular with a large public, Bergson was somewhat like Marcuse at Berkeley in the 1960s.

21   There is an artist who had a very distinct form of primitive fauvism: Henri Rousseau, with almost child-like depictions of jungles and wild animals. They are more like paintings of folk artist Grandma Moses than of his contemporary fauvists who, as Zolberg has noted (1997: 54), were more prone to see the primitive as "ferocious" than the nostalgic. Undoubtedly, both the nostalgic and the ferocious are components in the appeal of the primitive.

22   It would not be until the post-WWI setting that African objects were recognize rather than as *artifacts* as properly *art* deserving to be in an *art museum*, and the United States took the lead in this transformation (Zolberg 1997: 59).

Polynesia, etc.), the main storage of such objects as fetishes, masks, and so forth was in the Palais du Trocadéro. There a huge collection variously assorted was to remain until 2006, when due to the vigorous efforts of the French president Jacques Chirac, the collection of over a quarter of a million arts and crafts objects was moved to a more readily accessible location in Paris at the Quai Branly.[23]

The coming and "discovery" of functional and representational objects from distant lands was decisive for avant-gardism, albeit there has been controversy which need not bother us in this exposition as to just who should get credit for the initial discovery. What matters is that "tribal art" was discovered by the avant-garde (Matisse, Vlaminck but most decisively by Picasso) as a powerful "primitive" stimulus ca. 1906-1907. In passing, one might liken the electric shock reportedly felt emotionally by Picasso when early in 1906 he entered a room filled with uncared African masks and fetishes at the Trocadero as similar to the stimulus provided by Mauss in giving Durkheim a copy of Robertson Smith's *Religion of the Semites*. Picasso would respond to the stimulus of the primitive forms of representation by taking it in a short while to Cubism, while Durkheim took the stimulus of the "primitive" forms of religion of the Semites to his deepening analysis of the sacred as the ground of society.

The avant-garde artists readily incorporated from anonymous "primitive" artists a panoply of stylistic elements, such as distortions of the body, or depictions of dark cosmic forces that the community has to cope with, or primal erotic symbols of fecundity that appealed to avant-garde artists as an expression of deviance from mainstream Victorian cultural norms (Price 1989: 47).[24] The appeal of primitive art was not only what and how it depicted, abstractly, reality but also that it represented *communal* ideas conveyed through communal modes of expression (Price 1989:46). Although a *community of artists* was an ideal by some forerunners of the avant-garde we are discussing (notably Van Gogh in inviting Gauguin to take residence with him and have others join them), that did not materialize. But the communal aspect of tribal objects, of tribal art, was nevertheless and important source of ideological attraction, as much as it provided the avant-garde artists in self-identity. Concerning the latter, Antliff and Leighten have noted

> The concept of the artist as a 'primitive'– anti-rational, spontaneous, and above all 'authentic'– informed the entire Cubist movement throughout the pre-World War I period (2001: 57).

The "discovery" of tribal art, its masks and sculptures, occurred at a time of crisis in modern art when the traditional paradigm of visual representation seemed to have reached a dead end in advanced expressions, such as post-impressionism and

---

23   For a full discussion of the political process in the completion of the new Musée Branly, despite strong protest from other interested museums, see Price (2007).

24   Picasso's *Les Demoiselles d'Avignon,* drawn from his memory/image of a brothel in his native Barcelona, has at the right African women displaying raw sexuality.

pointillism. The stimulus (and shock value) of artistic primitivism was to get away from surface representation toward multiple perspectives (like viewing a *cube* from all sides) that could be depicted by juxtaposing elementary geometric forms. As a further extension, Picasso (and Braque), stimulated by African sculpture that broke with the unity of form and matter, took Cubism into another frontier of geometric abstraction in 1911-1912, with three-dimensional *collages*, objects and other bits of papers (especially fragments of headlines in newspapers).[25] This *synthetic Cubism* created another scandal when the avant-garde artists that rallied around it exhibited at the Autumn Salon in 1912 – the same year, it will be recalled, that Durkheim published *his* scandal, *The Elementary Forms of the Religious Life.* Like the avant-garde Cubists, Durkheim probed ethnographic materials for the underlying, elementary forms of reality. And, as I shall discuss in a concluding section, in the process of his exploration of deep structures – or forms – of social organization, Durkheim opened positivism to new frontiers that, like Picasso, he dared cross. But before a final evaluation of Durkheim and the avant-garde, there is need to look at a complementary contemporary avant-garde movement.

The Primitive in Performance Art

"Primitivism" also figured in the radicalization of ballet performance and ballet music. Just at the time the Fauves were doing radical innovations calling up archaic elements in their paintings, traditional ballet had seemingly reached an impasse with its forms of elegant choreographic story-telling, including stereotypical gender roles of feminine grace and male virility.[26]

A wind of change blew into Paris from the east in the early years of the decade, in the form a ballet group organized by the Russian impresario Sergei Diaghilef (1872-1929). Diaghilef did much to introduce Western art to Russia and conversely, staging art exhibits and musical productions by leading composers. As an aftermath of the political upheavals in Russia in 1905-06 and his incurring the

---

25   The appeal of Cubism and its stimuli in African and Oceania sculptures quickly became widespread beyond France, to modernists in Europe and the United States (Brancusi, Modigliani, Klee, Nolde, among many others). For detailed discussion and illustrations, see Rubin (1984).

26   Of course, "classical ballet" – *Giselle, Swan Lake, Les Sylphides* – is still the staple of the repertoire. But I am drawing attention here to radical new forms of modernism in the performing arts, with emphasis on the ballet. A "native American" radicalization of dancing in the performing arts is undoubtedly that introduced by Martha Graham in the 1920s, with at least surface similarities (e.g., angular movements, spontaneity) with the later Ballets-Russes. But relating different threads of modern dance is beyond the scope – and ability – of this essay. For a keen sociological presentation of the development of ballet in light of Weber's master concept of rationalization, see Phillip E. and Sandra N. Hammond, "The Internal Logic of Dance: A Weberian Perspective on the History of Ballet," *Journal of Social History*, vol. 12, 4 (Summer 1979): 591-608.

displeasure of the Russian Imperial Court, Diaghilef took a ballet group he had formed and toured Europe with great success (Lifar 1954). Diaghilef commissioned leading modernist composers to provide music for new ballets. In one ballet with music from the composer Ravel, *Daphnis and Chloe*, the choreography boldly utilized dance forms drawn from ancient Greek vases; it was a success, drawing attention from a leading member of the Fauves, Matisse, who depicted this in one of his most famous paintings, *The Dance*. Diaghilef had assembled a team with diversified great talent, but the name that retains above all the others was the young choreographer and dancer Nijinsky, barely twenty. The Ballets-Russes troupe under Diaghilef also had great success in its 1911 season with the performance of *Petrushka,* by a young Russian composer inspired by old Russian folk tales, Igor Stravinsky. As Lieven notes (1936: 130), Diaghilef decided to make his Ballets-Russes a permanent European organization, and Russian themes became dropped in favor of a greater rapprochement with the West.

The break with Russia and the break with the past, the search for something different took place in 1912 – the same year as Picasso took Cubism to a new dimension of representation, and the same year, to reiterate once more, as Durkheim took positivism on a radically new dimension.

In the case of ballet, following the success of *Daphnis and Chloe,* it was *The Afternoon of a Faun*, which caused a scandal. Debussy had composed the music after a poem by the symbolist Mallarmé; the "story" was a rather simple one of nymphs that are discovered by a semi-human creature who aroused from sleep chases after them. Besides innovative and colorful stage scenery, and the scantily clad and tight-fitting colorful costume of the male as background, what caused both an aesthetic sensation and a scandal against public morality was the extraordinary dancing of Nijinsky, who had daringly choreographed the ballet with erotic movements. The more explicit than implicit sexual innuendos in the chasing of nymphs reached a climax in a closing scene, with an uproar in the audience springing when "the Faun's final phallic movement... played a decisive part in the success of the ballet," (Lieven: 1936: 175). The Faun's sexual manipulation of a nymph's scarf had launched a "succès de scandal", especially given the location in a theatre used to middle class conventional representations. However, that scandal paled in comparison with Diaghilef's next production with "primitive" themes of sexuality and violence.

At its premiere on May 29, 1913, the production of *Le Sacre du Printemps (The Rite of Spring)* caused one of the great scandals in the world of performing arts. Diaghilef had commissioned Stravinsky for an original score, and the combination of the music, Nijinky's choreography, and the theme of the ballet – primitive rituals culminating in the sacrificial sacrifice of a virgin – was altogether so jarring that it sharply divided the audience into proponents and opponents, with an ensuing riot the police could not quell.[27] It is hard using print media to convey the combination

---

27   For a fuller accessible description of this work, see http://en.wikipedia.org/wiki/ The_Rite_of_Spring.

of dissonant, rhythmic music, scenery evoking primeval scenes, and Nijinsky's choreography of convulsive-like movements seeking to produce a "savage, almost terrifying impression", but for one eye-witness,

> The *Sacre* is a prehistoric vision, confused, awe-inspiring, but true. To appreciate the choreography of this ballet at its true value it is necessary to have seen the negro dances of primitive African tribes (Lieven 1936: 191).

This is echoed by another historian of the ballet:

> The heavy, angular movements, so far removed from the elevation of the classical ballet, gave by their very brutality an impressionof barbaric religious ecstasy born of a mixture of fear and joy and not devoid of a certain stark beauty (Lynham 1947: 130).

To the best of my knowledge, neither Diaghilef nor Nijinky nor Stravinsky had read *The Elementary Forms of the Religious Life*, and in the absence of knowing ticket holders for the premiere of *Rite of Spring,* it is equally unlikely that any Durkheimian was in the audience at its premiere at the Théâtre des Champs-Elysées. Yet, the ballet's scenes and its score are a perfect companion piece to Durkheim's description (following Spencer and Gillen) of tribal gathering in ritual activity among the Australian which generate collective effervescence. Some excerpts will illustrate this fit:

> The very act of congregating is an exceptionally powerful stimulant. Once the individuals are gathered together, a sort of electricity is generated ... and quickly launches them to an extraordinary height of exaltation ... from every side there are nothing but wild movements, shouts, downright howls, and deafening noises of all kinds... The sexes come together in violation of the rules governing sexual relations ... (Durkheim 1912:217-20).

The dramatic passages in this section of "The Elementary Beliefs" where Durkheim provides an account of the genesis of the sacred in primitive rituals are of course well known and highlighted in various utilizations of the power of the sacred, whether in the sociology of social movements or the sociology of religion or other vistas of the sociological imagination. I would suggest, however, that whether in a classroom setting or in one's own office, an enhanced reading anew of *The Elementary Forms* might profitably be done listening to Stravinsky's score and imaging the performance of Nijinsky and his troupe.

Closing Consideration: Durkheim, the Avant-Garde and Primitivism

I have contented in this essay that Durkheim's great masterpiece, *The Elementary Forms of the Religious Life* has a context that previous sociologists have neglected, the cultural context of avant-garde art in pre-war France. The creative activity of various avant-garde movements was oriented to challenging the status quo, to changing forms of depicting and perceiving reality. There is a patent affinity on the one hand between the Cubists' radical depiction of abstract geometric forms, including drawing from African masks body representations such that concave surfaces come to replace naturally convex ones, and, on the other, Durkheim drawing from ethnographic data of Australian aborigines to go beyond positivism to find elementary forms of social structure. It is this affinity occurring in the same condensed time period in Paris that I find intriguing, albeit there is no obvious direct linkage between Durkheim's avant-garde sociology and avant-garde art.

Further, there is an important divergence that may be noted in the political orientation of the avant-garde artists and that of Durkheim and the Durkheimians, and this in how each made capital of "primitivism" or the primitive. Patricia Leighten in her important study of the avant-garde in France, *Re-Ordering the Universe, Picasso and Anarchism 1897-1914,* has convincingly shown the influence of anarchism (formulated in the 19th Century by Kropotkin, Bakunin and Proudhon) on various artists and literary figures, from the Symbolists to the Cubists.[28] A major anarchist "mentor" of the avant-garde artists was Kropotkin who saw them as an avant-garde in changing human consciousness and moving society forward and away from the materialism of the age (Leighten 1989: 50). Picasso came to France from his native Barcelona with a strong anarchist cultural background and kept it in his radical explorations, as did others of his entourage. Even in his later years of great public (and commercial) success, he still saw himself "as a true revolutionary" though he rarely used his art work for political propaganda (save during the Spanish Civil War with his dramatic abstract canvas of the Nazi bombing of Guernica. in 1937). At the end of World War II Picasso joined the French Communist Party and kept his membership for the rest of his long life.[29]

Durkheim was hardly in sympathy with anarchism, which for him was social disorder, chaos, anomie. And if the Cubists had welcomed Poincaré's discussion of non-Euclidian geometries indicating there is no *a priori* geometrical space (Antliff and Leighten 2001: 72), Durkheim in the *Elementary Forms* may be seen

---

28   Among the well-known painters with strong anarchist tendencies seeking in their work to provide images of a future society were Pissaro and Signac (Herbert 2001). The latter was a long-time member of the Anarchist-Communist Party and an anti-war protester during World War I.

29   For a sophisticated Marxist sociological exposition of Picasso and Stravinsky as creative artists seen ultimately as reinforcers of contemporary bourgeois society and its contradictions, see Raphael (1980: 115-46).

as seeking to salvage the Kantian *a priori* categories (space, time, etc.) as essential epistemological bases on which our bases of knowledge rest – for Durkheim, the *a priori* are located in the very structures, or forms, of social organization: they are, in that sense, communal. But he was equally critical of individualism based on the market place, and used ethnographic materials of "primitive society" to seek bases of societal renovation, a task that needed to be completed by moral education (his chair, if not his mission at the Sorbonne, was one of sociology *and* education). World War I put an end to his mission, though his prize pupil and nephew Marcel Mauss was to continue the effort with an essay that has become a classic in its own right, *The Gift: The Form and Reason for Exchange in Archaic Societies* (1924; available in translation by W.D. Halls, New York: W.W. Norton, 2000). It has become a foundation work for exchange theory but also in its conclusion is a subtle manifesto for the democratic socialism that underlay much of the social philosophy of the Durkheimians.

Perhaps it is well to end this by first suggesting there is a slender nexus between the Durkheimians and avant-garde art. In 1930 Bataille published a short-lived review called *Documents*, with an issue entitled *Homage to Picasso* (*Hommage à Picasso*), and various testimonials addressed to Picasso were provided by a wide range of intellectuals and artists.[30] One of the testimonials was from Marcel Mauss, which merits reproducing in full:

> I am asked to join this homage which more competent others send you. Should I tell you that I was at the start of this century one of the young men seduced by your paintings and drawings and which even succeeded in convincing some amateurs? or do the organizers of this symposium, knowing my modest knowledge of art termed primitive, Negro or other (which is art *tout court*), simply want that I tell you how much your paintings and drawings bring us to the purest sources of impression and expression?[31] Marcel Mauss, Directeur d'études à L'École des Hautes Études.

---

30   Picasso never rested on his early and late Cubist laurels but kept experimenting in the 1920s, including working with Diaghilef and Jean Cocteau on designing ballet stage scenery, and, in another direction, painting shockingly grotesque distortions of the human face and body (Butterfield 2007). The stimuli for the latter may have been the sights of maimed World War I veterans and/or some of the African masks he had first seen in storage at Trocadero.

31   I have translated this from the original French: "On me demande de m'associer à l'hommage que d'autres plus compétents vous adressent. Est-ce pour vous dire que j'étais, aux premières années de ce siècle, un des jeunes gens que votre peinture et votre dessin séduissaient, et qui même réussirent à convaincre quelques amateurs ? Ou bien ceux qui dirigent la publication de ce florilège, sachant mes modestes connaissances en art dit primitif, nègre ou autre, (qui n'est que l'art tout court), veulent-ils tout simplement que je vous dise [sic] combien votre peinture et votre dessin nous rapprochent des sources les plus pures de l'impression et de l'expression?". Marcel Mauss, "Hommage à Picasso",

However brief this message is, it is most suggestive that at least in the case of Mauss, and perhaps other young Durkheimians of the period, the work of the avant-garde was known. Indeed, Mauss might well have visited a museum or an art gallery at the some time during September 17-October 8, 1911 as when Max and Marianne Weber visited Paris and enjoyed the cultural scene, including modern art and the theatre! Weber, Marianne recounted in her biography, was an enthusiast for art, purchasing in Paris paintings of contemporary artists Georges Desvallieres and Félix Valloton (the latter associated with the turn-of-century Nabis group of artists that preceded the *Fauves*); in fact, she added, "Max hunted down the whole modern painting not only in museums and galleries, but also at art dealers,".[32]

A lasting thought for this venture in historical sociology is to recall Nisbet's observation: "Scientists Marx, Weber, Durkheim, and Simmel were without question. But they were also artists, and had they not been artists ... the entire world of thought would be much poorer"(*Sociology as an Art Form*, p. 7).

Durkheim, however he might not have had a feeling for modern aesthetics the way that Mauss, and particularly Weber and Simmel (the latter's "formal sociology" of abstracting form from concrete content has striking affinity with Cubism)[33] showed, did live in a period of great artistic creativity, of avant-gardism prodded and stimulated by "the primitive". His own great work, produced at the very same time as *synthetic Cubism* and the artistic scandals of the Ballets-Russes, was a scandal for traditional religionists, by valorizing the genesis of the sacred in primitive communal settings of totemism rather than in the more evolved redemptive religions sometime grouped as the Abrahamic faith communities. *The Elementary Forms of the Religious Life* is also a multidimensional sociological masterpiece bridging sociology and philosophy, positivism and interpretive

---

Documents, 2, 3 (1930) : 177. I am grateful to W.S.F. Pickering for giving me this important reference of Mauss.

32   I am very appreciative of Professor Rainer Lepsius of the University of Heidelberg, drawing on Marianne Weber's biographical account (*Max Weber: A Biography)*, to bring this to my attention in a personal communication (November 2, 2007). Weber's aesthetic taste welcomed modern art in other than painting, as Lepsius notes, "Weber was also interested in modern music, as for example in operas by Richard Strauss." His interest there is shown in a lengthy essay relating the evolution of music to the rationalization process: *The Rational and Social Foundations of Music,* translated and edited by D. Martindale, J. Riedel and G. Neuwirth, Carbondale, IL: Southern Illinois University Press, 1958.

33   Simmel's broad interest in the cultural sphere and its nexus to the "inner life" led him to publish a detailed interpretive essay: *Rembrandt: an essay in the philosophy of art*, trans. and edited by A.Scott and H. Staubmann, with the assistance of K.P. Etzkorn, New York: Routledge 2005 (1916). The editors in their introduction signal Simmel's viewing "his intellectual engagement with art as a sort of treasure trove for his theoretical concerns" (p. xii). That Simmel most likely had knowledge of avant-garde Cubism and its geometric abstractions is strongly suggested in Coser's discussion of Simmel wanting "to develop a geometry of social life" (Lewis A. Coser, *Masters of Sociological Thought, Ideas in Historical and Social Context.* New York: Harcourt Brace Jovanovich, 1977, p. 180).

sociology, social structure and social change. By drawing on the primitive as an ingress on the modern, *The Elementary Forms* opened up in advance of its times the "cultural turn" in sociology. It qualifies Durkheim as a creative avant-garde artist.

References

Alexander, Victoria D. 2003. *Sociology of the Arts. Exploring Fine and Popular Forms.* Oxford and Malden, MA: Routledge.

Antliff, Mark and Patricia Leighten 2001. *Cubism and Culture.* New York: Thames & Hudson.

Butterfield, Andrew 2007. "Recreating Picasso," *The New York Review of Books,* 54, 20 (December 20): 12-16.

Dumont, Louis 1972. "Une Science en Devenir," pp. 8-21, in *Marcel Mauss,* special issue of *L'Arc,* 48 (Aix-en-Provence, France).

Durkheim, Emile 1995 (1912). *The Elementary Forms of Religious Life.* Translated with an introduction by Karen E. Fields. New York: The Free Press.

—. 1998. *Lettres à Marcel Mauss,* Philippe Besnard and Marcel Fournier, eds. Paris: Presses Universitaires de France.

Elderfield, John ed. 1994. *Les Demoiselles d'Avignon.* Special issue, Studies in Modern Art 3. New York: The Museum of Modern Art, distributed by Harry N. Abrams.

Francastel, Pierre 1949. "Art et Sociologie," *L'Année Sociologique,* 3rd series, 2 (1949): 491-527.

Gephart, Werner 2000. "The Beautiful and the Sacred: Durkheim's look at the elementary forms of aesthetic life," *Durkheimian Studies/Etudes Durkheimiennes,* 6, n.s., pp. 61-84.

Herbert, Robert L. 2001. "An Anarchist's Art," *The New York Review of Books,* 48, 20 (December 20). http://nybooks.com/articles/14967.

James, Wendy and N.J. Allen eds. 1998. *Marcel Mauss. A Centenary Tribute.* New York and Oxford: Berghahn Books.

Jones, Sue Stedman 2002. "Durkheim and Bataille: constraint, transgression and the concept of the sacred," *Durkheimian Studies/Etudes Durkheimiennes*, 7, n.s., pp. 53-63.

Kerensky, Oleg 1970. *The World of Ballet.* New York: Coward-McCann.

Kurasawa, Fuyuki 2003. "Primitiveness and the flight from modernity: sociology and the avant-garde in inter-war France," *Economy and Society,* 32:1, 7-28.

Leighten, Patricia 1989. *Re-Ordering the Universe. Picasso and Anarchism, 1897-1914.* Princeton: Princeton University Press.

Lieven, Prince Peter 1936. *The Birth of Ballets-Russes.* Boston and New York: Houghton Mifflin.

Lifar, Serge 1954. *A History of Russian Ballet.* London: Hutchinson.

Luhmann, Niklas 2000 (1995). *Art as a Social System*, Eva M. Knodt, trans. Stanford, CA: Stanford University Press.

Lynham, Deryck 1947. *Ballet then and now. A history of the ballet in Europe.* London: Sylvan Press.

Menger, Pierre-Michel 2000. "L'Art, les pouvoirs de l'imagination et l'économie des désires dans la théorie durkheimienne," *Durkheimian Studies/Etudes Durkheimiennes*, 6, n.s., pp. 61-84.

Nandan, Yash 1977. *The Durkheimian School. A Systematic and Comprehensive Bibliography*. Westport, CT and London: Greenwood Press.

Nisbet, Robert A. 1976. *Sociology as an Art Form*. Oxford: Oxford University Press.

O'Toole, Roger 2002. "Durkheim and the problem of art: some observations," *Durkheimian Studies/Etudes Durkheimiennes*, 8, n.s., pp. 51-69.

Pickering, W.S.F. 2000. "Durkheim, the arts and the moral sword," *Durkheimian Studies/Etudes Durkheimiennes,* 6 n.s., pp. 41-60.

Price, Sally 1989. *Primitive Art in Civilized Places*. Chicago and London: University of Chicago Press.

—. 2007. *Paris Primitive. Jacques Chirac's Museum on the Quai Branly.* Chicago and London: University of Chicago Press.

Raphael, Max 1980 (1933). *Proudhon, Marx, Picasso. Three Studies in the Sociology of Art*, trans. Inge Marcuse, ed. John Tagg. New Jersey: Humanities Press; London: Lawrence & Wishart.

Rubin, William 1994. "The Genesis of *Les Demoiselles d'Avignon,*" pp. 13-144 in John Elderfield, ed. *Les Demoiselles d'Avignon.*

Rubin, William ed. 1984. *"Primitivism" in 20ᵗʰ Century Art: affinity of the tribal and the modern*, 2 vols. New York: Museum of Modern Art; Boston: Distributed by New York Graphic Society Books.

Schlanger, Nathan 1998. "The Study of Techniques as an Ideological Challenge: Technology, Nation and Humanity In the Work of Marcel Mauss," pp. 192-212 in James and Allen, eds, Marcel Mauss. A Centenary Tribute.

Simmel, Georg 2005. *Rembrandt: an essay in the philosophy of art*, trans. and edited by A. Scott and H. Staubman, with the assistance of K..P. Etzkorn. New York: Routledge.

Strenski, Ivan 2006. *The New Durkheim*. New Brunswick, NJ & London: Rutgers University Press.

Willener, Alfred 1971. *The action-image of society; on cultural politicization*, A.M. Sheridan-Smith, trans. New York: Pantheon.

Zolberg, Vera L. 1997. "African Legacies, American realities: art and artists on the edge," pp. 53-70 in Vera L. Zolberg and Joni Maya Cherbo, eds., *Outsider Art. Contesting Boundaries in Contemporary Culture.* Cambridge and New York: Cambridge University Press.

Chapter 10
From Durkheim to Managua: Revolutions as Religious Revivals[1]

I

Although an infrequent class of social phenomena, revolutions have been of great interest to students of political modernity and social change. The general breakdown of a social regime and the attempted establishment in its wake of a new social order, this taking place within a compact time frame, continue to be an intriguing topic of historical and sociological research (Goldstone 1980, 1982; Taylor 1984; Zimmermann 1983).

The low incidence but high interest in revolutions at the macro level bears resemblance to the low incidence but high sociological interest in suicides at the micro level. Needless to say, it is Durkheim who very boldly placed suicide (more correctly, suicide rates) in the sociological consciousness not only by demonstrating that it can be analyzed as a social phenomenon but also that some aspects of it are an ingress to core features of modernity. If this seemingly irrational act can be shown to have socially conditioned patterns, then is it not less plausible to seek a sociological, accounting of a collective act – revolution – an accounting that would bring to light underlying patterns operative in historical revolutions? While various paths and models have been used to "make sense" of revolutions (particularly drawing from Marx and Weber), one source that has not been common currency is Durkheim, perhaps because of his image as a founder of "functionalism," with its conservative connotation.[2]

I would like in approaching contemporary revolutions to give his due to the author of *The Elementary Forms of the Religious Life;* this is of course recognized as a sociological classic that continues as a leaven (Jones 1977; Tiryakian 1981), but it has not been thought of in the context of political sociology. As the title of the present chapter suggests, it will be the purpose here to treat one manifestation of revolutions that has remained outside the gaze of sociological scrutiny: namely, revolutions as religious revivals.[3] Although Durkheim himself does not offer a

---

1   Published in Jeffrey Alexander, ed. *Durkheimian Sociology.* New York: Cambridge University Press, 1988, pp. 44-65.

2   For relevant discussions, see Moore 1978; Lacroix 1981; Coenen-Huther 1984; and Fenton 1984.

3   There is one recent study of revolutions, Billington's *Fire in the Minds of Men* (1980), which highlights the religious factor in European revolutions, from the French to

theory of revolutions, *The Elementary Forms* not only contains elements of a cyclic theory of societal renewal but also clearly makes use of the historical instance of a major social revolution, the French, to suggest the possibility of modern societal renovation.

Drawing from his analysis, this chapter will examine social revolutions as carrying out at various levels what may be viewed as aspects of the process of *dedifferentiation,* the obverse of the more familiar master process of *differentiation* (Luhmann 1982). If Durkheim in *The Elementary Forms* places "the religious life" – which he also saw as "the serious" side of the human condition – as the hub of society, so shall we view the religious sector as intrinsically involved in revolutionary movements. The process of dedifferentiation (Tiryakian 1985) at the societal level involves a transformation of consciousness, one in which the relatively distinct individual consciousness of everyday life becomes sentient with others in a common situation and in a common enterprise; this transformation is characterized by a high level of energy, for the individual and for the aggregate. It is a process in which the profane becomes transformed into a sacred context (the "transvaluation" of mundane values) – quite the obverse of the secularization process that has preoccupied so much of the sociology of religion and its image of "modernization."

It may be that the above remarks will evoke the impression that rather than "revolution" we are presenting jaded if not dated discussion of the "counterculture" and "altered states of consciousness" associated with the drug culture. Assuredly not, although the transformation of social consciousness does link theoretically the "counterculture" and "revolutions"; the empirical referents for this chapter postdate the counterculture movement of the 1960s and early 1970s.

The end of the 1970s and the beginning of the present decade witnessed major global shock waves: the oil crisis of 1979, double-digit inflation in industrial countries, a severe debt crisis in Third World countries, and, of still growing significance, the rise of East Asia (and particularly Japan) as a new economic center of industrial productivity successfully challenging the established Western center (Tsurumi 1984). Politically, a major global trend of the past ten years seemed to be a conservative swing in Western democracies, with a few exceptions where social democratic parties prevailed (e.g. France, Spain, Greece).

On the whole, the recent sharp economic constriction seemed to entail or go with greater political prudence, unlike the 1930s, or, for that matter, unlike the 1960s when the cornucopia of economic abundance and unlimited growth seemed to foster political radicalization. There is a set of anomalies to this conservative swing, the set which constitutes the empirical basis for our theoretical reflection. The set is comprised of three nation-states which underwent social revolutions between 1979 and 1981, and in which the religious factor has been central – not in mystifying the revolution, as a Marxist perspective might have it, but in catalyzing the revolutionary movement. The three are Iran, Nicaragua, and Poland. Each revolution is, of course, the fruit

---

the Russian.

of a specific socio-historical trajectory and each revolution has features distinct to its particular context.[4] Yet it is their world-significant import and their common denominators which are sociologically intriguing.

The Iranian Revolution, which toppled the imperial regime early in 1979, sought not only to transform a Westernizing bourgeois yet authoritarian regime into a theocratic "Islamic Republic," but also to export this project throughout the Islamic world, thereby sending shock waves throughout the Middle East (Ramazani 1986). The Polish Revolution, uneasily contained since December 1981, was revolutionary at two levels at least during its peak 1980-81 period. Internally, this was the first instance within a communist country of state-recognized institutions whose existence and autonomy were outside the monolithic power structure of the state and its party. This had been the basis of the socialist revolution laid down by Lenin; the workers' challenge of state authority in the Solidarity movement was thus a "revolution" within the socialist revolution. Externally, just as Iran threatened a domino effect for the Middle East (at least, for Sunni and/or conservative regimes), so did Poland and its Solidarity movement threaten a crack in Russian hegemony throughout Eastern Europe: Solidarity's appeal to the workers in other satellite countries and the appeal of nationalism constituted a potential spark in a tinder box. As to Nicaragua, the Sandinista Revolution was a demonstration that urban and rural populations could unite into an effective opposition movement that could neutralize a militarily superior regime – in this respect, a situation very similiar to that of Iran. But, equally significant, the Sandinista Revolution contained a model of socio-economic transformation and development that clearly challenged the typical "dependency" relation of Central America's export economies vis-à-vis the United States. Just as the Soviet Union applied every pressure, including military shows of strength on the Polish border, so has the Reagan administration done nearly everything to destabilize economically and otherwise the Sandinista government, so as to prevent a domino effect in the region.

The future of these contemporary revolutions is hard to discern, particularly because of their respective external environments. Polish nationalism and the democratization of the regime are severely constrained by Russia looking askance upon any threat to its security system (especially with Polish windows to the West, including a Polish pope who has entered into cordial diplomatic ties with the United States). Nicaraguan nationalism, seeking internal social reforms and external autonomy from American hegemony, has become the bête noire par excellence of the Reagan administration, the latter extending rather than innovating a traditional American interventionist policy in Central America. Iran has been deadlocked in a

---

4   There is an abundant literature on each revolution. Among works that I have found particularly informative on Iran see Bakhash 1982; 1984; Fischer 1980; Keddie 1981. For Nicaragua: Booth 1982; LaFeber 1983; Walker 1982. For Poland: Ash 1984; Ruane 1982; Szajkowski 1983; Touraine et al. 1983.

war with Iraq, but if that should cease tomorrow, Khomeini's Iran would remain as much of a sore spot in the Gulf region as was Mossadeq's Iran in the 1950s.

Exogenous forces are operating to untrack the projects of these three revolutions, and it is perhaps more likely than not that before the end of the century the respective revolutionary movements will remain only in collective memories rather than having become institutionalized in new, long-term social arrangements and societal reorganization. After all, if we look at the totality of historical revolutions, and not just at our three contemporary instances, weight must be given to Orwell's sober observation, "All revolutions are failure, but they are not all the same failure" (quoted in Ash 1984:275).

Perhaps revolutionary movements arc failures in the same sense as charismatic movements fail in carrying out the total transformation of the world contained in the promise of charisma.[5] Yet, revolutionary movements are also successes, for their inception and early phases punctuate the historical process with new beginnings, with the possibility of new bases of societal organization and restructuration.[6] Again, let me invoke Durkheim, the seeming conservative sociologist, who in the Conclusion of *The Elementary Forms* anticipates for modern society "hours of creative effervescence, in the course of which new ideas and new formulae are found which serve for a while as a guide to humanity" (p. 475). And where does

---

5   Indeed, one can consider revolutionary movements as a sub-set of charismatic movements, with charisma residing in the movement itself, rather than specific individuals. This assertion, which complements rather than contradicts the Weberian perspective on charisma, is based on the following suggestive passage in *The Elementary Forms* that parallels Weber's conceptualization:

> We say that an object, whether individual *or collective*, inspires respect when the representation expressing it in the mind is gifted with such force that it automatically causes or inhibits action, without regard for any consideration relative to their useful or injurious effects ... This is why commands generally take a short, peremptory form leaving no place for hesitation; it is because ... it excludes all idea of deliberation or calculation; it gets its efficiency from the intensity of the mental state in which it is placed. It is this intensity which creates what is called a moral ascendancy (1961:237-8, emphasis mine).

6   Note, for example, the following pertaining to the Sandinistas' launching of the Literary Crusade in Year 1 of the Revolution:

> Implicit in this process of transformation was the vision of a new society and of an educational model that would help bring about its realization. According to revolutionary thinking, that vision rested principally on the intelligent, creative involvement of a new kind of citizen in new participatory forms of social organization. Essentially, it called for the formation of the "new man" and the "new woman," a revolutionary citizen inspired by the goals of community service rather than individual gain ... The new social order meant creating a different set of institutions which would respond to the interests and needs of the majority (Miller 1982:247-8).

he look in retrospect for this inspiration? At the French Revolution and the civil religion which it promulgated but could not successfully institutionalize:

> the French Revolution established a whole cycle of holidays to keep the principles with which it was inspired in a state of perpetual youth. If this institution quickly fell away, it was because the revolutionary faith lasted but a moment ... But though the work may have miscarried, it enables us to imagine what might have happened in other conditions; and everything leads us to believe that it will be taken up again sooner or later (p. 476).

The societal transformations sought in the initial projects of the revolutionary movements in Iran, Poland and Nicaragua, those that received popular enthusiasm, may well falter and abort from internal and external factors. But that they were launched and that the religious factor played a central role in the launching have become irrevocably part of the contemporary scene and cannot be expunged from the world historical setting or dropped in an Orwellian "memory hole." If one takes into account that each occurred in a highly repressive regime that was either eventually toppled (Nicaragua and Iran) or forced to make previously unheard of concessions (Poland), then the actualization of the movements must also qualify as important historical moments that merit empirical and theoretical attention. In the context in which they have taken place, each represents a project of modernity, a radical alternative to being doomed to peripheral status as a client state of alien powers. Should the respective project not succeed, for whatever reasons, we can still affirm for the contemporary revolutions Durkheim's observation about the French Revolution: "But this experiment, though short-lived, keeps all its sociological interest" (p. 245).

II

To draw upon *The Elementary Forms* as the theoretical mainspring for interpreting contemporary revolutionary movements may seem like a far-fetched excursus into the sociological classics. After all, this is a work which is not only a fountainhead of modern functionalism but also a secondary analysis of ethnographic data pertaining to structures of primitive society. Yet, as already mentioned, the work contains several pregnant references to the French Revolution. Durkheim explicitly uses that historical happening, not only to illustrate the applicability of his theory of the genesis of the sacred as being at the heart of social renewal[7] but also to

---

7   Elsewhere (Tiryakian 1978) I have suggested that Durkheim might well have drawn upon other and closer collective experiences of the Third Republic – such as the trans-Paris funeral procession of the remains of Victor Hugo and the tumultuous pro- and anti- Dreyfus demonstrations – as occasions where great assemblies give rise to collective enthusiasm and sentiments of participating in a world that transcends the everyday, mundane sphere.

anticipate as one scenario of the future of modernity a religious effervescence that would provide a new set of guiding principles for the society of tomorrow.[8] To see its bearing for an understanding of contemporary revolutions and to see what validation these may offer Durkheim's analysis will be the purpose of the following reconsideration of aspects of *The Elementary Forms*.

Abstracting from the abundance of ethnographic materials crafted together by Durkheim into a unified sociological collage, the starting point of his analysis of the social order is his well-known dualism of things sacred and things profane: sacred and profane objects, sacred and profane activities, and, more generally, the sacred and profane worlds. In the "normal" setting of the social world, each has its own delimited sphere: it is in their confrontation, so to speak, that the drama of the social world – societal regeneration – takes place. Most sociologists of religion have implicitly considered the drama to be the intrusion of the profane in the sphere of the sacred: the enlargement of the sphere of the profane at the expense of the sacred is one major meaning of "secularization."[9] Durkheim's analysis, however, provides us with a complementary aspect: the enlargement, in extraordinary settings, of the sacred sphere, what may be termed the "sacralization" of aspects of the profane.

In his doctoral dissertation, *The Division of Labor in Society*, Durkheim had placed the world of work and its occupational structure as the key node of society. The socio-economic sphere in *The Elementary Forms* is that of the profane world *par excellence* (p. 346), but its image in this later work is considerably downgraded. The economic sphere fractionates individuals from each other into a social life which is "uniform, languishing, and dull" (p. 246), and "too great slavishness of daily work" (p. 426) leads to mental fatigue which requires recreation from other sources. What also needs renewal from sources outside the everyday world is the renewal of non-kin social solidarity.

Recall that the sphere of the sacred for Durkheim is the one in which the religious life takes place: it is generated – and regenerated – by great collective gatherings which provide actors with the direct consciousness of belonging to and participating in something greater than individual lives.[10]

A related point Durkheim makes is appropriate for an understanding of the onset of revolutionary movements. In book II, chapter 7, Durkheim talks about the increased energy and the increase in force which individuals feel when they assemble together. He makes clear (pp. 240ff) that this effervescence leading to

---

8   Obiter *dictum,* this is a striking parallel to Weber's own foreseeing as one alternative to the mechanized, bureaucratized petrification of capitalistic society the possibility of a new charismatic renewal.

9   Luckmann's perspective (1967) as to the growing centrality of the "privatization" of the religious in individual autonomy is the reciprocal of Durkheim's noting (1961[1912]:347) the rudimentary aspect of the individual cult.

10   "Society is able to revivify the sentiment it has of itself only by assembling" (*The Elementary Forms*, p. 391).

"this exceptional increase of force" (p. 241) is not limited to primitive society; it is also "characteristic of revolutionary or creative epochs" (p. 241). And much later in his analysis, Durkheim, in discussing the genesis of the philosophical notion of causality, reiterates the importance of the group assembling in giving rise to the consciousness of *power,* which stems from the moral forces of the collectivity (pp. 408ff). Durkheim's sociological analysis echoes the French adage, "l'union fait la force": the act of coming together, of uniting in collective assemblies, generates societal consciousness for the actor and in doing so provides him with exultation and a feeling of force or energy which, on an aggregate basis, conveys a sense of power. The power to do things, and, in certain circumstances, to transform (or re-form) the social order.

How does this relate to an understanding of revolutions? A revolutionary movement entails the sustained interaction of large numbers of persons; it entails the coming together and welding of various social fractions into a larger whole having consciousness of itself in a collective purpose. The social space and social time of the everyday world is transformed into an extraordinary setting which will become the axis *mundi*, to borrow from Eliade (1959), of the renovated social order. It is important to bear in mind that revolutionary movements unite actors *against an ongoing social order*; the power or collective force which the actors feel in uniting is essential if there is any chance that collective behavior may succeed in overcoming an established social order that commands important economic and military resources. The power that a revolutionary movement generates is, ultimately, an enthusiastic conviction that the overthrow of the established social order is morally right and just. Since Durkheim's analysis is in the context of rituals, it takes us only part of the way in looking at contemporary revolutions, which intend to alter drastically rather than reaffirm and renovate, the present order.[11]

Just what is revived? For Charles Grandison Finney, the great exponent, theoretician and practician of religious revivals in the Age of Jackson, a revival, which requires the excitement of protracted meetings, seeks ultimately to rekindle the desire of self to be united with God.

> The state of the world is still such, and probably will be till the millennium is fully come, that religion must be mainly promoted by these excitements. How long and how often has the experiment been tried, to bring the church to act steadily for God, without these periodical excitements (Finney 1960:10).

> A revival ... brings them to such vantage ground that they get a fresh impulse towards heaven. They have a new foretaste of heaven, and new desires after union to God; and the charm of the world is broken. (Ibid.:16).

---

11   Of course, revolutions often develop elaborate rituals: for interesting materials on the French Revolution in this vein, see Ehrard and Viallaneix 1977 and Hunt 1984.

Durkheim's analysis provides a sociologistic translation of the above. Instead of solidarity with God needing renewal, it is solidarity with society which has to be periodically revived, and this consciousness or sentiment conies about in assemblies (Durkheim, p. 391), just as for Finney. For Durkheim, in fact, all organized groups ("political, economic or confessional") need to have periodical reunions (p. 240) lest commitment to the group fall into desuetude.

Where Durkheim uses 'society," I would propose that technically it is better to follow Talcott Parsons and use "societal community" or, as he notes in the case, of modern society, "nation," to designate

> the collective structure in which members are united, or, in some sense, associated. Its most important property is the kind and level of solidarity which characterizes the relations between its members (Parsons 1968:461).

Sociological analysis of "nation" has been underdeveloped despite important early conceptualizations by Weber and Mauss, respectively (Tiryakian and Nevitte 1985), with the tendency until recently to accept uncritically the coupling of "nation" with the juridical and organizational "state."[12] The nation should be seen as a political and cultural "total social phenomenon" (in Mauss' expression), having intersubjective and objective features which taken together provide a matrix for social identity (one's nationality) and for differentiated social institutions that are in turn constituted by differentiated role-sets.

In the everyday, profane world, consciousness of belonging to the "nation" is subordinated to belonging to and participating in more differentiated structures. Actors occupy different positions in social space, with important differentials of power and resources that characterize the social stratification system. It is in extraordinary settings – typically, settings of crisis (such as wars, the holding overseas of hostages, and so on) – that these differentials are suspended if not eliminated and that consciousness of common membership in a single "nation" emerges to the fore as the basic structure underlying public intersubjectivity. It is particularly in the modern period of the past two centuries that "nation" has become salient as the societal community, and revolutionary movements as well as nationalistic movements have used it tacitly or explicitly for the purpose of social mobilization. "Nation" is more than secular grouping; it has tended to become a surrogate for the deity, with "In the name of the nation," or "In the name of national unity" replacing "In the name of God" as a call for collective action and sacrifice.

To extend the Parsonian conceptualization, revolutions and revivals may be viewed as representing "cycles of affective activity" in contradistinction to cycles

---

12   For recent discussions that bring back the centrality of "nation" as a social category, see Nielsson 1985, Tiryakian and Nevitte 1985, Armstrong 1982, and the review essay by Waldron 1985.

of "instrumental-adaptive" activity.[13] The latter entails processes of differentiation, the former of dedifferentiation (Parsons, Bales and Shils 1953:167). The religious revival which concerned Finney so much is also central in Perry Miller's brilliant analysis of the formation of the American national character: Miller saw in the evangelical fervor (of the 1830s) "the primary force in maintaining 'the grand unity of national strength'" (Miller 1965:95). Miller emphasizes the significance of the "great awakening" in reviving consciousness of belonging to the same American polity, of having common values and a shared purpose.

This is pertinent to the notion of dedifferentiation because the setting for the revival (typically in the American case, the campsite or outdoor tent meeting) placed participants on the same social plane, emphasizing the social equality between actors.[14] A religious revival and a genuine social revolution tend to devalue if not abolish social rankings, and this typically occurs in settings of high affectivity of "enthusiasm." With the dissolution of the structures and strictures of the everyday, profane world (its destructuration), there emerges the discovery of the societal community as the fountainhead of the social body.

In terms of the Parsonian A-G-I-L four-function schema of action systems, dedifferentiation would suggest a phase movement of action from differentiated, institutional structures to the more primitive "L" cell of the religious-expressive sphere. The process of dedifferentiation seems in general to be attended by a high level of energy release,[15] and once underway, it tends to accelerate.

This combination can often take pathological forms which may paralyze the living system involved: cancer in biological systems, antinomianism in (some) movements of religious enthusiasm, anarchism or "mob rule" in some collective uprisings. Religious systems seem to be aware of consequences of the profane coming into contact with the sacred (which is, to be sure, the ultimate goal of religious activity) by setting up careful, institutionalized procedures (rituals) which regulate the nature of the interaction. Political systems also seek differentiated means (such as the divisions of government) to regulate or control the access to political power. Revolutionary movements, however, sweep aside the rituals or institutional procedures (which may have been swept aside by the prevailing regime) and this may be attended by great violence – against others in the case of social revolutions, or against the self in some religious movements of enthusiasm.

---

13   The periodicity which Durkheim noted in *The Elementary Forms* as characterizing oscillations between sacred and profane activity receives an important corroboration in Bales' research and analysis of phase movements in small groups (Bales 1953:123).

14   Recall that de Tocqueville's voyage to America, in which he noted both the vitality of religion and the importance of equality in the new republic, took place in the midst of the great revival.

15   Very broadly, we may think of processes of differentiation as evolving from L→I→G→A, and dedifferentiation as a reverse movement. The high intensity of "I-L" interchanges, we suggest, would be in Parsonian action terms the equivalent of Durkheim's notion of "collective effervescence."

While this aspect of dedifferentiation may well appear noxious; it is also necessary to bear in mind that historical collective beginnings – of religious as well as political collectivities – more frequently than not are marked by violence.

It is now time to take up a discussion of the revolutions in our contemporary setting which represent attempted new beginnings for three nations, new endeavors at social mobilization to include actors who were excluded by the respective regime from active participation. One may say that in the cases of Iran, Poland and Nicaragua, "state" had become phenomenologically differentiated from, and in fact pitted against, "nation"; the religious factor was important in launching the process of dedifferentiation as a process of societal renewal.

III

The previous discussion has developed the twofold argument that modern religious revivals and revolutionary movements in their inception are processes of dedifferentiation and that their political significance lies in delegitimating the present social order and uniting against it socially heterogeneous and scattered actors. The essential dynamics of this transformation of the everyday social world into the realm of the sacred is contained in *The Elementary Forms.*

Extending the argument, the nexus between religion and polity, including between religious and political movements, can be viewed as intrinsic – not only to previous historical periods but also to the setting of modern society (Merki and Smart 1983). The etymology of religion (*religare*, to bind back or bind together) suggests that societal bonds are grounded in the realm of the sacred. "Nation" as the modern societal community partakes of the sacred in providing the basic political bonds of societal actors. Restoring or redeeming the nation from bondage (from what is perceived as alien rule), restoring or providing the nation with autonomy, are primary endeavors of the revolutionary movement. To the extent that revolutionary movements take place in conjunction with an ongoing "church" or religious institution which has historical linkage with the nation as its common religion, that is, the religion of the great majority of the people, then that religious institution may well play an important catalytic role in the national "awakening" and consequent political mobilization. This seems strikingly illustrated by the contemporary revolutions in Iran, Nicaragua and Poland. It is not part of my argument that if revolutions have occurred in these three countries it is because of religious causes that were not present in earlier historical social revolutions. Fischer's observation on the Iranian Revolution here seems appropriate for all three countries:

> The causes of the revolution, and its timing, were economic and political; the
> form of the revolution, and its pacing, owed much to the tradition of religious
> protest (Fischer 1980:190).

In each instance, the years preceding the revolution were marked by sharply deteriorating economic conditions for the masses, and by the ruling elites using widespread cultural and physical repression – ranging from media censorship to the brutal use of the National Guard by Somoza and SAVAK by the Shah. In each case, the regime faced growing opposition from the religious sector, which underwent radicalization and which became in the 1970s the one area having a certain degree of autonomy from the centralizing and totalitarian tendencies of the regime.

In Iran the secularizing, Westernizing orientation of the Shah as much as his pro-American policies (for example, violating the Arab oil embargo in the wake of the Yom Kippur War) generated increasing opposition from the country's Shi'ite religious leaders, such as the ayatollahs Shari'at-Madari, Mahmud Taleqani and Ruhallah Khomeini, the latter having been forced into exile in 1964 until his dramatic return in 1979. In between, various clandestine movements had sprung up, including secular leftist factions, but the ones with greatest popular appeal were those which interpreted the situation in terms of widely understood Islamic symbolism and tradition. Effective opposition to the Pahlavi regime was provided by the writings of such intellectuals as Jalal Al-i Ahmad and Ali Shari'ati, who redefined an autonomous Iranian cultural identity liberated from the disease of "Westoxication." Along with this, the writings of Khomeini (particularly *Islamic Government*) were widely distributed, read and heard on smuggled cassettes by a growing number of religious students. Shi'ism and its Holy City of Qom thus became important levers against official society. As Harney points out in his review of Bakhash,

> Khomeini been a forgotten exile in Iraq. Religious leaders within Iran had kept in touch with him over the years and in this way a network had been created which in effect amounted to a parallel society and authority within Iran (Harney 1985:65) .

In Nicaragua, the combination of Vatican II, the rise of liberation theology and the Latin American Bishops' Conference at Medellin (Colombia) in 1968 set the stage for a dramatic reorientation in the 1970s of the Catholic Church, a traditional basis of regime support in Latin America. This entailed withdrawal of regime support by the primate of the Church (Archbishop Obando), particularly following the earthquake of 1972 in protest at the appropriation by Somoza of international relief. Throughout the 1970s, an increasing number of the clergy – Catholic and Protestant Evangelical – turned socially and politically active in organizing "base communities" for the rural and urban poor, in staging protests in and out of churches, and even became participants in the opposition underground movement that had developed in the 1960s, the FSLN (Sandina National Liberation Front).

> By late 1972 church people were involved in the initial stages of the anti-Somoza struggle ... there were significant contacts between the FSLN and some people

in the church. The clergy and the hierarchy had been involved in conflictive situations, particularly in protest over human-rights abuses, and the hierarchy had taken some steps ... to move from its traditional posture of legitimation. (Berryman 1984:64)

In many areas, the churches came to be the only source of refuge. By providing refuge, the churches came under attack, and so became a focal point of popular resistance ... So, in the insurrection the weight of the institutional Church was perceived in the popular imagination as anti-regime. Meanwhile, much of the Evangelical leadership within the country openly embraced the FSLN as the legitimate representative of the Nicaraguan people (Dodson and Montgomery 1982:163).

As to Poland, the Catholic Church as associated with national identity for centuries, and, particularly after Poland's partition, had developed a double sense of mission: not only the strictly religious mission of the keeper of the faith until Christ's return, but also keeper of the national heritage until the return of an autonomous and integral Poland. Even after the communist take-over, the Church had deep roots and profound appeal in the rural areas as well as the newer industrial areas. For this reason, a certain *modus vivendi* was established in the post-Stalin years between the regime and the Church headed by Cardinal Wyszynski, with the Church having a de facto recognition, which permitted it to criticize openly aspects of the regime which the Church saw as abuses of the Polish people. It was thus an exceptional lever within the communist bloc of countries:

Even for those [intelligentsia] who were by no means religious, the Church offered the only opportunity of openly expressing their disapproval of the Government by attending Sunday mass. The Church pulpit became a unique source of the uncensored word, of a voice eminently concerned for the material and non-material well-being of the people of Poland (Szajkowski 1983:3).

I have used the past tense, but the situation still prevails in Poland today (1988), since the Solidarity Revolution of 1980-81 ended in defeat (or stalemate?), leaving the Church today in a situation similar to the pre-1979 setting.

Thus, Adam Michnik, a foremost intellectual dissident liberated from prison in 1984, commented about the present Polish situation:

I saw churches that served as oases of spiritual independence and provided home for centers of aid to the victims of repression...the Catholic Church is the only institution in Poland that is simultaneously legal and authentic, independent of the totalitarian power structure and fully accepted by the people. The pope is for the Poles the greatest teacher of human values and obligations (Michnik 1985:44-6).

Just as many clergy in Somoza's Nicaragua used churches and masses to express cultural opposition, so even today is this the case in Poland, as exemplified by the weekly "mass for the Fatherland" at the "Christian University of the Workers," organized near Krakow by Father Jancarz, continuing for steelworkers and intellectuals a tradition begun by Father Popieluszko for steelworkers in Warsaw, before his murder in 1984 (Michnik, p. 43; Ash 1985:5).

To be sure in the respective pre-revolutionary settings of Nicaragua, Iran, and Poland, the religious sector was not the sole source of opposition to the regime. A revolutionary movement, as any broad-based collective current, has different streams. The religious factor is significant in providing the movement with a moral force and symbolic means to neutralize and delegitimate the established regime and to affirm the legitimacy of the opposition. By so doing, it provides members with the courage and motivation that is needed to band together in active opposition and to risk their lives, if necessary, in seeking to topple the regime. This is particularly true in the case of the Catholic Church (and the Evangelical missions in Nicaragua) and Shi'ism, respectively, because of their emphasis upon the acceptance of suffering and martyrdom in emulation of their founders – Christ for the former, All and his son Husayn, for the latter).[16]

---

16   Note, for example, these passages in Fischer's discussion of the Iranian Revolution: "The theme of martyrdom was of course central to the revolution" (Fischer, p. 214), and "Muharram [December 1978] began with an explosion. For three consecutive nights, men in white shrouds signifying their willingness to be martyred went into the streets in defiance of the curfew" (p. 204).

In the Central American situation, the murders of fellow Maryknoll and other priests and nuns in Guatemala and El Salvador, climaxed by the assassination of Archbishop Romero, have made the theme of martyrdom in the service of the oppressed and the poor particularly salient to the clergy participating in the Sandinista Revolution.

Note, for example, the interweaving of Nicaraguan realities and the Christian passion in Ernesto Cardenal's remarkable *The Gospel of Solentiname*:

> Jesus before the Sanhedrin is like Thomas Borge, the Sandinista leader, who has been put on trial; the Roman soldiers are like Somoza's National Guard or like Green Berets ... There is an extensive comparison between the death of Jesus and that of Sandino ... (Berryman 1984:10).

In the case of Poland, the theme of martyrdom and sacrifice have many important symbols drawn from the historical experience and suffering of that country. A very important figure is Stanislaw Szczepanowski, patron saint of Poland; this eleventh-century bishop of Krakow was slain, while saying mass, by a tyrannical ruler whose immortal rule he had defied. Szajkowski notes about the bishop, "For Poles he remained for centuries a symbol of civic courage and religious zeal, as well as of national identity" (p. 62). Upon his accession to the papacy, John Paul II, whose see had been Krakow, sought to visit Poland in May 1979 to take part in the ceremonies for the 900th anniversary of Stanislaw's martyrdom. The regime, all too aware of the symbolism, had the visit put off until the following month.

Durkheim's analysis of the societal setting in which collective regeneration takes place is rather bare, and it is not clear just what incites or leads the Australians to come together; nor does Durkheim discuss the preconditions for the collective effervescence of revolutionary epochs. But the revolutionary settings of Iran, Nicaragua and Poland suggest that the "dullness of life" of the everyday, secular world, which Durkheim noted, was a function of decreased standards of living for the majority of the population *and* increased political and cultural repression by the regime. Grievances against the respective regimes had accumulated over the years, with episodic outbreaks and riots.

In all three countries religious leaders made common front with secular ones in denouncing the immorality of the regime. The opposition movement that grew in each country in the 1970s had a comingling of clergy, laity and secularists. The presence of recognized religious leaders in the midst of the opposition is highly significant in uniting and encouraging individual actors to engage in opposition to the regime. Durkheim talks about the phase of the profane social world and the "dispersed condition in which the society finds itself" (Durkheim, p. 246). It is not just economic differentiation which disperses (stratifies, fractionalizes) the societal community: it is also in the nature of repressive and totalitarian regimes to disperse actors and to seek to prevent them from coming together. On the other hand, the religious leaders in the three societal settings we have been talking about played a crucial role in the welding of the opposition into a cohesive, committed social body. Note the passage in *The Elementary Forms:*

> To strengthen those sentiments which, if left to themselves, would soon weaken;
> it is sufficient to bring those who hold them together and to put them into closer
> and more active relations with one another. (pp. 240-1)

Durkheim, without using the term "charismatic leader" goes on to talk about the role of the man able to enter into communion with the crowd; dominated "by a moral force which is greater than he and of which he is only the interpreter," he is able to generate an "exceptional increase of force" and "passionate energies" (p. 241). Durkheim might well have in mind as examples for this analysis Desmoulins or Danton during the French Revolution or Jean Jaurès in his own days. But in our contemporary setting, the catalytic agents of the revolutionary movements have been religious figures as much as secular ones.

So, for example, the election of Karol Wojtyla as pope in October 1978 was greeted in Poland as a miracle and "triggered off an unprecedented demonstration of national and civic awareness" (Szajkowski 1983:60). Even the Polish Communist Party (PUWP) sent to John Paul II a congratulatory message with a nationalistic ring. The collective effervescence, which rose to a peak in 1981 in such manifestations as the Solidarity Congress, the ceremonies of the 1956 uprising in Poznan, and the March general strike,[17] may be said to have been triggered off in June 1979 by the return home of John Paul II:

> This papal visit to Poland was a psychological earthquake, an opportunity for mass political catharsis. The Pope expressed in public what had been hidden for decades, the people's private hopes and sorrows, their longing for uncensored truth, for dignity and courage in defense of their civil and human rights (Szajkowski 1983:72).

> ... his return visit ... brought millions of Poles, particularly the young, together in massive demonstrations of national unity and religious fervour (Sanford 1985:8).

In Iran, the exiled Khomeini (in nearby Iraq until the authorities, becoming worried about Shi'ite radicalism, forced him to leave for Paris in October 1978) became the national rallying point for various sectors of society, including secular intellectuals, particularly after the death in 1977 of Ali Shari'ati. Collective effervescence grew in intensity in 1978 with marches, processions and strikes against the Pahlavi regime; banners in these demonstrations always included a picture of Khomeini.

In Tehran on 2 December 1978, the first day of Muharram (a month of special significance for Shi'ism since Husayn's martyrdom took place then) was placed under curfew. Returning home from mosques, people began shouting anti-Shah slogans and from their roofs began chanting "Kill the Shah!," "God is Great!" and "Bring Back Khomeini!"

> The cry was picked up as others in the same and adjacent neighborhoods took up the clamor. Spreading from quarter to quarter throughout the city, in Tehran at least, the entire populace seemed to be ignoring the curfew ... The chants were hypnotic, and as hysteria seemed to grow, people almost lost control (Green 1982:127).

The Iranian Situation (but also the Polish one since John Paul II is a very effective national symbol of Polish unity even away in the Vatican, witness the respective visits of both Polish authorities and Lech Walesa there) indicates that the physical presence of religious figures is not necessary in galvanizing the cohesion of the

---

17 "At eight o' clock on Friday 27 March the factory sirens sounded from Gdansk to Jastrzebie and Poland stopped work. For the next four hours Polish society demonstrated its unity and self-discipline in the largest strike in the history of the Soviet bloc" (Ash 1983:157). A departmental colleague who happened to be in Poland in early September 1981, told me that during the week he was there the Polish sociologists, no less than the general population, were having "a collective experience of a high."

revolutionary movement. It is important that different groups unite feeling his presence, which acts as a symbol of national unification.

Collective effervescence in Iran may have reached a zenith the day in February 1979 when Khomeini returned, greeted by two million people, and it may have reached a climax in Nicaragua on 20 July 1979 when the FSLN definitively took over Managua after the collapse of the Somoza dynasty. However, the effervescence of a revolutionary movement is part of an accelerating process, which this essay has discussed in terms of dedifferentiation. The Iranian Revolution and the Sandinista Revolution became successes in 1979, as did the Polish Revolution in 1980-1 (in terms of the legal recognition of unions and other major regime concessions to groups outside the party).

Collective effervescence as part of the renewal of the societal community, in opposition to official society, is a dramatic surfacing of interactions between groups and individual actors that take place well before a peak is reached or success achieved in overcoming the regime. What is involved is a twofold process of "demoralization" of the existent regime and welding together strands of the opposition into a single moral community, which is defined by the leaders of the movement as "the authentic nation." The task of the revolution, of course, is not achieved by the peak of the collective effervescence. The process of unification, of defining the new moral community which will renew the nation previously submerged in an alien regime, has to be complemented by a new phase of differentiation involved in institutionalizing the revolutionary movement, that is, in restructuring the societal institutions in accord with the principles of the movement.

The latter phase of contemporary revolutions lies beyond the scope and intention of this chapter. As mentioned in the introductory section, the eventual outcome of the respective revolutionary situations is hard to prognosticate, to a large extent because of exogenous factors, albeit the latter are paradoxically of some importance in maintaining the cohesion of national solidarity. The virulent opposition of Washington to Sandinista Managua, of Moscow to Solidarity, and of Sunni Islam to Khomeini's Iran, functions – as in earlier revolutions faced by invasion from counter-revolutionary forces – to provide the new regime with popular support, which might otherwise dissipate. In the case of both Nicaragua and Poland an exogenous variable is the relation of the indigenous Catholic Church to the Vatican, with John Paul II showing increased opposition to liberation theology and to the political involvement of the faithful in social movements. These and various other particular aspects of the empirical cases call for a different line of analysis than that attempted in these pages.

In conclusion, I have tried to frame an important cluster of large-scale social phenomena in our own immediate period within a conceptual frame that derives from a sociological masterpiece. Durkheim's *Elementary Forms* is a magnificent sociological testament of the significance of the religious factor in the organization (and dynamics) of human society. Yet Durkheim himself was very ambivalent towards the surviving organized religions of his day, particularly the Catholic

Church. How would he view the contemporary situations that we have interpreted in this chapter? I would like to think he would find very apt the following attitude of Adam Michnik (intellectual and adviser to Solidarity), described by Alain Touraine:

> If he had been a Frenchman at the beginning of the twentieth century, he told us, he would have taken part in the fight against clericalism and would have been in favour of the separation of Church and state. But, he added, it is impossible to compare a democratic situation with a totalitarian one. In the latter, the Church is a force resisting absolute power; it protects civil society against the state, and therefore plays a fundamentally democratic role, even when it continues to adopt culturally conservative positions which reinforce its hold over the population (Touraine *et al.* 1983:46).

Postscript: the Philippines Revolution of 1986

Subsequent to the preparation of the above chapter, the Philippines underwent in February 1986 a dramatic series of political events that makes this a striking fourth contemporary instance of the role of religion in revolutionary situations. To recall the salient features of the Philippine Revolution, the twenty-year-old regime of Ferdinand Marcos had become increasingly incapable of dealing with economic deterioration and massive popular discontent. Under pressure from the United States to demonstrate popular support, Marcos called for a "snap" election on 7 February, and the National Assembly which his KBL party controlled declared him the winner on 14 February. However, in the days that followed, a unified Roman Catholic Church, the "institutional Church" of the country since the Spanish colonial period, took an unprecedented active role which led to the ultimate delegitimation and deposition of the Marcos regime and to the subsequent legitimation of Corazon Aquino as the rightful new president.

Prior to the elections, in many rural areas not controlled by the guerrilla forces of the Communist National Democratic Front, the Church had virtually become the only vocal government opposition; several priests, ministers, and lay leaders had been killed, with the evidence pointing to the military (Peerman 1986:228). The electoral campaign itself contributed to the collective effervescence, as the Aquino campaign was forced to utilize "unconventional means of generating public awareness and indignation" (Chanco and Milano 1986:31). The color yellow became the symbol of the "people power," with shredded pages of the yellow pages of phone books thrown from tall buildings during rallies, and a popular jukebox hit, "Tie a Yellow Ribbon," as one of the battle hymns. The radio network of the Catholic Church, Radio Veritas, provided live coverage for the opposition campaign during the entire four-day revolution unlike other official media such as television networks supportive of Marcos (Chanco and Milano 1986:2). More important in the delegitimation of the *ancien régime* were major pastoral letters by the bishops, beginning with Jaime Cardinal

Sin, the chief prelate, whose letter, read in all churches on 18 January 1986, virtually accused the party in power of attempted fraud and intimidation. Even while the national assembly was declaring Marcos the official winner, Ricardo Cardinal Vidal and Bishop Claver, speaking for the Catholic Bishops' Conference, declared that "a government that assumes or retains power through fraudulent means has no moral basis ... the church will not recognize President Marcos even if he is proclaimed winner" (Buruma 1986:11).

The bishops' forceful Valentine Day's declaration proclaiming the moral obligation of the people to right the fraudulence of the regime and its call for "active resistance of evil by peaceful means" was a momentous occasion. As Peerman has observed, "never before had the bishops of any nation condemned a government as unworthy of allegiance and champion a revolution – albeit a nonviolent one – against it" (Peerman 1987:4) Indeed, the "institutional Church" was a crucial factor in the promotion of the February revolution, including the remarkable over-throwing of a repressive regime with non-violent means of delegitimation. The state of collective effervescence that characterized the cases of Poland, Iran, and Nicaragua is also indicated for the Philippines in the following statement: "that revolution did come, in four tense but exhilarating days in late February. Despite its potential for tragedy, the virtually bloodless uprising took on the aspect of a religious festival, with colorful banners flying, nuns saying the rosary, and people extending food and flowers to the enemy" (Peerman 1987:4).

References

Armstrong, John A. 1982. *Nations Before Nationalism*. Chapel Hill, NC: University of North Carolina Press.

Ash, Timothy Gorton 1984. *The Polish Revolution: Solidarity*. New York: Charles Scribner's Sons.

—.1985. "Poland: The Uses of Adversity." *New York Review of Books* 32 (June 2.7): 5-10. Bakhash, Shaul. 1982. "The Revolution Against Itself." *New York Review of Books* 30 (November 18):19-20, 22-6.

—.1984. *The Reign of the Ayatollahs: Iran and the Islamic Revolution.* New York: Basic Books.

Bales, Robert F. 1953. "The Equilibrium Problem in Small Groups." In Talcott Parsons.

Bales R. F. and Edward A. Shils *Working Papers in the Theory of Action* pp. 111-61. New York: Free Press.

Berryman, Phillip 1984. *The Religious Roots of Rebellion, Christians in Central American Revolutions* Maryknoll, NY: Orbis.

Billington, James H. 1980. *Fire in the Minds of Men. Origins of the Revolutionary Faith.* New York: Basic Books.

Booth, John A. 1982. *The End and the Beginning. The Nicaraguan Revolution.* Boulder, CO: Westview.

Buruma, Ian 1986. "Bishops in Open Defiance," *Far Eastern Economic Review* (Hong Kong) 131 (27 February): 11-13.

Chanco, Pedro A. and Benjamin H. Milano 1986. "A Different Kind of Revolution." *Communication World* 3 (September): 3 1-3.

Coenen-Huther, Jacques 1984. *Le Fonctionalisme en sociologie: et après?* Brussels: Editions de l'Université de Bruxelles.

Dodson, Michael and T. S. Montgomery 1982. "The Churches in the Nicaraguan Revolution." In Thomas W. Walker, ed., *Nicaragua in Revolution,* pp. 166-80. New York: Praeger.

Durkheim, Emile 1961 [1912]. *The Elementary Forms of the Religious Life.* Trans. Joseph Ward Swain. New York: Collier.

Ehrard, Jean and Paul Viallaneix eds 1977. *Les Fêtes de la Révolution.* Paris: Société des Études Robespierristes.

Eliade, Mircea 1959. *The Sacred and the Profane. The Nature of Religion.* New York: Harcourt, Brace.

Fenton, Steve 1984. *Durkheim and Modern Sociology.* Cambridge: Cambridge University Press.

Finney, Charles Grandison 1960 [1835]. *Lectures on Revivals of Religion,* edited by William G. McLoughlin. Cambridge, MA: Belknap/Harvard University Press.

Fischer, Michael M. J. 1980. *Iran. From Religious Dispute to Revolution.* Cambridge, MA: Harvard University Press.

Goldstone, Jack 1980. "Theories of Revolution: The Third Generation." *World Politics* 32(April): 425-53.

—.1982."The Comparative and Historical Study of Revolutions." *Annual Review of Sociology* 8:187-207.

Green, Jarrold D. 1982. *Revolution in Iran. The Politics of Countermobilization.* New York: Praeger.

Hunt. Lynn 1984. *Politics, Culture, and Class in the French Revolution.* Berkeley, Los Angeles and London: University of California Press.

Jones, Robert A. 1977. "On Understanding a Sociological Classic." *American Journal of Sociology* 83 (September): 279-319.

Keddie, Nikki R. 1981. *Roots of Revolution. An Interpretive History of Modern Iran.* New Haven: Yale University Press.

Lacroix, Bernard 1981. *Durkheim et le politique.* Paris: Presses de la Fondation Nationale des Sciences Politiques, and Montréal: Presses de l'Université de Montréal.

LaFeber, Walter 1983. *Inevitable Revolutions. The United States in Central America.* New York: W. W. Norton.

Luckmann, Thomas 1967. *The Invisible Religion: The Problem of Religion in Modern Society.* New York: Macmillan.

Luhmann, Niklas 1982. *The Differentiation of Society.* New York: Columbia University Press.

Merki, Peter H. and Ninian Smart eds 1983. *Religion and Politics in the Modern World*. New York: New York University Press.

Michnik, Adam 1985. "Letter from the Gdansk Prison." *New York Review of Books* 32 (July 18): 42-8.

Miller, Perry 1965. *The Life of the Mind in America. From the Revolution to the Civil War*. New York: Harcourt, Brace and World.

Miller, Valerie 1982. "The Nicaraguan Literary Crusade." In Thomas W. Walker, ed., *Nicaragua in Revolution*, pp. 241-258. New York: Praeger.

Moore, Wilbert E. 1978. "Functionalism." In Tom Bottomore and Robert Nisbet, eds., *A History of Sociological Analysis*, pp. 321-61. New York: Basic Books.

Nielsson, Gunnar P. 1985. "States and Nation-Groups." In E. A. Tiryakian and Ronald Rogowski, eds *New Nationalism of the Developed West*. London and Boston: Allen and Unwin.

Parsons, Talcott 1986. "Social Systems." In David L. Sills, ed., *International Encyclopedia of the Social Sciences*, vol. 15, pp. 458-73. New York: Macmillan and Free Press.

Parsons, Talcott, R. F. Bales and Edward A. Shils. 1953. *Working Papers in the Theory of Action*. New York: Free Press.

Peerman, Dean 1986. "'People Power' in the Philippines." *The Christian Century* 103, no. 8 (5 March): 228-9.

—.1987."Corino Aquino: Religious Newsmaker No. 1." *The Christian Century* 104, no. 1 (7-14 Jan.): 3-4.

Ramazani, R. K. 1986. *Revolutionary Iran: Challenge and Response in the Middle East*. Baltimore and London: Johns Hopkins University Press.

Ruane, Kevin 1982. *The Polish Challenge*. London: British Broadcasting Corporation.

Sanford, George 1985. "Poland's Recurring Crises: An Interpretation." *The World Today* 41 (January): 8-11.

Szajkowski, Bogdan 1983. *Next to God ... Poland, Politics, and Religion in Contemporary Poland*. New York: St. Martin's Press.

Taylor, Stan 1984. *Social Science and Revolutions*. New York: St Martin's Press.

Tiryakian, Edward A. 1978. "Emile Durkheim." In Tom Bottomore and Robert Nisbet, eds, *A History of Sociological Analysis*, pp. 187-236. New York: Basic Books.

—.1981. "*The Elementary Forms* as 'Revelation.'" In Buford Rhea, ed., *The Future of the Sociological Classics*, pp. 114-135. London: Allen and Unwin.

—.1985. "On the Significance of Dedifferentiation." In S. N. Eisenstadt, ed., *Perspectives on Macro-Sociological Theory*, pp. 118-134. London and Beverly Hills, CA: Sage.

Tiryakian, Edward A. and Neil Nevitte 1985. "Nationalism and Modernity." In E. A. Tiryakian and Ronald Rogowski, eds, *New Nationalisms of the Developed West*. London and Boston: Allen and Unwin.

Touraine, Alain, François Dubet, Michel Wieviorka, and Jan Strzelecki 1983. *Solidarity. An Analysis of a Social Movement: Poland 1980-1981*. Cambridge:

Cambridge University Press, and Paris: Éditions de la Maison des Sciences de l'Homme.

Tsurumi, Yoshi 1984. "The Challenges of the Pacific Age." *World Policy Journal* II (Fall):63-86.

Waldron, Arthur N. 1985. "Theories of Nationalism and Historical Explanation." *World Politics* 37 (April):416-33.

Walker, Thomas W. ed., 1982. *Nicaragua in Revolution.* New York: Praeger.

Zimmermann, Ekkart 1983. *Political Violence, Crises, and Revolutions: Theories and Research.* Cambridge, MA: Schenkman.

Chapter 11
Sexual Anomie, Social Structure, Societal Change[1]

The concept of *anomie,* re-introduced into sociological parlance in 1893 by Durkheim (1964) in pretty much the same sense as it was used in the late sixteenth century (Merton 1949), has proven itself extremely heuristic for modern sociological analysis, from Merton's own seminal essay on non-conformity, to Duvignaud's theory of anomie and mutation (1970). Indicative that new wine may continue to pour out of the venerable Bordeaux cask from which Durkheim first drew his conceptualization is the perspective recently provided by Simon and Gagnon (1976). They argue that the Mertonian approach, formulated first in the 1930s, was imprinted by a period of general scarcity; consequently this has to be complemented by an "anomie of affluence" which would recognize the capacity of advanced industrial societies to sustain long periods of affluence and technological growth. Their provocative analysis has been most recently extended by Abrahamson whose study of sudden wealth found an inverse relationship between anomia and acceptance of gratification; that is, unlike what Durkheim had posited, larger amounts of sudden wealth "lead to lower anomia" (1980:56).

The present essay endeavors to demonstrate yet another manifestation of the vitality of Durkheim's analysis of anomie by first redirecting attention to Durkheim's discussion of sexual relations as constitutive of social structure, and of the disruptions occasioned by sexual anomie. These observations, scattered in various of his writings, are related to more general theoretical concerns regarding social organization. We will then take the notion of "sexual anomie" and examine in the light of it present features of the social landscape.

Sexual Anomie in Durkheim's Analysis

Durkheim's treatment of sexuality, its social manifestations and significance in modern society, seems to occupy a minor place in his analysis; by extension, the pathology of sexual life, its deviation from a state of sexual health, was not an acute concern in his analysis of conditions making for social order and disorder. At least, this is an inference we can make from a knowledge of his sociological activities and of his times. His religious orthodox family background, his highly

---

1   First published in *Durkheim Lives!* special issue in honor of Everett K. Wilson, *Social Forces,* 59, 4 (1981: 1025-53).

stable, happy, and uneventful married life to a devoted wife, and his living in a "Victorian" period when sexuality was structured in very routinized and conventionalized relationships between men and women meant that Durkheim, unlike Simmel,[2] did not take as problematic (or interesting) relations between the sexes. Certainly when it came to sex, Durkheim was far more ascetic than Max Weber who experienced first hand the force of eros. Weber wrote some insightful passages concerning the tensions between religion and sex, particularly between eroticism and a principled ethic of religious brotherhood, viewed as competitors for this-worldly dominance.

Yet Durkheim's writings on sexuality and sexual anomie are worthy of consideration, not only because they can provide some historical perspective on what sociology at the turn of the century saw in terms of the question of sexuality but also because, reciprocally, Durkheim's position can serve as a mirror for us today on our own situation.

Durkheim's treatment of anomie begins in Book III, chapter 1 of his *Division of Labor in Society* and the emphasis is on structural malintegration between social functions. A fuller treatment is given in his subsequent epochal study, *Suicide*, where in Book II, chapter 5 is the well-known presentation of anomic suicide. There is no need to go over the familiar terrain at the beginning of the chapter where Durkheim discusses *anomie* manifested in economic suicide: unbridled wants and economic appetites are loosened in periods of sharp economic disturbances, crises and booms alike.

It is the latter part of the same chapter which usually receives short shrift by commentators, albeit we can note such recent exceptions as a very extensive and penetrating critique of Durkheim's inconsistency by Besnard (1973) and a utilization of Durkheim's reasoning by Austin and Bologna (1980) to formulate hypotheses concerning the recent effect of women's emancipation on female suicide rates.

In discussing what he terms "domestic anomy" Durkheim at the same time gives us a generalized perspective of human nature and some unexpected data on the functions of marriage – data which could have led to a profound rethinking and revaluation of our perspective on domestic life. Durkheim did not fully utilize his own findings and interpretations because, essentially, they constituted too much of an "anomaly" for the dominant bourgeois cultural paradigm concerning sexual regulation and marriage.

Earlier Durkheim had indicated that man in terms of his biological/animal nature is prone to unlimited desires and wants, which can only make him despair and provoke his unhappiness. Durkheim is talking about economic objects. Economic life, the work setting, which predominates the public setting in which men act, is of course in its normal course regulated by laws and norms that bind men in cooperative solidary association. Economic crises, whether crashes or booms,

---

2   See Georg Simmel, *On Women, Sexuality, and Love*, translated with an introduction by Guy Oakes. New Haven: Yale University Press, 1984.

essentially sweep aside the normative framework from men's consciousness, and one sad result is the increase of suicide from those who participate heavily in the industrial or commercial world (1963: 258). But now Durkheim extends this view that unsocialized or desocialized man is prey to desire the infinity by discussing sexuality. In a revelatory passage, Durkheim contrasts the sexual life of the married and unmarried men (note well that women do not enter into this crucial discourse). The unmarried man aspires to everything and is satisfied with nothing; this life of bachelorhood is typified by Don Juan. Durkheim underscores the "morbid desire for the infinite which everywhere accompanies anomy" (1963: 271) as frequently taking a sexual form. The single man (and we infer Durkheim is talking about the person whose adult life is spent as single, not an early stage in the adult life cycle) does not really give of himself to anyone and reciprocally has no title to anyone. He is uncertain of the shape of the future (again, Durkheim is expressing himself in the subdued Victorian language of the day when he means that the single man does not know what or with whom tomorrow's sexual relations will be shared), and this condemns the single man to constant change.[3] Durkheim concludes that this state of sexual anomie of the single male "inevitably increases the possibilities of suicide" (1963: 271).

What provides regulation of sexual desires is marriage. Durkheim is not so naive as to view sexual desires as "merely the physical instincts which this intercourse" between the sexes involves but all sorts of derived feelings that civilization has woven around the basic physical desire. Marriage regulates the life of passion, especially modern monogamic marriage. If this restricts the physical enjoyment of the married man, it has its benefits since it provides man with certainty (about today and tomorrow's sexual partner); it provides man with a certain peace of mind, with regularity and constancy. And so Durkheim will find in looking at the domestic side of man's social being the complement of the public side. Both support Durkheim's basic moral contention, namely that the discipline of society of which man must subject himself is not only necessary for social organization but beneficial for man. Beneficial to man means fundamentally that man lives better by submitting to social discipline, and living better is evidenced by not killing himself – as Besnard has noted in his discussion, the suicide rate is for Durkheim a salient indicator of social happiness or social health. In brief, we can say that Durkheim approaches marriage as being beneficial to man by socializing his sexual conduct in regulated channels, and that this stabilizes man.

It is apparent that Durkheim takes marriage as the normal sexual relationship between man and woman; marriage is the social condition and regulation of intercourse between the sexes. And this implies that *sexual anomie* will refer to that which deregulates the conjugal bond, e.g., divorce, separation, and death of the spouse. The deleterious effects of sexual anomie will be noted in terms of their manifestation in differential suicide rates. Durkheim further observes that for

---

3   Durkheim is explicit in stating this typifies Don Juan, but it is equally applicable to the polymorphous sexuality of De Sade.

different European countries, those having high rates of divorce and separation have higher rates of *suicide* (1963: 259), and he also notes that suicide among the divorced is markedly higher than among the widowed, the married, and the unmarried. So far so good, in terms of Durkheim's general positive evaluation of marriage.

The fly in the sociological ointment comes in comparing what Durkheim labels "the coefficient of preservation"[4] of husbands and wives in the same country. He notes that the easier divorce is to obtain and the more frequent its occurrence (in Baden and Prussia, in comparison to Italy and France), the higher is the coefficient of women in comparison to husbands; in other words, the greater the occurrence of sexual anomie (as manifested in divorce), the lower the suicide rate of wives, and correspondingly, the higher that of husbands. Marriage, in other words, protects or "immunizes" (again to use Durkheim's physiological/biological discourse in discussing societal conditions of health/pathology), but it is not mutually beneficial to men and women, at least in terms of suicide.

In countries where divorce is forbidden or only recently permitted, the suicide rate of married women exceeds that of unmarried women, while in the same countries, the suicide rate of unmarried men exceeds that of married ones. Inversely, where divorce rates are high, married women have a lower suicide rate than unmarried women, and husbands have a higher rate than unmarried men. Durkheim uneasily draws consequences from these empirical observations. The first is that in certain societies the prevalence of divorce is associated with a rise in the suicide rate of husbands but not wives.[5] This means not only that marriage is not of mutual benefit, but also, by inference, if ease of divorce is an emergent or modern aspect of marital relations, then one can propose that the modernization of marital relations in terms of the spread of divorce is harmful to men but beneficial to women. If Durkheim takes a dim view of divorce, it is – at least in terms of his discussion in *Suicide* – because of its disruptive effect of increasing the suicide rate of men.

In accounting for the empirical observations, Durkheim stresses that where divorce is prevalent, matrimonial regulations are less effective in curbing the sexual passions of man. The argument here implicitly rests on the notion that if "divorce is in the air," so to speak, if it is a rather common option, then married men will be less at peace, less content morally, and less restrained in their (sexual) desires; the net effect is to reduce the immunization of marriage from suicide. There will be a tendency for a convergence of suicide rates between married and unmarried

---

4   This is the ratio of suicide rates of the unmarried to the married of the same sex in the same country. Durkheim's methodological discussion of this relative index used in making national comparisons is worth noting (1963).

5   Durkheim observes in passing that although husband and wife "have the same object as parents, as partners their interests are different and *often hostile*" (1963: 269; emphasis added).

men, with the net result being an increase in suicides and, equally deplorable, adds Durkheim, a decline in the voluntary commitment to monogamous marriage.

Durkheim engages in further reasoning on the matter, which may not ingratiate him to feminists, but which needs to be noted as part of his perspective on sexual anomie. If there is an observable differential consequence of divorce, if divorce has a greater negative impact on men than women, it is because women's sexual needs are more directly physiological, whereas men's sexual needs are more tempered by the intellect and the imagination. "Being a more instinctive creature than man, woman has only to follow her instincts to find calmness and peace. She thus does not require so strict a social regulation as marriage, and particularly as monogamic marriage." (1963: 272).

Moreover, Durkheim notes in studied Victorian discourse that the double standard operates to man's benefit within the context of monogamic marriage:

> Man himself doubtless suffers from this immutability; but for him the evil is largely compensated by the advantages he gains in other respects. Custom, moreover, grants him certain privileges which allow him in some measure to lessen the strictness of the regime. There is no compensation or relief for the woman. Monogamy is strictly obligatory for her ... The regulation therefore is a restraint to her without any great advantages (1963: 272).

Divorce is therefore a welcome relief for the wife, by giving her an option which is an alternative to suicide and which makes her marital situation more flexible than when divorce does not exist or is not frequent.

Given this astute sociological analysis, one wonders why Durkheim continues to speak of "conjugal anomy" or "matrimonial anomy" if his data and analysis indicate that divorce – the major form of matrimonial deregulation for Durkheim – is not that injurious to the health of half of the sexual partners! In concluding passages in this chapter of *Suicide*, Durkheim unwittingly leads one to wonder why women should seek marriage. In reviewing the evidence and anterior discussions of his analysis, he comes down to the provocative statement that "woman can suffer more from marriage if it is unfavorable to her than she can benefit by it if it conforms to her interest. This is because she has less need of it" (p. 275). Even more radical is his conclusion that although marriage and its function are seen as a sacrifice of man of his "polygamous instincts," in fact (or in the light of sociological analysis), it is man who benefits more from marriage than woman, and by accepting monogamy, "it was she who made a sacrifice" (p. 276).

Although "anomie" ceases to appear in Durkheim's vocabulary as he stepped into the twentieth century,[6] there are writings subsequent to *Suicide* which are

---

6   Durkheim's explicit use of the term "anomie" was written in that period in the 1890s when France witnessed a wave of urban terrorism referred to as "anarchism," much like that seen from "the new left" in the aftermath of the 1968 movement, especially in

pertinent in drawing out his observations on sexual deregulation and social structure.

A proposal by the brothers Margueritte[7] to allow divorce by mutual consent occasioned Durkheim to revisit his Suicide data nearly ten years after its publication. Although disclaiming being a reactionary in responding to the proposal, it may be remarked that Durkheim's sociological argument in opposing the liberalization of divorce is complementary to the argument used one hundred years previously by the great reactionary De Bonald.[8]

Durkheim goes over familiar territory in inveighing against extending divorce. The argument is that further liberalization and extension of divorce, though it might make marriage a closer reality to the wishes of the marriage partners, would undermine the principle on which marriage rests and would become a graver social ill than the individual evils it pretended to alleviate (1978: 240). Why? Because where divorce is frequent, so is suicide, and inversely. We need not bother to detail his statistical reasoning.[9] What may be noted is the restatement of his earlier findings. Marriage provides married men with an immunity from suicide not enjoyed by bachelors, and to be married with children is an even greater insurance. Marriage integrates men more with life by exercising a moral influence; it produces peace of mind, an inner balance in men by regulating the passions and giving man "a moral posture which increases his forces of resistance" (1978: 247).

Unfortunately, such is not the case for women; Durkheim observes that divorce does not appear unfavorable to married women but on the other hand, Durkheim later acknowledges that marriage has only a slightly beneficial effect on women (in terms of the tendency toward suicide, to be sure). In rather outright male-limited perspective, Durkheim generalizes about the condition of the married woman.[10]

Germany and Italy. The anarchist movement seems to have receded from the scene with the emergence of the Dreyfus crisis of 1898.

7   Paul Margueritte (1860-1918) and Victor Margueritte (1866-1942) were two highly prolific writers of the Third Republic. Interspersed with a variety of novels, military histories, and short stories are various tracts they published together espousing the feminist movement and its militancy in emancipating women from the yoke of marriage. I cannot tell from Durkheim's reference to them which of their writings he has in mind. The catalogue of the Bibliothèque Nationale indicates several publications ca. 1905-06.

8   The latter's study of divorce should be seen as a prototype of structural-functional analysis and is one of those unsung sociological classics which would merit a modern edition and translation.

9   It is in his careful attention to the relationship between the 1906 essay of Durkheim with the earlier materials in *Suicide*, and the noting of contradictions in the data analysis that Besnard's critique of Durkheim (1973) is most trenchant. Essentially, Besnard faults Durkheim for dropping a sociological theory in trying to deal with the suicide of women; at best, he argues, *Suicide* remains an "unfinished work," and the 1906 essay finishes off the attempt by faulty reasoning.

10   In terms of data presented (1978: 245) Durkheim might have noted that if we compare the suicide rate of married to unmarried women, by age and by locale, in all

"She stands somewhat beyond the moral effects of marriage. Just as she benefits from it only a little, she suffers by it only a little" (1978: 247).

It does seem startling to read that women are marginal to the moral effects of marriage, especially if we take into account the broader cultural context of Durkheim's day, when marriage, foyer, and hearth were seen as the territory of women. The implication or conclusion of Durkheim's reasoning would be that marriage is a male institution and that consequently, in terms of the criteria of moral health and happiness, women should forego or leave marriage in favor of public life, leaving domesticity to men! Such a conclusion might be drawn today, not so much from a "reactionary" stance as from a radical one.

Durkheim, of course, could not face up to the implication if not contradiction of his analysis. He therefore "bracketed," so to speak, how half of the species fares with marriage, and generalized in terms of how the male half would fare with the deregulation of marriage by allowing divorce by mutual consent.

He consequently viewed divorce by mutual consent as making shambles of marriage, since "a regulation from which one can withdraw whenever one has a notion is no longer a regulation" (1978: 247). If such a practice became institutionalized, marriage would lose its prophylactic role of curbing the passions, and consequently anomic suicides would increase. Divorce by mutual consent, intended to lessen the moral miseries of the married partners, would have the unintended result of demoralizing the latter and marginalizing them further from life.

The conclusion of Durkheim in this essay deserves mention. Durkheim the sociologist rejoins Durkheim the moralist (Wallwork 1972) in stressing that conjugal and domestic relations cannot be dropped at the whim of consenting individuals: man's happiness and satisfaction of sexual wants, like the satisfaction of his economic wants, depend upon his being regulated, moderated, disciplined. Marriage serves this basic function.[11] But the last paragraph of the essay has a more poignant tone for it shows that Durkheim, like Cicero, is well aware that times have changed and that public opinion today "sees all regulation as an evil

---

instances save one (the age group 70-80 in Paris), married women have lower rates than unmarried ones. He does not make clear whether "unmarried women" refer only to spinsters/ never married or whether it is a general category that would include widows and divorcees. In any case, the data he does present could be taken to indicate that marriage does provide women with protection from suicide, although the effect is not as sharply marked as in the case with men.

11   It is remarkable that Durkheim, secular sociologist and son of an orthodox rabbi, rejoins almost literally the conclusion of the devout Catholic De Bonald who, in the concluding summary of his own study of divorce observes, "Le mariage est une loi portée contre l'inconstance de l'homme, un moyen de réprimer l'intempérance de ses désires ... la fin du mariage est la reproduction, et surtout la conservation de l'homme, puisque cette conservation ne peut, en général, avoir lieu hors du mariage, ni sans le mariage. L'effet du mariage est donc la perpétuité du genre humain; car le genre humain se compose, non des enfants produits, mais des hommes qui sont conservés."

to which one must sometimes be resigned but which one must attempt to reduce to a minimum" (1978: 252). The Victorian era had ended and concomitantly, the appeal of neo-Kantian asceticism, with which the official discourse of both the Third Republic and Durkheimian thought are so replete (Tiryakian: 1978), had waned from public commitment. Much as Durkheim had marshaled sociological reasoning to prop public support for the normative framework of society, for the voluntary acceptance of wise regulations, he viewed with foreboding that "this new assault upon marriage will achieve its ends;" which might lead to a repetition of the chaos which ensued from the widespread acceptance of divorce and deregulation of marriage during the peak of the French Revolution. Durkheim's admission in "Divorce by Mutual Consent" that public opinion is moving against all regulations, even those involving marriage, is one which bridges the distance separating Durkheim from our own social world; in fact, by virtue of it we can almost view him as our contemporary.

To complete a discussion of Durkheim's relevance for approaching the theme of sexual anomie, we now turn to two other pieces of his. In the first issue of *L'Année Sociologique*, Durkheim chose the occasion to devote an essay accounting for the near universality of the incest taboo (1898); in doing so, he touches on significant aspects of the sexual basis of social organization. Explicating these will be useful in evaluating features of our contemporary setting which from Durkheim's perspective might be termed as manifestations of sexual anomie.

A fundamental aspect of human society is the prohibition of incest; among the basic regulations of social life are the prescriptive rules which forbid sexual relations between members of the same clan (or family, or kin group), and as a corollary, prescriptive rules of marriage enjoin sexual partners to belong to an external clan group from the other. Durkheim notes (1898: 40) that these basic regulations of sexual contact, especially the injunction forbidding sexual contact between members of the same family, are similar to religious prescriptions regulating contact between the sacred and the profane.

He gives a great deal of attention to ethnographic materials that pertain to the ubiquitous phenomenon of the separation of the sexes at various levels. One such aspect is the sexual division of labor, with inter- dictions as to what men and women can do. Other cultural forms of sexual separation may be observed in language: some words are taboo for men when they speak to women, and even, in some societies, men and women may use different languages (1898: 46). The ritual separation of the sexes is grounded in a sort of repulsion which the sexes have for each other, manifested in their mutual avoidance; in societies where totemism is present and with it, sexual totems, Durkheim points out that the two sex totems are taken as rivals and even enemies (1898: 44). It is apparent from his discussion that Durkheim reflects and observes as a constitutive feature of sexual relations the element of antagonism, of the "war of the sexes." But there is another side of the coin to repulsion and antagonism.

It is that sexual relations equally attract together men and women. The basis of sexual intercourse is the pleasure that each member of the couple gets from the other, and this is a spontaneous occurrence, which, Durkheim observes, excludes the ideal of obligation and rule. Where the idea of duty and moral constraint is lacking, there the way is open for deregulation; consequently, "it is not surprising that the mutual attraction of the sexes and what results has often been felt as a danger for morality" 1898: 60). In brief, Durkheim's analysis suggests that a fundamental source of normative breakdown (deregulation or anomie), at least potentially, is sexuality because of its hedonistic or pleasure principle basis which is at odds with social actors submitting their conduct to the system of normative regulations which make possible social organization. Marriage, for Durkheim, is the societal solution which provides a regulation of sexual attraction; sexual attraction is at the basis of marriage but marriage obligates the united individuals to carry out certain duties.

Durkheim tacitly holds that the sexes have different sets of attitudes towards each other. A "spontaneous" attitude is that of physical attraction, but there are other sentiments, such as respectful affection. The forbidding of incest, Durkheim argues at one point, is to prevent such nobler sentiments from being corrupted: "given our present ideas," he remarks, "a man cannot make his sister into his wife without her ceasing to be his sister" (1898: 61). Yet, that is not an explanation of the incest taboo, for we may feel the same sort of affection towards both sister and wife and Durkheim is well aware of those unusual circumstances where incest is permitted and prescribed.

The analysis of Durkheim is framed by the basic sacred/profane differentiation of the social world. In this context, sexual relations = profane, family = sacred. That is, the family or clan is generally the center of religious life, so that clan relations are religious ones. But sexual relations cannot take place within the family because the latter is subject to strict rules of conduct; sexuality, or the passionate activity of humans, thereby went outside the family and expressed itself freely on the other side. Durkheim adds that with time, sensuality may have become a good deal more complex and spiritual or aesthetic but still remains in opposition to family morality: "Ideas related to sexual life have closely tied into the development of art, poetry, to all the vague dreams and aspirations of the mind and the heart, to all the manifestations, individual or collective, where imagination enters for the main part" (1898: 61).

Incest taboo, then, has a basic function of keeping sexual relationships and family relationships distinct; the former are amoral since they are based on pleasure, the latter are the foyer of morality based on sentiments of obligation and mutual duties. This primitive differentiation has become accentuated in historical development, adds Durkheim, right to the present. On the one hand, "sexual sensuality" has developed but our morality, stripped of every passionate element, stressed the Kantian ethic of the categorical imperative (1898: 67). It should be reiterated that Durkheim is writing this in the *fin-de-siécle* European society where sexual life and domestic life, especially in the middle and upper strata of society, were sharply differentiated.

Earlier in his analysis he had developed the proposition that what underlies the incest taboo and the practice of exogamy is the strong ambivalence which men have felt towards blood, endowing it with supernatural values. Since women are periodically "the theater of bloody manifestations," as Durkheim put it (1898: 50), men's feelings about blood become attached to women, leading to the carefully prescribed separation of the sexes. But if blood is perceived as a supernatural substance, that which gives vitality to organisms, and if women manifest a closer involvement with blood than men, doesn't this argue for women being of a higher state, of a higher religious value than men? Durkheim readily sees this implication: 'Primitive men had a choice of two interpretations he had to see in women either a dangerous magician or a born priestess" (1898: 55).

This opens up an extremely suggestive line of symbolic analysis (the image of woman as witch, on the one hand, as head of a public cult, as in the case of Mary Mother of God on the other). It raises the possibility that woman, being closer to the ultimate grounding of life, is not so much the mate of man as man is the mate of woman. However, Durkheim adds that given the inferior position that woman occupies in public life, primitive man did not accept the hypothesis of the religious superiority of woman, and therefore treated her more as a dangerous magician. Sexual separation and sexual segregation, including the sexual division of labor, then, are institutional practices or social structures that really exist more to benefit or protect men from women than vice versa. Durkheim does not state this but such is a warranted conclusion from his analysis.

Durkheim concludes his essay by observing how much of the contemporary aspects of sexual relations are historical derivatives of the primitive attitudes toward incest and blood. The separation of the sexes, he points out as features of modern society, is reflected in the school system and in social gatherings; the invisible barrier between the sexes is also present in each sex having its appropriate clothing and in the restriction of occupational opportunities for women albeit, Durkheim adds, they may have the skills to perform forbidden or restricted functions. Moreover, in men's relations with women, a special language and special manners are adopted. These rituals of deference and demeanor, to borrow from Goffman (1967), highlight and reaffirm the importance of sexual segregation and separation, which Durkheim suggests is a partial reflection of the fact that "thousands of years ago, our fathers made of blood in general and menstrual blood in particular the representation we have discussed" (1898: 68).

The primitive beliefs and prejudices may have dropped by the wayside of social evolution, but not before leaving their marks on sexual relationships, notably, adds Durkheim, with the touch of mystery with which men live to surround women. It is the element of mystery, of the unknown which each sex views the other that is perhaps the principal charm of relating to the other sex, and this could only with difficulty be maintained if men and women intermixed freely; hence the reason why public opinion resists innovators who seek to end the sexes living in dual spheres. Durkheim adds to this insightful analysis that the mysterious attraction of women for men, including the ideas and customs which regulate the interaction between the sexes, constitutes "a recreational need of social existence"; however, such needs are not innate or unchanging and they may be neutralized in the future by other needs, since they are less profound than those which underlie ideas pertaining to incest (1898: 69n).[12]

For Durkheim, then, the separation of the sexes is a constitutive feature of social organization, one resting on profound mixed sentiments. On the one hand, men see women as dangerous, in exactly the same fashion as the profane is a source of contamination for the sacred;[13] on the other, there is the impulse of sexual pleasure which seeks relations with the opposite sex. What Durkheim's discussion points to is the problematic nature of sexuality for the social order, since sexuality is both necessary for the reproduction of society but at the same time contains the possibility of destructuring the normative framework of social reorganization. The complex attitudes of the sexes toward each other (or at least of men towards women, since it is for the most part men who have done the talking about sexuality, including speaking as women, in plays and novels) attitudes which provide social definitions and taboos of sexuality entail all the manifestations of the "purity and danger" element discussed by Douglas (1966). The sentiments or attitudes towards the opposite sex are not so much a consequence of physiological or even individual psychological impulses; rather they may be seen fundamentally as an instance of what Merton and Barber called "sociological ambivalence" in reference to "incompatible normative expectations of attitudes, beliefs, and behavior assigned to a status or to a set of statuses in a society" (1963:95). The antagonism between the sexes, which Durkheim seems to take as one characteristic of sexual relations, could be interpreted as an expression of sociological ambivalence towards the sexual other who on the one hand is the object of pleasure but on the other hand may also be perceived as a source of disruption of the social order. There is thus a state of tension at the heart of sexuality, which Durkheim's essay brings into relief, though it does not become the object of a more comprehensive treatment of sexuality and social organization.

Durkheim did return to this line of analysis some years later in an extensive review (1903) of Ernest Crawley's *The Mystic Rose*, an important study of sexual taboo and its relation to primitive forms of marriage. Though Crawley rejected Durkheim's emphasis on blood as a major factor in the sexual interdictions

---

12   One instance of the correctness, of Durkheim's prediction is that industrial manpower shortages during the World War I, to say nothing of World War II, necessitated the recruitment of women into jobs and occupations which before had been considered off limits for women. The collective survival as a need certainly takes priority over recreational needs of the individual.

13   Durkheim implicitly grounds his analysis in taking the perspective of men. One could equally say that if women are considered as holier (because of or as manifested in their greater involvement with blood, the liquid of life), then it is men who may be the agents of profanation if they violate the social barrier between them, rather than the other way around.

separating the sexes, Durkheim found it an important contribution, particularly because of an argument Crawley introduced concerning the role of marriage in relation to sexual taboo. Briefly, sexual segregation, or the barriers between the sexes which are ritually prescribed or by social convention and mores, in effect would render marriage impossible. There is thus a basic dilemma for men (what might be termed the dilemma of sexuality): either violate serious moral and religious prescriptions or else renounce at the same time "the most powerful of instincts" (the phrase is Durkheim's) as well as the imperative necessities of social life (1903: 356). Crawley proposed, and Durkheim accepts this, that matrimonial practices are rituals which reduce the danger inherent in sexual intercourse; the union of the sexes is dangerous, it can engender harmful effects, hence the need at marriage for neutralizing or purifying the sexual act. At the same time, there are more positive rituals which create or cement the ties that unite the couple. In brief, we may point out that the Crawley/Durkheim perspective on marriage having a complex set of rituals which have as a function to permit interaction between two heterogeneous partners, that is to unite the sexes, is of the same order as the later Durkheimian analysis of religion (1961). It will be recalled that in the latter there must be avoidance of contaminating the sacred, manifested in "negative" rituals of purification that are preparatory for the "positive" rituals involved in interacting with the sacred.

Durkheim's *Elementary Forms of the Religious Life*, although void of the term "anomie," does have a couple of passages pertinent to our discussion. The work as a whole is a treatise on the fundamental forms of social organization, taking the religious life to be the infrastructure of human society. There is a very crucial dialectic between sex and society or sex and religion. On the one hand, the everyday social world is characterized by the segregation and separation between the sexes (as noted in Durkheim's earlier analysis), and this separation is sanctioned and prescribed by religious morality. On the other hand, in extraordinary periods when the collectivity interacts maximally, when there is a collapse of the sacred and profane so that the everyday world is transformed into an exulted sacred plane, the separation of the sexes is eliminated. Sexual interaction is then carried out, even if this interaction violates all the customary norms regulating sexual conduct.

This is brought out in Durkheim's discussion of the Australian corrobbori, a recreational gathering that differs from strictly religious ceremonies by being open to women and uninitiated males. Social interaction is very intense and becomes effervescent to the point that

> The sexes unite contrarily to the rules governing sexual relations. Men exchange wives with each other. Sometimes even incestuous unions, which in normal times are thought abominable and are severely punished, are now contracted openly and with impunity (1961: 247).

A further passage describes the religious ceremony among the Australian Warramunga, who are divided into two phratries, the Uluuru and the Kingilli.

During the evening of the fourth day of their gathering the Uluuru brought up their wives and allowed the Kingilli to have intercourse with them. The import of this, Durkheim notes, is that since these women were Kingilli themselves, the sexual unions violated the basic exogamic rule which structures the everyday social world. Such extraordinary sexual comportment is attended by the wildest excitement. It is at this point that Durkheim develops his provocative interpretation of the religious idea being born in the midst of social effervescence (1961: 250). In brief, what would seem to be the epitome of sexual anomie – the suspension of basic sexual regulation, including the incest taboo – appears in the generation or regeneration of the sacred.

This phenomenon among primitive Australians is one that recurs in other ritualized extraordinary moments of social life, for example the Roman saturnalia and later Mardi Gras festivals. This is also observable in various religious sects that manifest what is appropriately termed *antinomianism,* that is sexual intercourse which is taken by members of the sect as pure, as manifestations of the spirit, but which would be denounced and repressed as promiscuous, incestuous, illicit by the larger or everyday public society. Lastly, this antinomian behavior – understanding by this the breakdown and/or violation of everyday sexual regulations while done in the context of an extraordinary social effervescence – is also observable on certain occasions when the societal community is passing or has passed through a major societal crisis. For example, the declaration of the armistice or the end of World War I and World War II were attended by public spontaneous demonstrations at which the normal regulations of sexual conduct between strangers were suspended (and one can extend this to say that during wartime, which is an extraordinary situation in which there is a greater public awareness and appeal to the sacred, norms of sexual regulation are greatly loosened).

Durkheim did not draw out the implications of the ethnographic materials which suggest that sexuality and social organization are profoundly intertwined. Sexual regulations are for Durkheim part and parcel of the structuring of everyday society, and we must remember that the mature industrial, modern society of his time was one characterized by a well-defined normative differentiation of the sexes, by a rather elaborate set of prescriptions concerning sexual interaction. In this basic consideration, Durkheim's bourgeois world was not that different from the primitive social world of the Australians. Although there were stirrings in his own day – a second wave of the feminist movement that mainly took the form of the suffrage movement, but also of liberalizing the customs attending marriage and divorce – it was not until after World War I, and particularly in our own recent period that sexual regulations, and correspondingly, the deregulation of sexual conduct, really took on an amplitude of major proportions. We will now briefly consider some aspects and implications of the vast sexual revolution that, after capitalism,[14] is the most far-reaching revolution of modernity.

---

14   Although I cannot locate the reference, I believe that it is Lenin who credited capitalism with being an irreversible revolution which transformed unalterably the social

Sexual Changes and Deregulation

Changes that have taken place in sexuality, in sexual conduct and attitudes, constitute probably the most dramatic and significant transformations of the social world in the present century. On a more immediate note, I would also argue that of the various components of the "protest movements" that shook up so much of Western societies in the 1960s – educational, political, civil rights, religious, cultural factors – it may well turn out to be dimensions of the "sexual revolution" that have emerged as a long-term continuing source of structural change whose thrust has not been blunted by the passage of time. I would like to very briefly go over some of these facets and see to what extent or in what ways the notion of "sexual anomie" is appropriate.

First, in terms of Durkheim's own writings, it might be said that sexual anomie is manifest in the frequency, or rather, increased frequency in marital deregulation. As can be seen in Table 11.1, the United States has the highest divorce rate of various modern countries, followed by Russia. At 4.02 per 1,000 population, the divorce rate is now considerably higher than previous periods in this century: 1.6 in 1920, 2.0 in 1940, 2.6 in 1950, 2.2 in 1960, and 3.5 in 1970 (U.S. Census 1975: 58). Related to this, we may note that the number of unmarried couples living together has been increasing rapidly, from 327,000 to 660,000 in the period 1970-76 alone (Jones 1977). In Sweden, which has been given to major forms of changing traditional sexual patterns of gender roles, the percentage of non-married couples rose in just five years from 6.5 to 18 percent in 1974, with a corresponding decrease in number of marriages from 61,000 in 1966 to 37,500 in 1973 (Frappat 1976). In Durkheim's day, singlehood – whether labeled "bachelor" or "old maid" – carried with it connotation of deviating from the expected norm of being an adult. Since today there are about 47 million persons over 18 who are single, and half of these have never married, it is becoming less defensible to stigmatize singlehood as a deviant civil status.

Changes in marital and conjugal patterns relate to other major changes involved in sexual relations. As a very general and far-reaching trend, we may observe that, particularly since the 1960s, there has been a significant increase in the corning together of the sexes, both in the private and in the public sphere. In the private sphere means, very simply, that sexual intercourse between unmarried partners seems to become more the norm than the exception (refer to Table 11.4), and this reflects in part the 'liberation" of women stemming from the massive introduction of birth control devices. In the public sphere means the increased participation and interaction of women with men in the work setting, in higher education, in the recreational and leisure spheres.

---

world. Aspects of the sexual revolution, which will be touched on later in this article, have as far-reaching implications for societal transformation as did capitalism in an earlier period of modernity.

Table 11.1   Divorces and Divorce Rates, Selected Countries, 1974-78

Country	1974		1976		1978	
	No. Divorces	Rate*	No. Divorces	Rate*	No. Divorces	Rate*
United States	970,000	4.62	1,077,000	5.02		
Bulgaria	11,567	1.33	11,311	1.29	12,799	1.45
Canada	45,019	2.00	54,207	2.34		
Cuba	20,238	2.23				
Czechoslovakia	30,415	2.07	31,561	2.12	33,222	2.20
Egypt	73,425	2.02	76,479	1.97		
Japan	113,622	1.04	124,512	1.11		
Mexico	13,594	.23	16,668	.27		
Sweden	27,208	3.33	21,702	2.65	20,260	2.44
Venezuela	4,018	.35	5,683	.46		
United Kingdom	112,740	2.29	125,724	2.56		
USSR	743,398	2.95	860,688	3.35		

Rate is the number of final decrees granted per 1,000 mid-year population.
Source: United Nations (1979: 431-34).   No entry for a given year indicates data were not reported.

There has been somewhat more than a doubling of the percentage of women in the labor force from 1900 to today; alternatively, if somewhat less than one in five employed in 1900 were women, by the mid-seventies the figure was approaching one in two (Forisha 1978). More relevant to our analysis is the more recent and dramatic trend of mothers to find employment outside the home. According to Forisha, whereas in 1948 32 percent of mothers of school-age children and 13 percent of mothers of preschool children were working, by the mid-seventies these figures had increased to 52 and 32, respectively.

What this suggests is a breakdown of the compartmentalization of women in the domestic sphere, including mothers. Modern industrial society, in its formative and mature period, had to a major extent domesticated women, understanding by this the relative confinement of women's work to the home – either as the mother and core of the foyer or as the auxiliary domestic servant.

Oakley (1976) presents interesting historical materials on the changes brought about in the sexual division of labor by industrialization. Prior to the industrial revolution, the married woman worked in the family industry with unmarried girls and boys doing domestic work under her supervision. Industrialization, by separating the place of home from the place of work, also cut down on the employment of married women. Oakley points out that in the early nineteenth century factory work, in comparison to domestic service, cotton manufacture, dressmaking and millinery, laundry work and teaching – main sources of female employment in that order according to the 1841 British census – provided the best wages and working conditions for women. Until the 1840s, she notes, there was no significant ideology that woman's work should be confined to household work and childcare, coupled with the ideal of the husband as the sole breadwinner, which implies the married woman's total economic dependence on the husband; however, in the 1840s the factory reform movement led to the withdrawal of women and children from the factory. This coincided with the inaugural of the reign of Victoria, who was to give to the ensuing maturing age of modernity a whole cluster of major norms of social relationships, including the idealization of the domestic life.

Therefore, if women, including married women, are entering the work setting in increasing numbers, this may be viewed as a return to the pre-industrial cottage industry period when women were more economic partners of men in the household. Of course, the increasing participation of women in the public work sphere may also be reflected in the rise of divorces, since getting away from male economic dependency by finding remunerative work could be a factor in many cases of women seeking divorce where previously they submitted to marital abuses and tensions for lack of alternatives. To be sure, equality of employment and of wages does not yet obtain in advanced modern societies, as may be gleaned from Table 11.2.

One factor reflected in this earnings differential is the sex-linkage of certain occupations. Oakley mentions that since 1900 there has been little change in the United States in the degree of occupational sex differentiation, and she also notes in Britain the disproportionate concentration of women in a small number of industrial groups. Confirming this, Kreps reported in 1971 that one-fourth of all employed women in the United States work in five occupations: secretary-stenographer, household worker, bookkeeper, elementary school teacher, and waitress.

Nevertheless, if the pace of change in the division of labor is not as rapid as advocates of equalization desire it, the direction of change is certainly in the direction of breaking down the sexual division of labor, at least in modern advanced societies. We are used to seeing women serving on the police force, or as truckdrivers, as bartenders, as personal bankers and stockbrokers, and so forth. For women to engage in work which previously was defined as men's work is certainly an important feature of the "sexual revolution." The structural change in the sexual division of labor is of vast importance at the social psychological level, since so much of self-identity has derived from this division. That is, men's identity has been to a major extent a function of where they stand in the production process of industry, women's identity a function of where they stand in the reproduction process (i.e., single, married, married with children). Although somewhat of an exaggeration, still it is not too much of one to state that in most societies, pre-industrial as well as industrial, the paramount manifest social function of women has been the maternal role – to beget heirs and reproduce the supply of labor (through woman's labor). Of course, this function has been honored and idealized as intrinsic, yet one feature of the modernization process has been the development

Table 11.2 Earnings of Female Workers as Percentage of Male Earnings

Country	All Manufacturing
Countries Other than United States (1975)*	
Australia	73.4
Finland	73.1
Ireland	60.4
Norway	78.0
Sweden	84.8
United Kingdom	66.5
United States (1968)*	
Occupational Category	
Professional and technical	65.9
Nonfarm managers, officials, and proprietors	54.5
Clerical	65.1
Sales	40.5
Operatives	59.2
Service workers (except private household)	55.0

Source: International Labor Office (1978:18).
**Source*: Kreps (1976: 2).

of maternal care and maternal love as value-added elements of being a woman (Badinter).

We may now be witnessing questioning and, on the part of an important number of women, a rejection of childbearing and childrearing as a primary role of female identity. New options, particularly in higher rungs of the occupational structure, may be more appealing. Furthermore, whereas the cultural system until quite recently reinforced the social function of childbearing and childrearing as major vehicles of woman's identity in society today the cultural system – reflected in public life, in advertising, in mass media and recreational spheres – is either ambiguous as to the role set of maternity or else in some of its orientation promotes the desire for women to emancipate their bodies and their selves from traditional roles. In the process, then, having children is no longer the honored calling of being a woman but rather may become seen as a chore, as a trap. This may be accentuated in viewing marriage itself as a trap or as a drag, on the one hand, and with the welfare state's encouragement in legitimating and even funding of abortion, on the other.

One result of this rejection of maternity is indicated in the incidence of abortion. Table 11.3 below provides some raw data for various countries.

Table 11.3   Legally Induced Abortions, Selected Countries, 1968-77

Country	1968	1970	1975	1977
United States	. . . .	180,119	1,034,200	. . . .
Bulgaria	113,454	142,335	143,450	. . . .
Canada	. . . .	11,152	49,311	. . . .
Czechoslovakia	99,886	99,766	81,671	88,989
France	. . . .	. . . .	. . . .	150,931
Hungary	201,096	192,283	96,212	89,096
Japan	757,389	732,033	. . . .	. . . .
Sweden	10,91+0	16,100	32,526	. . . .
United Kingdom	23,641	86,565	106,224	. . . .

Source: United Nations (1979: 281)

However much comparability is difficult in these statistics, they are suggestive in showing a dramatic rate of increase in anglophone countries and Sweden during the past decade, with the most marked increase being in the United States, which now has more abortions than any other country included in the United Nations data.

Undoubtedly, given Durkheim's stress of the *conscience collective* and of collective representations, we may surmise that he would have been interested in surveys of public opinion attitudes pertaining to sexual matters, especially if time series were available. Although we cannot present data pertinent to the various changes just discussed, still the General Social Surveys conducted by NORC are suggestive of recent changes and continuities in the views towards various sexual issues held by a national sample of Americans. Below we present selected data drawn from materials presented by Davis.

The time interval is rather short but it is suggestive that the trend towards acceptance of sexual deregulations is not uniform. On the one hand, there is slight or increasing support for women participating more fully in the public sphere (items A, B, F); on the other, there is decreasing support for facilitating abortion and divorce (items C, D, E).

Durkheim might have interpreted trends concerning changes in women's sphere of identity in the breakdown of sexual segregation, and in the increased intermingling of women and men in public places as some aspects of sexual anomie.

But perhaps we should give Durkheim more credit than that. As an upholder of the sociological over the biological perspective Durkheim might well consider that a woman's role, like a man's role, is not so much a determinate function of biological imperatives and instincts as it is conditioned by social expectations which are dynamic rather than immutable.

Table 11.4 Selected Sexual Attitudes in The United States, 1974 and 1978

	1974		1978	
	N	%	N	%
A. Women should take care of running their homes and leave running the country up to men.				
Agree	509	34	473	31
Disagree	922	62	1,009	66
Other (not sure, etc.)	53	4	50	3
B. If your party nominated a woman for President, would you vote for her if she were qualified?				
Yes	1,150	78	1,217	79
No	283	19	275	18
Other	51	3	40	3
C. Should a pregnant woman be able to get a legal abortion if the family has a very low income and cannot afford any more children?				
Yes	776	52	696	45
No	641	43	773	51
Other	67	5	63	4
D. Should a pregnant woman be able to get a legal abortion if she is not married and does not want to marry the man?				
Yes	711	48	606	40
No	709	48	867	57
Other	64	4	59	4
E. Should divorce be easier or more difficult to obtain than it is now?				
Easier	472	32	405	26
More difficult	624	42	629	41
Stay as it is	308	21	412	27
Other	80	5	86	6
F. Attitude toward premarital sex relations.				
Always or almost always wrong	653	44	612	40
Wrong only sometimes	337	23	304	20
Not wrong at all	439	30	578	38
Other	55	4	38	2

Source: Davis (1978: 30-36).

Consequently, Durkheim might have – with some reluctance to be sure – realized that structural and ideational features of changing sexual relations and identity are grounded in the nature of the modernization process, and that the liberation of women (and men) from ascriptive statuses, though anomic from a traditionalist perspective, may also be conducive to a renovation of the social fabric. This in terms of a lessening of the distance between the two sexes, of reducing the tensions that come from sexual status inconsistency (e.g., women more intelligent than men having a subordinate status in the household or at work) and other factors that contributed to the state of structured antagonism between the sexes, a state that Durkheim took as a more or less characteristic condition. On the contrary we might now, with the breakdown of traditional social structures and social attitudes that regulated for previous eras the basic forms of relationships between the sexes, be poised for a major stage of social evolution, one whose creative agents will be women as much or even more than men.

Such a new situation – that is, in effect, the breakdown of the spatial, social, and psychological segregation of women – could only from a traditionalist perspective be called "sexual anomie." Such a perspective was grounded in a variety of assumptions that were taken to be rooted in biological nature but may well turn out to have been culturally induced – for example, that women are more emotional, more passive, less intelligent and rational, have less physical strength, and so forth. Such assumptions or "myths" did lead to observable differences but this may not have been so much a function of biological determinacy as results of the socialization process which carried out the cultural code.

Sexual Anomie Reconsidered: The Return of Androgyny

Does it make sense to speak of sexual anomie today? Changes in the sexual division of labor, portending a greater equalization of occupational roles in the next century, and even changes in marital relations (e.g., a greater number of unmarried couples living together, continuing high rates of divorce) are not anomic as such, since they are in the direction of ameliorating and enhancing the fuller participation of women in the larger society. This should be seen not as an epiphenomenon of advanced modernity but perhaps as one of the central features of it: the upgrading of the social status of women into one of equal participation and contribution in the public sphere. Of course, there are dysfunctions involved in any changes in social stratification, including the major subsystem of sexual stratification. Moulton, for example, has discussed a variety of effects of the new feminism on women and men. For women this includes performance anxiety, role conflict between personal, sexual identity and a woman's professional identity, retention of domestic dependency when joining or rejoining the workplace, etc. For men, effects of women's assertion in the sexual sphere seems to produce a variety of sexual anxieties, including among colleges males and young adults manifestations of impotence and sexual withdrawals (Moulton 1976).[15]

Just as the relationships between the (declining) aristocracy and the ascending bourgeoisie was marked with ambivalence, conflict, and ultimately accommodation over the course of several generations, so also may we opine that changing sexual stratification and behavioral patterns will follow a similar course and take several generations before a new modus vivendi is attained. The present transition period, attended by a good deal of ambiguity in changing normative expectations of sexuality and gender roles is one that could, thus, be termed a period of "sexual anomie," as an extension of Durkheim's analysis of anomie.   But it should be kept in mind that if increasing equality or equality of opportunities is both an ideological and structural goal of modern society, irrespective of the political regime in which it unfolds, then, to reiterate, the transformation of women's relations to men into one of greater equality of expression – economic, political, recreational, and sexual – should be seen as progressive or in keeping with trends of modernity, and not as anomic.

However, the above liberal/optimistic perspective has to be tempered somewhat by considering deeper aspects of the sexual revolution.

The sexual differentiation of the world is as ubiquitous in the human social world as it is in the animal biological world. This is reflected in a great many languages throughout the world which classify objects by gender. Durkheim and Mauss in a seminal essay (1903) had launched a cognitive sociology decades before ethnomethodology began investigating the categorization of the everyday social world as a constitutive feature of the everyday world. For Durkheim and Mauss, logical categories were intellectual products of underlying social categories; they unfortunately glossed over the primacy of sexual differentiation as the basis of the division of things into genera (23n). Nonetheless, we can add to their analysis by stressing how fundamental to the classification of the world is the ascription of gender identity.

It therefore might be of major significance that as a reflection of changes in sexual comportment and attitudes, it has become increasingly problematic as to what are the social meanings of sexuality and gender (Katchadourian). At the popular cultural level, this is reflected in "unisex" phenomena ranging from convergent hairdressers and hairstyles to convergence in clothing that can be worn interchangeably by men and women.

At the deeper ideological level, the blurring or de-differentiation of gender identity is reflected in a variety of predominantly feminist writings on the theme of *androgyny* (Ferguson; Forisha; Heilbrun; Singer; Trebilcot). In terms of existing forms of sexual and gender differentiation, whether in capitalist or socialist

---

15   The problem of adjusting to new patterns of sexual relationships would appear analogous or structurally similar to the adjustments that colonizers have to make to the colonized, and vice versa, in the aftermath of political independence, when the political status of each vis-à-vis the other is reversed.

countries, industrial or pre-industrial ones, the ideology of androgyny deserves to be seen as a truly revolutionary one. The ideology is directed against the sexual division of labor at home and at work and the attending stereotypes of masculine and feminine behavior which taken together perpetuate "patriarchal power relations between men and women" (Ferguson, 51). As ideology it is directed against the present prevalent form of the nuclear family which is the source of reproduction of heterosexuality in terms of parental socialization of children; it is an advocacy for developing bisexual personalities (Ferguson). Trebilcot talks of two forms of androgynism, the first as one social personality wherein masculinity and femininity coexist openly in the same person. The second, or "polyandrogynism," which also opposes that sex should underlie gender characteristics, prescribes that each person should have a variety of options ranging from "pure" femininity to "pure" masculinity, as well as any combination of the two (72). The resultant behavior would be "process oriented" rather than a "static, sex-typed" one, one that rejects any conformity to normative expectations of gender roles in favor of a completely open system of relating sexually to the world (Forisha).

This theme of androgyny, which seems such a recent aspect of the feminist counter-culture, is one that has an ancient heritage in the deviant esoteric subculture of Western civilization (Tiryakian, a). Since a good deal of the contemporary feminist radicalism is oriented to attacking the legitimizing of male dominance, it is worth noting that this has taken two forms. On the one hand, modern male dominance or "patriarchy" has been interpreted from a Marxist analysis of capitalist development (e.g., Bland et al.; Hartmann; Interrante and Lasser. For a lucid critical overview, see Burris). On the other hand, the diagnosis of the inequality and subordination of women has been approached from a theological critique of masculine/paternal symbolism of God which is at the heart of the orthodox Judaic-Christian traditions.

In advocating an androgynous conception of the deity to overthrow the masculine symbolisms of Father and Son of Christianity, or the masculine symbolism of Lordship in Judaism, today's radical feminists are thus, knowingly or not, espousing formulations of ancient heretical Gnostic feminism, which has been recently discussed by Pagels. Among these ideas is the one of God as "a dyad who is both masculine and feminine," of Genesis as the narration of "an androgynous creation," of human nature as "androgynous," and so forth. In examining Gnostic texts and historical materials pertaining to Roman society at the beginning of the Christian era, Pagels draws out the abortive tendencies of providing women with social equality both in the domestic and in the public spheres. Had Gnosticism triumphed over orthodoxy (or had some version of it become the new orthodoxy of later Roman society and ultimately of Western civilization), religious symbols of legitimating the social order would certainly have been strikingly different from those which for centuries in both Catholic and Protestant countries have been core features of the general cultural paradigm.

Concluding Considerations: Sexual Anomie and Social Change

I think it not unfair to state that mainline sociology, in both its theoretical and empirical branches, has implicitly taken sex for granted. By that I mean that, until quite recently at least, little import was given to sex as a significant dependent, much less as an independent variable, certainly in comparison to occupation, education, ethnicity, age, or religion. This benign neglect of sexuality in the sociological consciousness of major factors involved in social organization and social change is the cognate of viewing history in terms of political, economic, religious and other factors, with sexuality being relegated to incidental or titillating events or backstage events of otherwise little historical significance.

In the past 15 or 20 years at the most we have been witnessing and experiencing a vast array of changes in the public depiction of sexuality as well as in domestic sexual relationships, to say nothing of the organization of pressure groups seeking to alter and transform the legal code dealing with sexual relationships (e.g., the decriminalization of prostitution, of incest, of sodomy), including affirmative action on behalf of "sexual minorities"; and in the wake of this, we have seen individuals and groups rising in reaction to direct moral crusades against pressures for overhauling sexual regulations. We have noted in an earlier section some of the structural and social-psychological changes that have taken place in recent years. Vast as they seem in comparison to previous periods, it might be well to realize that coming years will likely witness major transformations and social conflicts involving changes in sexuality and gender roles.

Consider, for example, just two distinct possibilities among several that only a few years ago would have seemed "unthinkable." The first is that in the near future genetic engineering may be developed so that, in *Brave New World* fashion, women would no longer have to bear children in order for society to reproduce its members in the laboratory, doing away with the need for female "confinement" altogether. Second, a judicial interpretation of unconstitutional sexual discrimination that would make it illegal to have as a normative standard in the work place or in classroom instruction the advocacy of heterosexuality. The consequences of institutionalizing changes such as these and others (e.g., the eradication of gender ascription in language, such as "manpower," "chairman," etc.) could have polar results. On the one hand, a sharp accentuation of the prominence of sexuality the more there are changes designed to do away with sexual regulations. On the other hand, dialectically, the greater the nature of transformations in sexuality and the more ambiguous sexuality may become as a source of interpersonal identity, the more trivial it will become to the point of nearing zero marginal utility.

It would seem that if sociology is to rise to the occasion of significant changes or attempted changes in the sexual grounding of the social order, it will have to rethink many of its assumptions and models as to the parameters of social organization. Rather than an epiphenomenon of social structure and social change, the problematics of sexuality, including individual and collective identity, might well be viewed as core problems of modernity.

To conclude this essay, Durkheim gave relatively minor attention to sexuality, yet the theme of sexual anomie which is found in his writings is extremely heuristic in posing fundamental questions about changes in the social order. At the beginning of the twentieth century W.E.B. DuBois defined the problem of the century as being the question of race relations. That problem has been muted though not solved, since the North-South acrimonious debate at the international level is one involving both economic development and race relations. But as this century draws to a close and a new millennium looms two decades away, it is the contention of this writer that the question of sexual relations – of the meaning, forms and social regulations of sexuality – will become an equally central problem for the further development of modern society.

There appears to be at present, at least to this observer, a profound ambiguity. On the one hand, the extent of normative deregulations concerning sexuality suggest some uneasy parallels with the late Roman Empire, with the closing decades of the *ancien régime*, and even, following Stefan Zweig's description, with Weimar Berlin (Mitchell). On the other hand, it is also possible to visualize as Unwin (1934) had envisioned it years ago, a combination of placing the sexes on a level of complete legal equality and altering social and economic organization, such as to draw fully on the creative abilities of women as much as men while at the same time channeling sexual activity into a revitalized monogamy (Unwin).

Undoubtedly Emile Durkheim would have found in this situation, this ambiguous cross-road of modernity, a crucial challenge for an informed, objective sociological response. His sociological intuition correctly led him, as Hans Joas (2008: 143) has brought to our attention, to view sexuality – the sexual act, tout court-- as an important intersection of the sacred and the profane, as "constitutive of morality" (*foncièrement moralisateur*). Changes or attempted changes in the normative regulations of sexuality should therefore be seen as a critical field for the study of societal change.

References

Abrahamson, M. 1980. "Sudden Wealth, Gratification, and Attainment." *American Sociological Review* 45 (February): 49-57.

Austin, R. L. and M. Bologna 1980. "Durkheim, Women's Liberation and Female Suicide." Paper presented at the annual meeting of the American Sociological Association.

Badinter, Elisabeth 1980. *L'Amour en Plus*. Paris: Flammarion.

Besnard, Philippe 1973. "Durkheim et les femmes ou le *Suicide* inachevé." *Revue francaise de Sociologie* 14 (janvier-mars): 27-61.

Bland, Lucy, Trisha McCabe, and Frank Mort 1979. "Sexuality and Reproduction: Three 'Official' Instances." In Michele Barrett, Philip Corrigan, Annette Kuhn, and Janet Wolff (eds), *Ideology and Cultural Production*. New York: St. Martin's Press.

Burns, V. 1980. "The Dialectic of Women's Oppression: Notes on the Relation between Capitalism and Patriarchy." Paper presented at the annual meeting of the American Sociological Association.

Davis, James Allan 1978. *General Social Surveys, 1972-1978: Cumulative Codebook*. Chicago: National Opinion Research Center, University of Chicago. Distributed by Roper Public Opinion Research Center, Yale University.

De Bonald, Marquis 1805. *Du Divorce*. 2d ed. Paris: Adrien Le Clere.

Douglas, Mary 1966. *Purity and Danger. An Analysis of Concepts of Pollution and Taboo*. London: Routledge & Kegan Paul.

Durkheim, Emile a:1893. *The Division of Labor in Society*. New York: Free Press, 1964.

—. b:1897, *Suicide*. New York: Free Press, 1963.

—.c:1898, "La Prohibition de l'Inceste et ses Origines." *L'Année Sociologique* 1(1896-97):1-70.

—. d:1903, Review of Ernest Crawley, *The Mystic Rose, A Study of Primitive Marriage* In *L'Année Sociologique* 6(1901-02):352-58.

—. e:1906, "Divorce by Mutual Consent." In Mark Traugott ed., *Emile Durkheim on Institutional Analysis*. Chicago: University of Chicago Press, 1978.

—. f:1912, *The Elementary Forms of the Religious Life*. New York: Collier, 1961.

Durkheim, Emile, and Marcel Mauss 1903. *Primitive Classification*. London: Cohen & West, 1963.

Duvignaud, Jean 1970. "Anomie et Mutations Sociales." In Georges Balandier (ed.), *Sociologie des Mutations*. Paris: Anthropos.

Ferguson, Ann 1977. "Androgyny as an Ideal for Human Development." In Mary Vettenling-Braggin, Frederick A. Euliston, and Jane English (eds), *Feminism and Philosophy*. Totowa, N.J.: Littlefield, Adams.

Forisha, Barbara Lusk 1978. *Sex Roles and Personal Awareness*. Morristown, N.J.: General Learning Press/Scott, Foresman.

Foucault, Michel, 1976. *Histoire de la Sexualité*. Vol. 1: *La Volonté de Savoir*. Paris: Gallimard.

Frappat, Bruno 1976. "La Suède au masculin-féminin." *Le Monde* (Paris), February 5-11, 8.

Goffman, E. 1967. "The Nature of Deference and Demeanor." In Erving Goffman, *Interaction Ritual: Essays on Face-to-Face Behavior*. New York: Doubleday Anchor.

Hartmann, H. 1976. "Capitalism, Patriarchy, and Job Segregation by Sex." In Martha Blaxall and Barbara Reagan eds, *Women and the Workplace*. Chicago: University of Chicago Press.

Heilbrun, Carolyn C. 1973. *Toward a Recognition of Androgyny*. New York: Harper Colophon.

Hobsbawm, E. J. 1970. "Revolution is Puritan." In Philip Nobile (ed.), *Theories, Vagues and Canons*. New York: Random House.

International Labor Office. 1978. *Women at Work* Geneva: ILO newsbulletin.

Interrante, J., and C. Lasser 1979. "Victims of the Very Songs They Sing: A Critique of the Recent Work on Patriarchal Culture and the Social Construction of Gender." *Radical History Review* 20 (Spring/Summer): 25-40.

Joas, H. 2008. *Do We Need Religion? On the Experience of Self-Transcendence.* Boulder and London: Paradigm Publishers.

Jones, George F. 1977. "Can Carter Revitalize the American Family?" *U.S. News and World Report*, February 28, 35.

Jung, C. G. a;1963. *Mysterium Coniunctionis.* Bollingen Series XX. New York: Pantheon.

—. b;1967. *Alchemical Studies.* Bollingen Series XX. Princeton: Princeton University Press.

—. c;1968. *Psychology and Alchemy*, 2d ed. Bollingen Series XX. Princeton: Princeton University Press.

Katchadourian, Herant A. ed. 1979. *Human Sexuality. A Comparative and Developmental Perspective.* Berkeley: University of California Press.

Kreps, Juanita M. (ed.). 1976. *Women and the American Economy. A Look to the 1980s.* Engiewood Cliffs: Prentice-Hall, for The American Assembly.

Lukes, Steven 1969. "Durkheim's 'Individualism and the Intellectuals," *Political Studies* 17March:14-30.

Merton, R. K. 1949. "Social Structure and Anomie." In Robert K. Merton, *Social Theory and Social Structure.* New York: Free Press.

Merton, R. K., and E. Barber 1963. "Sociological Ambivalence:' In Edward A. Tiryakian (ed.). *Sociological Theory. Values, and Sociocultural Change.* New York: Free Press.

Mitchell, Juliet 1974. *Psychoanalysis and Feminism.* London: Allen Lane.

Moulton, Ruth 1976. "Some Effects of the New Feminism – On Men and Women." Paper presented at Joint Meeting of the American Academy of Psychoanalysis and the American Psychiatric Association.

Oakley, Ann 1976. *Woman's Work.* New York: Vintage/Random House.

Padgug, Robert A. 1979. "Sexual Matters: On Conceptualizing Sexuality in History." *Radical History Review* 20 (Spring/Summer): 3-23.

Pagels, Elaine 1979. "The Suppressed Gnostic Feminism." *New York Review of Books* 26 (November): 42-49.

Simon, W., and J. H. Gagnon 1976. "The Anomie of Affluence: A Post-Mertonian Conception." *American Journal of Sociology* 82 (September): 356-78.

Singer, June. 1977. *Androgyny. Toward a New Theory of Sexuality.* New York: Doubleday Anchor.

Sorokin, Pitirim A. 1956. *The American Sex Revolution.* Boston: Porter Sargent.

Thomas, William 1 1907. *Sex and Society. Studies in the Social Psychology of Sex.* Chicago: University of Chicago Press.

Tiryakian, F. A. a:1974. "Toward the Sociology of Esoteric Culture." In Edward A. Tiryakian ed., *On the Margin of the Visible: Sociology, the Esoteric, and the Occult.* New York: Wiley Interscience.

—.b:1978. "Emile Durkheim." In Toni Bottomore and Robert Nisbet eds, *A History of Sociological Analysis*. New York: Basic Books.

Trebilcot, J. 1977. "Two Forms of Androgynism." In Mary Vetterling-Braggin, Frederick Elliston, and Jane English eds, *Feminism and Philosophy*. Totowa, N.J.: Littlefield, Adams.

United Nations 1979. *Demographic Yearbook 1978*. New York: U.N. Publications ElF 79X111 I.

Unwin, J. D. 1934. *Sex and Culture*. London: Oxford University Press/Humphrey Milford.

U.S. Bureau of the Census 1975. *Historical Statistics of the United States, Colonial Times to Present*. Bicentennial Edition. Washington: Government Printing Office.

Wallwork, Ernest 1972. *Durkheim. Morality and Milieu*. Cambridge: Harvard University Press.

Weber, M. 1915. "Religious Rejections of the World and Their Directions." In Hans H. Gerth and C. Wright Mills eds, *From Max Weber: Essays in Sociology*. New York: Oxford University Press/Galaxy.

Chapter 12

No Laughing Matter: Applying Durkheim to Danish Cartoons[1]

Introduction

Danish readers of the daily *Morgenavisen Jyllands-Posten* (in English, *The Morning Newspaper "the Jutland Post"*), the largest-selling newspaper in Denmark, opened up the paper on Friday morning, September 30, 2005, and probably enjoyed reading its contents, which besides local and international news has special features. In addition to daily comic strips, the Friday issue has some special sections, including "Kultur Weekend", an in-depth analysis connecting culture to politics and international events.

On that particular day, the culture section had an article entitled "Muhammeds ansigt" ("The face of Muhammad"), illustrated with a dozen cartoons drawn by members of the Danish editorial cartoonists union at the invitation of the culture editor, Flemming Rose. Not all cartoonists who had been invited had accepted, some out of respect for a Muslim ban depicting Muhammad, some out of fear of reprisal. The latter was perhaps in keeping with the earlier strident indictment (in fact, a death sentence) by the Ayatollah Khomenei of Salman Rushdie for his alleged blasphemous *The Satanic Verses* (1988), perhaps because of the November 2004 assassination of Dutch film director Theo van Gogh after his short film *Submission* (English translation of "Islam") dealing with violence against women in Islamic societies. Several if not most of the cartoons were jocular in mood, and only one had a sinister appearance of Muhammad with an allusion to terrorism. Two weeks before, another Danish newspaper had published an article decrying the reticence of artists to illustrate a children's book on the Qur'an and the life of Muhammad, for fear of violent retribution. For the *Jyllands-Post* culture editor in his presentation of the cartoons there was more to this than a laughing matter, for self-censorship, arising from Muslim objections, was to enter a slippery slope "incompatible with contemporary democracy and freedom of speech".[2]

---

1   Prepared for this volume and presented as the Mayhew Memorial Lecture, University of South Carolina, Columbia, SC, April 3, 2008. My thanks to Mathieu Deflem for his support of this project.

2   Retrieved from http://en.wikipedia.org/wiki/Jyllands-Posten_Muhammad_cartoons.controversy. Unless otherwise indicated, I have taken this as the basis in this section for materials on the history of the Danish cartoons events, compiled from a large number of references.

Probably for most of the readers of the *Jyllands-Post*, the cartoons were light-hearted satire and caricature, in the long Western tradition of political and sometimes religious cartoons lampooning public figures, even heads of state and, at different times, the episcopate, including the Pope – although at times, some proposed cartoons have been "killed" by media editors in anticipation of readers' sensitivity (Wallis 2007). However, this particular set of Danish cartoons was to ignite a massive wave of violent reaction in Europe, the Middle East, and as far as Southeast Asia, with 50 killed overseas; Muslim protests and violence would in turn launch a counter- reaction, beyond the frontiers of tiny Denmark. The upshot was to lead the Danish Prime Minister Anders Rasmussen to view the situation as "Denmark's worst international crisis since World War II", which if it did not lead to war, did generate bitter acrimony from Muslim religious prayer leaders (*imams*) in Denmark, eleven ambassadors from Muslim-majority countries seeking a meeting with Rasmussen, and the boycott of Danish goods in several Muslim countries that cut Danish exports by one-sixth.

Thus, the publication of the cartoons outraged not only Danish Muslims (5000 of whom demonstrated in the streets of Copenhagen on October 14) but Muslims across in Europe and elsewhere as well. Religious fire was added to the fuel by radical Danish imams, who might have felt stymied by Danish authorities in government and in the courts for not taking sanctions against the blasphemers. The imams proceeded to gather a dossier of Muslim grievances at hostile acts of "Islamophobia". Besides public insults, some acts of violence, and alleged discrimination in housing and employment, the dossier included additional cartoons even more offensive than the original dozen, published in another Danish newspaper, with one of them said to show the Prophet with the face of a pig. As it turned out later, the latter was in fact a fax image received from France showing a pig-squealing contestant at a local country fair, but the dossier when shown in Muslim countries provoked intense sympathy for the Danish Muslim community and equally intense furor at the *Jyllands-Posten.* A December summit meeting of the 57 member states of the Organization of Islamic Conference (OIC) at Mecca expressed its deep concern and condemnation of the "desecration of the Holy Prophet Mohammad in the media of certain countries" and called on "all governments to ensure full respect of all religions and religious symbols,"[3] Besides consumer boycott of Danish exports, violent protests in February 2006 even took the form of fire set to the Danish and Norwegian embassies in Syria and to the Danish Embassy in Lebanon, and the assassination of a Catholic priest on February 5 by a 16-year old youth in a Turkish Black Sea port.

Simultaneously, Muslim outrage and demands for apologies and state sanctions against the journal led to a reciprocated outrage in the West at the perceived overreaction to lampooning and a more dangerous attempt at censure of freedom of

---

3   Final Communiqué, Third Extraordinary Session of the Islamic Summit Conference, "Meeting the Challenges of the twenty first century, Solidarity in Action," Mecca, Saudi Arabia, December 7-8, 2005. http://.oic-oic.org/ex-summit/english/fc-exsumm-en.htm

expression provided by the media. Demands by Muslim organizations in Denmark that the Danish Criminal Code apply its long-standing blasphemy law against the *Jyllands-Posten* were rebuked by the Regional Public Prosecutor who concluded that Danish case law "extends editorial freedom to journalists when it comes to a subject of public interest." An even sterner denunciation was the manifesto *Together facing the new totalitarianism* appearing on March 1, 2006 in the French satirical newspaper *Charlie Hebdo* signed by 12 writers (including Rushdie and French philosopher Bernard-Henri Lévy), warning of "Islamism" as a reactionary totalitarian ideology, a force of darkness that can only lead "to a world of injustice and domination: men over women, fundamentalists over others."[4] The normally staid *New York Times* fumed in an editorial "It is time for moderate Muslims to abandon the illusion that they can placate the Islamists by straddling the fence ... It is they who must make it clear to their people that blowing up mosques, beheading hostages and strapping on belts of explosives are far, far greater evils than a few drawings in a distant paper," (February 25, 2006).

It may be facile to see this episode and its reverberations through the prism of an irrational "clash of civilizations" (Huntington 1996).[5] However, a deeper analysis deploying Durkheimian analytical tools culled from his seminal *Elementary Forms of the Religious Life,* and in particular the binary concepts of "sacred" and "profane", will later give us the opportunity of showing the relevance of classical theory to our contemporary world. What is of particular concern is a sociological understanding of the bearing of the sacred in the cultural changes regarding collective identities.

My approach here is very much in the vein of the "cultural sociology" which Jeffrey Alexander, from a Durkheim launching pad, has done much to advance over the years (Alexander, 1988; 1992). Making sense of social interaction – the basic stuff that sociology deals with – is to understand the symbolic patterns which are the environment of every action. There is an "inner" aspect to meaning that is complementary to its "outer", material aspect. The "inner meaning" that sociologists seek to recover (or "uncover") is not the idiosyncratic attitudes of individuals but the *organized sets of symbolic patterns* meaningfully understood by social subjects (Alexander, 1992: 296).[6]

---

4   http://news.bb.co.uk/1/hi/world/Europe/47644730.stm). A Danish translation appeared immediately in the *Jyllands Posten,* which only a few weeks before had issued an apology for the publication of the cartoons.

5   Huntington's catchy phrase in fact headed an editorial in the *Wall Street Journal* regarding the cartoons controversy denouncing the violence as showing the "premodernism of much of modern-day Islam" in the light of the Western tradition decrying the injustice of Socrates being executed for blaspheming the gods of Athens. The editorial affirmed "When British Muslims carry placards reading "Butcher those who mock Islam", they are making their differences with that tradition depressingly plain," (February 11, 2006).

6   The stress on understanding the "inner meaning" of social phenomena is very compatible with Max Weber's central notion of *Verstehen,* derived from Dilthey's differentiation of the human sciences seeking to "understand" the meaning of "culture"

What I seek to do in this essay is to treat the Danish cartoons and the reactions they gave rise to as a *text* which needs to be *interpreted* in terms of its sociocultural *context*. The sociocultural context that I will deal with before moving on to apply Durkheimian analysis is that of Muslims in Europe and their host society. Not being Muslim, nor having direct access to Arabic sources, I do not claim to have "insider's knowledge", either of European Muslim scholars such as Tariq Ramadan (Ruthven 2007) and Humayun Ansari (2004) or of non-Muslim European specialists on Islam, such as the late Maxime Rodinson (1987) or Olivier Roy (2004; 2007). Still, in the sociological spirit of dispassionate inquiry, I seek to provide the reader with a more complete sociological understanding than the reportage that accompanied the Danish cartoons controversy. It is in the vein of the "thick description" popularized by anthropologist Clifford Geertz in tying together multiple, complex symbolic structures, for example in his analysis of Balinese cockfights (2000: 412-53), or, following Geertz, in the analysis of Alexander applying Durkheim's sacred/profane dichotomy to technological discourse (Alexander 1992).

Before undertaking this application of Durkheim, it will be necessary to lay out the context of contemporary, post 9/11 Muslim Europe, essentially a new world for both Islam and for modern Europe.

The New Europe(s)

In March 2007 widespread celebrations took place all across Europe as 27 member states of the European Union, from the six oldest members (Belgium, France, Germany, Italy, Luxemburg and the Netherlands) to the newest (Bulgaria and Romania) feted fifty years of the Treaty of Rome. Half a century before, the Treaty of Rome had sought a new economic entente in Western Europe to avoid the dismal fate of the Versailles Treaty at the end of World War I. The European

---

in contrast to the natural sciences seeking to explain external causal relations operating in "nature" (for a recent critical discussion of "culture" in the German tradition, see Lepennies, 2006). The divergence from Weber is that he applied interpretive understanding to fathoming the *cognitive orientation* of actors to the world, whereas Alexander, in his critique of Habermas, emphasizes that objectivity is nested in more irrational, primordial motivations of personality. As he states it, "the ideas that inform even modern society are not cognitive repositories of verified facts; they are symbols that continue to be shaped by deep emotional impulses and molded by meaningful constraints," (Alexander 1992:304).

While Weber's approach was immensely heuristic in its application to understanding the "elective affinity" between religious orientations and the ethics of economic practices across civilizations, the cultural studies interpretive approach that Alexander opts for, in line with Clifford Geertz (2000), is more in keeping with Durkheim's understanding of both cognitive *and* emotional aspects of religion, as Fish (2005) has recently emphasized. In turn, this latter perspective seems to me to have more relevance in understanding the emotions generated by the Danish cartoons.

Economic Community, born in 1957 (with a 1952 prototype as the European Coal and Steel Community), has had major steps in its evolution (signified by name changes), becoming in 1993 the new European Union (EU).[7] Two noteworthy if not epochal steps have taken place in the present decade: (a) in January 2002, 13 of the member states adopted a new currency, the *euro* (symbol €) with its own coinage and banknotes replacing in the economically disciplined eurozone the previous national currencies, and (b) following the Treaty of Nice (2003), the EU expanded by ten countries, eight of which only 15 years before had been firmly wedged in the Soviet Empire.

From many perspectives, structural transformation of the "New Europe" that has attended the development of the European Union is one of the great successes of economic and political *integration* in modern history. This is even more so since the sizeable enlargement of the EU has taken place by peaceful means: no war has broken out between any member states, and consensus-building has remained a priority along the way. Perhaps reflecting its combined Social Democrat and Christian Democrat leanings as a major continental mainstream, the EU's regional development policy has increased the standard of living of the relatively poor countries (such as Ireland, Greece and Portugal among the early members) and promises with regional development funds to do the same for the newer Eastern European countries. EU is fulfilling its motto *in varietate Concordia* ("united in diversity"), an apt expression of its philosophy as both a supranational and intergovernmental body.

The structural transformation of a new Europe also reflects equally profound but more subtle multidimensional changes at the levels of *identity*. Gerard Delanty (1995) has suggestively argued that the traditional idea of European unity has been historically constructed over the centuries in opposition to the "other", where the "other" has been at various stages the "Orient", "East", or "Islam". One can extend his broad analysis to include historical antipathies at a more specific level. So, for example, Anglo-Franco conflicts (and ambivalence) were instrumental in the definition of their respective national identity from the Medieval period into the dawn of the Twentieth Century;[8] correspondingly, an aggressive German militarism in the nineteenth and twentieth centuries, which led to three savage wars between 1870 (and the annexation of Alsace-Lorraine 1871-1918) and

---

7   For detailed information on the making, composition, and present conditions of the European Union, see Dinan (1999), Cram, Dinan, and Nugent (1999), Gerven (2005), and Giorgi, von Homeyer, and Parsons (2006). The chrysalis of the European Union was the postwar vision of Jean Monnet and Robert Schuman who believed that economic integration of Germany and France was necessary to avoid further wars: putting the vision to practice resulted in 1952 in the European Coal and Steel Community, whose success was the background to the Treaty of Rome.

8   "Time and time again, war with France brought Britons … into confrontation with an obviously hostile Other and encouraged them to define themselves collectively against it," (Colley 2005:5; see also Kumar 2003: 162-64).

1940, gave for France primacy to "the Huns" (*les Boches*) as the modern Other. Yet, starting with the cordial postwar relations between DeGaulle and Adenauer, and subsequently the development of the EU and the complementary Council of Europe, there has produced a remarkable sustained transformation from hostility to multi-task cooperation between France and Germany, be it in the control of trafficking of women or in their significant opposition in 2003 to the Iraq War.

While European public opinion has not been unequivocally supportive of the EU – partly because it is viewed by some as a vast impersonal bureaucracy in Brussels – there has nevertheless been a significant change in the acceptance of a *European identity* beyond the EU (Herrmann, Risse and Brewer 2004). It is not a zero-sum game with other, more local collective identities. However, to be a European, to feel oneself a citizen of Europe, may well be on its way among a younger generation born since the coming of the EU to be compatible with a regional identity as well as a national identity.[9] And the symbols of this emergent new collective identity – a composite of economic and cultural dimensions – are already in place: the euro (€) and its 13 member states Eurozone (as of 2007 having a stronger currency than the US dollar), the European flag, and an anthem derived from Beethoven's *Ode to Joy*. Further, a constitution that would incorporate previous treaties is having another round of drafting after failure of ratification in two referenda in 2005.[10] What is worth noting is a new "grand narrative" in Europe, what Shore aptly views in his study of the cultural politics of the EU as the promotion of the past millennia in Europe being a "moral success story" of cultural continuity, moral ascendancy and "unity in diversity"; this is further symbolized by the acronyms "ERASMUS", "SOCRATES" and "LEONARDO" as acronyms for major educational exchange programs which invoke key figures of the Western cultural heritage (Shore 2000: 57).

Asssuredly, the project of European integration and unity in cultural diversity is not completed: challenging has been the accession in short order of Eastern European states with vestiges of a communist/authoritarian past, different linguistic backgrounds, and lower levels of socioeconomic development requiring substantial funding from the West. All things taken into account, European unification has already accomplished more than any visitor to the European scene – except some visionary like Saint-Simon at the end of the Napoleanic Wars (Saint-Simon

---

9   This is indicated in the German university study showing the rejection of a traditional "nationalism" while as an emergent symbol of identity being *German-in-Europe* (Ezell, Seeleib-Kaiser and Tiryakian 2003).

10   It might be remembered that the first constitution of the United States was drafted in 1777 but only came into force in 1781 as the Articles of Confederation and after seven years redone in its present form in 1788. The question of small-state versus large-state representation was as much a source of controversy then, as it was in formulating the European Constitution. Ironically, the question of religion was more acrimonious in drafting the European Constitution than in the American case, although "the separation of church and state" has become more contentious in the United States in recent decades.

1814) – could have imagined at the end of World War II. The "new Europe" of today, with the stimulus of economic modernization in the EU and with equal political and cultural concerns in the parallel Council of Europe for broadening both human rights (especially regarding minorities) and the European cultural heritage, comes close to the model of "internationalism" espoused by Durkheim's nephew, Marcel Mauss. In 1920 the latter had differentiated the term from "cosmopolitanism" which is, he argued, a denial of nation, and from "nationalism" as an ideology which isolates the nation. Internationalism, he stressed, is an ensemble of ideas and sentiments that directs relationships between nations and societies (Mauss 1969)[11] That is pretty much what the European project, however haltingly, has sought to realize by consensus through its institutions and nascent collective identity.

A prosperous, integrated Europe, based on consensus, predominantly secular, responsive to the needs of its citizens and its minorities while protecting the rights of individuals for self-expression is thus *one* of the new Europes on the scene today, in fact and in the popular imagination.

The "Other" New Europe

Side by side with this seemingly idyllic if not utopian construction is another new Europe, the Europe that has become transformed from the nineteenth century region of emigration to the twenty first century region of immigration. More strikingly, it is the new Europe of Muslim immigrants having come to the fore of discussions of integration and identity.[12] What I would like to argue is that if the EU is at the base of a new and predominantly positive pan-European identity for "old Europe", particularly for the young generation, a case can be made for Islam having become the basis of a salient collective identity for Muslim immigrants in Europe faced with structural and social-psychological barriers of integration

---

11   *"L'internationalisme est ... l'ensemble des idées, sentiments, et règles et groupements collectifs qui ont pour but de concevoir et diriger les rapports entre les nations et entre les sociétés en générale"* (Mauss 1969: 630).

12   For the sake of brevity, I am leaving out of this discussion the several waves of migration that have changed the "socioscape" of Europe into a new region of immigrants. Included in these movements are the immigrants who came to the former colonial métropoles (London, Paris, Brussels, Amsterdam) at the end of empires; the large number of "guest workers" from the "South" of Europe (such as Spain, Portugal, Yugoslavia, Greece) before that broad region underwent economic growth; and, with the collapse of the Soviet Empire and the relaxation of border control, immigrants from Eastern Europe, particularly Poland. If immigrants came primarily for economic reasons, even with low-grade employment, some also came to seek asylum in periods of violent ethnic strife and regime change at home. For a broad coverage of Muslim institutions and organization in Europe, see Maréchal, Allievi, Dassetto and Nielsen 2003; and Allievi and Nielsen 2003. Both of these volumes, of course, were published before the Danish cartoons affair.

in their host societies. The violation of this identity, global in its dimension, will take us directly to the relevance of Durkheim's relevance in understanding the Danish cartoons confrontation. Before interpretation, however, there is need for further descriptive materials regarding Muslim immigration as a feature of "the new Europe".

The pronounced economic reconstruction of Europe after World War II and continuing development in subsequent decades has made the region – initially the "North" (Great Britain, France, Belgium, Germany, the Netherlands and Scandinavia), and later the "South" (Portugal, Spain, Italy, Greece) – one of "high income countries" as measured by the World Bank. The success of the Marshall Plan, coupled with an aging population and one which had suffered high casualty rates in World War II produced a shortage of labor for European reconstruction. The "supply" in the 1960s and early 1970s came not from a single country but several regions: predominantly from Central Europe (mainly Yugoslavia), Northern Africa, the Middle East (in particular Turkey) and South Asia (India and Pakistan mainly). The oil crisis of 1972-73 led to an economic slowdown in Europe, and restrictions on further labor needs from outside Europe. However, the doors were left open for family reunification bringing additional immigrants (estimated at 500,000), and yet another wave of immigration from Muslim countries came in the 1980s and 1990s with those (about 400,000) seeking political asylum away from the violence of severe conflicts and wars in Afghanistan, Iran, the Middle East, Yugoslavia (especially Bosnia-Hercegovina), and several African countries (Pauly 2004). Last but not least have been large numbers of illegal immigrants, in the range of 120,000 and 500,000 yearly (Savage 2004: 26).

Not only did this add a considerable ethnic mix to Europe, but in the process opened up the controversies surrounding "multiculturalism", collective identities, and integration into the European mainstream versus granting autonomy and governance to cultural and social practices of non-traditional Europeans (Christiansen and Hedetoft 2004; Rex and Singh 2004). Of the various immigrant communities that have generated the greatest challenge to integration were the multiple ethnic (coming from North Africa, the Middle East, and Asia) but single faith Muslim communities.[13] Cumulatively, amidst diversity of origins and trajectories, with a "new" religious identity in the face of global factors and, especially for the second and third generation of European-born who feel alienated from mainstream European society, they have (re)introduced Islam as a strong cultural presence. It is one whose strength besides its monotheistic communal faith also resides in its demographic advantage in former Christian, now secular Europe.

---

13   Some of these, such as the Bosniaks and the Albanians had just discovered or recovered their religious belonging after a communist period that had taken religion out of both the public and the private sphere. As noted by Kelly, "if the ethnicization of politics in Bosnia and Herzegovina is recent, then the notion of a distinct Muslim Bosnian identity and hence a Bosnian Muslim community may also be relatively recent," (Kelly 2004: 207).

Table 12.1 Percentage of Muslims in European Countries, 2005 Estimates

Country	Total Population (in millions)	Muslim Population (in millions)	Percentage Muslim (%)
Albania	3.1	2.2	70.0
Austria	8.2	.34	4.1
Belgium	10.3	.4	4.0
Bosnia & Hercegovina	3.8	1.5	40.0
Denmark	5.4	.27	5.0
France	62.3	5-6.0	8-9.6
Germany	82.5	3.0	3.6
Italy	58.4	.825	1.4
Macedonia	2.1	.63	30.0
Netherlands	16.3	.95	5.8
Spain	43.1	1.0	2.3
Sweden	9.0	.3	3.0
Switzerland	7.4	.31	4.2
Turkey	68.7	68	99.0
United Kingdom	58.8	1.6	2.8

Source: BBC News, December 23, 2005. http://news.bbc.co.uk/2/hi/europe/4385768.stm. These should be read with caution as there is no uniform census taking of Muslim populations in Europe.

At first glance, the Islamic presence in Europe seems minimal, as can be seen in Table1 indicating the population size of various countries and the percentage of the population that is Muslim.[14]

In the European Union only Bulgaria (its newest member as of 2007) has ten percent or more of its population Muslim (not shown in table but estimated at

---

14   Religious count has been notoriously difficult to establish in various countries and regions. Muslims in Europe present no exception. In the case of Denmark alone, Simonsen indicates that the Muslim population is 3% of the total or about 159,000 adherents (Simonsen 2002: 122), while the BBC News put the figure at 270,000 Muslims or 5% of the population in 2005 (BBC News 2005:3).

13%, a large part of which have been there for centuries[15]). Of other EU countries, France has had perhaps the longest contacts with the Islamic world, going back in modern times to Napoleon's failed conquest of Egypt and the later conquest of Algeria, with an influx in France of a heterogeneous population from North Africa and the Levant of intellectuals and other professionals, service workers, and unskilled laborers.[16] It has the largest Muslim total population in Europe (except of course for Turkey), with an estimated five to six percent of France's population. [17] Aside from Albania, Bosnia & Hercegovina, and Turkey, only the Former Yugoslav Republic of Macedonia has a significant (and growing percentage) of Muslims, with nearly one-third of its population.

Although the percentage of population that is Islamic in Europe may not appear problematic, it becomes more so when some additional demographic factors are taken into account. One is indicated in Table 12.2 showing differential fertility rates of Western European countries in comparison to Muslim countries which have been or are likely to be centers of emigration due to various factors, from high levels of unemployment to political crises and regime changes resulting in large numbers of displaced persons seeking asylum.

What is striking about Western countries is that *they are all below the level of replacement, customarily thought of as 2.1 children per woman.* France comes closest to replacement with a fertility rate of 1.98, with the Scandinavian countries, including Denmark, a good deal lower, and a virtual collapse in fertility of countries that have been thought of as "Catholic" with historically high fertility – Portugal, Italy, Spain and Poland. If we compare Muslim countries that have since World War II and more recently sent immigrants to Europe, most in the Middle East and South Asia have fertility rates above replacement. Yet it must also be noted that Turkey, Iran, and the Maghreb countries of Algeria, Morocco and Tunisia are at levels similar to Western European countries.

A second demographic aspect is religious. Europe, which in the popular image is a "Christian" region, has been continuing its nineteenth century post-Enlightenment trend of secularization (Chadwick 1975). Most recently, the debate

---

15   http://www.nationsencyclopedia.com/economies/Europe/Bulgaria.html.

16   A "modern" Islamic presence in France owed a new start in 1895 with initiatives from followers of Auguste Comte's positivism (Sellam 2006:29). Late Victorian England did have a small but active Muslim community, headed in Liverpool by Quillam, a convert, stigmatized by the wider community (for materials on this, see Ansari 2004: 82-84).

17   Based on the 2002 Russian census, and realizing that a large number may not be practicing, nearly ten percent or around 14, 340,000 of today's Russia is Muslim from a multitude of ethnic groups. See "Islam in Russia," http://en.wikipedia.org/wiki/Islam_in_ Russia. I leave out Russia from this discussion because its vast territory and equally complex culture straddle Europe and Asia. Yet, the prolonged war against Chechen insurgents, the large influx of Chechens and other Muslim immigrants in Moscow (whose 2.5 million Muslims is the largest of any European City), and the precipitous demographic decline of ethnic Russians make for increasing tension not unlike in the rest of Europe (Mainville 2006).

Table 12.2   Differential Fertility Rates, Western European and Muslim Countries (2007)

Western European	Total Fertility Rate (children born/ woman)	Muslim	Total Fertility Rate (children born/ woman)
France	1.98	Afghanistan	6.64
Iceland	1.91	Senegal	5.00
Ireland	1.86	Iraq	4.07
Norway	1.78	Saudi Arabia	3.94
Denmark	1.74	Pakistan	3.71
Finland	1.73	Syria	3.31
Netherlands	1.66	Libya	3.21
Sweden	1.66	Morocco	2.62
United Kingdom	1.66	Jordan	2.55
Belgium	1.64	Albania	2.03
Portugal	1.48	Turkey	1.89
Germany	1.40	Algeria	1.86
Italy	1.29	Tunisia	1.73
Spain	1.29	Iran	1.71
Poland	1.26	Bosnia-Herzegovina	1.23

Source: The data have been adapted from 2007 estimates of the Central Intelligence Agency *The World Factbook, https://www.cia.gov/library/publicatins/the-world-factbook/ rankorder/2127rank.html.*

For comparison, the figure given for the United States is 2.09 and for the World as a whole, 2.59.

over the European Constitution, in seeking to define the European cultural heritage, led after bitter arguments from religious conservatives to dropping altogether reference to God and a Christian heritage, albeit all Western European countries have this in their cultural background (going back at least to Charlemagne and the Holy Roman Empire). The "defeat" in 2003 of those – particularly from Poland, Italy, Germany, Lithuania – arguing for an acknowledgment of God and Christian values in at least the preamble of the Constitution was a clear indication of the progress of secularization in various European settings, such as France and its enshrinement of *laïcité* (Roy 2007), the Scandinavian countries, and even post-Franco Spain.

While "secularization" is a troublesome, multidimensional concept bearing on modernity, it is undeniable that in Western Europe traditional religious beliefs and practices, anchored in mainstream religious organizations, have steadfastly receded, and particularly after the political and cultural turbulence of the 1960s. This does not necessarily mean that native Europeans are not "spiritual" or without faith, but more that there is ongoing "bricolage" of traditional religious and liberal (post-Enlightenment) elements, generating a "mutation" of religious memory, as European sociologists of religion have found in their research (Dobbelaere and Voyé 1990; Davie 2000; Hervieu-Léger 2003). The "memory" is kept alive in monuments, churches, holidays and perhaps at the beginning and end of life (baptism and funerals), but dims immeasurably in adult life such as sexual conduct.[18] Denmark, as a particular focus of this essay, is very much in this trend away from established religion, which in this case has been the state-supported Evangelical Lutheran Church. While officially 85% of Denmark's population is a member of the state church,[19] Danes (like others in Lutheran countries) are below the already low European average for church attendance, on the one hand, and beliefs in God, a soul, afterlife, heaven, hell, and the resurrection of the dead, on the other (Davie: 2000: Tables 1.1 and 1.2). It is in comparison to the sharp and continuing decline of traditional European (Christian) beliefs and practices that the Muslim minority community in Europe takes added significance.

Although estimates of the Muslim population in Denmark vary (as is the case for every European country, and keeping in mind that Denmark does not have religion in its census questionnaire), a reasonable figure is about 3.5% (U.S. Department of State, International Religious Freedom Report 2005) of Denmark's 5.4 million inhabitants (Denmark Statistical Yearbook 2007). It should be borne

---

18   It is perhaps because of the increased laxity of sexual mores and conduct that there has been a sharply growing number of European converts to Islam, which offers a sanctuary with its strict code of dress and behavior for men and women, a code that Victorians would recognize. Quantitatively, just as it is difficult to get accurate figures for the number of Muslims in Europe, so also we only have rough estimates for European converts. With that caveat, it is estimated that there are about14,000-16,000 in Britain, 15,000-20,000 in Italy, and that about 4,000 in France converted to Islam in 2006, with about the same number in Germany, up from 1,000 in 2005 (Reuters Foundation, AlertNet Factbox, "European Converts to Islam". http://www.alertnet.org/thenews/newsdesk/L06820042.htm).

Qualitatively, a little vignette is suggestive. One of the highest profile British convert, Yvonne Ridley, a former correspondent for a leading newspaper, who was raised a Protestant and converted after being kidnapped by the Taliban, was sharply questioned by a Danish reporter about Ridley's stress on modest clothing. She retorted, "Listen, darling, if you want to look like a slapper and a whore and dress like a tart, it's up to you, but don't expect me to do it, too," and added, "What's more liberating – being judged on the size of your IQ or on the size of your bust?" International Herald Tribune, August 16,2006. http://www.iht. com/articles/2006/08/16/nes/converts.php?page=2. As for white male British converts, one observer noted, Islam "speaks to their masculinity" and gives them an identity in the greater transnational and supranational Muslim community, a "togetherness which is inevitably going to be against the West, because of their identity with other Muslims," (*ibid.*).

19   http://www.um.dk/publikationer/um/english/denmark/kap1/1-14.asp.

Table 12.3   Danish Immigrant Population by Muslim Country of Origin, 2007

Region	Country	Men	Women	Total
Africa				
	Egypt	1148	725	1873
	Morocco	4863	4377	9240
	Somalia	8430	7763	16193
Asia/Middle East				
	Afghanistan	6117	5437	11554
	Iraq	14883	12487	27370
	Iran	8311	6240	14551
	Jordan	1026	896	1922
	Kuwait	945	774	1719
	Lebanon	12121	10841	22962
	Pakistan	10036	9208	19244
	Syria	1599	1642	3241

Source: Statistical Yearbook 2007, Table 18, *Statistics Denmark*, Copenhagen. The total shown includes both immigrants and their descendents.

in mind that the Danish Muslim community comes from a wide variety of national ethnic background, as can be seen in Table 12.3.

In the aggregate, this makes Islam the second largest religion in Denmark – just as it is in neighboring Sweden, as well as in Belgium, France, Greece, Italy, Portugal, and Spain (Savage 2004). It is in terms of size a small Muslim European population, far less than almost all the other Western EU countries. Like other Muslim populations, it has experienced in recent decades and is expected to experience in coming ones, an important increase relative to the declining non-Muslim population. Based on various sources, Savage projects that compared to 5 % earlier this decade, Muslims will comprise at least one-fourth of France's population by 2025 and 20% of Europe's population by 2050, perhaps even more as Europe's aging non-Muslim population is, according to UN projections, to decline from 728 million in 2000 to under 600 million by 2050 (Savage 2004: 28f).

Gross demographic trends are useful in providing ingress to social change as Durkheim himself realized full well in *The Division of Labor in Society* looking at the dynamics of solidarity in modern society. However, if the emergence of the European Union over the last 40 years since the Treaty of Rome has generated and is generating what may be viewed as a new European organic solidarity around the European common market and commitment to European values being formulated in a new European Constitution, the rapid and projected growth of a Muslim community is providing a major challenge for integration. The challenge stems from both endogenous factors in Europe and exogenous factors on the global scene.

Integration as a reflection of social organization entails both structural aspects of meshing in the division of labor, or economy writ large, and social-psychological aspects of solidarity producing a "we" perspective. Integration as a social fact and social value seems to have run into a wall regarding the Muslim immigrants, even where these have attained citizenship. At present, for non-Muslim Europeans, whether in Great Britain, France, Germany, Sweden and elsewhere, the Muslim population is perceived more as a threatening presence, as "the other", an unwelcome and perhaps dangerous neighbor to be kept at a distance (Kuper and Dombey 2007; Allievi 2003; Ansari 2004: 390). Widely shared by various (Western) commentators is the somber appraisal:

> A sense of foreboding and an atmosphere of failed integration and social conflict hang like a cloud over the 16 million or so Muslims living in Western Europe (Laurence 2006a: 252).

For Muslims in Europe, and particularly for the second and third generation who now constitute about half of the immigrant population, a study of 58 in-depth interviews with Muslims in 10 EU countries found them concerned over being "excluded from economic, social and cultural life" (EUMC 2006b:7). Brief, they are more likely to feel *in* Europe than *of* Europe.[20] What underlies this and how does this connect to the cartoons affaire?

A New Islamic Identity

If ambivalence towards the world of Islam has a long European history, punctuated by wars of conquest, sieges and periods of accommodation (as in *al-Andalus* Iberia), I would argue that a new Islamic identity and a new sense of community became a reality in the wake of the massive immigration of recent decades. The *ummah* (or *umma*), the global Islamic community, has always been there (as is the case for the faithful of any world religion), but subordinated to other bases of identity, such as ethnicity and nationality.[21] Several factors have operated to make an Islamic religious identity salient in the otherwise secular Europe.

---

20   "They do not feel at home in European societies and prefer to live among themselves, forming a relatively self-contained community," (Parekh 2006: 179).

21   So, for example, France, which in terms of its enshrined principle of *laïcité* does not acknowledge religion in the public sphere, had "Arabs" and "Algerians" along with "Sénégalais", etc. Now, however, and especially since *9/11* they tend to be called "Musulmans".

First, the traditional European pathways to gradual political integration – electoral participation in the political sphere, civic participation through public education, and identification with the nation-state via conscription – have proved grossly insufficient to make the new immigrants into European nationals (Laurence 2006: 253).[22] Given the concentration of the immigrants in urban areas (but in less desirable neighborhoods), states have adopted various strategies of integration to relate to these groups. These have been prompted by "fundamentalisms" in various guises appearing in the 1980s, in Christianity, Judaism, Hinduism, *and* Islam, and in doing so, posing new challenges for the authority of states (Marty and Appleby 1993). In taking notice of a growing presence of Muslims in Europe – including new converts – European states found it convenient, if not essential, to relate to the immigrant population via Islamic institutions and associations, first outside Europe, then at the local level. Overseas Islamic states accepted willingly to be "outsourced" in providing resources, from funds for building of mosques to *imams* who could address immigrant groups in their own language: one estimate of Saudi Arabian funding for 1975-2005 places this at more than $85 *billion* (Laurence 2006: 258).

It was a *mariage de convénience* between secular European states and wealthy Islamic states (such as Saudi Arabia, Libya), since European states lacked funds to provide for the religious needs of immigrants, especially where Islam is not recognized as a religion entitled to state funding (as in the case of France and Germany). For the Islamic states, providing monetary resources or religious personnel (imams), was also a way of keeping tabs on its overseas population and insulating it to the extent possible from both the corrosive influence of Western secular modernity and from radical Muslim clerics. Taking Sweden as illustrative, the imams served an ethnic congregation, rarely learned the language of the host society, and lived within the enclosure of their respective community, insulated from the modernity and reality of Sweden, such as education and employment opportunities for women (Roald 2002: 111).

Related factors served to give salience to the religious ties of the immigrant population. First, a series of cultural and political crises between 1979 and 2005 profoundly impacted Muslims within and without Europe. Outside Europe, the dramatic return to Iran in 1979 of the Ayatollah Khomenei gained global attention in overthrowing the modernizing regime of the Shah that was viewed as authoritarian, corrupt, and putting the interests of big Western oil companies ahead of the spiritual and material needs of the Shia majority. The ability of the revolutionary regime to withstand an American attempt to restore the Shah led to the demonization of Khomenei in the American press, but to his becoming something of a David slaying Goliath in Islamic circles. Nearly ten years later,

---

22   Why and how these democratic pillars of civic engagement have been inadequate is a complex matter. In Great Britain which has probably the highest political integration in Europe of Muslims, Ansari notes that Muslim politicians have "largely remained sidelines in terms of power," (Ansari 2004: 242).

Khomenei further became seen as a redeemer "who had saved Islam in the hour of trial" in issuing his 1990 famous *fatwa* calling for the slaying of Salmon Rushdie for publishing the blasphemous *Satanic Verses,* forcing Rushdie to rush into hiding overseas (McRoy 2006: 13).

The Middle East became even more than usual a cauldron of bitter conflict putting Muslim nations and populations at risk from what was perceived as "homeland". In late 1987, the grassroots Palestinian civilian *intifada* using stones against armored Israeli troops captured world attention and was seen as something of a success leading to the 1993 Oslo peace agreement. In 1991, the invasion of Iraq by the United States, having divided opinion in the United States until its declaration, had partial Islamic support from Gulf oil states afraid that Iraq's Sadam Hussein might want to expand his domain beyond the contested Kuwait oil field. At the same time, for many of the young Muslims in Europe (and elsewhere), Hussein became seen as more of a folk hero than a villain.

The horrendous civil war in Yugoslavia in the middle, and its aftermath in Kosovo at the end of the decade brought to European immigrants from that region the fear that Muslims might not be safe anywhere, including Europe (McRoy 2006: 24). Although the United States led NATO forces to rescue Muslim ethnic Albanians from Serbian "ethnic cleansing" of Kosovo, Muslims in Great Britain had felt incensed by the British government's earlier refusal to come to the aid Bosnians; some had even become apprehensive that the neglect of Bosnian Muslims might presage their own Holocaust in Great Britain (McRoy *ibid.*).

The turn of the century marked a further deterioration of Muslim integration in the European mainstream, as centrist governments adopted the xenophobic attitudes of ultra conservatives, and popular resentment of Muslims was fueled by the general economic slowdown in Europe with double-digit unemployment straining welfare measures. Shunted unemployed Muslim youths, with their parents' origin outside Europe, increasingly felt discriminated against in the labor and housing markets *because* of their religion, as seemingly typified to be the case in the French school system and labor market with the denial of Muslim women wearing their traditional *hajib* headscarf or *foulard* (EUMC 2006a: 40; Laurence and Vaisse 2006: 163-74). In England in the early summer of 2001 in former mill towns of Yorkshire (Bradford, Burnley, Oldham), now marked by the closing of textile mills, unemployed South Asian Muslim youths engaged in highly publicized rioting, while across the Channel, the severe riots in Paris *banlieus* (suburbs) in the fall of 2005 was also seen as a rampage of militant unemployed Muslims from the Maghreb and Africa.

The attack on New York on September 11, 2001 has of course entered the history books, which will continue to reverberate domestically and internationally for longer than can be envisaged in previous declarations of war (assuming it was a declaration of war). Despite a politically correct attempt by governments to differentiate between "moderate" and "radical" Muslims, and despite that Muslims in Europe overwhelmingly reject suicide bombing (Kuper 2007), it is clear that the American declaration of a "war on terrorism" has reinforced a latent "negative identity" for Islam across a wide spectrum of the European public. Together with "7/11" (the London bombings of subway stations and a double-decker bus in July 2005), "9/11" greatly contributed to enhanced "Islamophobia" and the consequent further discrimination and verbal attacks on European Muslims (EUMC 2006a; EUMC 2006b).

Although we could add many more violent episodes and events in Europe and elsewhere, the point I seek to make is that Islam and being Muslim have become salient markers of identity, globally as well as in Europe. For non-Muslims, it is a negative marker, with tacitly the burden of proof placed on a Muslim to show that Islam is not a dark force which, in addition to oppressing women, propels wars, conflicts, and terrorism (EUMC 2006 b). For Muslims, and particularly for second and third generation youths born in Europe (or if not born, converted), Islam has become a primary basis of solidarity and integration – not integration in the surrounding civil society so much as integration in the "imagined" world community of the *Ummah,* in effect, the pan- global Islamic nation.[23] If American sub-culture of the ghettos provides a modicum of identification between the youth of Maghreb background and their inner city counterparts in America via *rap, funk, hip hop,* and *rock* music, as indicated in one study, the same also noted that for these youth, the return to religion is a symptom of wanting to fill a void in the spiritual or social which they could not obtain away from their country of origin (Berhil 2003; Laurence and Vaisse 2006: 74-97).

As the reciprocal of the presumed fundamental conflict between "modern" West and "traditional" or "pre-modern" Islam, which some Orientalists, media commentators, and other observers have drawn, sociologists can view the new religious basis of solidarity among younger generations of Muslims in Europe as a contemporary instance of a classic theory of Georg Simmel. Namely, an unanticipated function of social conflict is to increase the cohesion and solidarity of a beleaguered minority (Coser 1956).

Enter Durkheim

In his seminal study on the origins and structures of religion as a social phenomenon (and tacitly, of society as a religious phenomenon), Durkheim provides an analytical framework which can assist in the broader understanding of the Danish cartoons affair. At the same time, the contemporary uproar can broaden the scope of Durkheim's analysis well beyond its original base in Australian ethnographic data.

In launching his study of the religious life as a composite of beliefs and practices – the cognitive and active aspects of religion – Durkheim introduces the

---

23   I am using "imagined" in the sense of Benedict Anderson's usage of the role of print media in the construction of nationhood on the periphery of empires (Anderson 1991).

basic differentiation that humans make of the objective world. On the one hand are collective beliefs in *profane* things, on the other, in *sacred* things; the two are in stark contrast to one another in how they are approached, and together, all things – material or ideal – can be classified as either sacred or profane (Durkheim 1995:34). He further insists that the heterogeneity between these two categories is *absolute*, even more so than between good and evil, which Durkheim considers as opposite species of the same genus (p. 36). Each sphere has its own energies, in opposition to the other, with the opposition conceived differently in different religions. Although Durkheim acknowledges the possible ritualized passage from one realm to the other, symbolized for example in rituals of initiation,[24] he stresses the fundamental real antagonism of the two, their being "hostile and jealous rivals," (p.37).

This initial dichotomy might appear to underlie Huntington's "clash of civilizations" (1996), here between Islam's view of the "Abode of Peace" (or Abode of Faith), and the "Abode of War" (or "Abode of Unbelief"), and tie in with an image of Islam militant activists carrying out a *jihad* against the modernity of the West. While this is partly operative, it not only calls for a deeper analysis but also overlooks that Islam has its own internal spheres of sacred/profane as much as do respectively Christianity and Judaism, for each traditionally has conceived of spheres that are "pure" and "impure', the first the sphere of the sacred, the second of the profane. Further, *jihad* very broadly denotes *struggle* or *resistance*, taken often against an external foe but also in a spiritual sense against an internal one (inside the Islamic community or ultimately against the dark side of self). The latter significance is a reflection of the dualism of human nature which Christianity and Judaism also recognize, as did Freud's more "secular" dualism of the superego-id conflict, and as did Durkheim in a later essay (Durkheim 1960). Although a greater part of the present day discussions regarding Islam and Islamic terrorism is grounded on viewing it as manifestations of *jihad* aimed at destruction of the West and its core elements, we need to keep in mind that it is not the whole picture and that there is a space where Islam and the other world faiths might find common ground. I will take this up at the conclusion of this chapter.

Extending Durkheim's discussion and its relevance for our study, the separation of the sacred and the profane is not immutable, for each is subject to the primary process of "contagion" (Durkheim's term, p. 328) of the other. They are complementary *forces*, "qualitatively different from the tangible things in which we localize them,' (p. 327): they are, he adds, *superadded* (*surajoutées* in the original text) to objects. One might speak of a dialectical relationship involved, with reciprocal processes of each seeking to penetrate the other sphere. *Profanation (or desecration)* are actions or processes which penetrate the sacred and thereby

---

24   Among other classical ethnological studies of these rituals, see Arnold van Gennep, *Rites of Passage*, Chicago: University of Chicago Press, 1960 and Victor W. Turner, *Revelation and Divination in Ndembu Ritual,* Ithaca, NY: Cornell University Press, 1975.

may be taken to undermine the potency or power of the sacred. Reciprocally, *sacralization* may be thought of as actions rendering sacred that which has been viewed as ordinary, profane objects. So for example, whether the garment of a great religious leader or the ground where a miracle is said to have taken place or the relic of a national hero are among the myriad of objects illustrating Durkheim's dictum:

> By a sort of contradiction, the sacred world is as though inclined by its very nature to spread into the same profane world that which it otherwise excludes (322).

Still, the "sacred" must guard against being violated or penetrated by the profane, that is, it must seek to prohibit, bar, and react against being sullied by acts of *profanation,* giving rise in traditional societies to rites which seek to purify, cleanse and keep away profane forces from the sacred.[25] Since the focus of the present essay is initially at least to understand the vehemence of the Muslim reactions against the Danish cartoons, I will pursue the phenomenon of profanation at greater length than the complementary process of sacralization.

Among kinds of actions which profane the sacred is *blasphemy,* the profanation of the sacred by verbal attacks.[26] In the more advanced cults or faith communities which Durkheim does not analyze, blasphemy may take the form of a human being seeking to either verbally attack or to abrogate the power of the divine transcendental by improper use of the name of the deity, as reflected in the interdiction "Thou shall not take the name of the Lord in vain". To protect against this and other violation of the sacred, "traditional" societies have institutionalized *tabus*, interdictions of conduct, the realm of what is forbidden (p.304). The most familiar tabus involve avoidance of contact with sacred objects. In small-scale societies living in a relatively closed environment, kinship relations are paramount in social organization and the most frequently observed tabus are sexual contacts between kin relatives. The Judeo-Christian Decalogue may be viewed as partly grounded in the interdictions of small-scale societies, partly in the social milieu of a more complex social organization. In our further evolved modern complex societies, while sexual tabus are still minimally observed, newer tabus enter into the public sphere, some very abstract, such as interdictions to utter certain words that are considered opprobrious and morally reprehensible and offensive. The expressions of such words or phrases are, in effect, acts of blasphemy, even if the "sacred" that is attacked is not a deity or its direct human representative.

---

25   This is extensively examined by Mary Douglas in her classical derivative of Durkheim's analysis, *Purity and Danger: an analysis of the concepts of pollution and taboo*, London: Ark, 1984 (1966).

26   "In addition to the things that are sacred, there are words and sounds that have the same quality: they must not be found on the lips of the profane or reach their ears," (p. 309).

What Durkheim has to say specifically about *modern* tabus or changes in the content of what is considered sacred and what is considered profane is brief, yet as we shall later note, very relevant for another dimension of the Danish cartoons matter. Presently though, it is the structure of their antagonistic and dialectical relationship underlying his analysis which is of importance. In particular, how do social actors experience or react to the intrusion of one sphere on the other? Very much part of his approach looking at the beliefs and practices of religious life as a social phenomenon is, as carefully noted by Fish (2005), the affective, emotive aspects.

However much Durkheim has been an influence on scholars looking at structural aspects of social organization, it should also be recognized that *The Elementary Forms of Religious Life* also highlights the power of the societal to harness and direct powerful emotions generated in social interaction in very special moments (p. 212). While "collective effervescence" (p. 220) as a setting for the genesis of the religious idea has led to applications in many modern settings (see for example in this volume my essay, "Collective Effervescence, Social Change and Charisma: Durkheim, Weber and 1989"), of more immediate interest here is that strong emotions are generated when the sacred is attacked by profanation.[27] Durkheim's analysis is suggestive that when a breaking of a tabu occurs, it is attended by a strong visceral collective reaction, albeit he does not follow up what sort of negative sanctions are levied against the perpetrator of the profanation, either in the traditional society in which he has embedded his study of religion, or in our modern world. It may be expected that there will be significant cultural and historical variations in the sanctions levied, and that the element of power differential may also be a factor: for example, if a community is relatively powerless in relation to another which commits desecration, the sanctions may be contained in verbal accusations, such as emotive cursing. In any event, we can extrapolate his analysis to formulate the following:

> *When the sacred is violated by others than community ritual experts, especially by those considered outside the societal community, it will be reacted with strong, negative emotions and sanctions against the miscreant.*

Why this should be so can be understood sociologically: profanation and sacrilege expose or wound the core of the social community. The pain inflicted on the community is as intense as the pain felt by the body when it threatened with invasion by a pathogen. Ultimately, it is the core of social integration and cohesion

---

27   Again, the focus of this essay precludes my considering the strong emotions of collective joy or exuberance, when sacralization occurs in "collective effervescence", for example the day of a great victory for a country, an athletic team, etc. At the individual level, as Durkheim noted (p. 215), sacredness is also conferred on certain persons of high position.

that the sacred symbolizes, and its breach must be rectified with all haste, lest the sacred become a mere aspect of the quotidian.

It is at this point that we make use of Durkheim in interpreting the situation of Islam and Muslims in Europe regarding the Danish cartoons affair.

Interpreting Violation of the Muslim Sacred

What then accounts for the extent and unanimity of the Muslim reaction, in Denmark and world wide, to the publication of a set of cartoons in a newspaper hitherto little known outside Denmark? Equally, what accounts for the massive denunciation, in Europe and elsewhere, of Muslim violence and reactions against the publication of the cartoons? I want to propose that there has been a profanation of the sacred in *both* instances, each involving a different set of elements defining the sacred and the profane. More than that, the contemporary situation, with the ambiguity of what constitutes collective identity for Muslims and non-Muslims respectively, each separately feeling the tugs of "primordial" and "civic" ties, is a milieu that can ignite the strong reactions to the violation of the sacred.

First, the Muslim sacred.

Holding aside various theological derivatives and interpretations, the central core of Islamic belief and practice, as McRoy notes (2006: 83) is the *Qur'an* (much as the Torah for the Jews and the Gospels for Christians), seen as the Word of God.[28] Over a series of revelations from the angel Gabriel, Muhammad, a former merchant, became entrusted to write down what God required of men; after a flight from Mecca to Medina, he was successful in setting up a community faithful to God's intention, the community of Islam (Lawrence 2006). Muhammad thus is seen by Muslims as a Prophet, a special Messenger of God, the last in a chain that goes back to Abraham and Moses down to Jesus. Muhammad is not a divine figure, having an acknowledged date and place of birth and death, but he is a specially revered figure for making accessible to humans the literal speech of God. Hence, to revert to Durkheimian terminology, if Muhammad is not in Islamic theology the founder of Islam, the community of all who hear and practice what is revealed in the Qur'an, he is in fact a prime *collective representation of Islam*, of the total global community, the *Ummah*.

It might be added that Islam, just as Judaism, had its beginning in a given territory which became a sacred heartland, giving it a sense of its faithful being chosen with a divine mission, like components of Judaism and Christianity (Davies 1982, Smith 2003). Through conquest and immigration, Islam has over the ages spread around the world, in areas where its adherents are the majority and in others where they are the minority. Although in the contemporary world there

---

28   For succinct explications and overviews of the Qur'an, its main adherents and structures, see McRoy 2006, Part 2, ("Islam and Islamism in Relation to Democracy and *Jihad*"), and Lawrence (2006).

is a multiplicity of recognized Islamic states, the separation of church and state so familiar in Western civilization tends to be absent in the Islamic world. Islam, I would propose, is a religion *and* a nation with seamless borders, an "imagined community" (Anderson 1991). The interpenetration of the two underlies the observation of Ivan Strenski:

> Not only do national boundaries mark the boundaries of a sacred precinct as 'tabu' to the intruder as any temple's holy of holies, but the accessories of nationalism – its flags, monuments, anthems and such – partake of the same transcendent religious glow of the nation as sacred being (Strenski 2006: 301).

Although for Islam there are tangible markers of the faith, such as the Dome of the Rock in Jerusalem, whose ground is equally sacred to Judaism (Lawrence 2006: 62-72), the land where traditionally Muslims have been the majority and live in observance of the Islamic code of law (the *Shari'ah)* is a core aspect of Islamic nationhood. Hence, the invasion and occupation of Islamic territory by non-Muslim military forces, as in Afghanistan by Russian troops in the 1990s and in the present decade by NATO, or in Iraq by the American-led coalition in the present decade is already for Muslims a breach of the sacred. But aside from the military occupation of Muslim countries (which for Muslims include Palestine, and particularly Jerusalem and the West Bank), Islam in recent years, and particularly since *9/11,* has in much of world media and by eminent secular and religious leaders, borne a negative image as having a propensity for violence and encouraging terrorism, a carrier of an AIDS-like virus. This stigmatization extends even to countries viewed as "moderates": for example, when Dubai, a Gulf emirate which is rapidly becoming a prime regional center of finance, sought in 2006 to purchase a company that would allow Dubai Ports World to operate several port terminals in the United States, strong political opposition in Congress blocked the transaction. To incidents such as this are added other forms of humiliation that have deepened a sense of grievance against the West: the treatment of Muslim combatants and detainees in Abu Ghraib prison in Iraq and in Guantanamo camps in Cuba in violation of the Geneva Convention, and the tongue lashing in lieu of a welcome address the president of Columbia University gave to the duly elected president of Iran in September 2007 when the latter visited New York to address the United Nations. Equally offensive, Salman Rushdie was rewarded for his writings by being awarded a knighthood at the Queen's Birthday Honours in June 2007, albeit he is no longer a resident of the United Kingdom, an action praised in some quarters but seen as a deliberate insult to the Islamic world.

Space limitation prevents a fuller discussion of the global situation of Muslims. On the positive side, the Islamic world is marked by demographic and economic growth: with 2006 UN data, Muslims, with higher fertility rates, now exceed Catholics as the largest global group of adherent (19.2% vs. 17.2%), and have the second largest number of adherents after Christianity (with varying estimates but around 1.3 billion).[29] The crescent flag is shown over several countries riche in natural resources in the Middle East, Central Asia, and Southeast Asia, with many new Islamic sovereign funds commanding large capital cross-border investments. On the other hand, the Islamic world is surrounded by suspicion of being actively or covertly a foyer of *jihad* terrorism which has to be met with a show of military force utilizing leading-edge technology and by all possible means of surveillance, of Muslims at home and abroad. Thus, globally, Islam is in a state of active tension with a hostile external *Dar al-Harb*, the abode of war.

The situation of Muslims in Denmark is prototypical of their uneasy situation in Europe. Although a small but growing community with second and third generation members that are more familiar with quotidian Danish life and culture than with that of the country of origin, they tend not to be accepted in civic engagement. In effect, since 9/11 in particular, Danish identity has drawn around "our common Danish values" which in effect reside in a glass bowl excluding the Muslim immigrants and their Danish-born progeny (Simonsen 2002: 127); Mouritsen 2006: 81-83). And as I have noted earlier, this exclusion in Denmark is both representative of the Muslim situation in Europe and of the global situation of Islam overseas (particularly in the United States and Great Britain). At the same time, and perhaps because of perceived "Islamophobia" in Denmark, Europe and elsewhere and the perceived mistreatment and discrimination of Muslims, the religious basis of collective identity – with the succor and encouragement of traditional religious leaders, the imam – has been strengthened, particularly among the second and third generations, and even become paramount over ethnicity and country of origin.

Thus, the publication of the Danish cartoons that set off massive Muslim protests in Denmark, Europe and overseas was a profanation of a traditional sacred tabu (the depiction of the Prophet) but in its defiling of a sacred figure, it was also a defilement of the entire societal community, the Ummah.

How can a set of cartoons have such import, and in a related vein, how can a minor "ordinary" novel (*The Satanic Verses*) become condemned as blasphemous and its author declared de facto an outlaw? [30] Durkheim's analysis of the efficacy of religious symbols as collective representations will take us deeper into a sociological understanding. He observes that collective representations can objectify, and "from the most commonplace object, they can make a sacred and very powerful being," (1995: 229). Further,

---

29   http://www/catholicnewsagency.com/new.php?n=12192.

30   In contrast, the author of an equally blasphemous literary attack on the Christian sacred, *The Da Vinci Code*, was publicly lionized and richly rewarded, with only minor protests from traditional religious organizations, and similarly for the BBC 2005 production of the blatantly anti-Christian *Jerry Springer – the Opera* at taxpayers' expense, defended as "a legitimate work of art," (Jenkins 2007: 280).

where religious force becomes objectified depends entirely upon what circumstances cause the feeling that generates religious ideas to settle here or there ... Finally, from the standpoint of religious thought, the part equals the whole; the part has the same powers and the same efficacy. A fragment of a relic has the same virtues as the whole relic ... (1995: 230f).

The Danish cartoons mocking and depicting Muhammad as a terrorist were thus a double profanation of the sacred. Not only did this violate a traditional Islamic injunction against the human figures of the Messenger of God. Its caricature of The Prophet was contextually a public ridicule and attack of the entire community, the Ummah, yet an additional symbolic act of violence to complement acts of violence on Muslims in Europe and outside Europe. The Danish cartoons and the failure of the Danish government to castigate the editor of the newspaper and the collaborating cartoonists was for the Muslim world a further defilement, one that released the strong emotive reactions that became manifest, first in Denmark in September 2005, then with the diffusion of the cartoons among Islamic countries, in other regions in February 2006.

Interpreting Violation of the Secular Sacred

The Danish cartoons affaire is revelatory of another sacred whose violation brings to light a further aspect of our modernity. Recall that at the beginning of this paper we mentioned that a proximate cause for the publication of the cartoons was the issue of self-censorship and possible fear that depiction of Muhammad would bring harassment and retribution similar to what happened to Rushdie and Theo van Gogh. Media reaction to the imams' condemnation of the cartoons was mixed, but regrets about blasphemy and offending Muslim sensitivity were minor in comparison the large-scale upholding of the freedom of the press and freedom of expression. That has become a core element of the modern secular sacred, which Durkheim had well noted in his extended discussion:

> Even the peoples most enamored of free thinking tend to place one principle above discussion and regard it as untouchable, in other words, sacred: the principle of free discussion itself. (1995: 215)

This is not the only element of our present contemporary sacred but it is of paramount significance, since free speech and free press are seen as portals of modern democracy; conversely, its violation – for example the Muslim public burning of *The Satanic Verses* – evokes a regime of tyranny. British Muslim denunciation of the Danish cartoons in the form of placards reading "Butcher those who mock Islam" was in turn denounced in a *Wall Street Journal* editorial upholding in contrast "The Western philosophical tradition... founded on the belief that the execution of Socrates for blaspheming the gods of Athens was an injustice," (*WSJ*, February 11, 2006).

Why freedom of expression, verbally, visually, and in print media has become such an important, if not the most important, ideological component of the secular sacred, would require a more extensive discussion than can be undertaken here. But perhaps it may be seen as the least common denominator for the prevailing liberal orientation of modern societies, even as a surrogate for democracy itself.

Conclusion

The "thick description" of the Danish cartoons offered here has sought to provide an interpretation of the meaning of the *situation* in which it took place. The situation has multiple interactive settings: the situation of Muslims and the host Danish society, the situation of Muslim immigrants in a changing Europe, and the evolving situation of Islam in the world but particularly vis-à-vis the West, with the latter both highly dependent on Middle East resources yet waging wars on traditional Islamic soil. For obvious reasons, only the analysis has been suggestive and far from comprehensive. It has had some focal points, however, which can open up broader sociological vistas, using the Danish cartoons controversy and Durkheimian analysis as a starting point.

The question of *integration*, so central in Durkheim's oeuvre from start in *The Division of Labor in Society* to *the Elementary Forms of Religious Life* is of equal importance today in the era of globalization, characterized not only by flows of capital and goods but also vast flows of people from different cultural backgrounds. The socioeconomic integration of countries and regions has been making remarkable strides in recent decades in Europe, North America and quite likely to come, in Asia. Muslims in Europe face major challenges being accepted as citizens and their host societies face equal challenges in accepting them as such, for both domestic and international reasons. Internally, Muslims in Europe face the problem of opening the door away from ghettoization by attending public education, participating in national identity other than national sports (such as German Muslims did in showing their support at the Berlin World Cup of 2006), and coming to grips with the "inner lines of conflict". Here the stand of European Muslims on the Danish cartoons ipso facto challenged the major achievements of the Enlightenment under girding the modern European Union: "equality and sexual determination of women and homosexuals, freedom of opinion and the press, and the rights of the secular vis-à-vis the sacral world" 2007: (Peter Schneider quoted in Jenkins 2007: 248).

With unequal economic development and with unequal rates of population growth, regions that have a surplus of population and a shortage of employment opportunities have sent significant numbers of emigrants to more fortunate countries. Economic integration was facilitated by the immigrants providing necessary services at lower labor costs. But economic integration is only a partial aspect of integration, and political and cultural factors, as previously suggested, have hardened the acceptance of the immigrant community by the larger host society, particularly as the economic climate of the past two decades has reduced growth and employment opportunities, in Europe and in North America. Of equal if not greater weight in the problematic of accepting Muslims in Europe as bona fide citizens, the unexpected terrorist attacks in the United States and in Europe in the present decade (and sporadic terrorist attacks associated with radical Islam as far away as Bali) have contributed to a "nativistic" if not xenophobic current viewing selected immigrant communities as potential dangers, rather than as welcome additions to cultural diversity.[31]

I have at length commented on this in drawing attention to the Muslims in Europe feeling marginalized, subject to "Islamophobia", out of place, differentiated by religion and clothing. Similarly, the problem of integration for the immigrant community is very much that of the *Hispanic* situation in the United States, who despite larger numbers also occupy lower rungs of employment, and have become subject of a "nativistic" current seeking to impose actual physical barriers preventing illegal entry into the United States. This is not the first time in American history when a quasi-hysterical reaction of a "moral panic" was launched against "aliens", such as Japanese and Chinese 100 years ago (the "yellow peril"). That the United States has had in the past a remarkable success with integration of immigrants with modest backgrounds and different cultures is of little help to increasingly harassed legal as well as non-documented immigrants from Central America who are starting to feel as an unwelcomed presence, much the same as Muslims in Europe (Collins 2007).

The question of integration common to both the Muslim minority in Europe and the Hispanic minority in the United States also opens reflection on the sacred in the contemporary world. Durkheim's analysis drew upon materials of a society very different from ours, but his analysis of the sacred had a much more general application than the sacred in Australian totemism. It is, in effect, an invitation to consider reflexively the sacred in our setting, particularly in its manifestations in what seems a highly secular age, which initially might seem bereft of the sacred. I have already used one clue from Durkheim in proposing that freedom of expression from censorship (free speech, free press) is a core aspect of the sacred (at least in theory, though in practice subject to limitation).

---

31   Illustrative is the declaration of a leader of the Dutch Labor Party in December 2005 that "unlimited migration and failing integration are a serious threat to solidarity and to the degree of welfare sharing we are proud of as social democrats," (Jenkins 2007: 247). It is a direct echo of a declaration ten years previously by a Danish spokesman for the Liberal Party that "there are Muslims in Denmark who support ... things which are against Danish Law or, at least, against current morality in Denmark ... we must take these facts into account when we decide granting asylum... because they represent a danger to the security of Denmark," (Hjarnø 1997: 295).

Limiting ourselves to the United States, its sacred sphere has other elements which provide the core identity of the American nation. The place and the figure of the deity have become increasingly muted with secularization and legal battles to minimize visual and verbal references to God in the public sphere. However, and particularly since *9/11*, the American nation and its paramount symbols – the flag and the national anthem – have come to preeminent places as collective representations of the nation. To profane either is met with the same emotive (or "primordial") reaction of furor and threats of violence as met the publication of the Danish cartoons. Such is what happened in 2006 when Mexican Americans sang *Nuestro Himno* as an intended manifestation that they shared and identified with the American cultural heritage of the Star-Spangled Banner, but which non-Hispanic Americans thought was a gross insult. In a similar vein, English as a language has become part of the sacred for American nationalism, rather than viewing it as a global instrumental language in exchange processes of capital and information. To protect English from profanation and competition, part of the nativistic movement seeks to make English the official language of the country. Thus one may say that in both Europe and in the United States, multiculturalism which a few years ago appeared as a new paradigm for advanced modernity, has come on trial from various sources.

The sacred is equally manifested in other major social groups, because, to continue with Durkheim's analysis, the sacred is fundamental to group identity, and particularly significant in the global age when the commingling of populations and the encouragement of individualism can negate collective consciousness aside from nationalism. Historical events and historical figures can become transcendent in collective memories, as did Christianity once in an age that produced martyrs following its Prophet and as did Islam in having its Prophet and its martyrs. More recently, Martin Luther King as a prophet and as a martyr has become a core element of the sacred for African-Americans, while the *Shoah* has equally become a core element for the Jewish community. In keeping with Durkheim's analysis, profanation of either will be met with the strongest emotive reaction as an attack on the entire community, particularly with the prompting of traditional elites.

This essay is also intended as an initial starting point in bridging a seeming chasm of two cultures of modernity. What is perhaps urgently needed is for liberals, Muslim and Westerners, to understand the perspective of the other, and to allow "voice" to prevail over "exit", to invoke Hirschman (1970). At present, it is lamentable that "dialogue" is not allowed to take place in the country that is the greatest proponent of freedom of expression, the United States. Woefully, the distinguished Swiss Ph.D. Muslim scholar Tariq Ramadan who has sought in numerous works to relate Islam and modernity with democratic values (Ramadan 2002; Ruthven 2007) and so mitigate a "clash of civilizations", has had his tenured appointment at the University of Notre Dame blocked by the State Department revoking his visa for alleged being an endorser of terrorism.

Ultimately, the challenge for sociology is to carry on the legacy of Durkheimian analysis oriented to providing bases for greater integration rather than further division and separation, within and across borders. In the present geopolitical climate, it is an awesome task.[32] We cannot refuse it. It's no laughing matter.

References

Alexander, Jeffrey 1992. "The Promise of a Cultural Sociology: Technological Discourse and the Sacred and the Profane Information Machine," pp. 293-323 in Richard Münch and Neil J. Smelser, eds, *Theory of Culture*. Berkeley: University of California Press.

Alexander, Jeffrey ed. 1988. *Durkheimian Sociology*. New York: Cambridge University Press.

Allievi, Stefano and Jørgen S. Nielsen eds 2003. *Muslim Networks and Transnational Communities in and across Europe*. Leiden and Boston: Brill.

Anderson, Benedict 1991. *Imagined communities: reflections on the origin and spread of nationalism*, revised and extended edition. London & New York: Verso.

Ansari, Humayun 2004. *'The Infidel Within'. Muslims in Britain since 1800*. London: Hurst and Company.

Armstrong, Karen 2007. "Balancing the Prophet," *Financial Times, Life & Arts*, p. 6 April 28/29.

Beckford, James A., Danièle Joly, and Farhad Khosrokhavar 2005. *Muslims in Prison: challenge and change in Britain and France*. Basingstoke (UK) and New York: Palgrave Macmillan.

Berhil, Mohammed 2003. *Les Jeunes en France entre Islam et Modernité*. Paris: Publibook.

Chadwick, Owen 1975. *The Secularization of the European Mind in the Nineteenth Century,* Cambridge (UK) and New York: Cambridge University Press.

Christiansen, Flemming and Ulf Hedetoft eds. 2004. *The Politics of Multiple Belonging. Ethnicity and Nationalism in Europe and East Asia*. Aldershot Hants, UK and Burlington, VT: Ashgate.

Citrin, Jack and John Sides 2004. "More than Nationals: How Identity Choice Matters in the New Europe," pp. 161-85 in Hermann, Richard K. et al., *Transnational Identities*.

Colley, Linda 2005. *Britons: Forging the Nation 1707-1837*, 2nd ed. New Haven, CT: Yale University Press.

32　It is heartening to note on the lighter side that, following the initiative of former UN secretary-general Kofi Annan and French cartoonist Plantu, in 2007 at various sites in Europe and the United States *Cartoonists for Peace* held meetings and expositions to draw attention to skillful cartooning of political subjects without hatred and disrespect for deep-seated convictions of their satirical target (www.cartooningforpeace.org).

Collins, Kristin 2007. "Hispanic People Feel New Hostility," *Raleigh (NC) News & Observer*, September 23, 1A.

Coser, Lewis 1956. *The Functions of Social Conflict.* New York: Free Press.

Cram, Laura, D. Dinan, and N. Nugent 1999. *Developments in the European Union.* New York: St. Martin's Press.

Davie, Grace 2000. *Religion in Modern Europe. A Memory Mutates.* Oxford and New York: Oxford University Press.

Davies, W.D. 1982. *The Territorial Dimension of Judaism.* Berkeley: University of California Press.

Delanty, Gerard 1995. *Inventing Europe. Idea, Identity, Reality.* London: Macmillan Press.

Dinan, Desmond 1999. *Ever Closer Union. An Introduction to European Integration,* 2nd ed. Boulder, CO & London: Lynne Rienner.

Dobbelaere, Karel and Liliane Voyé 1990. "From Pillar to Postmodernity: the Changing Situation of Religion in Belgium," Sociological Analysis. 51: S1-13.

Durkheim, Emile 1960 (1914). "The Dualism of Human Nature and Its Social Conditions," pp. 325-40 in Kurt H. Wolff, ed., *Emile Durkheim, 1858-1917.* Columbus, Ohio: Ohio State University Press.

—.1995 (1912). *The Elementary Forms of Religious Life,* translated with an Introduction by Karen Fields. New York: Free Press.

EUMC (European Monitoring Centre on Racism and Xenophobia). 2006a. *Muslims in the European Union. Discrimination and Islamophobia.* Vienna (Austria).

EUMC. 2006b. *Perceptions of Discrimination and Islamophobia. Voices from Members of Muslim Communities in the European Union.* Vienna (Austria).

Ezell, Elizabeth D., M. Seeleib-Kaiser, and E.A. Tiryakian 2003. "National Identity Issues in the New German Elites: A Study of German University Students," *International Journal of Comparative Sociology*, 44, 3: 280-308.

Fish, Jonathan 2005. *Defending the Durkheimian Tradition. Religion, Emotion and Morality.* Aldershot Hants, UK and Burlington, VT: Ashgate.

Geertz, Clifford 2000 (1973). *The Interpretation of Cultures.* New York: Basic Books/Perseus Books Group.

Gerven, Walter van 2005. *The European Union: a polity of states and peoples.* Stanford, CA: Stanford University Press.

Giorgi, Liana, Ingmar von Homeyer and Wayne Parsons eds 2006. *Democracy in the European Union: towards the emergence of a public sphere.* London & New York: Routledge.

Haddad, Yvonne Yazbeck ed. 2002. *Muslims in the West. From Sojourners to Citizens.* Oxford and New York: Oxford University Press.

Herrmann, Richard K., Thomas Risse and Marilynn B. Brewer 2004. *Transnational Identities. Becoming European in the EU.* Lanham, MD: Rowman & Littlefield.

Hervieu-Léger, Danièle 2003. *Catholicisme, la fin d'un monde.* Paris: Bayard.

Hjarnø, Jan 1997. "Muslims in Denmark," pp. 291-302 in Gerd Nonneman, T. Niblock, and B. Szajkowski, eds. *Muslim Communities in the New Europe*. Reading, Berkshire (UK): Ithaca Press.

Huntington, Samuel P. 1996. *The Clash of Civilizations and the Remaking of World Order.* New York: Simon & Schuster.

Jenkins, Philip 2007. *God's Continent. Christianity, Islam and Europe's Religious Crisis*, Oxford: Oxford University Press.

Kelly, Lynette 2004. "Bosnian Refugees in Britain: A Question of Community," pp. 199-212 in Agata Górny and Paolo Ruspini, eds. *Migration in the New Europe. East-West Revisited.*

Kumar, Krishan 2003. *The Making of English National Identity*. Cambridge: Cambridge University Press.

Kuper, Simon and Daniel Dombey 2007. "Religious fault line that divides Europeans," *Financial Times*, August 20: 3.

Laurence, Jonathan 2006a. "Managing transnational Islam: Muslims and the state in Western Europe," pp. 251-273 in Craig Parsons and Timothy M. Smeeding, eds. *Immigration and the Transformation of Europe*. Cambridge and New York: Cambridge University Press.

—. 2006b, *Integrating Islam. Political and Religious Challenges in Contemporary France*. Washington, D.C.: Brookings Institution Press.

Laurence, Jonathan and Justin Vaisse 2006. *Integrating Islam. Political and Religious Challenges in Contemporary France.* Washington, D.C.: Brookings Institution Press.

Lawrence, Bruce 2006. *The Qur'an, a Biography.* New York: Atlantic Monthly Press.

Lepennies, Wolf 2006. *The Seduction of Culture in German History*. Princeton: Princeton University Press.

Mainville, Michael 2006. "Russia has a Muslim dilemma: Ethnic Russians hostile to Muslims," *San Francisco Chronicle*, November 19.

Maréchal, Brigitte, S. Allievi, F. Dassetto, and J. Nielsen eds. 2003. *Muslims in the Enlarged Europe. Religion and Society.* Leiden and Boston: Brill.

Marty, Martin E. and R. Scott Appleby eds. 1993. *Fundamentalisms and the State. Remaking Politics, Economics, and Militance.* Chicago: University of Chicago Press.

Mauss, Marcel 1969. *Œuvres*. Vol 3, *Cohésion sociale et divisions de la sociologie*, edited by Victor Karady. Paris: Les Éditions de Minuit.

McRoy, Anthony 2006. *From Rushdie to 7/7: The Radicalisation of Islam in Britain.* London: Social Affairs Unit.

Modood, Tariq A. Triandafyllidou, and R. Zapata-Barrero, eds. 2006. *Multiculturalism, Muslims and Citizenship.* London and New York: Routledge.

Mouritsen, Per 2006. "The particular universalism of a Nordic civic nation. Common values, state religion and Islam in Danish political culture,: pp. 70-93 in Tariq Modood, A. Triandafyllidou, and R. Zapata-Barrero, eds, *Multiculturalism, Muslims and Citizenship* London and New York: Routledge.

Parekh, Bhiku 2006. "Europe, Liberalism and the 'Muslim Question'," pp. 179-203 in Tariq Modood, Anna Triandafyllidou and Ricard Zapata-Barrero, eds. *Multiculturalism, Muslims and Citizenship. A European Approach.* London and New York: Routledge.

Parsons, Craig A. and Timothy M. Smeeding eds. 2006. *Immigration and the Transformation of Europe.* Cambridge and New York: Cambridge University Press.

Pauly, Robert J., Jr. 2004. *Islam in Europe. Integration or Marginalization?* Aldershot, Hants (UK): Ashgate.

Ramadan, Tariq 2002. "Islam and Muslims in Europe: A Silent Revolution toward Rediscovery," pp. 158-66 in Yvonne Yazbeck Haddad, ed., *Muslims in the West. From Sojourners to Citizens.* Oxford and New York: Oxford University Press.

Rex, John and Gurharpal Singh eds. 2004. *Governance in Multicultural Societies.* Aldershot Hants, UK and Burlington, VT: Ashgate.

Roald, Anne Sofie 2002. "From 'People's Home to 'Multiculuralism': Muslims in Sweden," pp. 101-20 in Yvonne Yazbeck Haddad, ed., *Muslims in the West. From Sojourners to Citizens.*

Rodinson, Maxime 1987. *Europe and the Mystique of Islam*, translated by Roger Veinus. Seattle and London: University of Washington Press.

Roy, Olivier 2004. *Globalized Islam: the Search for a New Ummah.* New York: Columbia University Press/Centre d'Études et de Recherches Internationales.

—. 2007, *Secularism Confronts Islam*, George Holoch, trans. New York: Columbia University Press.

Ruthven, Malise 2007. "The Islamic Optimist," pp. 61-65, *The New York Review of Books*, 54, 13 (August 16).

Saint-Simon, Henri 1814. *De la réorganisation de la société européenne,* 2nd ed. Paris: A. Ėgron.

Savage, Timothy 2004. "Europe and Islam: Crescent Waxing, Culture Clashing," *The Washington Quarterly*, 27 (Summer): 25-50.

Sellam, Sadek 2006. *La France et ses musulmans. Un siècle de politique musulmane 1895-2005.* Paris: Fayard.

Shore, Cris. 2000. *Building Europe. The Cultural Politics of European Integration.* New York and London: Routledge.

Simonsen, Jørgen B. 2002. "Globalization in Reverse and the Challenge of Integration: Muslims in Denmark," pp. 121-30 in Yvonne Yazbeck Haddad, ed., *Muslims in the West. From Sojourners to Citizens.* Oxford: Oxford University Press.

Smith, Anthony D. 2003. *Chosen Peoples.* Oxford and New York: Oxford University Press.

Strenski, Ivan 2006. *The New Durkheim.* New Brunswick, NJ: Rutgers University Press.

Wallis, David, ed. 2007. *Killed Cartoons.* New York & London: W.W. Norton.

PART 3
Durkheim and Weber

Chapter 13

A Problem for the Sociology of Knowledge: The Mutual Unawareness of Emile Durkheim and Max Weber[1]

The social significance of ignorance and ignoring may have important latent functions which are as revealing of the social structure (and hence of social relationships) as positive knowledge.[2] I wish to present a simple but intriguing fact about the intellectual history of our discipline, one which I consider sociology's own prize detective story. The fact is that Durkheim and Weber, to the best of my knowledge, never refer to one another's writings or mention the other *when every circumstance would seem to indicate that they should have had full awareness of each other.*

1 Common Denominators Between Durkheim and Weber

It can be asserted with some degree of confidence that in today's perspective on the history of sociology, Durkheim and Weber appear as the two outstanding figures in the development of general sociological theory and in the establishment of modern sociology as an autonomous scientific discipline.[3] As we all know, their lives overlapped to a remarkable extent, with Durkheim born in 1858 six years before Weber and dying three years sooner in 1917 – each, in his own way, a victim of World War I.

---

1   First published in the *European Journal of Sociology*, 7 (1966): 330-36.

2   One of the rare treatments of this in the literature is Wilbert E. Moore and Melvin M. Tumin, "Some Social Functions of Ignorance," *American Sociological Review*, XIV (1949), 787-795. Essentially, they treat knowledge as a source of power and ignorance as a mechanism of social control used by the knower to keep his hierarchical position. The authors exclude from their discussion the act of ignoring the social other.

3   As an indication of the esteem in which they are held, note the following statement by Raymond Aron: "Max Weber is, without any doubt, the greatest of German sociologists" in *La sociologie allemande contemporaine*, (trad. amér. *German Sociology*, New York, The Free Press, 1957, p. 67), and the complementary phrase by Henri Peyre of Durkheim: "The greatest of French sociologists" ("Durkheim: The Man, His Time, and His Intellectual Background" in Kurt Wolff, ed., *Emile Durkheim, 1858-1917* (Columbus, Ohio State University Press, 1960), p. 3.

Their endeavors as sociologists evince major areas of congruence, not only in the sense of theoretical convergence along the lines so cogently argued by Parsons in his *The Structure of Social Action* or in a related manner as I have recently discussed their relation to existential phenomenology,[4] but in other major respects as well: the non-economic aspects of economic institutions were of much concern to Durkheim and a primary interest of Weber. The major preoccupation of both was to relate rigorously moral phenomena to other aspects of society; in particular, their cardinal substantive contributions lie in the field of the sociology of religion, albeit, paradoxically, neither was religiously "active" or "engagé." In spite of their personal indifference to established religion, their complementary research demonstrated beyond doubt the significance of the religious factor in the structure and dynamics of human societies.

Besides this general substantive interest, another important common denominator as far as their influence on sociology is their methodological writings (*Les règles de la méthode sociologique* and *Gesammelte Aufsätze zur Wissenschaftslehre,* respectively), which works have essentially a similar conception of the objective nature of sociological research. Also in this context, Durkheim and Weber saw eye-to-eye in rejecting biological and racial explanations of social behavior when this was still in vogue in the wake of Social Darwinism.[5] Further, they rejected the evolutionary optimism prevalent in some liberal intellectual circles prior to the Great War since they both recognized that the absence of a religious grounding for modern society implied the loss of a secure foundation by means of which the irrational potentialities of mankind could be harnessed in constructive channels.

Also in terms of professional roles, Durkheim founded in 1897 the most influential French sociological journal, the *Année sociologique*, while Weber was an associate editor from the start of the new *Archiv für Sozialwissenschaft u. Sozialpolitik*, whose first volume appeared seven years after the debut of the *Année*. Both journals had a similar format and a similar purpose: to present a few quality monographs and a comprehensive survey of contemporary social science studies, the latter so as to facilitate the unification and communication of materials relevant for the development of social science.

In political outlook, Durkheim and Weber were also remarkably close. Both had a sympathetic understanding of the working class and its spokesmen, yet both felt that socialism sought too facile a solution to the complexity of the modern social order. Both were intensely patriotic and gave fully of their energy to the war effort, but at the same time both were adverse to the imperialistic expansion of their

---

4   "Existential Phenomenology and the Sociological Tradition," *American Sociological Review*, XXX (1965), pp. 674-688.

5   On Weber here, see *The Methodology of the Social Sciences*, tr. and ed. by E. A. Shils and H. A. Finch (New York, The Free Press of Glencoe, 1949), p. 69; also H. H. Gerth and C. W. Mills, *From Max Weber: Essays in Sociology* (New York, Oxford University Press, 1958), p. 177. Durkheim's rejection of bio-racial interpretations of social phenomena is illustrated in Book I, chapter II of *Le Suicide*.

respective nations, even during the heyday of the popular acceptance of imperialism. Both were politically motivated by a commitment to social responsibility which transcends any interest group, to a genuine liberalism which goes deeper and wider than any political party or ideology. Durkheim was a confirmed republican throughout his life and Weber gravitated to this position in later life from an earlier support of the monarchy,[6] but neither was dogmatically and blindly the follower of a political creed. Their tremendous intellectual energy took them outside the academic walls and both were very much engaged in affairs involving the national welfare and social reconstruction – Weber being very much taken up with politics and the form of the Weimar republic, Durkheim with revising the curriculum of French higher education. As a result, in their lifetime both achieved a national reputation of outstanding eminence in intellectual circles.[7]

All in all, it would seem a most natural thing for Weber and Durkheim to have been aware of each other and to have mutually fructified their writings with references to each other's investigations.

2 Absence of References to Each Other

And yet, here is the astonishing thing: *The published works of Weber and Durkheim have no reference to each other.*[8] Now let me thicken the ingredients of this mystery further. The *Année* and the *Archiv* were the two leading European reviews of the social sciences, each designed to keep its readers abreast of important contributions. How did the colossus of French and German social science, respectively, fare in each other's journal?

First of all, having examined the issues of the *Archiv* during the time that Weber was on its editorial staff, *I have not found one single review of any of Durkheim's works*. Tönnies in 1905 gave an extensive review of the first six volumes of the *Année* and its structures, but only mentions Durkheim in passing.[9]

---

6   H. H. Gerth and C. Wright Mills, eds, *op. cit.* pp. 37-43.

7   No less an eminent figure than Karl Jaspers has said of Max Weber that he was "the greatest German of our age." Karl Jaspers, *Three Essays* (New York, Harcourt, 1964), p. 189.

8   There is a footnote reference on page III of Durkheim's *Sociologie et Philosophie* (Paris, Presses Universitaires de France, 1951) to a M. Weber. ("M" stands for "Monsieur"). This, however, was Louis Weber, secretary of the Société française de Philosophie and author of *Le rhythme du progrès*, but so far as I know unrelated to Max Weber.

    Professor Aron in a personal communication has informed me that when Marcel Mauss visited Max Weber at Heidelberg, he found in Weber's library a complete set of the *Année*. Mauss, in a conversation with Raymond Aron before World War II, told the latter that Weber "had borrowed many ideas" from Durkheim and his students.

9   Ferdinand Tönnies, "Soziologische Literatur," *Archiv für Sozialwissenschaft u. Sozialpolitik*, Bd 21 (der neuen Folge dritter Band), 1905, pp. 237-47. In that issue, Weber has the lead article with the second part of his Protestant Ethic essay.

In 1908 there was a citation of Durkheim's *Die Methode der Soziologie* translated by Werner Klinkhardt, but this gives only the section headings and is not a review. That the editorial board of the *Archiv* simply did not know of the head of the *Année sociologique* is practically impossible since in its first volume, the *Archiv* describes (p. 248 sq.) the bibliographic scheme of the *Année* and there is to be found the flattering statement (by Sombart) about the *Année,* "Dieses ausgezeichnete Jahrbuch." Since the *Année* was so closely identified with Durkheim,[10] why his works should receive such a seeming slight is indeed perplexing.

Incidentally, it may be of interest that the fact that Weber did not take cognizance of Durkheim was briefly noted in an issue of the *Année sociologique* which appeared ten years after Durkheim's death. In a sophisticated review article of a volume edited by Harry Elmer Barnes, *The History and Prospects of the Social Sciences* (New York 1925), the *Année's* reviewer contrasts the fragmentation of the social sciences in the United States and Germany with the unity of the social sciences perspective adopted in France by the Durkheimian school. He then makes the pregnant remark: "Le regretté Max Weber, s'il n'a guère cité Durkheim et l'oeuvre faite sous la direction de celui-ci, était beaucoup plus près de notre point de vue. L'état actuel des choses est presque en régression par rapport à cet auteur."[11]

But now, how does Weber fare in the *Année*? Here again the mystery is deepened. The whole Weber family was taken notice of by the editors of the *Année* but they seem hardly to have been held in esteem. The member of the illustrious Weber family that received the longest notice was Max's younger brother, Alfred, whose *Über den Standort des Industrien* (Where Industries locate?) was given a long but very negative review by Bourgin.[12]

As to Max Weber, his "Roscher und Knies" (1903) and the equally famous essay "Die 'Objektivität'" (1904) are listed but not discussed in the 5ᵉ section, devoted to "Economic Sociology" of the *Année* for 1903-1904 (vol. VIII, p. 539). This section was the joint responsibility of H. Bourgin and F. Simiand. Weber's seminal *Protestant Ethic* appears in the same section in volume IX of *L'Année* (1904-1905) with a very brief synopsis to the effect that this study "deals with how the economic superiority of Protestants follow from ethical dispositions rather than more contingent causes" (p. 471). The second part of Weber's *Protestant Ethic* (*Die Berufsidee des asketischen Protestantismus*) is cited in the next volume of the *Année,* volume X (1905-1906) and commented upon with a laconic Gallic sentence "étude fort intéressante dont les conséquences seraient à pousser" (p. 555). In the same volume there is notice given,

---

10   Indeed, Tönnies (whose *Gemeinschaft u. Gesellschaft* Durkheim had reviewed twenty years earlier) begins his 1905 review by noting: " *L'Année sociologique.* Publiée sous la direction de Emile Durkheim…".

11   *L'Année sociologique,* n.s., vol II (1924-1925), pp. 176-19 [2]. It has not been possible to find out who was the reviewer, as the copies of the issue end abruptly on page 192.

12   *L'Année sociologique,* XII (1909-1912), pp. 678-687.

without any comment, of the second and third parts of "Roscher und Knies." The bibliographical accounts of the section on "Economic Sociology" in this latter volume was the responsibility of Bourgin, Simiand, and a new addition to the team, Halbwachs. Apparently, not one of them seemed to find Weber's writings a worthwhile subject for a lengthy review!

And now let me introduce one last fact in this tantalizing puzzle. In volume XI of the *Année* (1906-1907) Durkheim himself gives a seven-page review of a work, *Ehefrau und Mutter in der Rechtsentwicklung*, written in 1907 by yet another Weber, this time Marianne Weber, Max Weber's wife! This book dealt with the historical situation of women and what should be the role of the woman today in the family. Durkheim's review shows little gallantry toward a female author : "What this book lacks," he observes curtly (p. 364), "is an organizing idea which would organize the facts according to a methodical plan and which would indicate the way they converge toward the intended conclusion." In his review he also criticizes the *Gesellschaft* view of marriage and association between legal partners which were advanced by Frau Weber; in keeping with his own general views he stresses in his criticism that the *solidarity* of the family has given respect to the role of women. Durkheim's notion of the organic unity of society, so dear to French social thought from Saint-Simon, de Maistre and Proudhon on, was bound to find itself repelled by Marianne's stress on *Gesellschaft*.[13] In this vein, it may be argued Durkheim could have had little sympathy with Weber's own tendencies toward nominalism[14] *(i.e.* for Weber the historical *individual* was the key unit of sociological analysis).

3 The Problem of their Unawareness

And it is at this point that we must leave this problem open-ended. Since everything points to the probability that Durkheim and Weber must have known of the existence of the other, why is there no cognizance of this in their writing? Why was there no exchange of ideas between the two who worked on so many overlapping problems? What sort of factors could account for a failure in communication (leaving out the formal linguistic factor since Durkheim read German and Weber must have read French because several of his bibliographical references in *The Protestant Ethic* and elsewhere are to French sources)? For heuristic purposes let me suggest a few possibilities.

One way we could interpret their mutual unawareness as judged from their writings is that this may have been not so much a case of mutual *ignorance* as a

---

13 After all, the form of relationship embodied in the notion of "Gesellschaft" is strikingly similar to Spencer's "contractual relations" which Durkheim had vigorously criticized in *De la division du travail social*.

14 Georges Gurvitch, Le concept de structure sociale, *Cahiers internationaux de sociologie*, XIX, n.s. (1955), 3-44.

case of *ignoring* each other. If this was indeed the case, conflicting *nationalism* is a background factor which immediately suggests itself.[15] Since each man identified with the totality of his country perhaps more than any other Frenchman or German of their days (a reflection of the societal perspective of sociology?), might they in spite of their commitment to the scientific criterion of universality have developed a nationalistic antipathy to each other, *precisely* because each saw in the other not only the major luminary of the social sciences in his own country but also a representative symbol of a hostile culture?[16] We do know in any event that Durkheim and Weber ardently supported their respective country's cause in World War I. Somehow, if it is due to nationalism and patriotic pride that Durkheim and Weber ignored each other in their professional writings, that would dampen their Olympian stature; however, in terms of the sociology of knowledge it would be worthwhile to see in this situation a manifestation of the "universalistic-particularistic" dilemma operative in the social structure of a scientific discipline.[17] Another possibility is that Weber has only in the passage of time become viewed as a sociologist, and that in his own days his professional identification was more that of an economic historian; this might reduce occasion for each to be aware of the other's sociologically relevant works.[18] Still, in that case the sociology of

---

15   Eugène Fleischmann has stated for some reason that "Le nationalisme était pour Weber la 'valeur' absolue par rapport à quoi se situe toute politique," in his "Métamorphoses webériennes," *Archives européennes de sociologie*, V (1964), pp. 126-129. However, I would take Weber to be a "cultural nationalist," in this respect much like Max Scheler. See also Gerth and Mills, *op. cit.* pp. 171-176 for Weber's views on the nation. As to Durkheim's position on nationalism and patriotism, see in particular his posthumous *Leçons de sociologie* (Paris, Presses universitaires de France, 1950), pp. 87-91.

16   From 1870 to World War I there was considerable concern and even alarm in France as to the spreading influence of German culture in various intellectual spheres. In 1902 the Kaiser called for "world supremacy" of the German mind. In response, Jacques Morland of the *Mercure de France* sent a questionnaire to various eminent figures asking them to assess the Germanic influence in their own area. Durkheim in his published answer stated that although in his early formative years he had learned from German social science the complexity of social reality, he felt that sociological studies were now lagging behind in Germany and that "je ne vois pas se produire d'impulsion nouvelle dans l'ordre des sciences sociales." The tone of his remarks is a rather negative evaluation. See *Mercure de France*, XLIV (1902), 647-648.

17   "[…] Si la pratique de la science, si la pensée scientifique exigent la tolérance, le savant en fait se montre fréquemment intolérant," Jean Pelseneer, "La psychologie du savant de génie," *Janus*, II (1964), 62-64. Among the numerous personal clashes in the history of science, the author mentions the antagonisms between Descartes and Fermat, Leibniz and Newton, Cantor and Kronecker, Jeans and Eddington. The Durkheim-Weber relationship might well be the classic sociological case, one of these instances characterized by, in the words of Pelseneer, "une opposition sourde".

18   Thus, Durkheim was listed as an advising editor of the *American Journal of Sociology* as early as its second issue (September 1895) and continued to be so listed until the interruption of World War I. While Simmel and Tönnies were also foreign editors of the

knowledge has another intriguing problem to iron out, namely, what accounts for changes in the image of a person's professional identification? What sociohistorical factors account for a person "drifting" after his death from one field to another? What factors make a discipline come to recognize somebody as one of their own (or obversely, to reject him)?

A more subtle question raised by all this is just what are the criteria used to determine what external stimuli (and by external we can include a different culture or a different perspective) are cognized by a writer or a school as being relevant for their own creative development. Concretely, did Durkheim know of Weber's sociological writings but ignore them because he considered them irrelevant for his own studies and *vice versa*? The practical consequence of this little problem in the intellectual history of sociology is that it can put us on our guards against perpetrating sins of omission – is American sociology, for example, aware of theoretical and substantive developments in French sociology or the latter of developments in say, British sociology? If not, is this due to the fact that mental products are so related to their sociocultural setting that even the towering figures of the same social science may operate from sufficiently different presuppositions concerning social reality and concerning what is socially relevant that they will know of each other without knowing each other? In any case we hope by this paper to have drawn attention to the sociological salience of silence.[19]

---

journal, Weber not only was not given this honorific position but furthermore none of his works was reviewed in the *AJS* as late as 1935. On the contrary, Durkheim's writings were frequently discussed in his own lifetime.

19   *Postscript:* Subsequent to this publication, Steven Seidman published in a research note an interesting finding: Weber had twice cited Durkheim in footnotes in *the German edition of General Economic History*, but Frank Knight's English translation had omitted these altogether. Seidman further suggests the citations were "derived from Weber's lectures and not interpolated after Weber's death," ("The Durkheim/Weber 'Unawareness Puzzle'," *Archives Européennes de Sociologie*, 18, 2 (1977): 356.

Chapter 14
Neither Marx nor Durkheim ...
Perhaps Weber[1]

I Introduction

In the formulation of macro theories of modern society, three figures have
provided the sociological profession with a patrimony of continuing importance
for reflection and research: Marx, Durkheim, and Weber. I take this occasion to
raise the question: Which one has a model of society that provides the best fit
with the sociohistorical phenomenon of the United States as a modern society?
The title of my paper anticipates its conclusion. I hope the ground covered in the
process of reaching it will provide readers with new food for thought and new
sprouts for research.

The first part of the title is an adaptation of the original title (*Ni Marx ni Jésus*)
of a fairly recent interpretation of American society by a French intellectual,
Jean-François Revel's *Without Marx or Jesus* (1971). Revel is a recent link in
the chain of French intellectuals and social scientists who have used their travels
in the United States as a basis for reflections on American society and who, in
several instances, have sought to draw lessons (or warnings) about the future of
modernity.[2]

Just as Max Weber came to the United States in part to seek renovation in the
aftermath of psychological depression, so, too, Revel came to the United States
roughly five years ago to get away from a state of depression and exhaustion, but
one with a different source. Like many other French left-wing intellectuals, and
like all of France, Revel had lived through the critical "events" of May 1968,
which at first appeared like the promised revolution on the eschatological horizon

1   Published in *The American Journal of Sociology*, 81, 1 (July 1975): 1-33. I wish
to thank the late Robert K. Merton for his thoughtful comments and suggestions on the
original draft of this paper.

2   Representative figures include André Siegfried, *America Comes of Age* (1927) and
America at Mid-Century (1955); Jacques Maritain, *Reflections on America* (1958); and
Claude Julien, *Le nouveau nouveau monde*, 2 vols. (1960). For a succinct discussion of the
meanings of the United States to French intellectuals, see Raymond Aron's discussion in
Joseph (1959, pp. 57-71). Alexis de Toqueville's *Democracy in America*, first published in
1835, is not only a classic in this chain but one which is still a stimulus for contemporary
American sociologists (see, for example, Neil Smelser's recent essay on de Tocqueville as
a comparative sociologist (1971).

of militant consciousness. If the start of the events was a trauma for liberals and conservatives, the collapse of the "movement" and the return to "normalcy" were no less traumatic for French radicals, just as had been the case almost exactly 100 years before with the crushing and collapse of the 1870 Paris Commune. So Revel came to the United States, in part at least, to see what had been the fate of the American "events" of 1968 and 1969 and whether they had been as futile a gesture in bringing about change.

Revel's observations and reflections in comparing the American with the French situation, and their respective outcomes, lead him to the conclusion that revolution in the modern world is blocked or stagnant everywhere but in the United States, where it is a dynamic reality operating *within* the institutional structure of society. A revolution, he proposes, if it is to be a sustaining one, cannot take place by a single coup at the top and in a single direction; it must be multidimensional, at the economic, political, cultural, and economic levels (1971, pp. 183-84). Revel sees the United States as the society most eligible for the role of the prototype nation for the achievement of the full aims embodied in the Principles of the 1789 Revolution. This is because the United States has the following necessary conditions: (1) it enjoys a high rate of economic growth and prosperity, (2) it has a high level of technological competence and basic research, (3) it is culturally oriented toward the future rather than the past, (4) it is undergoing a revolution in behavioral standards and in the affirmation of individual freedom and equality, and (5) it rejects authoritarian control and multiplies initiative in all domains, allowing the coexistence of diverse, mutually complementary alternative subcultures (p. 183).

Revel sees the United States as a mobile entity, characterized by a "diversity of cultures and contradictory moral systems" which is generative of collective and individual crises of increasing frequency (p. 262). These crises – numerous, permanent, and always new – are the essence of modern revolution; they are not repressed by the legal framework of the United States. The changes they bring about are broadened within the constitutional framework, which makes revolutionary action in the United States – unlike elsewhere in the modern world – profound, varied, fertile, or, in brief, creative (p. 185).

Revel finds that Left and Right in the United States exist in a creative tension; in Europe, or at least in France, they are characterized equally by a sterile conservatism which effectively blocks the possibility of a new political and cultural revolution (pp. 260-61). In concluding his book, Revel rejects the possibility that the unfolding American revolution will be affected by either Marxism or organized religion (the European poles of Left and Right). The Left's image of class warfare is inapplicable to the United States, not only because class differentiation is not the major basis of social differentiation here but also because the image is based on an essentially static or rigid society which is afraid of and resists structural change. The classical (or orthodox) Left operates from a Manichean view of the world; its typical attitude is that it exists within the context of a reactionary government in a reactionary country. He states on this point: "That attitude I would describe as characteristic of the 'conservative Left,' the Left that wants to maintain itself, its views and its future, unchanged in an unchanged world, less interested in destroying injustice than in proving triumphantly that every day brings further and further greater injustice" (p. 269).

Although Revel is less detailed on the classical Right, he sees it as unable to foment a counterrevolution in the United States because of this country's historical separation of church and state. There is no historical basis for restoring a social order based on the integral unity of ecclesiastical and secular powers, which is the primeval vision and basis of social action of the traditional (European) Right. So much for an outline of Revel's reflections on American society as an introduction to the body of the present essay. I do not wish to assess the correctness of his thesis that the United States is the world's major hope for bringing about the fulfillment of the Principles of 1789; Revel himself may have had second thoughts on the subject since the publication of his book. Nevertheless, in spite of its limitations, *Without Marx or Jesus* is a good starting point for viewing the United States from an observer's perspective, or to use a bit of phenomenological jargon, for "bracketing the natural attitude" of American sociologists.

Revel's analysis of the United States is complemented by that of another Frenchman, Jean-Jacques Servan-Schreiber, in *The American Challenge* (1968). He too is critical of both Left and Right in Europe for their resistance to change, for their mutual distrust of man's nature, for their distrust of the individual. He asserts that what primarily gives American corporations their edge over European competitors in Europe itself is, even more than their wealth, their much greater flexibility: this is the great American weapon (p. 6). Further, he later adds that "in an expanding economy, social justice is the condition of industrial dynamism" (p. 242); the United States is exceptional in its ability to commit itself simultaneously to both social justice and industrial dynamism.[3]

One last appropriate French analysis that I wish to cite is that of the well-known student of bureaucracies, Michel Crozier. This sociologist's most recently published study is a diagnosis of "the mechanisms governing the blockages and the processes of involution now paralyzing all advanced societies" (1973, p. vi). The frustration over a lack of tangible change that he shares with Revel and Servan-Schreiber led Crozier to write his sociological analysis, *The Stalled Society.*

3　A sociological audience might be interested in the fact that the originator of sociology, Henri de Saint-Simon, one of the great visionaries of the modern world, was similarly impressed with the American visit 200 years ago. Subsequent to fighting on the side of the revolutionaries, he wrote: "I perceived that the American Revolution signaled the beginning of a new political era, that this revolution was to determine necessarily an important progress in civilization in general and that it would shortly cause major changes in the social order which existed in Europe...It is in America, in fighting for the cause of industrial freedom, that I conceived for the first time the desire to see in my homeland flourish this transplant from another world" (1925, pp. xxii-xxiii).

From his observations of French society, including previous studies of the "bureaucratic phenomenon," Crozier develops a general image of modern advanced societies as characterized by structural blockages that inhibit real development. What modernity calls for in terms of values are creativity and nonconformity, along with rationalist vigor and social responsibility (1973, p. 51). But what in fact characterize the societal system are bureaucratic centralization, industries taking over the government or the army as their organizational model, paternalism, compartmentalized stratified groups, and the absence of freedom and initiative (p. 73). In particular, the stratification and centralization of the social system penalize innovations that might upset society's order and stability; the major systems of control which thwart creativity and innovations are the administrative, educational, and political systems (pp. 105-6). In the face of an implacable, stalled, hierarchic society, the events of 1968 resemble a modern Saturnalia more than anything else, or in the words of Crozier, the social crisis of 1968 is basically "a festival of face-to-face confrontations and challenges to authority" (p. 129).

Although Crozier seems to argue that all modern advanced societies are "blocked" (or "stalled"), he does find the United States an anomaly: "Being far more involved in the collective adventure than citizens of more stratified societies, Americans are forced to internalize all their social conflicts and contradictions far more thoroughly than members of society where responsibility for change can be thrust upon the leaders or upon a more coercive system" (p. 145).

To summarize the essence or spirit of the observations I have cited, the United States, then, is an interesting example of modernization as an ongoing process. It is, par excellence, the large-scale society where actual, continuous change in all sectors – economic, political, cultural, social – occurs. Tacitly, it is American society that comes closest to fitting empirically the general characterization of modernization advanced or summarized by one of the major theorists of modernization, S. N. Eisenstadt:

> Modernization implies not only the development of... various indices of social mobilization and of growing structural differentiation, but also the development of a social, economic, or political system which not only generates continuous change, but unlike many other types of social or political systems, is also capable of absorbing changes beyond its own initial institutional premises (1973, p. 25).

From these background considerations, we can now proceed to examine how appropriate the models of modern society of Marx, Durkheim, and Weber, respectively, are for an understanding of American society.

II Neither Marx ...

My discussion of Revel could serve to indicate the inapplicability of Marxist analysis for an understanding of the dynamics of American society. However, let me add some supplementary considerations concerning Marx and the United States.

Marx's conception or perception of modern society makes more sense, I propose, in a sociohistorical setting having a tradition of sharp social cleavages, with a cluster of status, class, and power stratifications institutionalized in a hierarchical arrangement of the social order. Marx implicitly and often explicitly based his analysis of the necessity for revolution on the European setting, where class divisions and class awareness were – and still to a large degree are – aspects of everyday life. The Marxist perspective, culminating in the vision of a future-at-hand revolution, has, of course been carried beyond Western industrial societies (which he took to be most ripe for revolution, given his interpretations of the historical process) to such societies as Russia and China. These societies too, though lacking a developed industrial proletariat and a well-developed industrial bourgeoisie, were characterized in their pre-revolutionary forms by clear-cut social demarcations and institutionalized bases of social differentiation. These constitute one prerequisite for the applicability of the Marxist model. Another equally important prerequisite, it seems to me, is the unwillingness of the ruling stratum to accommodate itself to desires for increasing power and participation among the disenfranchised, the "have nots," the upwardly mobile, the groups with rising expectations.

In one respect the United States might be the modern society most appropriate for Marx's analysis of modernity: in it, capitalism as an economic system is most fully actualized and routinized. And yet the United States has not behaved in a predictable Marxist manner; rather, in a crucial respect it stands out as an anomaly, as recently noted with more lament than glee by Szymanski: "Clearly, however, the United States working class has not realized the role expected of it by the classical Marxist tradition. Although most of the working classes of the other advanced capitalist countries have developed class consciousness and adopted socialist-communist politics, this has never been the case for the majority of the U.S. working class" (1974, p. 1474).

Why the United States has not behaved predictably is subject to a variety of interpretations, even Marxist ones. I suggest that one basic consideration is the fluidity of the institutional structure, coupled with the fact that social protest and demands for increasing participation by the disenfranchised have been given greater accommodations than in other advanced societies. I shall return to this point shortly, but first I would like to make additional remarks about Marx himself on the United States. He had a limited but interesting awareness of American society worth mentioning.

For a decade Marx was a foreign correspondent of the *New York Daily Tribune* (1851-62) and also wrote on the American Civil War for the Viennese *Die Presse* (Christman 1966; Marx and Engels 1937). Although his various writings in this context are not important contributions to sociological theory (unlike, say, the *Critique of Political Economy,* written during this period, or the earlier *Communist Manifesto* and the later *Capital*), they demonstrate his fantastic powers of political analysis. Even more, his observations on the course of the Civil War suggest to me that Marx deserves recognition as an outstanding military strategist.

Quite early, and before most people, Marx saw the struggle between North and South as "nothing but a struggle between two social systems, between the system of slavery and the system of free labor" (Marx and Engels 1937, p. 81). His sympathies lay with the North because its victory was "necessary for the emancipation of slavery and... for the emancipation of the working class – the growth of manufacturing was hindered by the Southern ruling class reinvesting surplus capital in chattels and land rather than railroads and factories" (p. xv). Marx was a signatory (if not the drafter) of the address that the International Workingmen's Association sent to Lincoln shortly after the latter's reelection, an address which states among other things: "The workingmen of Europe feel sure that, as the American War of Independence initiated a new era of ascendancy for the middle class, so the American anti-slavery war will do for the working classes" (p. 281).

Five years earlier, on January 11, 1860, Marx had written prophetically to Engels: "In my opinion, the biggest things that are happening in the world today are on the one hand the movement of the slaves in America started by the death of John Brown, and on the other the movement of the serfs in Russia" (p. 221).

His dispatches to *Die Presse*, for example those of March 26 and 27, 1862 (pp. 164-77), as well as his correspondence with Engels about the course of the Civil War (pp. 221-77), cannot fail to impress us with Marx's in-depth knowledge of the American scene and his assessment of the military situation (which turned out to be more correct than that of Engels, who at times despaired as to the outcome), including both what would be a winning strategy for the North and who were the really capable military leaders on both sides.[4]

For all his perspicacity concerning the course of the Civil War, Marx seems to have lost interest in the United States shortly after Johnson succeeded Lincoln. Although he drafted a laudatory address to Johnson on May 13, 1865, sent to the latter by the International Workingmen's Association, his letters to Engels at that time indicate he held Johnson in low esteem (pp. 276-77). Effectively, the "bourgeois republic" was of minor and passing interest to Marx, whereas Germany, France, and England continued to provide the major empirical foci of his analyses and theories of modernization. Would Marx have changed his general model of modernization in the light of the subsequent historical experience of the United States? (For example, is revolution

---

4   Thus in early 1862 Marx had discerned that Grant was the outstanding military figure for the North and would be far better than McClellan as commander-in-chief. He had also seen the importance of the border states in the winning of the war, and (still in 1862) indicated to Engels that it would not matter if the South captured Washington or the North captured Richmond: from a military point of view, he asserted, the war would be decisively won when the North captured Atlanta and the railroads in Georgia linking the Confederacy. This in fact turned out to be the winning strategy of Grant and Sherman!

as he saw it a historically necessary outcome of industrialization?) Perhaps he would have, perhaps not, and perhaps he would have seen the United States as the exception that proves the rule.[5]

In one sense, the American historical experience in this century demonstrates an essential thesis of the general Marxist model. In contradistinction to the Spencerian model, economic development and industrialization do not lead to social unity and increased social happiness for all strata; internal social conflicts (to say nothing of international military conflicts) and cleavages can be generated, directly or indirectly, by processes of economic development (albeit the lines of cleavage are not necessarily or most importantly along industrial class lines). It is after all in the past 20 years, marked by great economic and technological development (Spencer's source of optimism), that the United States has witnessed some very intense "protest" movements. Yet, where similar movements elsewhere have been met by military repression or by passive resistance of the ruling elites (who may go through the form of accommodation but do not in fact alter the distribution of social power), such movements and "crises" in the United States have led to significant institutional reforms and new sources of legitimated social power for protesters.

Before closing this section, let me reiterate that Marx's basic model of modern society is tacitly grounded in the historical status-stratified society of Europe, where sharply delineated status differentials are part of everyday social reality and authority is (willingly or grudgingly) seen or taken to be hierarchic in nature, vested in leaders who hold office. The medieval social order may still have such weight of tradition in Europe today that structural change, if it is to occur, has to take place in the classical Marxist revolutionary model of change. But the continuous adaptation in the United States to protest demands – which is part of the American reality – demands questioning of what we assume to be a "revolution."

In European imagery, "the revolution" is either a glorious achievement of the past, hallowed as the Creation of modern society, upon which the ship of state is anchored and which disguises the absence of real social development – or else it is placed in the eschatological vision of the future. In the United States, one might say, the revolution is not so much a sacred point of history as the continuous historical process itself, given what I see as a dominant value orientation of commitment to actualize change, not only in the technological sphere but also in the multifaceted social sphere. Commitment to technological change and economic development is widely shared by just about every modern country, but legitimation for experimentation within a wide range of social change is another matter. For better or worse, the United States, in its recent history, manifests the closest approximation of acceptance of the full spectrum of change on the part of

---

5   Marx did have an awareness of the United States as an anomaly in the developmental process of capitalism. This is suggested in his rather favorable 1857 critique of the American Henry Carey's political economy (Marx 1971, pp. 47-53).

ruling strata (I use the plural form deliberately, although a case can be made for talking about the "Establishment") of any existent large-scale society.

This is what Revel perceived, and this phenomenon in all its features lifts the United States outside the European mold which framed Marx's model of modern society.

III ... nor Durkheim

Durkheim's model of society is frequently judged to be in sharp contrast and antithesis to that of Marx. For Marx the central tendency, of modern society is for the social order to be constructed on the oppression, coercion, mystification, or alienation of those dominated by a ruling class, or, if you will, by fundamental class conflicts that cannot be remedied short of the abolition of private property, the ultimate source of labor and consequently status differentiation. For Durkheim, the central tendency of society is social solidarity based on new forms of structural interdependence, cemented by the normative consensus of shared collective representations. I am not about to question the acceptance of the Durkheimian perspective as a polar model of modernization, although there are some major overlooked convergences between Marx and Durkheim;[6] and certainly I am the last person to question the worth of Durkheim's seminal contributions to our understanding of social reality, such as his profound insights into the fundamentally symbolic nature of the social world, the integral nexus between deviance and conformity, and the specificity and irreducibility of sociocultural reality. For me, Durkheim is the *primus inter pares* of sociology's greats. Having said this to indicate that Durkheim makes a great deal of sense to me in general, let me go on to suggest what limitations I have found in the applicability of his model of society to an understanding of American society.

First, of the three major figures we are dealing with in this paper, Durkheim had the least exposure to and awareness of the modern American scene. He was, it might be said, abreast of American intellectual currents rather than American social currents. As a foreign advisory editor, he seems to have kept up-to-date with the *American Journal of Sociology*;[7] he was well versed in the American

---

6   Thus, in the concluding section of *Professional Ethics and Civic Morals* (1957, pp. 208-20), Durkheim argued that the evolution of social justice and egalitarianism, as cardinal features of the modernization of social morality, required the abolition of the inheritance of private property – certainly a key tenet of orthodox Marxism. If Marx was animated by the vision of a classless society, so also was the mature Durkheim, although from a very different set of considerations and with different means of realizing this structural transformation.

7   A basis for this assertion is the following: in the January 1898 issue of the *American Journal of Sociology*, Gustavo Tosti published a long and very negative review of Durkheim's *Suicide*. On February 6, 1898, Durkheim, then in Bordeaux, wrote a rejoinder,

ethnographic literature (Lukes 1972); and he made an intensive study of America's major contribution to philosophy, pragmatism, which he took very seriously as an intellectual challenge to Cartesianism.[8] Nevertheless, it is difficult to find in his writings references to the United States in its modern form.[9]

What difference does it make whether Durkheim did or did not have exposure to the institutional structure of the United States? To answer this, let me point out essential aspects of his model and image of modern society. I want to argue that his conceptualizations, like Marx's, were framed by the European historical experience, albeit he drew a different lesson from history.

A crucial aspect of modern society for Durkheim is the condition of *anomie*, a notion which has been incorporated into the American sociological vocabulary with as much facility and distortion as Marx's notion of alienation (Horton 1972; Israel 1971). Since "anomie" is such a familiar term, it will suffice to indicate briefly what it meant for Durkheim. Anomie is the state of normative or moral deregulation which afflicts modern society; among its consequences can be seen unbridled economic appetites which undermine the integrative tendencies of the modern division of labor, as well as pathologies of individual conduct, such as suicide. For Durkheim, anomie – or amorality – was at the core of the crisis of modern society, giving it a profound instability, and sociology's ultimate justification was to assist in social reconstruction by scientifically deriving or arriving at the moral system which would provide the necessary anchor of modern society.[10]

The concern with morality as a topic of sociological analysis, reflection, and research has been seen correctly in the recent literature on Durkheim (Tiryakian 1962; Wallwork 1972; Bellah 1973) as not only a major concern but also perhaps

---

which was published in the May 1898 issue. Piqued, Tosti went on to publish a rejoinder to Durkheim in the September 1898 issue of the *American Journal of Sociology*. Although Durkheim did not reply further, the test of time has given him the last word. From the first year of its publication, he was an "advising editor" of the *American Journal of Sociology* and remained one at least up to the outbreak of World War I (I am indebted to the editorial staff of the journal for this information).

8   Durkheim, it will be recalled, gave a detailed critique of pragmatism during a year-long course at the Sorbonne in 1913-1914. This course was published posthumously from student notes under the title *Pragmatisme et sociologie* (1955). It is amusing to note that the American philosophical challenge of pragmatism is reflected in the pragmatism of American corporations operating in Europe, which gave rise to Servan-Schreiber's warning to take the American challenge seriously.

9   I am uncertain whether Durkheim makes explicit reference to de Toqueville's *On Democracy in America*. The latter's stress on the importance of intermediary groups, central to his study *L'Ancien Régime*, may well have influenced Durkheim's belief in the need to revitalize those (such as professional associations) in any program of social reconstruction needed to give democracies a structural stability.

10   The concluding pages of *The Division of Labor* very clearly enunciate Durkheim's lifelong paramount concern.

the core nexus providing a fundamental unity to all his works, from his first articles (Durkheim 1886, 1887) through *The Elementary Forms of the Religious Life* (1961). His concern with morality as a fundamental aspect of social reality, as a core structure of social interaction, led him to an intensive analysis of the nexus between morality and religion, which he took to be essentially social in nature, albeit in a different sense, as he pointed out, from Marx's perspective (Durkheim 1961, pp. 471-72). Durkheim saw morality and religion as interrelated but analytically distinct; morality has traditionally derived from religion, but the nature of religion is to be a specific institutional structure. For Durkheim, consequently, the resolution of the normative crisis of modern society is to establish on empirical and theoretical grounds what are the appropriate moral system and the appropriate religion for modern society.

He offered no definitive answers. Such works as *Professional Ethics and Civic Morals* (1957) and *Moral Education* (1973) offer us a pretty good indication of his thinking about the necessary system of morality for modern society, whereas the appropriate religion remained much more elusive. In one sense *The Elementary Forms* is the most important achievement of the sociology of religion and the culmination of Durkheim's brilliant explorations of the structures of the social world. In another sense it is a scaffold and not a finished edifice, for he offers only the barest hints as to the religious institutional structure necessary for modern society. Intellectuals might not need such a structure, but Durkheim saw that its absence was deleterious for social organization. What form a "civil religion" should take was even more unclear for Durkheim than for Comte and Saint-Simon before him, both of whom had grappled with the same haunting problem; perhaps it was more unclear to Durkheim (though equally important) *because* he investigated the complexities of religion and society more thoroughly than his predecessors.[11]

Durkheim's image of religion and society is tacitly grounded in the common historical experiences not only of the predominant majority of European societies but also of most "traditional" societies. What in this context has marked such societies? Whether we think of classical Rome or Greece, whether we think of France, Great Britain, or Tsarist Russia, we are dealing uniformly with societies having a very close unity between polity and religion, between "church" and "state," between religious and political authority. We are dealing with a societal system possessing one publicly legitimated religious institution, one officially recognized "church," one institution which not only provided an important criterion of membership in the collectivity and the body politic but also was the major foyer, arbiter, and interpreter of moral conduct.

Of course, Medieval or pre-Reformation Europe seems to typify this system, but the post-Reformation world, even in countries which broke with obedience to the Roman pontiff, still fitted this characterization. To be sure, Durkheim (like

---

11   I view Robert N. Bellah's recent essay, "Civil Religion in America" (1970, pp. 168-89), as an important catalytic endeavor to redirect sociological attention to this crucial concern of Durkheim.

Saint-Simon and Comte) saw that the French Revolution was a decisive break in history; sympathetically understanding of the great contributions of Christianity to the development of Western civilization, he was certainly committed to the disenfranchisement of Catholicism from public education. A devout supporter of the Third Republic and its *laïcisme*, Durkheim was not a restorationist of traditional religion (i.e., Catholicism) in the same sense as his contemporaries of the Right (such as Maurras or Barrès). Nonetheless, unless I am in grievous error in my interpretation, given his tacit awareness of not only modern Western but also "archaic" and "classical" societies,[12] social reconstruction for Durkheim involved the public reinstitutionalition of a consensual moral system replacing the *status quo ante*; the latter had been proven inadequate for modern society by the outbreak of the Revolution of 1789. The present for Durkheim was a period of increasing anomie because of the absence of a regulating, institutionalized moral system.

Now, the United States represents an interesting anomaly[13] precisely because during the entire course of its historical experience it has never had an officially state-recognized and sanctioned religious institution;[14] it has never had *the* legitimate institution of religious authority, one which embodied or served as *the* foyer of morality and in turn legitimated political authority.

The absence of such a central religious institution (in the presence of which other religious institutions may exist in a tolerated, even de jure, "nonconformist" status but without a de facto recognition that they have the same intrinsic social worth) means that at the societal level the United States has not had an institutionalized or institutionally grounded moral system. From Durkheim's perspective this might well be seen as the very condition of anomie he decried as the fundamental source of social instability and malaise.

Perhaps Durkheim, had he studied America with the same thoroughness and objectivity he devoted to everything else, might have come to entertain two contrasting interpretations of the United States. I have suggested the first: it is easy to see this country as exemplifying the greatest degree of anomie, manifested in economic, political, sexual, and other spheres of conduct. Lacking a centralized, visible foyer of morality, American society may be viewed as highly amoral and running amok. Just as Marx might point out that the United States is highly unstable structurally because of the advanced state of capitalism, so could Durkheim see it as highly unstable structurally because of its advanced state of anomie. What is the contrasting interpretation?

---

12   In this context, see another important essay by Bellah (1964, pp. 358-74).

13   To be sure, the United States is not the only country having the peculiarity noted in the ensuing discussion. At the national level, Switzerland may be thought of as being in the same class of societies, although at the subnational (cantonal) level it may be seen as having historical features in common with the general European experience. In this regard, see the important study by Guy Swanson (1967).

14   I mean here a religious institution in the sense of "church" as used by Durkheim and Ernst Troeltsch, or "ecclesia" as used by Howard Becker and Milton Yinger.

It is that, during the entire historical experience of the United States, the moral system, by virtue of not having a specific religious institutional grounding, has been diffused in various sectors of society to a significantly larger extent than in other societies, hence that the United States is one of the least anomic modern societies. Aspects of social reality and spheres of social conduct outside what is usually thought of as religious life are subject to moral accountability in the United States – spheres of conduct including sexuality, economic and political conduct, even international relations. I do not mean to assert that social actors in the United States, individuals and collectivities, actually behave morally (i.e., in conformity with ethical norms of conduct) more than those of any other society. I do mean to say that practically all spheres of conduct and all aspects of social affairs are potentially and often actually subject to moral scrutiny and to a public accounting of whether actors' conduct, at the individual or collective level, is "moral" or "immoral." The delimitation of authority, punitive sanctions, and demands for social change are typically grounded in a moral justification and in the morality of the situation. Established institutional practices and established authority figures are seldom if ever considered immune from moral scrutinization.

In terms of the familiar Durkheimian model, we might reason that the modernization system carries with it a paralyzing "crisis of morality" as the traditional religious institutions which have fostered it lose their social significance and legitimacy; increasing social heterogeneity, a feature of modern society, should make morality more difficult and less visible. Yet I would argue that were all the evidence available, we might be able to demonstrate that, in this century, with sharply increasing social heterogeneity, moral accountability has become more and more salient in the public life of the United States – in such matters as the regulation of corporations, race relations, domestic life, environmental affairs, and the behavior of government officials. The mighty stream of moral accountability is always at the gate of the American forum!

I have said that a salient feature of American public life is the constant questioning of whether an institutional practice is in consonance with moral expectations; if it is decreed not to be, that becomes cause not only for reforming the persons involved but also possibly for altering the institutional structure giving rise to the morally abusive practice. Perhaps some might say that there has been a decline and a loss of "traditional" morality and an increasing ambiguity of moral norms. But perhaps also we should rethink the notion of anomie in our sociological vocabulary and ask ourselves whether what might possibly make sense in the European context is in fact applicable in the American context. Far from believing in a loss of a shared moral system held at an antecedent time, a loss inducing fragility and instability in the entire institutional framework of society, I have come to entertain a different perspective: the United States might be seen as exceedingly viable because its moral system has never been taken for granted or seen as well delimited, because its moral system has been institutionally extensive rather than specific or intensive. And if there is any merit to the above discussion, we should be prepared to rethink the presuppositions of the Durkheimian model, as its originator might be the first to do in a genuine positivistic spirit.

IV ... Perhaps Weber

Can we find in Max Weber a standpoint having a greater heuristic merit for a sociological approach to American society? I think so, but as the "perhaps" in my title suggests, the case of the United States calls for fresh consideration of the Weberian model of modernization. Let me first adduce the reasons why I think he has more to offer us than either Marx or Durkheim.

Weber had a much greater range of exposure to American society than either Marx or Durkheim. Interspersed in his writings are many references to the United States, often illustrative or comparative. We well know, further, that in *The Protestant Ethic and the Spirit of Capitalism* (1958b) he gave special attention to Benjamin Franklin as the typification of "the spirit of capitalism." Moreover, unlike Marx or Durkheim, he had an immediate, direct experience of the United States from which he gathered data concerning the Protestant sects and voluntary associations.

About 70 years ago (from September to December 1904) Weber made a short but extremely fruitful visit to the United States (Brann 1944; Weber 1958a, pp. 14-18). With his prodigious energy, he covered as much physical territory during his stay there as he covered intellectual territory in his library research in Germany. In about 100 days he visited a variety of academic institutions (Harvard, Columbia, Haverford, Tuskegee); he observed ethnic diversity in the metropolis as well as rural homogeneity; he even lived briefly with Indians in Oklahoma, where he was captivated by the nascent oil fields and their dynamic social milieu. No mere tourist, he came to see, ask questions, and become informed on a variety of major facets of American life. He used an equally great variety of informants, including academic colleagues, lodge members, taxi drivers, and relatives living in North Carolina.

Although greatly stimulated by what he saw and regenerated from the psychological doldrums in which he had floundered for many years previously, Weber did not view the United States through rosy glasses; he saw the good, the bad, and the ugly in the totality of American society. And for all the fantastic array of situations and places seen in a short period of time, his discerning acuity led him to observe that above the wonderful, energetic nation, there hovered a big dark cloud, that of race relations, particularly "the Negro question" (Brann 1944, pp. 26-27; Weber, 1958a, p. 16).[15] Had Weber found the time to develop

---

15   Weber thus echoed the prophetic statement made four years before by W. E. B. DuBois at the first Pan-African Conference: "The problem of the twentieth century is the problem of the colour line..." (quoted in Legum, 1962, p. 25). A reading of chap. 6 of Weber's *General Economic History* (1961) will testify to his knowledge of the Negro situation in relation to economic conditions; moreover, his references indicate that he had

his primary and secondary knowledge of the United States into a full-length structural and historical study of American society, he well might have provided us with a classic companion piece to de Tocqueville's *Democracy in America* or Lord Bryce's *The American Commonwealth.*

In itself, however, Weber's direct and rich experience of the United States does not warrant a preferential utilization of his interpretive scheme or frame of reference over that of Marx or Durkheim. I have wished to suggest that Weber knew more facts about and had greater familiarity with the United States than either of the others, but this is not sufficient ground.

The "goodness of fit" between Weber and American society, in comparison with Marx and Durkheim, is grounded in what may be taken initially to be a banal observation, namely, that the United States is a Protestant society and that Weber had a profound insider's understanding[16] of ascetic, this-worldly Protestantism, his conduct and thoughts exemplifying it in the same way as, say, Immanuel Kant's.

To say that Weber was of Protestant background and that the majority of the American population shares this background is indeed a banal observation. Even if I add that somehow American Protestantism and American capitalism have a historically demonstrable symbiotic relationship and that the former played the role of a "booster" for the full-grown emergence of the latter in the second half of the 19th century, this would still be a banal sociological observation. After all, Weber himself, impressed as he was with the dynamism of American society and the vitality of American sects, did not think the United States could remain immune from the "characteristic process of 'secularization' to which in modern times all phenomena that originated in religious conceptions succumb" (1958*a*, p. 307).

To go beyond the conventional perspective on Weber, we must rethink the implications of his intellectual Odyssey of Western civilization; we must be willing to find paths in his writings which he barely traced out in suggestive, programmatic form rather than finished, paved roads. Benjamin Nelson, in a recent and illuminating reappraisal of the Weberian enterprise (1973*b*), has expressed this view with great insight: "Weber always intended the notion of the 'Protestant ethic' to refer to the existential and cultural foundations of any society committed to the mastery of this world through intensive discipline and consensual organization of personal and social orders" (p. 83). That Weber concentrated on the historical linkages between the religious and the economic vectors of Western civilization and that he threw in for good measure, so to speak, civilizational comparisons to achieve the full delineation of the nexus between religious attitudes and economic development is quite true. But

---

consulted DuBois's writings in presenting his materials on the American South. For more on personal contacts between Weber and DuBois, see Nelson (1973*a*).

16   Undoubtedly, Weber would have applauded Merton's perceptive essay (1972) dealing with the limitations of "insiders' understanding" as a claim for absolute knowledge.

the relation between the Protestant ethic and modernization as an instance of the relation of religious *Weltanschauungen* and sociohistorical development is far broader than the nexus of that ethic to the economic sector, which was the major focus of his analysis. Weber himself did not methodically investigate the nexus between religion and polity in general or, more specifically, between the Protestant ethic and modern historical political development. Ben Nelson is convincing in arguing (1973*b*, p. 80) that Weber was committed tacitly to uncovering all the elements involved in the transformation of the modern world, and we can surmise that he had found in the Protestant ethic his Archimedean lever, which still has great heuristic value for us today. It is because the United States as a sociohistorical society most manifests or approximates the totality of what is contained in the deceptively simple expression "the Protestant ethic" that I think this country merits special attention.

To develop my argument further, we may view the Protestant ethic as an articulation of the general *Weltanschauung* of the symbolic cultural system framed by post-Lutheran Protestantism. Going further, the cultural system of the United States which has provided American society with its fundamental system of value orientations toward the empirical world has been grounded in what may be designated as 'Puritan" culture, and what makes the United States particularly interesting is that it represents not only "The First New Nation," to borrow Lipset's pregnant designation (1963), but equally important, the "First Protestant Nation" in terms of its underlying cultural system.[17] In contending that we should take a new look at the United States as *the first Protestant nation* (and perhaps, to add to its unique qualities, the only one), I mean that in terms of the totality of its historicity, the United States' major institutional structure and its system of value orientations have been those of the first society established on premises nurtured by and in keeping with the basic tacit dimensions of Puritan mentality. Of particular importance here is the relation between religion and polity as a starting point in this discussion.

---

17   Seymour Martin Lipset's *The First New Nation* (1963) is one of the most important sociological accountings of American society. I agree with a great deal of its perceptive analysis, whose scope is more comprehensive at the institutional level than what is sought in this essay. My major divergence from Lipset concerns "Religion and American Values" (chap. 4). On a minor point, I do not think Arminianism became accepted by Puritan theology, although it was a major challenge. More important, however, Lipset sees religion in America in conventional terms, that is, in its formalized, institutionalized form. I think this is one segment of the religious life in America, but I also see a "free-floating" or institutionally diffuse aspect of the religious life, which I take to be quite in keeping with the spirit of Protestantism, with the dedifferentiation of religious and secular activities. Consequently, I would question Lipset's statement that "the separation of the church and state has increasingly given religion *per se* a specific rather than a diffuse role in American society" (1963, p. 168), because I think quite the opposite is true.

In the European historical context, the success of the Reformation led to the establishment of Protestant countries, yet with an important carry-over of the Medieval (and pre-Medieval) assumption that church and state were indissoluble and solidary institutions. Thus, even after Westphalia, the religion of the ruler was the official state religion and he (or she) was sworn to uphold it. Structurally, the Protestant countries (Holland, Prussia, the Scandinavian countries, and, for the sake of inclusiveness Anglican England) were as committed to the principle of the establishment of church and state as countries remaining Catholic (France, Austria, Spain, etc.). Even the First Republic of France carried over this basic structure, for it established an official public cult of Reason.

It was the United States that from its very beginning as a nation-state embodied the principle of a formal separation between polity and religion at the level of the national regime; the federal principle recognized in spirit the equality not only of citizens but also of denominations before the law. Although the early history of the American Colonies showed a carry-over of the traditional principle of an established church for a given political entity, by the eve of the Revolution most of the colonies had accepted the new, "modern" viewpoint; once established at the national level, it was shortly carried out in the remaining states.

The United States may thus be seen as the first modern nation to embody a basic, latent Protestant premise involving the nature of the relationship between the religious and political sectors of society. The separation of church and state in the United States is one outcome and manifestation of Puritan world outlook. Stemming from the historical imprint it received in Europe in the sixteenth and seventeenth centuries, Puritanism developed in its formative period as a protest against established, ecclesiastical, traditional authority. Basic to the Puritan mentality, I suggest, is a deep-seated ambivalence toward external authority, leading to ambivalence toward both secular authority figures (partly because they may trammel the autonomy of self and conscience) and externalized institutions. It follows that a working out of Puritan values leads to the rejection of the sanctity of authority based on tradition (and for not-unrelated reasons, to a rejection of authority based on personal "charisma"); a consequence of this is the rejection of an institutionalized nexus between polity and religion. This ambivalence toward external authority not only is manifested in the separation of church and state in America,[18] but also expresses itself in the continuing American value orientation of ambivalence toward institutionalized authority.

To view the United States as Protestant in spirit by virtue of the principle of the separation of church and state is really a mere initial step in coming to grips with the full import of the Puritan cultural matrix of the United States. Weber placed before us a Jacob's ladder, but he himself did not ascend (or descend) all the rungs; he did not examine the specificity of the Puritan cultural matrix in American

---

18   Weber, in beginning his essay, "The Protestant Sects and the Spirit of Capitalism," notes the separation of church and state in the United States but does not examine "the practical importance of this principle …" (1958*a*, p. 302).

society as the latter's paramount cultural system. One of the peculiarities of the Puritan mold, at least as I interpret it, is that it is not easily recognizable as a religious cultural mold: the separation of church and state leads to blurring of the differentiation between the religious life and the secular life, a blurring of sacred and profane activities and social objects – a blurring which itself is a cardinal feature of the Protestant ethic.[19]

Weber saw the modernization process of Western civilization as having two interrelated underlying tendencies: rationalization of all spheres of conduct and secularization, that is, the differentiation of the religious impulse and religious attitudes from "practical" social activities. A great deal of our sociological thinking has been molded implicitly in this broad image. Rather than accept it uncritically, we should take a fresh look at it. One fruitful start might derive from coming to grips with the cultural system of the United States. Puritan in its inception and gestation period, Puritan even thereafter, the United States is an intriguing society for analyzing elements of the Puritan cultural system to which Weber sensitized us but which he himself did not systematically analyze.

V Some Manifestations Of Puritan Culture

On the basis of the preceding sections, let me now seek to illustrate some historical and contemporary manifestations of Puritan culture in the United States, thereby, I hope, suggesting some new casks for the Weberian wine.

A Nature and Wilderness

Cultural systems, like most things, do not exist in a vacuum. The categorization of the physical environment, of "nature," is an extremely important function of any cultural system, providing important channels of socially organized conduct toward nature.[20] I wish here to suggest that the American historical experience, from the Colonial period to the present, has as a major collective representation an interesting and complex orientation toward nature, linking it with "wilderness," and that this orientation is rooted in religious imagery which evolved from its

---

19   Highly pertinent here is the observation of Nelson (1973*b*, pp. 98-99): "The influence of the Protestant ethic in America is sometimes very easy, sometimes very hard to uncover ... The reason for this may be put simply: in our land Protestantism seems to take form less sharply differentiated institutions than to express itself at every point in the social and cultural life process in a volatilized form. Rather, as a way of life, Protestantism secretes itself in all the conventionalized structures which are then taken-for-granted ways of proceeding in the worlds of education, business, and law."

20   Taking off from Durkheim and Mauss (some would say way off), Claude Lévi-Strauss' *Mythologiques* volumes of the past decade are explorations of the complex culture/nature interplay.

European base to a distinct American Puritan perspective that still has efficacy today in organizing collective action.[21]

"Wilderness" as polar to "civilization" is a biblical theme common to both Old and New Testaments; in this sense, wilderness had been seen, in the context of later Western civilization, as a refuge that nature offered from the corruption of civilization, a temporary abode of trial and purification. This traditional imagery persisted in the collective experiences of Protestant sects and proto-Protestant sects (such as the Waldensians) in Europe and also in the initial experiencing of North America by its early Puritan settlers (Williams 1962).

However, the meaning of "wilderness" and "nature" underwent an important historical transformation as the result of a Puritan cognitive breakthrough.[22] The first phase of the breakthrough took place in England in the theology of radical Puritanism, which came to see nature as withdrawn from the direct government of Christ, pending his return. As Williams notes: "This interpretation of nature liberated it as a realm free for scientific inquiry and for decisive human action. In some cases this eschatological view had also the effect of endowing man with a special responsibility for this realm in the interim" (p. 83).

The full import of this new way of perceiving nature unfolded only gradually on the North American scene.[23] At first, seeing the Atlantic as a geographical boundary between two worlds, the Puritans perceived wilderness as behind them; it was the corrupt Old World civilization, from whose stifling and oppressive institutional structures (particularly those of religion and polity) they were fleeing. Subsequently, wilderness was seen in still traditional imagery: as the wild nature of the physical environment, a setting of ordeals and tribulations, a temporary abode in the search for the "Promised Land."

However, in the course of the 18th century, a new conceptualization emerged. Nature *qua* wilderness took on a "value-added" aspect: it became seen as the permanent physical actuality of the American scene. Not only that, but the conquering of nature *qua* wilderness came to be seen as *the* divinely assigned task, the mission of the American people as a collectivity.

Whereas in the traditional European mentality nature was godly, sanctified by the work of Creation (hence, even in later Romantic thought, a refuge from the burdens of civilization), in America the imagery of nature contained in the dominant cultural system took on a very different meaning. Nature *qua* wilderness was not sacrosanct but a realm which had to be methodically, systematically

---

21   Major background materials in this context are to be found in Williams (1962), Nash (1975), Heimart (1953), and Miller (1956).

22   My use of the concept of cognitive "breakthrough" is indebted to Talcott Parsons' discussion of it in his "Introduction" to Weber's *The Sociology of Religion* (Parsons 1963, pp. xxix-xxiv).

23   See also Mosse (1960) for this and other tenets of radical Puritan thinking in the seventeenth century.

conquered and harnessed by strictly human means.[24] Conquering and civilizing nature became incorporated in the Puritan value system as a goal of transcendent, paramount importance (Nash 1973, p. 37; Heimert 1953, p. 382).

What is the sociological relevance of the wilderness theme in Puritan culture? First, in reference to Weber himself, we all know how very pregnant he took to be the notion of "calling" (*Beruf*), at the core of the "Protestant Ethic" (Weber 1958b, chap. 3). Weber, however, does not seem to have been attentive to subtle but significant changes in the Puritan conception of calling (Michaelsen 1953).[25] Of special interest here is the adaptation of this concept to the American experience: the methodical conquering or taming of nature *qua* wilderness became a *collective* life task of the emergent nation. What really gave sense to the American community, to the community which became after the first colonial generation increasingly heterogeneous socially and religiously, and ever increasingly so after the United States as such came into being, was unremitted devotion to the never-achieved (even unachievable) task of the total conquest of wilderness. Perforce, the notion of calling became transformed from an individual matter to a fundamentally collective enterprise.

The collective calling of the conquest of wilderness retained its significance beyond the New England colonial period, even into and beyond its importance for the "winning of the West" of the nineteenth century (Nash 1973). If the physical frontier as an environmental factor disappeared from the scene, did this lead to the demise of perceiving wilderness as a reality of the world? I think not, for the reason that wilderness is a basic frame of Puritan mentality and the Puritan cultural system; it is intrinsic to the Puritan mind to look for or find wilderness where others might see just nature or even civilization (both of which are essentially stable states, or, if you will, static categories). Wilderness, if you seek it, can always be found. Consequently, Americans have found new frontiers of wilderness both inside and outside the United States. Outside, it has been found in underdeveloped areas of both the Third World and the Old World. Inside, it has been found not in virgin lands but in the overdeveloped areas of civilization, in the urban sprawls of the great metropolitan areas (including the ghettos) whose decay stamps them as being characterized by an encroaching wilderness, one which calls for renewed

---

24   The colonial Puritan imagery of wilderness is marked by ambivalence. Nature *qua* wilderness is not an object of love or devotion. Nor is it an object of indifference or hatred. It is something initially hostile but redeemable by men's powers of transformation (reason, science, and technology). Transformed, it will yield fruits, but fruits which are imperfect since they are man made.

25   I am not concerned here that from Luther and Calvin's period to that of Baxter the religious meaning of "calling" may have altered in such a way as to make it more consonant with emergent modern capitalism. Such changes do not in any way invalidate the heuristic use of "calling" made by Weber in accounting for the development of the spirit of modern capitalism.

efforts of collective conquest, such as are manifested by a war on poverty.[26] Shifts in the content and referents of the image have taken place, but wilderness has lost none of its cultural significance.

The conquering of wilderness as a collective calling may thus be seen as a central element in the American Puritan culture. Its meaning is grounded in the this-worldly orientation of ascetic Protestantism. The blurring of the distinction between sacred and secular inherent in this orientation manifests itself here in the blurring of the economic meaning, on the one hand, and the moral-religious meaning, on the other, of conquering wilderness. In any case, American Puritan culture has sought and found in the ceaseless task of grappling with and conquering the wilderness the collective enterprise of purification of the world.

Conquering nature *qua* wilderness may further be seen as a key factor in the stress in American society on change as a valued end of action (Weber's *Wertrationalität*). If the Puritans could not participate in changing the world, they would surely feel unworthy and dissatisfied; just as surely, they cannot accept the world as a finished product, nor can they reject it and leave it alone. Since the task of transforming nature *qua* wilderness is a ceaseless, even frenzied, toil with no objective criteria for ever being able to judge it finished, the this-worldly activism of Puritanism may thus be shown to be the persisting cultural ground of American society's commitment to social change as much as to technological change. American dynamism or active commitment to change and experimentation (which so impresses foreign observers such as Revel) may thus be understood more adequately in terms of the spirit of Protestantism, and, more particularly, as related to the Puritan collective calling of the conquest of wilderness.[27]

The existential salience of being in a "wilderness-condition," as Cotton Mather put it (Heimert 1953, p. 379), uncovers other related features of American Puritan culture. One of particular interest here is that this condition leads to an acceptance of adversity and even disasters as having religious worth and meaning (since the wilderness is a situation of tribulations par excellence); they may be seen as divinely ordained ordeals which test, purify, and regenerate the collectivity.[28] In relating the Puritan ethic to the American Revolution, Morgan (1968) has shown

---

26   An expression of this is symbolized in the title of a noted work on American urbanism, Sam Bass Warner, Jr., *The Urban Wilderness* (1972). Moreover, President Kennedy's program for a Peace Corps was first thought of as a training program to develop young Americans to tackle the new frontier in the United States (personal communication from Professor W. W. Rostow).

27   However exalted this task of the conquest of wilderness may seem in the abstract, it has brutal consequences for those who happen to be dwelling in the wilderness – I have in mind the American Indians of yesteryear and today's victims of urban redevelopment.

28   Puritan mentality, in its historical development in America, was heavily imprinted by identification with the biblical Jews (Heimart 1953, p. 380; Miller 1954, pp. 463-91). The Puritan divines shared the prophets' belief that ordeals of adversity are necessary to regenerate the purity of the collectivity, and, as a corollary, that affluence contaminates the moral purity of the collectivity.

that the Puritans saw virtue in frugality and adversity and that they really felt more at ease in a condition of adversity than in one of material success, the latter, paradoxically, being a source of greater anxiety than the former. If Puritan culture is seen as thriving in adversity taken as a challenge, an ordeal of purification, may not this attitude be manifested in such contemporary phenomena as the general reaction to the energy crisis and the Watergate crisis? Perhaps even the hippie movement of a few years ago partook of Puritan culture in displaying a preference for the adversity of wilderness frontier over the decay of civilization affluence.

In the context of the Puritans' finding virtue in adversity, let me draw attention to one other American phenomenon. At various points in the Colonial period, situations of great adversity and threatening calamity brought forth "jeremiads," days of collective fasting and humiliation. The very political beginning of the United States was marked by a jeremiad. In 1775 the Continental Congress meeting in Philadelphia recommended that July 20 of that year be observed in all colonies as "a day of publick humiliation, fasting, and prayer"; purified by a national confession of sin and transgression, the American people could then meet the threatening calamities of political adversity (Miller 1968).

Lest we think of jeremiads as curious fossils of the early period of the United States, it is interesting to note that three times during the great national ordeal of the Civil War Lincoln proclaimed days of "humiliation, fasting, and prayer" at the request of Congress. It is even more interesting to note, as an indication of the persistent vitality of Puritan culture, that the political crisis stemming from the prolonged Watergate investigations an ordeal for not only the defendants but for the nation as a whole, was also seen as a critical time calling for a jeremiad! I have in mind the bipartisan Senate resolution passed in early 1974 which called for April 30, 1974, being set aside as "a National Day of Humiliation, Fasting, and Prayer."[29]

Perhaps this resolution should be seen as a quaint anachronism, though a hard-nosed Puritan could also point to the fact that the 1974 jeremiad was successful (if not in its observance, in its consequences). More to the point, it can also be seen as a continuing expression of national identity, a reaffirmation of deep-seated collective values grounded in Puritan culture, one which cannot be divorced from the concept of wilderness.

The sociological significance of wilderness cannot be found in the grammars of European sociology, neither that of Marx, nor that of Durkheim, perhaps not even that of Weber. But it should be of major importance in the sociological interpretation of American society, and I hope I have been able to suggest how the

---

29   A Rip Van Winkle Puritan, awakening after a sleep of two centuries, would find himself at home reading the following: "Because of the spiritual failure of the American people, the Senate resolution said, 'It therefore behooves us to humble ourselves before almighty God, to confess our national sins, and to pray for clemency and forgiveness'" (*Report from the Capital*, 1974).

Weberian perspective is of heuristic value in sensitizing us to themes of Puritanism, such as that of wilderness, other than those he himself analyzed.[30]

B Voluntarism

The second broad instance of Puritan culture to which I wish to draw attention is the theme of "voluntarism," which, like wilderness, did not originate in America but was reworked into a new American framework.

The principle of voluntarism developed in American Puritan culture as a formulation of social conduct, a social theory concerning most specifically the relation of the actor to the state but also his relation to other social institutions (such as marriage). In hammering out the social dimensions of a theology appropriate to New World conditions, the Puritan mentality reinterpreted traditional Western cosmology, including the two interrelated religious doctrines of Original Sin and the Covenant.[31] Original Sin became interpreted not as a condition of human bankruptcy but as one in which man is born owing God a debt which he can freely pay in worldly actions. That man can voluntarily discharge his debt in an important injunction and motivation for this-worldly activism, the opposite of a fatalistic acceptance of the situation into which one is born. As to Covenant theory, the voluntaristic principle became manifested in the notion that "the Puritan state could be wholly contractual, it could be the product of man's volition, and subject to the laws of their reason, and yet be directed and ruled by God. In society as in physics, free will and absolute decree went hand in hand" (Miller 1954, p. 421).

Freedom of action for the self thus received an important religious legitimation, and our emphasis on civil liberties can be shown to derive from basic Covenant premises of the Puritan mind. But a radical individualism is alien to Puritan thinking, a fact which deserves noting because of the ambiguity of the term "individualism." The antinomian tendency was limited by the Puritans' perspective on voluntarism as having meaning in the context of community; freedom of action also entailed the acceptance of social duties and obligations (Miller 1954, pp. 425, 427). The political conception of American society, from the early to the later Puritans, became grounded in the voluntaristic principle (initially a strictly religious principle that adults should freely choose God, that is, in the context of the Reformation, the sectarian principle of religious choice) that the pure society was "... erected upon the belief that the right sort of men could of their own free

---

30   This discussion has just scratched the surface of the sociological importance of the concept of wilderness for delineating interrelated aspects of American society. Viewed structurally and dynamically, the wilderness theme may be seen as what Marcel Mauss aptly termed a "phénomène social total," whose comprehensive sociological analysis, like that of the "gift," exposes deep structures of society otherwise hidden from view. In this context, see the concluding section of Mauss (1954).

31   For significant materials on Puritan social doctrine, see Miller (1954, pp. 398-431).

will and choice carry through the creation and administration of the right sort of community" (Miller 1956, p. 147).

We thus find in Puritan social theory central features of the American perspective on the relation of self to organized society. Loyalty to political authority is limited to rulers or officials abiding by the law. Loyalty ends and dissent begins when the administrators of the state transgress the law. The state is neither the result of divine creation (as in traditional European thought) nor a divine emanation (as in Hegel) but the product of men's concerted actions. Freedom of action is a cardinal aspect of Puritan social theory, but it does not mean that the actor can do as he pleases without regard to civil duties. On the contrary, his actions are always to be judged in terms of their service to the community, which is the corporate (or fiduciary) agent of God in this world until such time as He might decide to reenter it directly. The community is an organic reality but one resting on freely-arrived-at contractual relationships between free agents – the community is not a suprahuman entity.

Voluntaristic theory, framed by Puritanism, became a cardinal feature of American society, both pre-Revolutionary and post-Revolutionary. At one level, the United States has come close to approximating a society of voluntary associations, of secondary groups formed by the free association of adults – a fact of American life which certainly impressed de Tocqueville. At another level, much of the political dynamism of the United States in the past two centuries owes much to the strength of voluntarism in American society. The thrust for social change and social reforms, a feature of the American scene, reflects the strength of voluntary associations, or, as the social historian Berthoff has remarked in retrospect: "Movements for reforming society were a special province of voluntary associations. Each group conceived of its cause as the vanguard of the progressive, egalitarian, individualistic, and optimistic spirit of the times" (1971, p. 255).

Voluntarism, grounded in Puritan social theory, underlies the basic American value orientation of individualism; as previously indicated, the spirit of the latter is that it should be oriented to service and benefit for the larger community. It would take an essay in itself to document adequately all the social manifestations and consequences of the voluntaristic principle in the evolution of American society. Of particular importance here is the degree to which American capitalism reflects the theme of voluntarism and service, differentiating it in important respects from the development and attitudes of European capitalism. Quite aside from social legislation, I have in mind the acceptance of social and civil responsibilities in the form of establishing from the profits of enterprise educational institutions (including so many of our major universities), large-scale foundations which are given autonomy from their corporate sponsors, public libraries and museums, etc. I do not point this out as a justification of the economic system of American capitalism itself (which in its economic practices is as ruthless as any other form of modern capitalism). However, the pronounced element of social service in American capitalism cannot simply be dismissed as "blood money" but must be seen as related to the Puritan social ethic.

In the rest of this section, I would like to illustrate how the theme of voluntarism, rooted in Puritanism, is itself manifested in American sociological thought. In other words, let us try to bring the Protestant ethic as close to home as possible.[32] Let me boldly assert that I consider George Herbert Mead the most important native-born contributor to micro-sociology and Talcott Parsons the most important native-born contributor to macrosociology. I assume that their writings are familiar to the reader. Even if some disagree with my contention, I trust all will agree that both are major influences on present American sociology.

Mead has provided us, essentially, with a paradigmatic approach to socialization: the genesis of the social self, its actualization in role behavior, the significance of symbols in social interaction, etc. (Mead 1934). Neither self nor society are fixed, static givens; they are emergent features of reality. Although there is no explicit mention of voluntarism in Mead, his approach to self and society is highly voluntaristic. It underlies his view of "... human society not as an established structure but as people meeting their conditions of life; it sees social action not as an emanation of social structure but as a formation made by human actors ... it sees group life ... as a process of building up joint action" (Blumer 1969, pp. 74-75).

Mead places a strong stress on the volitional capacities of the individual for self-development, for freely accepting and internalizing the rules of the game. Ultimately self-consciousness structures what the actor chooses to become, but what he chooses, fundamentally, is to become an active and productive social being. Society is neither a blessing nor a curse but an on-going community of actors. Mead's social realism has a different image of society from those of Marx and Durkheim, respectively. Yet his stress on the inherent subjectivity of action is not an acceptance of nominalism (i.e., a belief that only individuals as such constitute or "construct" social reality), nor is it an invitation to behavioristic reductionism. Thus, in his discussion of perception, Mead clearly notes that in the evolutionary process human perception is distinguished from that of animals and that if humans perceive objects symbolically, "the precondition for such a development ... is that there should be a community perspective, that there should be objects which exist in their relationship to the group" (1938, p. 203).

To emphasize the point, self-development is contingent on the internalization of common meanings, which in turn presupposes an organized community, a rationally organized society (Mead 1938, p. 518). In keeping with Puritan social theory which stressed personal achievements against ascribed privileges based on birth (characterizing the Medieval social order), Mead sees democratic society as favorable to and necessary for self-development and self-expression. He argues that personality development requires "the removal of castes" (1934, p. 318),

---

32   In the broader academic context, note the cogent remarks of Shils (1971): "Universities are still the scene of the "Protestant ethic," even if they are not as Christian as they were a century ago ... the scholar and scientist is like the Puritan entrepreneur ..."

which also allows the actor to make a maximal functional contribution to the societal community:

> ... the sense of the self obtained through the realization of a function in the community is a more effective and for various reasons a higher form of the sense of self than that which is dependent upon the immediate personal relations in which a relation of superiority and inferiority is involved (1934, p. 316).

Brief as my discussion of Mead has perforce been, I hope it has suggested that his formulation of self and society is not only an intellectual expression of central features of the value patterns of American society and their actualization in it but also consonant with the basic social premises of the American Puritan orientation to the world.[33]

How does the line of analysis developed in the course of this paper and particularly in this section inform us about Talcott Parsons, about whose extensive writings equally voluminous tracts have been written? I hope to introduce a new dimension in the interpretations of Parsonian theory by proposing that his contributions to macrotheory mesh with and complement Mead's contributions to microtheory; that both express, at a high level of abstraction, central sociocultural realities and value orientations of American society; and finally, that the existential foundations of Parsons's approach to social reality are as consonant with, if not as rooted in, Puritan culture, as Mead's.[34]

I have stressed that Puritan social doctrine gives cardinal importance to the principle of voluntarism. Recall that this theory of individualism contains both the sanctioning of freedom of action in the social sphere (ranging from voluntary assent in religion to voluntary assent in matters of political authority) and also the injunction that the individual's freely chosen worldly actions be of service to the community in the realization of common ends. Now, it is worthwhile noting that both of these elements, which run tacitly throughout Parsons' mature writings, are explicit in the "young" Parsons. It is Parsons who over 40 years ago prepared the article entitled "Service" which appeared in the *Encyclopedia of the Social Sciences* (1934), an article in which he gives a succinct account of the structural and historical aspects of service, including the secularization of the idea in the

---

33   A more explicit reference to Puritan culture is found in a passage of Mead that deserves to be noted: "There have been two attitudes of the American which have largely determined his reaction to science – the philosophy of history given by Puritan theology and the will to understand the physical world about him that he might control it. Back in his mind lay some version of the plan of salvation as his interpretation of the world ..." (Mead 1938, pp. 625-26).

34   In no way is this meant to be an "unmasking" of Parsons such as Gouldner appears to intend in *The Coming Crisis of Western Sociology*. It is meant to add to our understanding of the intellectual frame of Parsons' sociological conceptualizations, not to negate them as "ideology."

hands of Calvinism. In passing, we might note an amusing coincidence: the article by Parsons is the last in a volume; the first in the same volume (by M. James) is …"Puritanism"!

The second early work relevant to our discussion is his classic study *The Structure of Social Action* ([1937] 1949). From this seminal work Parsons' later "general theory of action" and analysis of institutions evolved. We should note that the foundation of the theoretical frame of reference it advances (a synthesis of analytical elements in Marshall, Pareto, Durkheim, and Weber) involves a very important critique of both utilitarianism and empirical positivism. More crucial perhaps is the explicit formulation of its action frame of reference, clearly announced, from the earliest pages of Parsons' treatise, to be voluntaristic: "The central focus of attention is in the process of development of one coherent theoretical system, that to be denoted as the *voluntaristic theory of action*" (p. 11; emphasis in the original).

From what source is this vital ingredient, voluntarism, obtained? From certain passages and suggestions in the text (pp. 53-55, 63, 87-88), it is not unlikely that the inspiration for the term has its roots in Puritan social thought. To be sure, Weber and Troeltsch, whom he had studied intensively, are European intellectual influences that may have contributed to Parsons's theoretical formulation of voluntarism, but his own cultural heritage is probably the primordial factor underlying the emergence of the concept of voluntarism.[35]

After *The Structure of Social Action*, voluntarism seems to have dropped out of Parsons's vocabulary. But just as explicit consideration but not the themes of alienation and anomie drop out of the later Marx and the later Durkheim, respectively, the theme of voluntarism is still in the background of Parsons' approach to institutional structures. His interpretations of American society, particularly its set of value orientations, give cardinal importance to "instrumental activism" (1960, p. 172), which is very much related to the earlier voluntarism. Further, in various essays (1969) he has continued to emphasize the importance of "voluntariness" in associations.

I think this is important in several respects for a proper understanding of Parsons, The notions of "community," of "normative obligations," and of "service" are important elements of Puritan social theory, and the same elements appear (perhaps in a more secular form but nevertheless in the same grammar) in Parsons' sociological analyses and interpretations. His early critique of utilitarianism in *The Structure of Social Action* is highly consonant with the Puritans' awareness of the societal dysfunctions of economic individualism, of money making as an

---

35   To be sure, Troeltsch, who gave so much attention to voluntarism in his landmark study of the sociology of religion (1960), was himself steeped in the Protestant culture of Germany.

end in itself; however much support Protestantism gave to economic conduct, the Puritans disapproved of merchants seeking only their own enrichment.[36]

If we keep in mind that the Parsonian theory is grounded in the voluntaristic assumption of social action (and has remained so), we should be able to correct the faulty image that this theory views the actor as a passive agent who is determined by social structure. Examination of comparable passages would show that Parsons' perspective on self and society complements Mead's. Nor should Parsons' later analysis of social structures as analytical aspects of social reality lead us to think that his image of concrete society is that of a "static" entity. Reflecting the dynamics of American society and its commitment to change, Parsons' later evolutionary perspective is consonant with both Mead's view of society and the Puritan social doctrine that human society is the active product of men, one which is never completed in the realization of common ends. The American openness to change is reflected in Parsons' own explicit programmatic statement of a general theory of action calling for a theory "equally applicable to the problem of change and to those of process within a stabilized system" (1951, p. 535).

To end this treatment of Parsons on a reflexive note, it may be advanced that the sociology of Parsons is much more attuned to the realities of American society than some recent critics have alleged (and more perceptive of these realities than some critics) because it has existential roots in the underlying cultural system of Puritanism, from which American institutional life and values have emerged.

VI Conclusion

In the course of this paper we have covered much territory, some very familiar and, for a sociological essay, some not so familiar. Let me admit that it has not been an easy journey for me, if only because most of my own sociological roots are in the Old World and my existential roots are not in the Puritan culture which I have emphasized. But perhaps it is because I am not a straight insider that the depth of Puritan culture underlying the United States has come to impress itself on me.

I have not meant to suggest that American society is totally integrated in terms of Puritan culture, for that cultural system has lost its monopoly; nor do I mean that American society is more "stable" because of the presence of Puritan culture. In brief, I do not mean that for sociological purposes all things judged interesting about American society could be dealt with had we sufficient knowledge of all the interrelated elements of Puritan culture.

I do mean to imply, however, that the Puritan cultural system is of the utmost importance for the sociological analysis of American modernization and modernity. The modernization process of the United States in the past 200 years

---

36 "... the merchant sometimes demeaned his calling by practicing it to the detriment rather than the benefit of society ... As the Puritan Ethic induced a suspicion of merchants, it also induced ... a suspicion of prosperity" (Morgan 1968, p. 237).

shares many features with those of other countries. Yet it also has a specificity in the sense outlined in this paper, namely, the distinct, paramount cultural system of American Puritanism. Neither Marx nor Durkheim in terms of their respective frame of reference might do much with it ... perhaps Weber.

Perhaps more than anything else, to add a concluding note, what is so sociologically intriguing about American society is its profound ambiguity.[37] Highly permissive, it is also highly oppressive; highly capitalistic, it is also highly socialistic in its implementation of egalitarian principles; highly secular, it is highly religious; it has not changed its political regime in 200 years, yet its political life is marked by progressive changes. From its very beginnings ambiguity was stamped on the United States, for the character of the American Revolution was highly ambiguous and cannot be reduced to a simple "conservative" or "radical" image.[38]

I suggest that the ambiguities of American society are related to ones intrinsic to American Puritan culture. In the nearly two centuries preceding the events of the 1770s, the Puritan cultural system was not fashioned in a final form but continued to evolve out of basic considerations as new conditions called for enlarging and modifying elements that had originated in European society. Not a static cultural system on the eve of the Revolution, it has not been static in its wake, yet it remains – even if only marginally visible – the cultural roots of American society which, though deeply buried, still throw out new growth. It is perhaps the very ambiguity of the Puritans' search for meaning in the wilderness which imparts a Sisyphus aspect to American society.[39] Like Sisyphus, the United States is perpetually achievement oriented, albeit the fulfillment of the task always escapes it.

The Puritans of the pre-Revolutionary period had come to this painful realization, which nevertheless led them to accept the permanence of their "wilderness-condition." Perhaps because of this core ambiguity as to the meaning of the collective enterprise,[40] there is a never-achieved aspect of American society. Not glorifying "revolution" or "counterrevolution" as ends in themselves, the United States, as Revel sensed, has been the most historically active of societies because of the elusiveness of the moral and social revolution to which Puritan culture is committed.

I hope, in the light of materials presented in this paper and not necessarily because of its conclusion, that current American sociology will take a new look at American society, both in terms of its development and in terms of contemporary

---

37   For comparative purposes, see the sensitive work of Georges Balandier (1966).

38   I rely here on the assessment of the noted historian Robert R. Palmer (1959, 1: 235).

39   The Sisyphus metaphor was suggested to me by reading Rollin Chambliss' application of it to George Herbert Mead's perspective (Chambliss 1963).

40   Perry Miller has stated this essential ambiguity eloquently: "Can a culture, which chances to embody itself in a nation, push itself to such remorseless exertion without ever learning whether it has been sent on its business at some incomprehensible behest, or is it obligated to discover a meaning for its dynamism in the very act of running?" (1956, p. 217).

features, and this by means of an intensive and extensive examination of Puritan culture. After such an examination, we can continue, in the apt phrase of Perry Miller, our never-ending "errand into the wilderness."

References

Balandier, Georges 1966. *Ambiguous Africa.* London: Chatto & Windus.

Bellah, Robert N. 1964. "Religious Evolution." *American Sociological Review* 29 (June): 358-74.

—.1970, "Civil Religion in America." pp. 168-89 in *Beyond Belief.* New York: Harper & Row.

—. ed. 1973. *Emile Durkheim on Morality and Society.* Chicago: University of Chicago Press.

Berthoff, Rowland T. 1971. *An Unsettled People: Social Order and Disorder in American History.* New York: Harper & Row.

Blumer, Herbert 1969. *Symbolic Interactionism.* Englewood Cliffs, N.J.: Prentice-Hall.

Brann, Henry Walter 1944. "Max Weber and the United States." *Southwestern Social Science Quarterly* 25 (June): 18-30.

Chambliss, Rollin 1963. "Mead's Way out of the Basic Dilemma in Modern Existential Thought." *Journal of Social Psychology* 60: 213-20.

Christman, Henry M., ed. 1966. *The American Journalism of Marx and Engels.* New York: New American Library.

Crozier, Michel 1973. *The Stalled Society.* New York: Viking.

Durkheim, Emile 1886. "Las études récentes de sciences sociales." *Revue philosophique* 22: 61-80.

—. 1887. "La science positive de la morale en Allemagne." *Revue philosophique* 24:33-58, 113-42, 275-84.

—. 1955. *Pragmatisme et sociologie.* Paris: Vrin.

—. 1957. *Professional Ethics and Civic Morals.* London: Routledge & Kegan Paul. First published in French in 1950.

—. 1961. *The Elementary Forms of the Religious Life.* New York: Collier. First published in French in 1912.

—. 1973. *Moral Education.* New York: Free Press, First published in French in 1925.

Eisenstadt, S. N. 1973. *Modernization, Change, and Modernity.* New York: Wiley.

Heimert, Alan 1953. "Puritanism, the Wilderness, and the Frontier." *New England Quarterly* 26 (September): 361-82.

Horton, John 1972. "The Dehumanization of Anomie and Alienation: A Problem in the Ideology of Sociology." pp. 135-51 in *Humanistic Society: Today's Challenge to Sociology,* edited by John F. Glass and John R. Staude. Pacific Palisades, California: Goodyear.

Israel, Joachim 1971. *Alienation from Marx to Modern Sociology.* Boston: Allyn & Bacon.

Joseph, Franz M., ed. 1959. *As Others See Us: The United States through Foreign Eyes.* Princeton, N.J.: Princeton University Press.

Leguns, Cohn 1962. *Pan Africanism: A Short Political Guide.* New York: Praeger.

Lipset, Seymour Martin 1963. *The First New Nation.* New York: Basic.

Lukes, Steven 1972. *Emile Durkheim, His Life and Work.* New York: Harper & Row. Marx, Karl. 1971. *The Grundrisse.* Edited by David McLellan. New York: Harper & Row.

Marx, Karl, and Frederick Engels 1937. *The Civil War in the United States.* Edited by Richard Emmale. New York: International.

Mauss, Marcel 1954. *The Gift: Forms and Functions of Exchange in Archaic Societies.* New York: Free Press. First published in French in 1923-24.

Mead, George Herbert. 1934. *Mind, Self, and Society.* Chicago: University of Chicago Press.

—. 1938. *The Philosophy of the Act.* Chicago: University of Chicago Press.

Merton, Robert K. 1972. "Insiders and Outsiders: A Chapter in the Sociology of Knowledge." *American Journal of Sociology* 78 (November): 9-47.

Michaelsen, Robert S. 1953. "Changes in the Puritan Concept of Calling or Vocation." *New England Quarterly* 26 (September): 315-36.

Miller, Perry 1954. *The New England Mind: The Seventeenth Century.* Cambridge, Mass.: Harvard University Press.

—. 1956. *Errand into the Wilderness.* Cambridge, Mass.: Harvard University Press.

—. 1968. "The Moral and Psychological Roots of American Resistance." pp. 251-74 in *The Reinterpretation of the American Revolution 1763-1789,* edited by Jack P. Greene. New York: Harper & Row.

Morgan, Edmund S. 1968. "The Puritan Ethic and the Coming of the American Revolution," pp. 235-51 in *The Reinterpretation of the American Revolution,* edited by Jack P. Greene. New York: Harper & Row.

Mosse, George L. 1960. "Puritan Radicalism and the Enlightenment." *Church History* 29 (December): 424-39.

Nash, Roderick 1973. *Wilderness and the American Mind.* Rev. ed. New Haven, Conneticut: Yale University Press.

Nelson, Benjamin 1973*a*. "Max Weber, Dr. Alfred Ploetz, and W. E. B. DuBois." *Sociological Analysis* 34 (Winter): 308-12.

—. 1973*b*. "Weber's Protestant Ethic: Its Origins, Wanderings, and Foreseeable Futures." pp. 71-130 in *Beyond the Classics: Essays in the Scientific Study of Religion,* edited by C. Y. Glock and P. S. Hammond, New York: Harper & Row.

Palmer, R. R. 1959. *The Age of the Democratic Revolution: A Political History of Europe and America, 1760-1800.* Vol. 1. Princeton, N.J.: Princeton University Press.

Parsons, Talcott 1934. "Service." pp. 672-74 in *Encyclopedia of the Social Sciences*, R. A. Seligman, editor-in-chief, vol: 1.3, New York: Macmillan.

—. 1949. *The Structure of Social Action.* New York: Free Press. First published in 1937.

—. 1951. *The Social System.* New York: Free Press.

—. 1960. *Structure and Process in Modern Societies.* New York: Free Press.

—. 1963. "Introduction." Pp. xix-xvii in Max Weber, *Sociology of Religion.* Boston: Beacon.

—. 1969. *Politics and Social Structure.* New York: Free Press.

—. 1974. *Report from the Capital* 29 (January): 1.

Revel, Jean-François 1971. *Without Marx or Jesus.* Garden City, N.Y.: Doubleday. Published in French as *Ni Marx, ni Jésus*, in 1970.

Saint-Simon, Henri de 1925. *Lettres d'un habitant de Genève à ses contemporains.* Paris: Alcan.

Servan-Schreiber, J. J. 1968. *The American Challenge.* New York: Atheneum.

Shils, Edward 1971. "Academic Appointment, University Autonomy, and the Federal Government." *Minerva* 9 (April): 161-70.

Smelser, Neil J. 1971. "Alexis de Tocqueville as Comparative Analyst." pp. 19-47 in *Comparative Methods in Sociology*, edited by Ivan Vallier. Berkeley: University of California Press.

Swanson, Guy E. 1967. *Religion and Regime.* Ann Arbor: University of Michigan Press.

Szymanski, Albert 1974. "A Reply to Friedman, Stevenson, and Zeitlin." *American Journal of Sociology* 79 (May): 1462-76.

Tiryakian, Edward A. 1962. *Sociologism and Existentialism.* Englewood Cliffs, N.J.: Prentice-Hall.

Troeltsch, Ernst 1960. *The Social Teaching of the Christian Churches.* New York: Harper.

Wallwork, Ernest 1972. *Durkheim: Morality and Milieu.* Cambridge, Mass.: Harvard University Press.

Warner Sam Bass, Jr. 1972. *The Urban Wilderness.* New York: Harper & Row.

Weber, Max 1958a. *From Max Weber: Essays in Sociology.* Edited by Hans H. Garth and C. Wright Mills. New York: Oxford University Press.

—. 1958b. *The Protestant Ethic and the Spirit of Capitalism.* Translated by Talcott Parsons. New York: Scribner's. English edition first published in 1930, from the original German essay published in 1904-5.

—. 1961. *General Economic History.* New York: Collier.

—. 1963. *The Sociology of Religion.* Boston: Beacon.

Williams, George H. 1962. *Wilderness and Paradise in Christian Thought.* New York: Harper.

Chapter 15
Durkheim and Weber: First Cousins?[1]

The late Max Weber, if he rarely cited Durkheim and the work done under the latter's direction, was much closer to our point of view. – Marcel Mauss, *l'Année Sociologique*, n.s. II (1924-25), p. 186.

I Introduction: Strasburg as a Strategic Setting

This *Durkheim-Weber* symposium is an historic reunion of two lineages, of two major clans: French-speaking and German-speaking sociology who have not met in a dialogic encounter situation, such as one envisioned for sociology by Donald Levine (Camic and Joas 2004). As far as I know, there has not been in the recent past a joint conference bringing together representatives of French-speaking and German-speaking sociologists similar to various conferences bringing together American and German sociologists.[2]

That this meeting of sociologists coming from both sides of the Rhine and even overseas is taking place in Strasburg, regional capital of Alsace and meeting point of French and German cultures with its own historical identity, has something genial if not inspirational, for reasons pertinent to the history of sociology. Strasburg has a special niche as an intersection of French and German sociology, comparable, say, to the niche that New York and the New School for Social Research occupied

1   Revised from a welcome address "Durkheim et Weber: cousins germains?" presented at the international symposium *Durkheim-Weber*, held in Strasburg, France, April 8-9, 1991, and published in Monique Hirschhorn and Jacques Coenen-Huther,eds., *Durkheim, Weber. Vers la fin des malentendus*. Paris: l'Harmattan, 1994.

2   For example, the conference *Theories of Social Change and Development* organized by the theory sections of the American Sociological Association and the Deutsche Gesellschaft für Soziologie at Berkeley, California in 1986, which led to the volume by Hans Haferkamp and Neil Smelser, eds, *Social Change and Modernity* (Berkeley: University of California Press, 1992). The following year, Hans-Peter Müller (Humboldt University) organized at Werner Reimers-Stiftung in Bad Homburg an Anglo German conference on "The Normative in Durkheim". The success of these was the stimulus for an ongoing dialogue between anglophone and German-speaking sociologists.

John Craig does make passing mention of philosopher Maurice Blondel and Maurice Halbwachs, both at the University of Strasbourg, taking part at the "Franco-German conferences at Davos of 1928-31," (Craig 1983, p. 280), and in the course of which Halbwachs got to meet Sombart. Unfortunately, I have not been able to track down these conferences and what collaborative work, if any, they achieved.

as a meeting ground in the 1940s between American sociologists and French and German refugee social scientists.

Where this first conference of German-speaking and French-speaking sociologists is taking place also adds a symbolic significance. The selection of Strasburg has enabled the symposium to take place in the building of the Council of Europe where the European Parliament also meets: recall in this context that the vision of a larger Europe "without frontiers" was envisioned first in 1814 by Henri de Saint-Simon, our sociological progenitor and mentor of Auguste Comte.[3] The unification of Europe had its beginning then in the former's vision of a post-Napoleon Europe with industry replacing military conquest, and Saint-Simon's vision for the construction of a new Europe even included a transnational deliberative body of government![4]

The great common market of a Europe without economic frontiers also implies that a parallel market of ideas be open without linguistic or nationalist barriers, which is not always the case in sociology, despite a common longing for the discipline to be a science. Meeting where the deliberations of the European Parliament take place will be a stimulus for sociologists from various countries, and particularly from the French- and German-speaking worlds, to engage in a renovated sociological encounter "without frontiers".[5] As a measure toward this encounter we may reflect on aspects of the history of sociology where invisible frontiers may have existed, particularly in critical locations or between actors strategically placed for the exchange and diffusion of sociological studies, which may be thought of as "cultural goods".

A glaring "invisible barrier" producing silence rather than lively interaction across national and linguistic frontiers existing in the history of sociology is, as I noted a quarter of a century ago, that Weber and Durkheim seemed to have ignored each other.[6] Yet, everything in terms of their elite position in the sociological world of pre-war Europe would lead to think these contemporaries could have and should have known one another: intellectually and ideologically, they can be

---

3   *Oeuvres complètes* de Saint-Simon et Enfantin, Paris, 1865-1876, vol. 15, pp. 153-248.

4   The stimulus of European unity in cultural diversity anticipates a "new world" for the twenty-first Century, a theme I had proposed as incoming president of l'Association Internationale des Sociologues de Langue Française (AISLF) in 1988 and which became the theme of the 15th World Congress of AISLF, in Lyon, France (*Les Nouveaux Mondes et la Sociologie*, July 6-11, 1992).

5   In fact, the Strasburg symposium led to the publication of the volume, *Durkheim, Weber. Vers la Fin des Malentendus,* Monique Hirschhorn and J. Coenen-Huther, eds., (Paris: L'Harmattan 1994).

6   Edward A. Tiryakian, "A Problem for the Sociology of Knowledge: The Mutual Unawareness of Emile Durkheim and Max Weber" (1966). Reproduced in the present volume with an added postscript.

viewed as ... "first cousins", only dimly aware of each other.[7] As a background preparation for our present meeting, I would like to develop further my initial probe of their seeming mutual unawareness as case materials beyond the sociology of knowledge.[8]

If they did not physically meet nor apparently take cognizance of one another in their lifetime, although there were settings where they might actually have been at the same time, how about subsequently in the post-World War I era (they both may be said to be victims of the war)? In summary fashion I will look at just the French context of the reception of Weberian analysis, leaving it to German colleagues to consider the receptivity or lack of receptivity of Durkheimian sociology before WWI and in the Weimar period.

For present purpose, as background to this symposium, we can take the *oeuvre* of Durkheimian sociology – its methodology and substantive works – and in parallel fashion, the *oeuvre* of Weberian studies, as major *cultural innovations* respectively in sociology, that have had lasting importance, comprising today a sort of common analytical "toolkit" used by sociologists in very different countries with different national traditions. If scientific discoveries and paradigms, as well as technological innovations, can diffuse very rapidly beyond frontiers, such is frequently not the case with cultural bases of innovations. In a recent article, Kaufman and Patterson open up some important general considerations regarding the dynamics of cultural diffusion,[9] which I believe are heuristic for considering the subdued extent of the diffusion of German sociology in France during the first half of the twentieth century. A shortcoming of the diffusion literature they surveyed is that beyond the institutional framework there are important considerations overlooked, such as the power relation between change agents and "adopters", and cases where "innovations are transmitted but eventually rejected, as well as cases where adoption might have been expected but did not occur," (Kaufman and Patterson, 2005: 83).

Taking this basic framework to our central symposium theme, what were the opportunities for Weberian studies to diffuse in France before and after World War I, and who were the main change agents in a structural position to assist or hinder the diffusion of Weberian studies? Strasburg, as well as Paris, is in several respects a key nodal point for examining the diffusion of "national" sociologies across the Rhine.[10]

---

7   The reader may bear in mind that "cousin-Germain" in French has a dimension which the English equivalent "first cousin" does not provide.

8   For a complementary and more extensive discussion of the blockage of Weberian studies in France, see Monique Hirschhorn, *Max Weber et la Sociologie Française* (1988).

9   Jason Kaufman and Orlando Patterson,, "Cross-National Cultural Diffusion: The Global Spread of Cricket," *American Sociological Review*, 70 (February 2005): 82-110. Concretely, they examine why the traditionally English sport of cricket spread to many but not all countries having close colonial and other ties to Great Britain.

10   A broader comparative study of the diffusion process would consider Berlin and Heidelberg as nodal points.

II Simmel, Halbwachs, Gurvitch

Georg Simmel, near the end of his life, received his first regular academic appointment as professor in Strasburg in 1914, where he died four years later. While a lecturer in Berlin he had been invited by Durkheim to contribute an essay to the first volume of the *Année Sociologique*.[11] Apparently Durkheim was not pleased with the "formal sociology" of Simmel, since, unlike the *American Journal of Sociology* that regularly published his essays after its initial one (also in 1896-97), Simmel apparently had no further ties to French sociology in his lifetime. He might well have felt rebuffed even after death, since his name does not even appear in the Index of the first volume of the *Année* that Mauss edited in 1923-24 albeit a number of his important works (such as *The Philosophy of Money*) were being published posthumously. What he taught at Strasburg, and whether he included Durkheimian studies during the wartime years when nationalism ran high on both sides, needs investigation (as well as what, if anything, he taught about Durkheimian sociology before 1914). For the time being, one can only say that unfortunately Simmel is a sort of "missed link" between German and French sociology.

After World War I, with Alsace and its educational institutions returned to French authority, it is at the "new university" in Strasburg where he was professor of sociology and education that Maurice Halbwachs taught a long time, from 1919 until 1935. As a young professor there in the 1920s extending the Durkheimian approach to economic sociology and demography, he was the first to introduce the thought of Max Weber in France, in advance of Parsons bringing Weber to the attention of American sociologists.[12] As long as Halbwachs was at Strasburg, French sociology had a conduit to Weberian analysis, with the tacit sanctioning of Mauss in his overall editorial capacity .

Halbwachs, thoroughly familiar with German, as editor in the Economic Section of the *Année Sociologique* (which he shared with Simiand) had already before World War I published listings and brief reviews of Weber, including a consecutive and positive two-part mention of *The Protestant Ethic and the Spirit of Capitalism* (in volume 9, p. 471, and volume 10, p. 555). From a young disciple (first of Bergson then of Durkheim) before World War I, Halbwachs became an important anchor man for the surviving post-war Durkheimians. His early interests in religion had many sides, including in 1925 an extensive though not original condensation of

---

11   "Comment les forme sociales se maintiennent," *L'Année Sociologique,* I (1896-97): 71-109.

12   Maurice Halbwachs, "Max Weber: un homme, une oeuvre," *Annales d'Histoire,* 1(1929): 81-88. More broadly, Deyon credits Halbwachs with his publications to have brought to France knowledge of German language and civilization (Deyon 1997). Although beyond the purview of this Franco-German symposium, an important comparative question of diffusion is why after a late start in Weberian studies did American sociological interest in Weber grow rapidly and even today is far ahead of France?

Durkheim's *Elementary Forms* for a new generation of students.[13] Interest in Weber grew markedly under the general editorship of Marcel Mauss in the new series of the *Année*, which journal unfortunately lasted not even two complete volumes. But in the first of these (volume 1, 1923-24), Halbwachs gave ample scope to Weber's then recent publications , not only in extensive reviews of *Gesammelte Aufsätze zur Sozial-und Wirtschaftsgeschichte* (Weber's studies of ancient agrarian societies) and *Wirtschaftsgeschichte* (the economic history Weber had taught in 1920), but also in bringing in Weber in several adjoining reviews, notably that of the French translation of Sombart's *The Jews and Economic Life* (which Halbwachs notes he had already reviewed the original German edition in volume 12 of the *Année Sociologique*, the last to appear in Durkheim's editorship).[14]

Even as he developed his interests in demography and economic stratification, he also continued explorations in religious motivation as factors in economic development and collective consciousness. One may note that among the essays which make up the posthumous volume *The Psychology of Social Class*, Halbwachs again made extensive use of both French translations and German original editions of Sombart and especially of Weber in accounting for the transformation of collective mentalities and morality that have led to the modern industrial and entrepreneurial spirit.[15]

Halbwachs moved on from Strasburg in 1935 to become professor in Paris at the Sorbonne, and eventually gained the ultimate recognition in the French hierarchical academic milieu by a Chair of Social Psychology at the Collège de France in 1944.[16]

---

13   Maurice Halbwachs, *Sources of Religious Sentiment* (1925), New York: Free Press, 1962.

14   In his lengthy review of Sombart (*L'Année Sociologique* 1923-24, 1, ns., pages 745-48) which indicates Weber's sociology of religion as an important influence, Halbwachs opines that both Weber and Sombart err in attributing a causal relation between religious factors in all their form and economic facts. There may be in some religious sects and in some ethnic traditions some conditions favorable for aptitudes in economic conduct favorable for capitalism, he states, but it is the latter which is of interest in tracing the development of capitalism.

15   Halbwachs also promoted knowledge of Weber outside sociological circles. In 1925 he published an extensive account of the 1920 German edition of the *Protestant Ethic* essay in his article *Les origins puritaines du capitalisme* (*Revue d'histoire et de philosophie religieuse*, University of Strasburg Theological Faculty, March-April 1925: 132-57).

See "Urban Environment and Industrial Civilization, Part I", pp. 41-65 in Halbwachs, *The Psychology of Social Class* (1955), trans. C. Delavenay, with an introduction by G. Friedman. New York: The Free Press, 1958. It might be noted that Halbwachs in this essay also makes good use of other accounts of modern capitalism including Veblen, Tawney and Schumpeter.

16   War-time France and the German occupation had no respect for academic freedom and Halbwachs, always outspoken politically, was arrested by the Gestapo shortly after his appointment and perished in a concentration camp the following year. One is tempted to say

When Halbwachs was named professor at the Sorbonne in Paris, it was Georges Gurvitch (one of the founders in 1958 of the International Association of French-Speaking Sociologists, AISLF) who succeeded him at Strasburg. Gurvitch in turn later became Professor of Sociology at the Sorbonne and the most important French theorist in the post-war years. After a stay in Germany escaping from the Bolshevik Revolution, he had come to France having acquired a thorough knowledge of German philosophy, particularly the strong phenomenological current of the 1920s.[17] While features of the phenomenological approach are recurrent in Gurvitch's later theoretical analyses (such as the "multiplicity of social times" and the "depth levels of social structure"[18]), and while Marx and Fichte provided much inspiration for him, the same cannot be said of Weber. Gurvitch severely criticized the latter methodologically (for Weber's nominalism) and substantively in Weber's approach to law, religion and historical sociology.[19]

***

Having indicated this linkage in the 1920s and for some of the 1930s in the figure of Halbwachs, it might open up a path for archival research. Did Halbwachs in the courses he taught at the Sorbonne bring in German sociology and figures like Sombart and Weber? And reciprocally, was there in Weimar Germany a link to French sociology, and particularly to Durkheim? I can only speculate at this point that little if any attention may have been given, partly because Durkheim's positivism would not find a favorable soil in the first postwar decade, partly because in the subsequent Nazi period, its racist ideology would preclude acceptance of the head of a school who was both French and Jewish. And after World War II, despite the valiant efforts of Raymond Aron and later Julien Freund (himself at Strasburg) to bring the best of German sociology and Weber to the attention of students,[20] there was a long frost in the relation of French and German sociology,

---

that a precious link relating French and German sociology was severed. Happily, in recent years, translations of his writings have begun to appear in German, as noted by Jaisson and Baudelot (2007: 13f).

17   *Les Tendances Actuelles de la Philosophie Allemande*. Paris: Librairie J. Vrin, 1949 (new printing of 1930 edition).

18   For a brief overview of Gurvitch's sociology, see Phillip Bosserman, *Dialectical Sociology*. Boston: P. Sargent 1968; see also, Richard Swedberg, *Sociology as disenchantment: the evolution of the work of Georges Gurvitch*. Atlantic Highlands, N.J.: Humanities Press.

19   "Le monumental effort de Weber se solde donc par un formidable échec au point de vue sociologique," in his Chapter "Histoire de la Sociologie" in Georges Gurvitch, ed. *Traité de Sociologie*, vol. 1 (Paris: Presses Universitaires de France, 1958, p. 58.

20   See for example Aron's lucid *La Sociologie Allemande Contemporaine*. Paris: Presses Universitaires de France. 1966, and his "Introduction" to Max Weber, *Le Savant et le Politique*. Paris: Librairie Plon, 1959; for Julien Freund, see *The Sociology of Max Weber*, New York: Pantheon, 1968, and *Études sur Max Weber*. Geneva: Droz, 1990. Freund in his

a frost partly due to the bitter memory of yet another occupation of France by Germany, the third in less than a century. But beyond this, dominant aspects of French social theory in later postwar decades in the form of academic Marxism and postmodernism (Foucault, Althusser, Lyotard, Baudrillard and others) might have created a gulf between Durkheimian and Weberian studies.

Whatever the antecedents for the lack of diffusion of Weberian studies in France and reciprocally, now, however, the coming of the European Union with the 1992 Treaty of Maastricht, an historic "Entente Cordiale" between France and Germany, and a new generation for which the frontiers of the past have lifted are propitious conditions to rediscover a common ground to meet "the other".

III A Common Ground

The title of my piece seeks to point to a certain kindred concern between the two great contemporaries who inspire modern sociology as much epistemologically as ontologically. Bringing them together on a common ground, a historical meeting ground from which a dialogue can develop, is the raison d'être for this symposium. The superficial kindred nexus is not only because Durkheim spoke German but also because his name suggests his ancestors might have came from the other side of the Rhine.[21] Deeper kindred ties, however, exist because it is not wrong to say that Durkheim and Weber worked on adjacent fields of research, fields of research which practically abut on each other. To extend the metaphor, one can say that between the sociological field of Durkheim and that of Weber, there are certain ditches but also certain bridges.

The three major themes of this symposium – *theory of action, methodological orientation*, and lastly, *science, morality (morale) and politics* – allow us to have a real dialogue regarding the gaps and the bridges. Let me briefly point out some bridges, since several texts presented have already indicated points of divergence such as the "methodological individualism" of Weber contrasting with the "sociologistic" tendency of Durkheim (a divergence admirably refuted by Boudon in his presentation[22]), or again, the importance of historical documentation with the former in comparison to the preference for ethnological data with the latter.[23]

1988 preface to Hirschhorn notes the "reticence" if not "resistance" in France to Weber for epistemological and political reasons, and this well after the end of World War II.

21   Perhaps even from *Bad Turckheim,* although there is also a town Turckheim in Alsace. In any case in the archives of Epinal (where Durkheim was born and returned periodically) one can see the name of the family spelled " Turckheim".

22   Raymond Boudon, "Durkheim et Weber: Convergences de Méthode," pp. 99-122 in M.Hirschhorn and J. Coenen-Huther, eds *Durkheim, Weber. Vers la Fin des Malentendus.* Paris: L'Harmattan, 1994.

23   Hirschhorn after noting points of convergence comes down to stressing their basic divergence, even regarding Kant, by stating "the intellectual universe of Max Weber

The first theme of this symposium is the *theory of action*. Here, I wish to stress the work of Talcott Parsons in showing a convergence of Durkheim and Weber with a common voluntaristic approach to action, which is a refutation of a strict determinism sometime associated with Durkheim but more in keeping with Marxist structuralism.[24] Richard Münch has well noted the centrality of a Kantian ethics in Parsons's action theory.[25] One can expand this in pointing out that in the context of modern, urban industrial societies undergoing "disenchantment", a new appreciation of Kant (including neo-Kantianism) was essential for the European generation of Durkheim and Weber. It represented the safeguard of a transcendental morality outside the seemingly outdated frames of traditional religion on the one hand, and the immorality of the laissez-faire economics of the market place, on the other. Kant is, so to say, the great moralist of modernity, as much for the Third Republic as for Wilhelmine Germany, with his concerns to establish transcendental ethics (the "categorical imperative") and the conditions for a lasting peace.[26] As a normative derivative from Kantian ethics, to act with responsibility is to make choices and to exercise clear-mindedly one's functions in society; it is to exercise the freedom of the actor in the institutional context of the moment with its constraints. That connection to Kant seems to me a major bridge between Durkheim and Weber, establishing a link between texts such as *L'Éducation Morale (*especially chapter 7) and the conclusion of *Les Formes Élémentaires,* on the one hand, and on the other, *Politik als Beruf* and *Wissenschaft als Beruf.*[27] On a philosophical plane, Kant was an inspiration for each.

Regarding the theory of action which is central to Durkheim and Weber, Hans Joas at this conference has opened up an important consideration with a theory

---

and Durkheim differ," (Hirschhorn 1988: 43). In my original discussion of their seeming unawareness I thought the same, but have come to reconsider, as my discussion in the present paper will indicate.

24   Talcott Parsons, *The Structure of Social Action*, 2 vols. New York: The Free Press, 1968: 81f.

25   Richard Münch, "Talcott Parsons and the Theory of Action. I. The Structure of the Kantian Core," *American Journal of Sociology*, 86, 4 (January 1981): 709-39 , and "Talcott Parsons and the Theory of Action. II. The Continuity of Development," *American Journal of Sociology*, 87, 4 (January 1982): 771-826.

26   See for example, Immanuel Kant, *Toward Perpetual Peace,and other writings on politics, peace and history*, edited with an introduction by P. Kleingeld. New Haven: Yale University Press, 2006.

27   Emile Durkheim, *Moral Education: a study in the theory and application of the sociology of education,* foreword by P. Fauconnet, trans. by E.K. Wilson and H. Schnurer, ed. E.K. Wilson. New York: Free Press, 1961 (1934), and *The Elementary Forms of Religious Life,* trans. with an introduction by Karen E. Fields, New York: Free Press, 1995 (1912); Max Weber, *Politics as a Vocation* and *Science as a Vocation* in Hans Gerth and C. Wright Mills, trans., eds, *From Max Weber: Essays in Sociology*, New York: Oxford University Press.

of creativity.[28] He finds elements of this in Weber's concept of charisma and in Durkheim's reworking of the sacred which can bring forth new ideals and new institutions. I venture that his approach, rooted in the pragmatism of Dewey and Mead, does go beyond both the normative emphasis in Parsons and the utilitarian aspect of classical *homo economicus*, but still leaves space for a Kantian approach to ethics in advanced modernity. This is a theme that merits fuller attention in our theory dialogue.

The second theme of the symposium deals with *methodological orientations*. Durkheim and Weber had the merit of stating explicitly the question of method in sociology, the former in his *Rules of the Sociological Method*, the latter in various essays (available in French or English) such as *Roscher und Knies und die logischen Probleme der historischen Nationalökonomie* and *Die Objectivität sozialwissenschaftlicher und sozialpolitischer Erkenntnis*. There are here both many overlapping fields and many ditches. The positivism of Durkheim seems to agree with a causal and deterministic perspective on "social facts". His sociologism appears to attribute to sociological research normative implications for modern society. Weber, on the contrary, stresses the impossibility of reaching via (scientific) research value choices that would guide social action. He puts the stress on the individual, but, like Durkheim, he refuses to explain psychologically social institutions.[29]

It is ironic that Weber was termed an idealist and Durkheim a materialist. That in itself would deserve a long debate. Weber's sociology of religion did not seek to substitute a religious interpretation of history in place of an economic one. Weber, it might be said, refused monocausality in providing evidence for the conditioning of the cultural by the economic life and the mode of production, and conversely. As to Durkheim, one cannot really say that either his conception of society conditioned by a demographic factor of population density (in *The Division of Labor in Society*) or that of the religious life as ultimately generated in an exceptional social interaction of the collectivity, leads to a form of materialism. Although coming to the question of methodology from different venues, Durkheim and Weber seem to me to end up in convergence rather than divergence. For both, society as an historical reality is not only the result of interactions between institutions but it is also an intersubjective reality. For Weber, more than for Durkheim, society at the

---

28   "La théorie de l'action chez Durkheim et chez Weber: le problème de la créativité," pp. 53-71 in Hirschorn and Coenen-Huther, *op. cit.* See also Hans Joas, *The Creativity of Action.* Chicago: The University of Chicago Press, 1996. For a broader overview on action theory than under discussion here, see Michael W. Macy, "Action Theory," pp. 1-4 in Bryan S. Turner, ed., *The Cambridge Dictionary of Sociology.* Cambridge: Cambridge University Press, 2006.

29   *"Objectivity' in Social Science and Social Policy,"* pp. 50-112 in Max Weber, *The Methodology of the Social Sciences*, trans, and edited by E.A. Shils and H.A. Finch, New York: Free Press, 1949 (1904).

psychological level is composed of intersubjective realities.[30] Durkheim does not speak of understanding (*Verstehen*) as a method, but his brilliant "dynamogenesis" analysis in *The Elementary Forms* is undoubtedly a sociological hermeneutic of interpreting the collective experience of the sacred.

At bottom, Durkheim and Weber converge in viewing the future of modernity as open-ended. Durkheim in *Les Formes Elémentaires* leaves open the possibility of new ideals coming from unexpected social movements in the stirring of modern society, as took place in the early days of the French Revolution, and as perhaps he witnessed renovated in the Dreyfus affair. Weber in the equally well-known conclusion of *The Protestant Ethic* is cognizant that the rationalization process can deplete the cultural capital so much but that a return of the irrational, or new prophets, can also bring a new enchantment. And both Weber and Durkheim were sensitive to new turns in modernity having the potential of creativity, as well as an equally socially destructive "dark side".

Lastly, the third conference theme is a very large one: *science, morality, and politics*; each of these three warrants a colloquium but for the moment I will only briefly allude to them as other presentations will treat them more adequately.

Politically, Durkheim was a lifelong republican; Weber, after Germany's debacle in World War I, became one. Had they both survived, they might have become post-war architects of a new viable European republican regime as an alternative to the collapse of the Third Republic and Weimar Germany. In their lifetime, passionate as each was in the political affairs of their country, they did not seek political office. They were intellectuals through and through. Let's return briefly to the importance of the *Kathedersozialismus* in the forming of Durkheim and Weber. In 1873, Wagner, Schmoller, Brentano, Knapp and others established the *Verein für Sozialpolitik*[31] to reinject in economic life a dose of idealism and to stimulate a social action oriented toward workers seeking to better their conditions of life and work, while avoiding state intervention. A new social science came out of these concerns, as was to be the case later, at Chicago, with American sociology. Weber became a member of the *Verein* shortly after the stay of Durkheim in Germany, and his first empirical study on the condition of agrarian workers was commissioned by this association.[32] Certainly, neither Durkheim nor Weber wished for the classroom to become a place of political indoctrination. However, it must be added that on the political plane, both were drawn close to that of the *Kathedersozialismus* orientation, basically a form of democratic socialism. Both

---

30   On this, see Alfred Schutz, *The Phenomenology of the Social World,* trans. George Walsh and Frederick Lehnert, introd. G. Walsh. Evanston, IL: Northwestern University Press.

31   Originally founded in opposition to laissez-faire social policy, it is still in existence today as a politically neutral, interdisciplinary society with research and publications in all fields of economics. For details, see http://www.socialpolitik.org/vfs.php?mode=informati onen&lang=2.

32   Marianne Weber, *Max Weber, A Biography*, pp. 127-29.

were concerned with science, morality and politics, without confounding them as did many of their and our contemporaries, yet fully aware of the tensions in keeping the spheres of morality, science, and politics distinct, as shown in various writings and discourses.[33]

So, then, here very briefly are some markers for this present encounter of Durkheim and Weber and their contemporary heirs: Strasburg as a site of confluence of German and French culture, Kant as a philosophical inspiration, the *Kathedersozialismus* as a sociopolitical stimulus – a lot of elements in common for a new, and, hopefully this time, sustained dialogue between sociological first cousins.

References

Camic, Charles and Hans Joas, eds 2004. *The Dialogical Turn. New Roles for Sociology in the Posdisciplinary Age. Essays in Honor of Donald N. Levine.* Lanham, MD: Rowman & Littlefield.

Craig, John E. 1983. "Sociology and related disciplines between the wars: Maurice Halbwachs and the imperialism of the Durkheimians, " pp. 263-89 in Philippe Besnard, ed. *The sociological domain. The Durkheimians and the founding of French sociology*, with a preface by Lewis. A. Coser. Cambridge & New York: Cambridge University Press, Paris: Éditions de la Maison des Sciences de l'Homme.

Deyon, Pierre 1997. "Maurice Halbwachs et l'histoire de son temps," pp. 17-20 in Christian de Montlibert, ed., *Maurice Halbwachs 1877-1945.* Strasbourg: Presses Universitaires de Strasbourg.

Hirschhorn, Monique 1988. *Max Weber et la Sociologie Française*, préface de Julien Freund. Paris: Éditions de l'Harmattan.

Jaisson, Marie and Christian Baudelot. 2007. *Maurice Halbwachs, sociologue retrouvé.* Paris: Editions Rue d'Ulm/Presses de l'École Normale Supérieure.

---

33   For Weber, see his classical "Politics as a Vocation," and "Science as a Vocation" in Hans Gerth and C. Wright Mills, eds, *From Max Weber: Essays in Sociology.* New York: Oxford University Press, 1958; Wolfgang J. Mommsen, *Max Weber and German Politics 1890-1920*, M. S. Steinberg, trans. Chicago and London: University of Chicago Press, 1990 (1974). For Durkheim, see his *Professional Ethics and Civic Morals,* trans. Cornelia Brookfield, London: Routledge & Kegan Paul 1957 (1950); *Emile Durkheim on Morality and Society*, edited with an introduction by Robert N. Bellah, Chicago: University of Chicago Press, 1973; W. Watts Miller, *Durkheim, Morals and Modernity.* Montreal & Kingston, London: McGill-Queen's University Press, 1996.

Chapter 16

Collective Effervescence, Social Change, and Charisma: Durkheim, Weber, and 1989[1]

Introduction

The dynamics of social change may be said to constitute the *Urgrund* or original matrix of sociological reflection, starting with Saint-Simon seeing the need of a "social physiology" science to make sense of the social turmoil attending the post-1789 European scene. Two hundred years later, and hundreds if not thousands of sociological writings later, the topic of social change retains all its pregnancy, prodded in just a few recent years by the unexpected transformations of seemingly monolithic structures of power. Clio has been immensely generous: to her children in the West she gave the events of "1968" and to those in the East she gave the events of "1989,"[2] both immense historical moments, unpredicted by almost all social scientists irrespective of their ideological persuasion. Much of the contemporary world may be seen as resultant of these two moments of social change, or at least profoundly affected by them. While we search and sift through the still-settling dust in terms of changing institutions, social arrangements and collective identities, we can only agree with Sztompka's recent framing of contemporary social change as signifying an ontological "becoming of the very mechanism of becoming", that "social becoming changes its mode in the course of history" (Sztompka 1993: 230).

Let me restate this in a more prosaic manner. While some historians and many social scientists have sought to provide neat models, causal or otherwise, to account for what may happen in the future in the image of their interpretations of the dynamics of what happened in the past, the seemingly staid present continues

---

1   First published in *International Sociology*, 10, no. 1 (September 1995): 269-81.

2   I use "1968" to denote both an extraordinary year and a period of time, roughly 1967-1972, marked by intense sociocultural and sociopolitical challenges to established states, for the most part of the liberal-industrial kind, with universities as epicenters of attempted revolutions. I use "1989" to indicate a similar extraordinary year/period marked by the predominantly successful challenges to established socialist states that had Marxism-Leninism as an official ideology and the Communist Party as the sole recognized political association. "1989" may be said to have started with the reforms "from above" launched by M. Gorbachev shortly after he took office and the policy of *glasnost*, or open discussion and criticism of policy, and *perestroika*, or attempted structural changes in the economy; it came to an end in late 1991 with the dissolution of the Soviet Union.

to surprise us. The events of "1968," which ultimately must be thought of as a cultural revolution that challenged the legitimacy of established authority everywhere, particularly in the West, and the events of "1989" – ultimately an extension of "1968" in the political and cultural spheres – were major surprises. No less a surprise recently is the rejection of apartheid for a democratically elected government of South Africa, and the peace initiatives in the Middle East which may lead to Israel becoming recognized by more Arab states as a potential partner in the development of the region. Nor, in this quick enumeration of surprises in a presumably "disenchanted" world of modernity, should we overlook the rapid spread in the past quarter of a century (or less) of Islamic fundamentalism as a force threatening established "secular" states, some of which, like Algeria, Egypt and Turkey, had their "modern" or "modernizing" revolution a good while ago. And for good measure, mention should also be made of various forms of nationalism, including "ethnonationalism" (Connor 1994), that have taken place as domestic challenges to regimes of very different sorts: liberal, authoritarian and communist alike.

From this initial reflection we see that the condition of modernity cannot be accounted for in terms of any determinate equation or unilinear trend, for "surprises" entail unexpected reversals or changes in direction. Once the "surprise" happens, of course, social scientists are not at a loss to provide rational accounts of why what took place happened in the way it did. That, in a sense, is not as challenging a task as a more serious challenge, namely to accept that as part of the historical process, as part of the historicity of the human condition, surprises will happen: agencies and social structures combine and recombine in new ways. That is very much part of social becoming changing its modes of becoming. Sociologists have tacitly accepted this by espousing the principle of "the unintended consequences of purposive action" (which goes back at least to Durkheim and Wundt). Sometimes, however, we tend to forget that it does take individuals and not just anyone to undertake a purposive action that will set in motion an important train of actions that affect a collectivity, even if the impact is not readily apparent or if its long-term consequences differ from short-term intentions and consequences.

For example, in terms of some of the 'surprises' we have witnessed in recent years, if the leaders of South Africa in 1992-93 had been other than Mandela and De Klerk, or those of Israel and the Palestine Liberation Organization other than Rabin and Arafat, or in the Soviet Union in the late 1980s other than Gorbachev, we can say that the dramatic initiatives that have brought important structural changes would not have occurred. And if they had not, we might be left with accounts as to why they did not take place when the rest of the world was moving towards new paths of social change. Inertia, in the sense of a social system or a collectivity failing to make adaptive changes, has sometimes been attributed to "national character" or to the force of "tradition" prevailing. There is some truth in this; most of the time, most members of society are conservative in their orientation to the everyday world. Yet, on some occasions a significant number of persons are sufficiently willing to change their orientation to the everyday world and take risks to reject the institutional structure and arrangements that reproduce the world, and real structural changes *do* take place.

There are two major foci of investigations to deal with the mechanisms or dynamics which underpin real structural changes: those dealing with *revolutions* and those dealing with *charisma*. These are well-trodden sociological avenues and there is little need to go over familiar signposts. In this paper I would like to propose that the events of 1989 provide new wines for these familiar casks.[3] More concretely, the following deserve particular consideration:

Sociological models and images of revolutions, from Marx and de Tocqueville on down, have taken these large-scale transformations to entail violence: either civil war or external war or the latter as a precondition for the exhaustion of the state, permitting a revolutionary take-over. Yet, in 1989, the Soviet system began to crash with minimal violence and no major external war (unless it is argued that the Afghanistan war had a crippling effect on the Soviet state).

From the nineteenth century on, socialism was seen as a progressive force, with its vanguard, or avant-garde, in the form of the revolutionary party, taking the lead in revolutionary change. Once a socialist revolution or seizure of power took place, a certain irreversible development beyond "bourgeois" society was assumed to happen. Yet, in the past five years, not only in the Soviet Union and its former satellites but also in far-flung regions of Africa and Southeast Asia, democratization in the form of market economy and sanctioning of political parties other than the Communist Party has taken or is taking place, leading to new ways of accounting for the unexpected "demise of state socialism."[4]

What is the bearing of charisma in this new revolutionary period of change? Revolutionary periods of earlier times, including those of the Third World in the anti-colonial movements in this century, have recognized charismatic leaders – Robespierre and Danton, Lenin and Sun Yat-Sen, Castro, Che Guevara and Mao Zedong, for example – but the revolutionary periods of "1989" and "1968" are characterized more by the absence of charismatic figures. Is there a place for the notion of charisma in accounting for the dramatic changes of East Europe?

In trying to come to grips with these questions, we might begin to provide a meaningful interpretation of the dynamics of the historical changes we have witnessed by recombining the analyses of Weber and Durkheim. Essentially, I first propose that "charisma" and "collective effervescence" are complementary notions (if not obverse sides of the same coin) and second, that using them in combination provides an important ingress to understanding how social actors even in coercive secular states that have a monopoly of power are able, in certain exceptional circumstances, to rise and disarm the state.

---

3   Although I will not deal with them here, for purpose of economy, I view the global cluster of politico-cultural events of "1968" as complementary and antecedent to those of 1989, even if the former occurred primarily in non-Communist countries.

4   See the special issue on "The Theoretical Implications of the Demise of State Socialism," *Theory and Society* 1994.

Convergence of Durkheim and Weber[5]

Although Durkheim's sociological realism contrasts with Weber's methodological individualism, I argue that a reading of key passages in their respective treatment of how the ordinary world of everyday life is transformed will show sufficient overlap to establish an important theoretical convergence – a convergence different from the one that Parsons (1937) established in his classic synthesis. This convergence, with the focus on the dynamics of change provided by a situational analysis of "charisma" and "collective effervescence," can be applied successfully to understand the dynamics of the "revolutions" of 1989. We need now to reconsider the basic classical texts of Durkheim and Weber. Key passages are to be found in Durkheim *EFRL* (book II, chapter 7, "Origins of these Beliefs, contd.") and Weber *ES* (vol. I, chapter 3, the initial discussion of "Charismatic Authority," and vol II, chapter 14, the later discussion of "Charisma and its Transformation").

We are all familiar with Weber's main emphasis on charisma as a type of authority that challenges traditional and rational, particularly bureaucratic, authority (*ES*: 244). Historically speaking, Weber saw charismatic leadership as a particularly potent revolutionary force in "traditionalist" or "prerationalistic" periods (*ES*: 245). Much of his analysis of charisma deals with its routinization over time in offices and institutions, including occupations and social stratification.[6] Although Weber gave a passing nod to the presence of charismatic revolutionary leadership in Germany in the wake of World War I, he was skeptical that charisma could overcome the forces of growing economic interdependence and the routinization of life (*ES*: 252).[7] What seems to propel charisma to its routinization is "naturally the striving for security," on the one hand, and the need for "some definite order" in the administrative staff on the other hand (*ES*: 252). I discuss later how this observation has to be modified in light of the changes we have witnessed in the past quarter of a century, and particularly those pertaining to "1989." Let me finish this brief exposition by noting in Weber's discussion some of the characteristics of the social setting in which the charismatic figure appears: it is not during routine, ordinary institutional times but "in moments of distress" (*ES*: 1111), or alternatively,

---

5   For Weber, I am using *Economy and Society* (1978; hereafter *ES*) and Gerth and Mills (1958). For additional material see Eisenstadt (1968). For Durkheim I am using *The Elementary Forms of the Religious Life* (1965; hereafter *EFRL*).

6   See Eisenstadt's (1968) discussion in his introductory essay, "Charisma and Institution Building: Max Weber and Modern Sociology."

7   In this respect, Weber's analysis of charisma might have left him unprepared for the eruption of charismatic leadership, both personal and collective, in different settings (traditionalist, colonial, industrial-liberal and industrial-socialist) of the contemporary world in the past seventy-five years.

from unusual, especially political or economic situations, or from extraordinary psychic, particularly religious states, or from both together. It arises from *collective excitement* produced by extraordinary events and from surrender to heroism of any kind 1121, my emphasis).

I refer to Weber's discussion later, but with mention of "collective excitement" in Weber, it is time to pass on to Durkheim. Just as Weber emphasised the "extra-ordinary" feature of the appearance of charisma, and how this is particularly in opposition to mundane economic considerations (*ES*: 244), so also did Durkheim situate the genesis of the sacred in a phase of social life which is "extra-ordinary," where "ordinary" is the everyday world of economic activity (*EFRL*: 246). Never mind that Durkheim's data are predominantly drawn from a non-Western traditionalist society (although he also put to good use historical material, from the extra-ordinary setting of the French Revolution[8]). Where Weber speaks of "moments of distress," Durkheim speaks of "periods in history when, under the influence of some great collective shock, social interactions have become much more frequent and active." And he continues: "That general effervescence results which is characteristic of revolutionary or creative epochs" (*EFRL*: 241).

Essentially, then, Durkheim and Weber both look at unusual, extraordinary periods for challenges to institutionalized authority, and for these challenges to take place, the actors involved must transcend the attitudes of everyday life: for Weber and Durkheim alike, actors must be capable of acts of heroism born out of enthusiasm. The assembling of the group is background to Weber's discussion of charismatic leadership, and it is foreground to Durkheim. Durkheim's discussion, without using the term, does make room for what we can recognize in Weber as charismatic authority. It is for Durkheim (but also for Weber) a special relational structure between an individual who is able to "put in play," so to speak, and to articulate the strong emotions, the aspirations, the pent-up feelings of the collectivity:

> This is the explanation of the particular attitude of a man speaking to a crowd, at least if he has succeeded in entering into communion with it. His language has a grandiloquence that would be ridiculous in ordinary circumstances; his very thought is impatient of all rules and easily falls into all sorts of excesses. *It is because he feels within him an abnormal over-supply of force which overflows and tries to burst out from him; sometimes he even has the feeling that he is dominated by a moral force which is greater than he and of which he is only the interpreter* (*EFRL:* 241, my emphasis).

---

8   Note for example Durkheim's reference to the historical night of August 4, 1789, when the National Assembly voted away feudal privileges. For a more extensive discussion of the French Revolution as Durkheim's "other" source of data in the *EFRL*, see Tiryakian (1988a).

If we juxtapose the texts of Durkheim and Weber, we may readily see the overlapbetween "collective effervescence" and "charisma." To be sure, they are not identical, partly because Weber's model of the charismatic figure whose followers have a duty to obey is based on religious saviors while Durkheim, talking here of "the demon of oratorical inspiration" (*EFRL*: 241) may have had in mind more political figures, not only Robespierre and Danton but Durkheim's own contemporary, the great socialist leader Jean Jaurès. However, the difference is slight.If we want to apply the convergence to the revolutionary situation of 1989, there is one more point to make: the effect of the extraordinary situation on the individuals who participate in the assembly, or, in Weber's term, in the "charismatic community." Durkheim proposed that in the revolutionary or creative moments of general effervescence,

> ... this greater activity results in a general stimulation of individual forces. *Men see more and differently now than in normal times ... men become different. The passions moving them are of such intensity that they cannot be satisfied except by ... actions of superhuman heroism or of bloody barbarism* (*EFRL*: 241, my emphasis).

Weber echoes and amplifies this somewhat by noting that charismatic belief revolutionizes men "from within" rationalization and rational organization revolutionizes "from the outside," whereas charisma, if it has any specific effects at all, manifests its revolutionary power from within from a central *metanoia* [change] of the followers' attitudes (*ES*: 1117, emphasis in original).

Weber, quite correctly, sees that charisma is *the* revolutionary force of history because of its nature of casting aside in its followers' attitudes towards the world "all notions of sanctity," including those born of rules either of tradition or of rational bureaucracy.[9]

In Durkheim and Weber there is one unstated aspect of the attitudinal transformation that merits our attention. It is that being in and part of the charismatic/effervescent tradition gives the charismatic community a sense of *power* – power not based on control of physical or material resources, but effective power nonetheless by virtue of being part of a moral community. One may say that this sentiment of empowerment, which occurs only in certain moments, transforms the group into a charismatic community, transforms, ultimately, social structure into agency; or, if I understand him correctly, what Touraine (1992) calls *subjectification*.

If the community is pitted against the holders of rational-bureaucratic or of traditional organizations in these circumstances, it may at certain moments be repressed by physical violence. This may prevent the toppling of the regime but

---

9   In terms of phenomenological analysis, charisma has the effect of setting aside the "natural attitude" of the *Lebenswelt*, of exploding the meaning structures which relate actors in their everyday life to the objects of their situation.

at the same time produce martyrs, from the early Christian martyrs to more recent ones, such as Imre Nagy in Hungary (1956), Jan Palach in Czechoslovakia (1969), Father Jerzy Popieluszko in Poland (1984) and the pro-democracy students who died in Beijing in June 1989. However, there are other moments when the forces of tradition or of rational bureaucratic organizations have so squandered or diluted the routinized charisma of their office (from which they draw their privileges) that they have *de facto* lost legitimacy. It is at such times that the feeling of empowerment that comes in the assembling and interaction of rank and file with spokesmen (to use these more neutral terms in place of "followers" and "leaders") becomes an especially potent lever of social change, of "social becoming." Such a period was "1989" in East Europe, as had been "1968" in West Europe.

"1989"

There are several striking aspects of the revolutions that shook the Soviet world in 1989. One is the rapidity with which the revolutionary process went through the entire system: the seemingly monolithic empire went through the shedding of the communist mantle from the East European periphery to the hinterland Central Asian region and even the Russian heartland within a three year span. Another is the absence of violence on the part of those seeking to topple the regime, matched by the amazing restraint of the authorities who had a short while before used violence to supplement the virtual monopoly of the media in propagating regime ideology. In these two respects, the events of "1989" are similar in their dynamics to the toppling of the colonial empires in Africa during the five-year period of 1957-62.[10]

The socialist societies of East Europe and the USSR, on the eve of the revolution, or what Ash (1990: 14) termed "refolution" in acknowledgement of the "reforms from above" interacting with popular pressures from below, had many features in common. Those that have a bearing on the analyses of Durkheim and Weber may be rapidly summarized in the following manner: Throughout the Soviet empire there was predominantly an absence and repression of civil society (Miller 1992). The conditions noted by Andorka (1993) for Hungary were typical: a lack of civility and self-reliance, a high level of distrust, *anomie* and powerlessness, even as the overall political system moved towards a "softer authoritarianism." The public sphere was monopolized by official ideology, and this was known and understood by all to be a system "living in lie," with official statistics meaningless. This was as true for thoseliving in the "centre" as for those in the "periphery." So,

---

10   It might be pointed out in passing that the African setting of the late 1950s and early 1960s was also one of collective effervescence and charismatic leadership, reflected in such figures as Jomo Kenyatta, Kwame Nkrumah, Sékou Touré, Hastings Banda and others.

for example, what Rose recently notes about the Russians was equally applicable to citizens of the Soviet republics, East and West:

> To protect themselves against claims of the state, many Russians practiced "defensive alienation." Apathetic conformity was the mask shown to authorities (1994 : 52).

Likewise, for instance, in the Baltics where "During the 40 years of soviet power Estonians had become remote from state power as well as from politics generally"(Rosimannus 1991). One difference between centre and periphery was that for many in the periphery (e.g., in the Baltics and the Central Asian Republics) the more important "modern," prestigeful and powerful occupations of the industrial and bureaucratic managerial sectors were assigned to non-natives and immigrants (Bankovskaya 1992). Even the early reform movement launched by Gorbachev did not produce the intended results but rather emphasized the faults of the system. What Gorbachev might not have realized, in retrospect, is that to ask people to speak up and make their views known is contingent on the people's basic commitment and trust in the system; this was lacking throughout the system, in the centre as well as the periphery.

Again, in the case of Estonia as prototypical, Estonians saw local state authorities as only representatives of "the occupation power and the essentially alien soviet regime and were implementers of the colonization and russification politics of the centre" (Rosimannus 1991).

As Rosimannus notes further, in 1984 the Estonians' index of contentment with the governing of society was 3.9 on a 7-point scale (which he cautions might have an upward bias because of respondents' fear of repression); by April 1988 it had fallen to 2.7, with discontent expressed towards "all the power structures embracing the system as such."

Five years or so before 1989, East Europe and the Soviet Union appeared to have a fixed political system, one that was recognized as repressive but, as Jeanne Kirkpatrick (1982) believed, not subject to change since it was "totalitarian" and not "authoritarian." Systemic change was not in the cards, at least not in the foreseeable future. It turned out, of course, that the "timelessness" (or "post-historical" in orthodox Marxist perspective) of the socialist system was deceiving, a time "*trompe l'oeil*" (or "deceptive time") in Georges Gurvitch's (1964) typology of social times, when things appear routine and ordinary but vast structural changes are covertly taking place.

It was in fact a period applicable to the conceptual framework derived from Durkheim and Weber. There were external, exogenous factors that played into the situation, and certainly the new reform leadership of the Communist Party was one of these. So too was the significance of television and other mass media which in the 1980s made the Soviet Empire much more porous than previously, and certainly made even those reputedly having the highest standard of living in the East, the East Germans, aware of the discrepancy between their economic conditions and those of "Wessies." So too was the presence of a hardline anti-Communist in the White House.[11]

But these exogenous factors, together with the internal decay and corruption of the regime – the extent of the latter, including the corruption of the environment not disclosed until after the end of the system – are not sufficient to account for the revolution. What played "an equally important part in this most unexpected social becoming was grass-roots social mobilization, with students and intellectuals playing an important role in what I view as movements of national renewal, digging deep into the seemingly buried cultural capital to restore or revivify collective symbols that had been thought laid to rest by the communist regimes. Social mobilization, the coming together of persons in public places, had been, of course, used by fascist and communist regimes, but the social mobilization seen in 1988-91 was on a voluntary basis, very much in keeping with Durkheim's discussion of the social assembly.

Given the fact that the state did have a monopoly of the means of violence, it was a remarkable set of acts of heroism to assemble, to protest peacefully. The demonstrators made use of the Helsinki Declaration of Human Rights, which the USSR had endorsed earlier in the decade for its own foreign political agenda – but which backfired.

Gathering in open public spaces signified many things: an overcoming of fear of repression, an overcoming of the compartmentalization of the private and the public spheres, ultimately, then, an overcoming of the alienation of the socialist system. As a keen eyewitness observer of the events of 1989 noted:

> … as they stood and shouted together, these men and women were not merely healing divisions in their society; they were healing divisions in themselves … The semantic occupation was as offensive to them as military occupation; cleaning up the linguistic environment as vital as cleaning up the physical environment. The long queue every morning in Wenceslas Square [Prague], lining up patiently in the freezing fog for a newspaper called *The Free Word*, was for me, one of the great symbolic pictures of 1989 (Ash 1990).

---

11   I well remember my first visit to East Europe in 1986. In the course of giving a talk at Jagiellonian University in Krakow, I saw some puzzled faces when I talked about the U. S. foreign policy toward Nicaragua. Afterwards some students came to me and asked, "We thought you were a good guy until you started attacking Solidarity." Astonished, I said, "How could you say that? I am completely supportive of what Solidarity stands for!" The students then told me, "When you criticized Reagan's policy towards Nicaragua because of their Marxist government, you are criticizing the person who wants Poland free from communism!"

Every setting, or nearly every setting, had its mass demonstration, althoughthe particulars of the occasion that led to the assembly differed.[12] Poland had led it in 1980, of course, with the Gdansk strikes, and a key stimulus was the visit of the first Polish pope in the previous year. In January 1989 protesters gathered around the statue of King Wenceslas in Prague to mark the death of the student Jan Palach who set fire to himself on 16 January 1969 to protest against the 1968 Warsaw Pact invasion of Czechoslovakia. On May Day, the official rally was disrupted by human rights groups in the historic Wenceslas Square. But social mobilization in Czechoslovakia reached a peak in November, particularly when Václav Havel assumed or became Durkheim's "interpreter" of collective sentiments. Ash (1990: 89) characterizes Havel in those days of November as "charismatic": "It was extraordinary the degree to which everything ultimately revolved around this man ... the one person who could somehow balance the very different tendencies and interests in the movement." In this extraordinary setting one can say that the charismatic community, the "people" with whom the charismatic figure interacts, becomes all inclusive:

> For those in the Magic Lantern, 'the people' meant first of all Prague. In a sense all of Prague became a Magic Lantern. It was not just the great masses on Wenceslas Square. It was the improvised posters all over the city, the strike committees in the factories, the Civic Forum committees that were founded in hospitals, schools and offices ... It was ordinary people on the streets (p. 90).

The numbers grew, almost exponentially; 300,000 people greeted Havel, Alexander Dubček and Cardinal Tomasek on November 24 with a spontaneous shaking of key-rings that produced "a sound like massed Chinese bells"; the next day, 500,000 came to the Letna football stadium in Prague, interacting with the speakers in a way that exemplified Durkheim's discussion. Citing Ash again:

> Various speakers address the crowd, one calls in the name of Jesus Christ to ask the crowd 'to stamp out the devil.' Then *in the extraordinary way these crowds have of talking back to the speakers* they give an almost instant response, 'The devil is in the castle, the devil is in the castle' [the Castle in Prague is the seat of the government] (p. 99, my emphasis).

In Hungary, the occasion of mass mobilization was the reburial on 16 June 1989 of Imre Nagy and four of his close associates; almost 300,000 people attended the state funeral at Rakoskeresztur cemetery before a nationally televised audience. A government commission had decided that Nagy, the popular leader of 1956, executed by the Kadar regime in 1958, was a genuine reformer and not

---

12   Unless otherwise noted, I have drawn my discussion of specific events in various countries from two reference sources: *Eastern Europe and the Commonwealth of Independent States 1992* and *Keesing's Record of World Events*.

a "counter-revolutionary traitor." The year before, on the occasion of the 140th anniversary of the Hungarian uprising against Austrian rule, 10,000 had marched to demand genuine reforms; a year later, on 15 March, 100,000 demonstrated in Budapest against the government, using the same occasion of the anniversary of the Hungarian uprising against an unpopular alien regime. Nagy's reburial was, in effect, a public resurrection of an autonomous Hungary, including the flying of the red, green and white national flags without the hammer and sickle. This was followed by other symbolic and real acts of autonomy, such as the September opening of the border with Austria to allow the exodus of East Germans and the October renunciation by the Socialist Party of Marxism in favor of democratic socialism – the first time in history that a ruling communist party had done so.

In Romania, which had not budged towards reform because of the tyranny of its Stalinist leader Ceausescu, an anti-government protest against the "systematization policy" of Romanian villages had focused on an ethnic Hungarian pastor, Laszlo Tokes, in the Transylvanian city of Timisoara. It is noteworthy that Romanians joined ethnic Hungarians in protecting the pastor from the police. Their vigil was the spark that set off demonstrations in Bucharest, Cluj and elsewhere against the brutal regime, and toppled Ceausescu during the last days of December 1989. Again, it was a collective act of heroism for the crowd to drown out Ceausescu with pro-democracy slogans during his speech at an official rally from the balcony of the Royal Palace in Bucharest, the sort of heroism which is involved in the sense of empowerment of the social assembly.

The meeting of the XIIIth World Congress of the International Sociological Association in Bielefeld, Germany, five years after the dramatic events of 1989 that paved the way for the surprise unification of Germany, is an appropriate additional marker of that *annus mirabilis*. The fall of the Berlin wall, a global media event that symbolized the end of an era of estrangement which had, symbolically, been announced by Winston Churchill in 1946, climaxed a year of surprises. Let me mention in passing the increasing frequency of public demonstrations in the former German Democratic Republic, with the active support of the church, during the summer months and into the fall preceding those November days. Since so many settings of collective effervescence had as part of the mobilization collective symbols, including religious ones, it is well to remember that St Nicholas Church in Leipzig was an important rallying point, a symbolic space independent of the public sphere. During September and October the regular attendance at the Monday evening "prayers for peace" grew in size into the tens and even hundreds of thousands.[13] Needless to say, a global audience of hundreds of millions saw the world's largest or most impressive "walkathon" on the weekend of 10-11 November 1989, when 2,000,000 East Germans flooded through breaches of the Wall (most of them returned after a quiet walk that ended the national cleavage).

---

13   "The epicenter of the revolution was in Leipzig, at the church of St. Nicholas and outside at the Karl Marx Platz" (Ash 1990: 67ff).

Although germane to the general framework of this paper, I will not dwell on the charismatic/effervescent setting of the late 1960s ("1968"). Nor on other recent settings, such as Nicaragua, Iran, and Poland in 1979-80 or the Philippines in 1985-86, where I would argue that the phenomenon of the commingling of charismatic leadership and collective effervescence took place as the empowerment of the societal community rising against unpopular regimes that had hitherto a virtual monopoly on the apparatus of power (Tiryakian 1988b).

Conclusion

I have sought to propose in this paper the convergent features in the sociology of religion of Durkheim and Weber, which may provide us with a new understanding of the dynamics of social change and collective action in the contemporary world. The days of collective effervescence and charismatic settings are not ordinary days, nor are they things of the dim past only. The events of "1989" discussed here, with a focus on the symbolic recapture of the public sphere by the nation *qua* societal community (Parsons 1969), are not sufficient in themselves to account for the demise of an extensive and well- entrenched regime as was the soviet regime. Obviously, antecedent factors of economic deterioration, the 1986 environmental disaster of the nuclear explosion in Chernobyl and a new generation of reformers in various countries all played a role in this demise; but the sparks of the implosion, so to speak, are the social mobilizations treated above, and these involve transformations of the attitudes of the everyday life for which the complementary analysis of Durkheim and Weber is essential.

The assembling of the collectivity in different public places in East Europe (and the former USSR) had been routinized in the soviet period (as it had been in fascist regimes) as secular command performances from the top (e.g., May Day parades or the celebration of the anniversary of the revolution). But in the extraordinary days of 1989 the assembling was spontaneous, it was an authentic coming together of the nation protesting the usurpation of the public sphere by the state. In the assembling, the individuals, either in place or watching on television, felt the empowerment that arises from the experience of a transcendent order (for a more extensive discussion of experiences of transcendent order, see Berger 1992).

East Europe and the territories of the former USSR have gained much in the way of political freedoms. They have (re)established the basis of national identity, but the "good surprises" of five years ago are giving way to a different cycle of events. If West Europe is trying to shake off an economic recession which has generated or promoted new minority nationalist movements, East Europe and perhaps even more acutely Russia are experiencing great economic and social distress. The national unity that characterized the moment of 1989 (or somewhat later for parts of the periphery) is undermined by degrading socioeconomic conditions for the older generation, lack of employment opportunities for the younger and a new meltdown of trust and confidence in large sectors of the population. Hence the appearance of Vladimir Zhirinovsky (Morrison 1994; Specter 1994), and the return to (elected) power by ex-Communists who are now social democrats in Lithuania, Poland, Hungary and elsewhere as indications that a new cycle of collective effervescence and charismatic authority may be on the way. The movements of 1989 were exhilarating and constructive, while they delegitimated an abhorrent system. But since then the democratization process in the self-liberated countries seems to be floundering and faltering, perhaps with the exception of the unification process in Germany and one or two other "success" stories. The next set might not be so constructive, for Durkheim and Weber were also aware of the possibility of "violent and unrestrained actions ... of bloody barbarism" – as we saw in Germany in the 1930s.

In this millenarian decade, social becoming will continue to surprise, and there may well be other occasions, in Europe and elsewhere, when the collectivity will leave their television sets and virtual reality games in order to assemble in the public space of reality to find themselves as a nation and define or redefine a common trajectory.

References

Andorka, R. 1993. "The Socialist System and its Collapse in Hungary: An Interpretation in Terms of Modernization Theory." *International Sociology* 8 (September): 317-337.

Ash, T. G. 1990. *The Magic Lantern. The Revolution of '89 Witnessed in Warsaw, Budapest, Berlin, and Prague*. New York: Random House.

Bankovskaya, S. P. 1992. "On the 'Birth-marks' of Socialism in Latvia,' in Nikula, J. and Melin, H. eds, *Fragmentary Visions of Social Change – Poland, Latvia, and Finland*. Tampere, Finland: University of Tampere, Department of Sociology and Social Psychology, Working Papers B:34.

Berger, P. L. 1992. *A Far Glory: The Quest for Faith in an Age of Credulity*. New York: Free Press.

Connor, W. 1994. *Ethnonationalism. The Quest for Understanding*. Princeton: Princeton University Press.

Durkheim, E. 1965. *The Elementary Forms of Religious Life* trans. By J. W. Swain. New York: Free Press.

Eastern Europe and the Commonwealth of Independent States 1992. London: Europa Press.

Eisenstadt, S. N. ed. 1968. *Max Weber on Charisma and Institution Building*. Chicago: University of Chicago Press.

Gerth, H. and C. W. Mills 1958. *From Max Weber: Essays in Sociology*. New York: Galaxy.

Gurvitch, G. 1964. *The Spectrum of Social Time*. Dordrecht: D. Reidel. *Keesing's Record of World Events*. 1989. 35(1).

Hechter, M. and I. Szelinyi eds 1994. "The Theoretical Implications of the Demise of State Socialism," *Theory and Society* 23 (2) Special Issue, April.

Kirkpatrick, J. J. 1982. *Dictatorships and Double Standards*. New York: American Enterprise Institute/Simon & Schuster.

Miller, R. F. (ed.) 1992. *The Development of Civil Society in Communist Systems*. North Sydney, Australia: Allen and Unwin.

Morrison, J. W. 1994. "Vladamir Zhirinovsky, An Assessment of a Russian Ultra-Nationalist." McNair Paper 30. Washington, D. C.: Institute for National Strategic Studies, National Defense University.

Parsons, T. 1937. *The Structure of Social Action*. New York: Macmillan.

Parsons, T. 1969. *Politics and Social Structure*. New York: Free Press.

Rose, R. 1994. "Getting by Without Government: Everyday Life in Russia." *Daedalus* 123 (Summer): 41-62.

Rosimannus, R. 1991. "State Power and Public Confidence in Estonia 1985-1991," *Emor Reports* (1, July-September): 15.

Specter, S. 1994. "Why Russia Loves this Man." *New York Times Magazine* 19 June.

Sztompka, P. 1993. *The Sociology of Social Change*. Oxford: Blackwell, p. 230.

Tiryakian, E. A. 1988a. "The Political Context of a Sociological Classic: Durkheim, Mathiez, and the French Revolution." *European Journal of Sociology* 29(2): 373-396.

Tiryakian, E. A. 1988b. "From Nicaragua with Love," in J. Alexander ed., *Durkheimian Cultural Studies*. New York: Cambridge University Press.

Touraine, A. 1992. *Critique de la Modernité*. Paris: Fayard.

Weber, M. 1978. *Economy and Society*, ed. Roth, G. and Wittich, C. Berkeley: University of California Press.

Chapter 17
On the Shoulders of Weber and Durkheim: East Asia and Emergent Modernity[1]

I Introduction

An interesting conjuncture has taken place during this momentous decade of the 1980s. On the one hand, Western commentators and analysts are grudgingly becoming more and more aware that the Pacific Rim, particularly the East Asian countries, is the most economically dynamic if not aggressive region. If, at the beginning of the decade, American Department of State officials and other public figures were praising "our Japanese ally," today I would judge the tone to be a more apprehensive and defensive one; the cover of a recent issue of *The Economist* depicting Japan as a huge sumo wrestler is symptomatic of a "Japan bashing" that is unfortunately not that far removed from refurbishing the image of the "Yellow Peril" which permeated the American image of Asia before World War I. On the other hand, and undoubtedly related to the first, is an uneasy *malaise* that America's "good times" are coming to an end, reflected in a recent poll of *The Wall Street Journal* (May 1, 1989) showing that "Americans who think the standard of living is falling narrowly outnumber those who think it is rising." Two years ago, a respected journalist commented on a speech given at Harvard University by Professor Paul Streeten of Oxford University; the latter having enunciated the thesis that *Pax Americana* was coming to an end, just as *Pax Brittanica* had after World War I. The journalist, Leonard Silk, noted that the United States has become "the world's biggest debtor today" *(Herald Tribune,* May 9-10, 1987) but that no other country was rushing in to take the role of "hegemon."

What was not mentioned during the Reagan era was that the commitment to "make the United States strong again" was done in the area of military defense expenditures, not in advanced technology, and that the military clout of America was shown against small Third World countries (Nicaragua, Grenada), reversing the David vs. Goliath biblical imagery of popular identification. One of the results has been the weakening of the dollar and the cheapening of American real assets, compounded by a rising trade imbalance with all East Asian countries,

---

1   Keynote address delivered at the annual meeting of the Korean Sociological Association, Seoul, Korea, June 1989. Published in Kim Kyong-Dong and Su-Hoon Lee, eds, *Asia in the 21ˢᵗ Century: Challenges and Prospects.* Seoul, Korea: Panmun Book Co., 1990, 3-25.

and an escalating U.S. deficit in the balance of payments on its current account in excess of 3% of GNP. The malaise is expressed in a number of works that look at internal manifestations of decline (to speak of "American decline" is as shocking to American ears as to murmur praises of "socialism") such as falling rates of investment, decline in productivity relative to other countries, failure of our educational system in training the next generation, etc. David Halberstam's *The Reckoning,* with a critical look at the ineptitude of the American industrial sector in responding to the challenges of its Japanese counterpart, and David Kennedy's *The Decline of the Great Powers* with its broad cyclical view are obverse sides of the same coin.[2]

Essentially, the United States is perhaps more ready today to acknowledge Oswald Spengler's *Der Untergang des Abendlandes (The Decline of the West)* than when this epochal study first appeared on the eve of World War I. Europe then was ripe for Spengler. Today, the United States is, if not ripe, ripening for such a perspective, one which fundamentally challenges the frame of reference of progress and America's sense of mission to the world as being a beacon light of progress. The decline (however relative) of America, the ascent (however relative) of East Asia, and the renovation of a "new Europe" are important interrelated features of our contemporary global setting. They do not exhaust the major regions which give our world its physiognomy but represent the relatively more positive settings of modernity. There are three regions which I view as the bleak side of modernity, and for which the decade of the 1990s seem to hold little promise for amelioration: (a) sub-Sahara Africa, which has had negative economic growth in the 1980s, compounded by the misery of civil warfare (after Uganda, the Sudan and Ethiopia) and the AIDS epidemic, (b) Latin America; crippled by external indebtedness and rising civil violence, and (c) the Middle East, where economic deterioration, religious fanaticism, and political intransigence provide little hope for a redress of this "cradle of civilization."

In the face of this rather complex assortment of regional development – in some instances, it might be better to speak of "regression" than "development" – it may be foolhardy to venture what the twenty first century will bring to the world. It is also very risky to assess what the next decade will bring because the historical process never runs in a well-defined channel. So, by way of a "mental experiment," who in 1959 among wise social scientists anticipated the turbulence of the protest movements of the 1960s? And who in 1969 among wise social scientists anticipated the swing toward conservatism that took place in most advanced industrial countries in the following decade? That is why, in 1989, it is

---

2   A work which brings into play both "the Yellow peril" and America's fiscal decline is Daniel Burstein's *Yen!* (1988). The essentially zero-sum relation between the two economic superpowers leads Burstein to state: "The Japanese challenge to American power is therefore an incendiary one ... the question of which nation wields greater influence on the world will have a direct impact on our pocketbooks, our way of life, our self-image, and our security" (1988:295).

risky for us to anticipate too much: sociologists are really at their best in providing sophisticated accounts of what has happened in the world, not in providing accurate forecasts of what will happen.

So much by way of an introductory caveat. In the section that follows, I will make some observations concerning perspectives on "development." I will then go on to invoke two classical figures of sociology to discuss modernity and East Asia. I will not provide new "facts" you don't already possess, but hopefully my interpretation of these factors will be provocative and help us to undertake the discussion of topics central to this conference.

II

The problematics and explanation of "development" are at the heart of the sociological enterprise. It is a theme as old as sociology itself, contained in the vision of Saint-Simon of a new industrial order emerging out of the debris of the *ancien régime* and running through the various social evolutionist currents of the nineteenth and twentieth centuries, from Spencer to Parsons. In spite of vigorous criticism along the way (e.g., Nisbet 1970), the search for a unifying paradigm of development has been a *leitmotiv* of the macrosociological imagination.

Along the way, particular paradigms have held sway with different groupings or "schools." The paramount paradigm of the nineteenth century was the one of "progress," which was widely shared by the heirs of the Enlightenment, the seedbed of "progress" mentality (Bury 1932). The historical process was read as a uniform text where recognizable stages of development flowed out of a pre-modern matrix of undevelopment ("darkness," "barbarism," "feudalism,"or what have you) through a tunnel of transition into the New Jerusalem of modernity – sometimes with travail (Marx), sometimes without (Spencer).

A century later, in the post-war world, the ability of various Western countries to modernize their social structures and reconstruct their economies without falling prey to Communist takeovers (after 1948-49) led social scientists in the United States to formulate different strands of what became in retrospect known as "modernization theory." The intended audience for this paradigmatic view of development was the elites of the "new nations," former units of colonial empires or Western spheres of influence, which were, so to speak, shopping around for blueprints of development beyond mere political independence. The major themes of modernization analysis were threefold: (1) economic development takes place within a sociocultural, institutional matrix that has to be transformed from a "traditional" to a "modern" setting; or in other words, economic development is part of a social totality and cannot occur *in vacuo*, (2) the transformation of society from an economy of scarcity to one of relative plenitude is a realizable project of actors acting in concert, one that will increase the happiness of the majority of societal members, (3) although the crucial forces of development and societal transformation are fundamentally endogenous factors, the optimal model for societies undertaking to modernize is one that corresponds to or approximates the historical experience of Western industrial-liberal regimes, marked by relative freedom of the market and relative freedom of access to the forum.

By the time "modernization theory" became recognized by that name, it was already under heavy attack from ideological sources linked with economic discrepancies. The attack had a prime center in Latin America in the late 1960s, with a secondary center in Africa. In the former, economists and economic sociologists formulated a "structuralist" perspective, having two branches (a "nationalist" and a "Marxist" one) which made a common front against "modernization analysis." The "structuralist" perspective reflected on the inability of Latin American societies to transform themselves socially and economically because of "structures of dependency." These environmental constraints are in effect straight jackets which First World countries (above all, the United States) and their agents (transnational corporations headquartered in the First World) have forced via world commodity markets onto Third World countries. The world market system which necessarily links Latin America to developed societies may be thought of as an unfair casino game where the "house" (the First World) keeps accumulating surpluses at the expense of losing players (the Third World). Therefore, "development" is a myth or a fraud; or rather, in a zero-sum world economy, "development" is asymmetrical in the sense that the more the advanced industrialized societies develop, the more the Third World countries pay the freight without benefiting. In Africa, the critique of "modernization theory" did not take the name of *dependencia*, but the analyses of Nkrumah, Amin, and Ziegler lashed out at "neo-colonialism" with a strikingly similar evaluation.

We can speak consequently of an "anti-modernization" paradigm, a paradigm of "non-development" where the problematics are to discuss why development does not take place in "new nations," and the answer is found to lie in structures of dominance that negate the capacity of societies to transform themselves into a better world for their ordinary citizens.

Building on top of Third World paradigms of non-development, Immanuel Wallerstein returned to the United States at the end of the Vietnam War (from self-imposed exile in Canada), and set up in an institution peripheral to the academic establishment, the Fernand Braudel Center at the State University of New York, Binghamton campus. The "world system" paradigm that he formulated – an ambitious attempt to reconstruct the historical development of capitalism as a world-conquering force (Shannon 1988) – became as near-hegemonic in macro-sociology in the 1970s as "modernization" had been in the late 1950s and early 1960s. Boldly proclaiming in a Zarathustra-like fashion the death of modernization (1979:132-7): "we are living in the historic world transition from capitalism to socialism" (Wallerstein 1979:135) and that "we may conjecture ... the socialist world-revolution of our time as ... a historically singular world-scale movement" (Hopkins and Wallerstein 1982:140) – statements which seem the inverse of the actual major shifts in socialist societies in the 1980s to market systems – there is no denial that Wallerstein, his journal *Review,* and various conferences and groups have produced a vast rethinking and research concerning the dynamics of large-scale economic development.

At the same time, the very economic determinism which undergirds the model is open to criticism on non-ideological grounds. There are two essential dimensions of any empirical social system (which are also dimensions of any complex processes of social stratification) that are basically missing in Wallerstein's world-system model: the dimension of the political sphere of action and of the cultural sphere. Wallerstein's redoing modern history conveniently trivializes Weber's more comprehensive accounting of the historical process of modernity, but if there is one thing to be learned from Weber's *Economy and Society* (1978) it is that of the interdependence and interrelatedness of the economic, political, and cultural (normative) spheres of human action, without one of these having causal primacy. Finally, one may say that if the "modernization" paradigm neglected exogenous or external environmental factors in development, the "world system" paradigm is equally remiss in giving play to endogenous factors, such as culture and politics, for societies or regions that are at the core of the world system.

The critical assumption of world-system theory is that if you were not in at the beginning when the capitalist game was set up, you are doomed to be a "field hand" or at best a "house hand" but never an elite (unless the game blows up). This denies the capacity of actors to act upon and transform their situation, even if they are "latecomers" in the game. And yet, just in the context of the "First World," "latecomers" can be shown historically to have the capacity of moving from "periphery" to "core," as illustrated in the case of Germany in the nineteenth century, while the reverse process is equally possible (witness Spain after the seventeenth century). But it isn't so much past history that renders the world system paradigm suspect in its claim of universality, as it is a more recent empirical phenomenon that constitutes a major anomaly. I will come back to this shortly.

Although I am sure there are others, two recent compendia on development merit acknowledgement. The first is a special issue of *Daedalus*, "A World to Make: Development in Perspective" (Winter 1988), and the second a state-of-the-art survey by Evans and Stephens (1988). The former does not seek a synthesis but offers interesting descriptive and retrospective essays, ranging from the ideological feature of development analysis (Sutton 1989) to the role of national and local governments in Third World development (Lewis 1989).

The essay by Evans and Stephens, which has broader sweep of development studies and which acknowledges the present diversity of orientations, proposes that a certain coherence in the profuse literature on development. They note that

> ... recent work has not aimed at charting progress along a presumed unilinear
> path of societal development but rather with uncovering, interpreting, and trying
> to explain distinctive patterns of development (1988:746).

They see as a paradigm synthesizing recent work what they call "the new comparative political economy" which takes as variables endogenous factors (class relations and the actions of the state) and exogenous factors (international economic and political conjunctures). Four critical issues are suggested as heuristic (but not comprehensive) and salient in developmental issues: (1) states and markets, (2) development and democracy, (3) accumulation and distribution, and (4) the world political economy and national development. Evans and Stephens conclude their survey by noting two perspectives that might emerge as competing or hopefully complementary orientations: cultural approaches to the study of social change and rational choice theory. Somehow, one feels that the authors are more likely to put out the welcome mat for the latter, as suggested in the following concluding remarks:

> There is an obvious complementarity between rational choice approaches and
> the work we have highlighted here ... the new comparative political economy ...
> defines the sociology of development not as simply the study of poor countries
> but the study of long-term, large-scale socio-economic and political change
> irrespective of the epoch or region in which it occurs (1988:761).

It is the absence of reference to normative and cultural change in that last sentence which I find revealing (and disturbing) for it is indicative of the limitations of a political economy approach to the question of development, no matter how well reasoned and how broad-based the particular approach is, such as that of Evans and Stephens.

It is precisely to fill this lacuna that I now reverentially alight on the shoulders of Weber and Durkheim to develop a perspective on East Asian development in the twenty first century.

III

My core argument in this paper is that to get a fresh perspective on "Asia in the Twenty-First Century" it is fruitful to resume the macrosociological analyses of Weber and Durkheim on development. We must be prepared to "stand on their shoulders" with the proviso not to remain there indefinitely. Weber and Durkheim had a broad and clear horizon from which to view the problematics of the development of modern society. Still, their view on East Asia was limited to an important extent by the fact that they shared with the great majority of their Western contemporaries a general Western ethnocentric bias. Consequently, while drawing upon Weber and Durkheim is very heuristic for the major theme of this conference, there is need to go beyond their perspective to upgrade our model of modernity.

Because Weber wrote extensive essays on Asian religions, which are available to English readers (1967, 1968), there have been extensive discussions and critiques of his interpretation of Asian development. It is not my intention to review this considerable literature, but I would like to make some passing observations on the reception of Weber's comparative analysis in terms of what we might view as three phases.

The first phase was during the first half or so of this century, when scholars engaged in the Weberian "thesis" controversy in terms of Western sociohistorical materials. Little consideration was given to either what Weber had said about religion and society outside the West or to how what he did say informed his analysis of societal change in the West. The second phase coincided with the accession of Third World countries to political independence in the late 1950s and 1960s. The "modernization" paradigm lay stress on immanent (or endogenous) factors bringing about structural transformations that would propel a society from a "tradition" to a "modern" cluster of institutional arrangements. Among endogenous factors were personality changes – "mentalities" and motivational states: what then would be needed to change structures were new "habits of the mind" (to adapt Tocqueville's "habits of the heart"). A fruitful ingress was Weber's discussion of the "Protestant ethic" which had generated a radical "innerworldly asceticism" that had swept magic aside and laid the soil for modern, rational capitalism. Hence, during this second wave of Weberiana, there was a stress on finding functional equivalents of the "Protestant ethic" in traditional society, or if not finding it, then seeking mechanisms of instilling the attitudinal complex of achievement-orientation, postponement of gratification, and the like to future leaders and potential native entrepreneurs.

This second wave had another side, or generated a negative reaction to Weber, which might have linkages to Third World anticolonialism. Weber was seen by some as one of the many promulgators of "Orientalism" (Said) a broad ideology of Western domination. If one reads Weber on China and India as saying that capitalism and rationality, the bedrock of modern civilization, could not develop on Asian soil because of encrusted anti-modern values and social organization, then Weber has little to offer in the way of understanding what has been happening in East Asia. Further, critics also charged that Weber was cut off from a deep understanding of Asian religion by his lack of reading ability of original Asian sources, and by his basically ahistorical typifications of Indian and Chinese societies.[3]

More recent scholarship has nuanced the criticisms of Weber so that we might speak of something like a neo-Weberian phase emerging. One figure in this trend is S. N. Eisenstadt who has undertaken a vast research project of comparative civilizational analysis (1986a, 1986b), with Weber as the major background figure.

---

3   Weber in his "Introduction" to his comparative studies of religion was very careful to point out the limitations of his knowledge and his reliance on the meager availability of translations of "real sources." "From all this follows," he warned, "the definitely provisional character of these studies and especially of the parts dealing with Asia" (1958:28).

Eisenstadt, taking a major cue from Weber, has been examining the transformative
capacity of civilizations stemming from "transcendental visions" that are located
in heterodoxies and which can act as levers of change against an established social
order. Such, after all, was a key source of the dynamics of Western civilization
with the Puritan sects providing the "breakthrough" (Parsons 1963) that provided
a radically new interpretation of salvation, one closely tied in to an ethic of "this-
worldly asceticism."

   In his examination of Chinese civilization (1983), Eisenstadt notes that the
institutional framework of imperial China was not differentiated into two spheres,
a cultural one and a politico-administrative one. This meant that the cultural elites
(foremost being the literati) did not have an autonomous sphere of action but
rather were closely interwoven and integrated with the political-administrative
center. Eisenstadt follows in many respects Weber's analysis, but objects to
Weber's image of China as a "patrimonial society." Unlike Weber, he finds a
good deal of far-reaching institutional or structural changes in China, including
movements of protest and change, which Eisenstadt sees as having "very strong
incipient transformative potentialities" (1983:395). If they did not succeed, he
argues, it is not because the society was mired in "traditionalism" so much as
the ruling coalitions developed sophisticated means of social control. Rebellions,
scattered through Chinese imperial history, were not linked with the heterodoxies
(Buddhism and Taoism), nor did they develop ideological or structural linkages
with the system's institutional elites.[4] It is only with the Communist revolution that
the transformative potentiality in Chinese society was able to radically reconstruct
the sociopolitical order.

   A second contemporary figure making use of Weber's analysis of China is the
sociologist Gary Hamilton. Hamilton acknowledges that "a Weberian perspective
offers the best starting point to an analysis of modern Asia," (Hamilton and Kao,
1987:289). Hamilton rejects criticisms of Weber that the latter erred in thinking that
Confucianism was incompatible with a capitalistic, industrial order. As Hamilton
points out, Weber saw that the Chinese could readily assimilate capitalism (better
than the Japanese, he thought). What Weber wanted to know for his comparative
analysis was why it did *not* originate in China, which in many ways was the great
competing this-worldly civilization, on par if not technologically ahead of the
West on the eve of the sixteenth century. Hamilton sees Weber's analysis of China
as heuristic but flawed because Weber was writing his study of Asian religions
from the perspective of his accounting for the dynamics of Western civilization.
His account of China, particularly of China's economic and social history, is
incomplete. Essentially, Hamilton argues that an economic history of China, or

---

   4   Weber was not neglectful of rebellions. He gave considerable attention to the Tai
Ping, "by far the most powerful and thoroughly hierocratic, politicoethical rebellion against
the Confucian administration and ethic which China has ever experienced ... the magical
and idolatrous fetters were broken and this was unknown elsewhere in China" (Weber
1968:219-22).

more broadly of Asian societies, must be written from the inside, not from the perspective of Western development:

> To develop an analytic understanding of Chinese society ... one needs to develop concepts and theories in the same way that they were developed in the West, i.e., through a close contextual analysis of the society in question. Once an understanding of the institutional conduct of the Chinese economy has been reached, then and only then is there a basis for cross-cultural comparisons designed to illuminate the Chinese economy (Hamilton 1985:71).

Hamilton's own detailed study of late imperial economy, its institutional framework in regional associations (1985), goes far in developing a new approach to Chinese economic history. In doing so, he spotlights major Western "misunderstandings" of the Chinese situation, such as characterizing the Chinese imperial state as "strong or weak" and viewing the Chinese economy as "a legally defined sphere of activity" rather than the moral terms which bound merchants together in clan associations (1985:84-85).

Also in this vein might be mentioned the recent institutional analysis that saw Oriental culture as stagnant. Hsiao is equally critical of world-system analysis, which cannot account for Taiwan's rapid move upward in the international market. He suggests the different models of development may apply at different periods of a given country's history, and to provide a more accurate account of Taiwan's successful post-1948 socioeconomic history, he brings out important cultural factors (p. 21). Nan Lin's institutional analysis gives centrality to the Chinese family as a "deep structure" in Chinese society (1989:18), whose key functions lie in the transfer of *authority* and *property,* which are critical resources for any society. His analysis leads to interesting comparisons between Chinese, Japanese, and Anglo-Saxon society. And what adds to his study is that Lin provides materials showing that in such areas as "voluntarism" (here taken as ownership of non-profit organizations), differences between Chinese-Americans, Japanese-Americans, and Korean-Americans prevail as much as they do in East Asia. The Chinese "are much less likely to operate or engage in voluntary associations that are independent of family concerns." (p. 62).

In showing the significance of the Chinese family in modern economic life, Lin (as does Hsiao in his study of Taiwan) is providing a mirror image of the one sketched out by Weber. The latter saw the sib as one of the forces of tradition thwarting "the free market selection of labor" necessary for modern enterprises (Weber 1968:95). Lin goes on to take up Weber's contention that China lacked a rational religion as a necessary step in the transformation of social organization. Pointing out that China was exposed to Christianity as early as the second century A.D., he states that the question to be asked is *"why did certain societies, such as China, not extensively adopt such religion?"* (p. 63, emphasis author's). It is essentially because the latter is incompatible with Chinese family practices, although, Lin adds, it is more easily adapted to Japanese and Korean worship practices (p. 66).

Weber's study of Asian development, or rather, lack of Western-style development, has led other scholars to probe deep in the cultural setting of East Asia to redress the image. So, for example, one of the most distinguished historians of Chinese science, Nathan Sivin, is critical of Weber and Joseph Needham for asking a misleading question: why didn't the Scientific Revolution take place in China? (Sivin 1982). Sivin brings out various fallacious assumptions in the posing of the question, not only the assumption of the backwardness of China as demonstrated in the fact that it did not develop modern science, but also the assumption of the uniqueness and universality of the science that did develop in 17th century Europe. Equally significant, Sivin faults Weber (and Needham) for being "relentlessly unsociological" in considering China (Sivin 1985:44). Related to this, Sivin points out that in accounting for the transformation of the West from tradition to modernity, Weber fixed his gaze on marginals (the Protestant sects) whereas when he looked at China, he kept his attention on the elite and its literary heritage (1985:46).

Finally in this cursory listing, the Harvard scholar Tu Wei-ming, with several associates, has undertaken recently a broad, cross-cultural study of "the rise of East Asia," one giving a major focus to "Confucian institutions" (MacFarquhar *et al.* 1987). Tu sees the merit of taking Confucianism seriously, though not positing a Confucian ethic" as the driving force of East Asian economic dynamism. Weber's study of China treated Confucianism as lacking the potential for cultural transformation to modernity. Tu has given extensive attention to the dynamics of neo-Confucianism, which Weber glossed over, and he has compared it to Heidegger's ontology (1983, 1988). Basically, what Tu and various others associated with him are beginning to do is to develop a research program which will look at how much of the variance of East Asian dynamics can be accounted for in terms of Confucian institutions, the way the Weberian problematic may be said to ask how much of the variance of Western modernity might be accounted for in terms of Puritan values and institutions.

IV

I will not spend as much attention on Durkheim as I have on Weber, partly because Durkheim himself did not engage in an intellectual encounter with Asia as did Weber.[5] Two of his close associates, Célestin Bouglé and Marcel Granet, made

5   Yet Durkheim did show interest and sensitivity to China and Japan in reviews he gave in his *Année Sociologique* to works about those countries. I find intriguing that in his review of Tokuzo Fukuda's book on *Social and Economic Evolution of Japan,* Durkheim likens Japanese evolution to that of the West and states, "The analogy between the Japanese sects and Protestantism is striking. That is to say that both developments alike resulted

extensive studies of Asian society. Bouglé wrote early in his career a series of essays on the Indian caste system (1971). He viewed the caste system as the inhibiting force of modernity, preventing innovations in the division of labor and inhibiting mobility, a condition for individual freedom. His summary judgment was the following:

> The caste system ... no doubt serves to raise a society out of barbarism. But it runs the risk of halting it rapidly and for a long time on the road to civilization ... In the area of economics also then, India presents a spectacle of a kind of arrested development (1970:176).

Bouglé did not engage in field work, but his work synthesized a great deal of materials available in the West about India and it had an important influence on providing a focus for the study of Indian civilization. Granet, on the contrary, was a Sinologist of the first rank, who took Durkheimian sociology's primary concern with relating collective representations to their social milieux to the study of Chinese thought. In several passages one may see Granet as another Westerner who looked for factors in Asian society that blocked development and modernity. So, for example, in analyzing Chinese language, Granet saw Chinese thought in its basic mode of expression being "almost necessarily turned toward the past" (1953:120). Further, because written and spoken Chinese is full of concrete images but lacking abstraction, it did not produce a theory of knowledge and therefore, unlike Western languages, traditional Chinese is impervious to modern science. Consequently, Granet added, if China wants to modernize it will be forced to construct a new language (1953:152f). Elsewhere, in providing an account of the history of Chinese civilization, from the ancient to the imperial period, Granet felt that "the evolution of morals ... went on by way of progressive drying up, and that, in the moral life, under the increasing weight of a conventional etiquette, spontaneity saw its part reduced to nothing." (1930:428).

Still, Granet (an eyewitness to the 1919 Revolution in Beijing) had hope for a Chinese awakening. In closing his *Chinese Civilization* he stated in words that were as applicable to his interim period as to the beginning of the imperial era (and perhaps as applicable today):

> but although by defining with increasing strictness its traditional ideals, the believers in orthodoxy wished to adorn it with a static dignity, it remains rich in youthful forces (1930:429).

And in the conclusion of his great study of Chinese religion, which far surpasses Weber's study in its scope and use of sources, Granet gives an insightful look

---

from general causes and that we are here, perhaps, in the presence of an abstract type of social evolution" (1980: 319).

at the contemporary (i.e., 1922) setting. He has interesting comments on Catholicism, Protestantism and Islam – the "imported" religions – and turns his attention to the indigenous ones. Noting that Confucianism was under fire by parliamentarians who wanted to substitute a state morality of positivism, Granet observes delicately,

> ... the virtue of Confucian teaching is to nourish a practical spirit whose ideal might be defined by the [Comtean] formula Order and Progress (1975:156).

Granet and Bouglé, though students of Durkheim, cannot be taken as complete surrogates, not at least for a perspective on the challenges of East Asia in the 21st century. The Durkheim problematic of modernity that is appropriate is the following: economic development is a feature of modernity which entails the transformation of society from a "mechanical" to an "organic" solidarity but, by itself, economic development is no guarantor of regulated social order. A regulated social order of modernity involves a normative framework freely accepted by its actors, one which is more an inclusive than a kin-specific framework. Tacitly, a Durkheimian perspective leads one to look for organic solidarity institutionalized in a modern civil society. There is no doubt that East Asian societies have achieved the means of economic transformation. What remains to be achieved is a civil society that is interactive with a civil religion. Arguably that is the Durkheimian challenge for East Asia. I am tempted to think that the "Confucian" nations have some natural advantages in achieving this, while maintaining a high level of economic and technological development. But the transition from an authoritarian order, one where decision and power comes "from the top down," to a more socially inclusive and participatory order is far from easy. It is particularly difficult if the freedom and autonomy that comes with civil society not be a dissolvent of the normative framework that provides a shared consensus and a curb of the tendency for *anomie* which is also the "fate of modernity."

Weber and Durkheim provided complementary perspectives on modernity. Their questions are as heuristic today as when they posed them, although their concrete analyses are, like most other nineteenth century grounded perspectives, flawed by the historical moment in which they were drawn. In particular, we are entering a new axial age, the age of the twenty first century, one in which our accounting of modernity may well have to begin with an East Asian focus it rather than a Western one.

Postscript

I have tried to convey that a view from the shoulders of Weber and Durkheim can help us obtain a broad perspective on Asian development. But we must also recognize that they can only carry us so far and that for the next period of interpretation and analysis, it is necessary to renovate the paradigm(s) of development. In particular,

I have argued elsewhere (Tiryakian 1985) that we must view the historical course of modernity as truly dynamic in the sense that centers of modernity are not fixated in a given locale and that East Asia may well become the new locale of global modernity. How does this relate to Korea? Durkheim and the Durkheimians, to my knowledge, did not have anything to say about Korea. Weber devotes only a few pages, showing an awareness of the Tong-hak movement and the Japanese colonization (1967:270), but basically he saw the Korean social order as "a copy of the Chinese" (1967:269).

So, ultimately, it is the task of Korean social scientists to come to grips with the sociocultural dynamics of Korean modernity, as Kyong-Dong Kim (1985) and Son-Ung Kim. (1988), among others, have begun to do. The challenge here is to indicate how the dynamics of Korean development relate to general cultural and institutional aspects of East Asian development as well as to the specificity of Korea's situation being neither Japan nor China. Of more global significance, Korea's development is that of being a country which has experienced a relatively recent colonial situation and which has shown an autonomous capacity for socioeconomic transition from an agrarian to an advanced industrial society. At the same time, it represents a culturally pluralistic society with a broad religious matrix in which "East meets West." To assess these elements as aspects of Korean modernity and the contribution of Korean modernity to a broader, twenty first century setting, is a fascinating challenge for Korean social scientists.

References

Bouglé, Célestin 1971 [1908]. *Essays on the Caste System,* trans. by D.F. Pocock. Cambridge: Cambridge University Press.

Burstein, Daniel 1988. *Yen! Japan's New Financial Empire and its Threat to America.* New York: Simon and Schuster.

Bury, John B. 1932. *The Idea of Progress.* New York: Macmillan.

Davis, Winston 1987. "Religion and Development: Weber and the East Asian Experience," pp. 221-280 in M. Weiner and S.P. Huntington, eds, *Understanding Political Development.* Boston: Little, Brown.

Durkheim, Emile 1980. *Contributions to L'Année Sociologique,* edited by Y. Nandan. New York: Free Press.

Eisenstadt, Shmuel N. 1983. "Innerwltliche Transzendenz und die Strukturierung der Welt. Max Webers Studie uber China und die Gestalt der chinesischen Zivilisation," pp. 363-411 in W. Schluchter, ed., *Max Webers Studie uber Konfuzianismus und Taoismus.* Frankfurt am Main: Suhrkamp.

—. 1986. *A Sociological Approach to Comparative Civilizations: The Development of a Research Program.* Jerusalem: Truman Research Institute.

—.n.d. (a). "Some Observations on Relations between Confucianism, Development and Modernization."

—.n.d. (b). "The Structuring of Social Protest in Modern Societies: The Limits and Direction of Convergence."

—. ed. 1986b. *The Origins & Diversity of Axial Age Civilizations.* Albany: State University Press of New York.

Evans, Peter B. and J.D. Stephens 1988. "Development and the World Economy," pp. 739-73 in Neil Smelser, ed., *Handbook of Sociology.* Newbury Park, CA: Sage.

Granet, Marcel 1930. *Chinese Civilization.* New York: Knopf.

—. 1953. *Etudes Sociologiques sur Ia Chine.* Paris: PUF.

—. 1975. (1922). *The Religion of the Chinese People.* New York: Harper & Row.

Hamilton, Gary G. 1985. "Why No Capitalism in China? Negative Questions in Historical, Comparative Research," in Andreas E. Buss, ed., *Max Weber in Asian Studies.* Leiden: E.J. Brill.

Hamilton, Gary G. and Cheng-Shu Kao 1987. "Max Weber and the Analysis of East Asian Industrialisation," *International Sociology,* 2 (September): 289-300.

Hsiao, Hisin-Huang Michael forthcoming. "Changing Theoretical Explanations of Taiwan's Development Experience: An Examination," in E. Tiryakian and T. Kashioka, eds., *East Meets West: Theoretical Perspectives on Asian Development.*

Hopkins, Terence K., I. Wallerstein *et al.* 1982. *World Systems Analysis.* Newbury Park, CA: Sage.

Kim, Kyong-Dong 1985. *Rethinking Development: Theories and Experiences.* Seoul: Seoul National University Press.

Kim, Son-Ung 1988. "The Role of Social Values and Competitiveness in Economic Growth: With Special Reference to Korea," pp. 76-92 in D. Sinhar and H. Kao, eds *Social Values and Development. Asian Perspectives.* New Delhi and Newbury Park: Sage.

Lewis, John P. 1989. "Government and National Economic Development," *Daedalus* 118 #1 (Winter): 69-83.

Lin, Nan 1989. "Chinese Family Structure and Chinese Society." mimeo.

MacFarquhar, Roderick, H. Rosovsky, Wei-ming Tu, and B. Vogel 1987. "The Rise of East Asia." mimeo. Cambridge, MA: American Academy of Arts & Sciences.

Nisbet, Robert A. 1970. "Developmentalism: A Critical Analysis," pp. 167-204 in John McKinney and E.A. Tiryakian, eds, *Theoretical Sociology.* New York: Appleton-Century-Crofts.

Parsons, Talcott 1963. "Introduction," pp. xix-lxvii in Max Weber, *The Sociology of Religion.* Boston: Beacon.

Schluchter, Wolfgang ed. 1983. *Max Webers Studie Über Konfuzianismus und Taoismus. Interpretation und Kritik.* Frankfurt am Main: Suhrk amp.

Shannon, Thomas R. 1989. *An Introduction to the World-System Perspective.* Boulder, Colorado: Westview.

Sivin, Nathan 1984. "Why the Scientific Revolution Did Not Take Place in China— Or Did It?" pp. 53 1-54 in E. Mendelsohn, ed., *Transformation and Tradition in the Sciences.* Cambridge: Cambridge University Press.

—. 1985. "Max Weber, Joseph Needham, Benjamin Nelson: The Question of Chinese Science," pp. 37-49 in B. V. Walker, et al., eds, *Civilizations East and West. A Memorial Volume for Benjamin Nelson.* Atlantic Highlands, N. J.: Humanities Press.

Sutton, Francis X. 1989. "Development Ideology: Its Emergence and Decline," *Daedalus* 118 #1 (Winter): 35-67.

Tiryakian, Edward A. 1985. "The Changing Centers of Modernity," pp. 13 1-47 in Erik Cohen, M. Lissak, and U. Almagor, eds., *Comparative Social Dynamics. Essays in Honor of S. N. Eisentadt.* Boulder, Colorado: Westview.

Tu Wei-ming 1983. "Die neokonfuzianische Ontologie," pp. 271-97 in W. Schluchter, Max Weber Studie, etc.

—. 1986. "The Structure and Function of the Confucian Intellectual in Ancient China," pp. 360-73 in S. N. Eisenstadt, ed., *The Origins & Diversity of Axial Age Civilizations*

—. 1988. "Confucius and Confucianism," mimeo. Extended version of a paper appearing in the Encyclopedia Brittanica, 15th ed., 1988.

Wallerstein, Immanuel 1979. *The Capitalist World-Economy.* Cambridge and Paris: Cambridge University Press/Editions de la Maison des Sciences de l'Homme.

Weber, Max 1958 [1904-1905]. *The Protestant Ethic and the Spirit of Capitalism,* trans. by T. Parsons. New York: Scribner's.

—. 1963. *The Sociology of Religion.* Boston: Beacon.

—. 1967. *The Religion of India.* New York: Free Press.

—. 1968. *The Religion of China.* New York: Free Press.

—. 1978. *Economy and Society,* 2 vols., Guenther Roth and Claus Wittich, eds Berkeley and Los Angeles: University of California Press.

Other Writings by Edward A. Tiryakian Relating to Durkheim

Book and edited works

Sociologism and Existentialism. Two Perspectives on the Individual and Society. Englewood Cliffs, NJ: Prentice-Hall, 1962.

Spanish translation, *Sociologismo y Existencialismo* (Buenos Aires: Amorrortu, 1968; Japanese Translation, Tokio: Misuzo Shobo, 1971; integral reproduction in *Perennial Works in Sociology* collection, New York: Arno Press, 1979).

Guest Editor, special issue, *"Durkheim Lives!"*, *Social Forces*, 59, no. 4. Editor, special issue, "The 100ᵗʰ anniversary of Durkheim's *Division of Labor in Society*," in *Sociological Forum*, 9, no. 1 (1994).

Articles

"Durkheim and Ethics," *American Sociological Review*, 25 (1960): 405-06.

" Introduction to a Bibliographical Focus on Emile Durkheim," *Journal for the Scientific Study of Religion*, 3 (1964): 247-54.

"Durkheim's Two Laws of Penal Evolution," *Journal for the Scientific Study of Religion*, 3 (1964): 261-66.

"Le premier message d'Emile Durkheim," *Cahiers Internationaux de Sociologie,* 43 (1967): 21-23.

"The *Elementary Forms* as *Revelation*", pp. 114-35 in Buford Rhea, ed., *The Future of the Sociological Classics*, London: Allen & Unwin, 1981.

"Hegemonic Schools and the Development of Sociology," pp. 417-41 in Richard C. Monk, ed., *Structures of Knowing: Current Studies in the Sociology of Schools*, Lanham, MD: Maryland University Press of America, 1986.

"Revisiting Sociology's First Classic: *The Division of Labor in Society* and its Actuality," *Sociological Forum,* 9 (March 1994): 3-16.

"Three Levels of Teaching Durkheim," pp. 29-50 in Terry F. Godlove, ed., *Teaching Durkheim on Religion*. Oxford & New York: Oxford University Press 2005.

Book Reviews

Review of Steven Lukes, *Emile Durkheim: His Life and Work*, in *American Journal of Sociology* , 79, no. 6 (1974).

Review of Robert N. Bellah, ed., *Emile Durkheim on Morality and Society,* in *American Journal of Sociology*, 80, no. 3 (1974).

Review of Ernest Wallwork, *Durkheim, Morality and Milieu,* in *American Academy of Religion*, 43, no. 2 (1975).

Review of Yash Nandan, *The Durkheimian School: A System and Comprehensive Bibliography* in *Contemporary Sociology*, 7, no. 4 (1978).

Review of Anthony Giddens, *New Rules of Sociological Method* in *American Journal of Sociology,* 83, no. 4 (1978).

Review of Mary Douglas, *Implicit Meanings* in *Sociological Quarterly*, 19, no. 2 (1978).

Review of Mark Traugott, ed., *Emile Durkheim on Institutional Analysis* in *Contemporary Sociology*, 8, no. 4 (1979).

Review of Jennifer M. Lehmann, *Durkheim and Women,* in *American Journal of Sociology*, 100, no. 5 (1995).

Review of N.J. Allen, W.S.F. Pickering, and W. Watts Miller, eds, *On Durkheim's Elementary Forms of Religious Life,* in *American Journal of Sociology*, 105, no. 1 (1999).

Review of Jonathan S. Fish, *Defending the Durkheimian Tradition: Religion, Emotion, and Morality* in *Contemporary Sociology*, 35, no. 5 (September 2006).

Index

Note: Numbers in brackets preceded by 'n' indicate the reference to a footnote, 'f' indicates the reference is carried over to the next page.